AS LEVEL
PSYCHOLOGY

To Sebastian with love

AS LEVEL

PSYCHOLOGY

Fifth Edition

Michael W. Eysenck

Psychology Press
Taylor & Francis Group

HOVE AND NEW YORK

Published 2012 by Psychology Press
27 Church Road, Hove, East Sussex, BN3 2FA

Simultaneously published in the USA and Canada
by Psychology Press
711 Third Avenue, New York, NY 10017

www.psypress.com

Psychology Press is an imprint of the Taylor & Francis Group, an informa business

British Library Cataloguing in Publication Data
A catalogue record for this book is available from the British Library

ISBN 978-1-84872-115-9

Typeset in India by Newgen Imaging Systems (P) Ltd
Printed and bound in Italy by L.E.G.O. S.p.A.

Contents

About the Author

Michael W. Eysenck is one of the best-known psychologists in Europe. He is Professorial Fellow at Roehampton University and Emeritus Professor at Royal Holloway, University of London. He is especially interested in cognitive psychology (about which he has written several books) and most of his research focuses on the role of cognitive factors in anxiety within normal and clinical populations.

He has published 43 books. His previous textbooks published by Psychology Press include *Psychology for AS Level (4th Edn)* (2008), *Psychology for A2 Level* (2009), *A2 Psychology: Key Topics (2nd Edn)* (2006), *Psychology: An International Perspective* (2004), *Psychology: A Student's Handbook (6th Edn)* (with Mark Keane) (2010), *Simply Psychology (3rd Edn)* (2012), *Fundamentals of Psychology* (2009), *Fundamentals of Cognition (2nd Edn)* (2012), *Perspectives on Psychology* (1994), and *Individual Differences: Normal and Abnormal* (1994). He has also written several articles on topics within the AS Psychology specification for the journal *Psychology Review*, and has given talks at numerous A-level conferences.

In his spare time, Michael Eysenck enjoys travelling, tennis, walking, and an occasional game of golf. He is a keen supporter of Manchester United Football Club.

Preparing for the AS Exam

Roz Brody

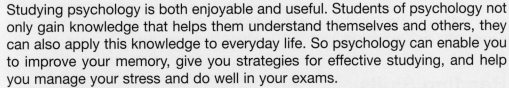

Studying psychology is both enjoyable and useful. Students of psychology not only gain knowledge that helps them understand themselves and others, they can also apply this knowledge to everyday life. So psychology can enable you to improve your memory, give you strategies for effective studying, and help you manage your stress and do well in your exams.

The study skills you need to be successful in the AS exam are based on psychological principles involving learning and memory. So you should already be well placed to gain maximum advantage in the exam room! This chapter is divided into two sections that address your own study skills and the ways in which the exam will be assessed and marked.

This chapter is designed to take some of the stress out of the exam by giving you hints on how to study, and letting you know what the exam involves and what the examiners look for. You will probably return to this chapter as you work through the rest of the book.

SECTION 1
HOW CAN I STUDY EFFECTIVELY?

Students of psychology should find it easy to develop good study skills because they are based on psychological principles. For example, study skills are designed to promote effective learning and remembering, and learning and memory are key areas within psychology. Study skills are also concerned with motivation and developing good work habits, and these also fall very much within psychology, although they are not part of your AS-level course. Most of what is involved in study skills is fairly obvious, so we will focus on detailed pieces of advice rather than on vague generalities (e.g. "work hard", "get focused").

Motivation

Most people find it hard to maintain a high level of motivation over long periods of time. We all know what happens. You start out with high ideals and work hard for the first few weeks. Then you have a bad week and/or lose your drive, and everything slips. What can you do to make yourself as motivated as possible? One psychological theory of motivation (Locke, 1968) suggested the following seven ways to set appropriate goals and maintain motivation:

1. You must set yourself a goal that is hard but achievable.
2. Once you have your goal, you need to commit yourself to it. Telling others about it can keep you motivated.

Section 1 will teach you how to develop your study skills, including increasing your motivation and improving reading skills using the SQ3R approach. There are also tips on how to manage your time to get the best results from your work. Section 2 is on how to do well in the exam. In this section you will find out how to discover your own personal learning style, and how your performance in the exam will benefit from this knowledge. There is also information on what the examiners will be looking for, and how they award marks.

NOTE: At the start of each chapter there is a list of specification content. Check this list to see what you could be examined on.

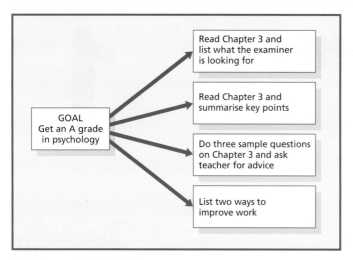

A major goal broken down into smaller goals.

3. You should focus on goals that can be achieved within a reasonable period of time (e.g. no more than a few weeks). Long-term goals like "I will get a grade A in my psychology exam" need to be broken down into a series of short-term goals (e.g. I'll read and summarise the key points of Chapter 3 by Friday", "I'll do two timed answers on this chapter in the next week").

4. Set clear goals, and avoid vague goals.

5. Obtain feedback on your progress.

6. Once you have achieved your goal, move on to slightly harder goals.

7. Be honest about any setbacks and try to work out what went wrong, rather than simply saying it was bad luck. We can and do learn from our mistakes.

Your attempts to motivate yourself are only likely to be successful if you make use of all seven points. If you set yourself a very clear, medium-term goal, and obtain feedback, but the goal is impossible to achieve, then you are more likely to *reduce* rather than *increase* your level of motivation.

Reading Skills

If you have ever turned over a few pages in a book and had no idea what you have just read, then this next section is for you. Studying psychology involves effective reading and being able to remember and use the information you have read. Morris (1979) described the **SQ3R** approach—Survey, Question, Read, Recite, Review, representing the five stages in effective reading—which has proved to be very useful. We will consider these five stages with respect to the task of reading a chapter.

Survey

The Survey stage involves getting an overall view of the way in which the information in the chapter is organised. If there is a chapter summary, this will probably be the easiest way to achieve that goal. Otherwise, you could look through the chapter to find out what topics are discussed and how they are linked to each other.

Set a realistic goal.

Commit to achieving the goal.

Enjoy your achievement!

Question

The Question stage should be applied to fairly short parts of the chapter of no more than six pages. The essence of this stage is to get you to think about the questions you want answered by reading the text, such as "What does the S and Q in SQ3R stand for?"

Read

While the read stage obviously involves reading the text to answer your questions, it is also very important to integrate any new information with your pre-existing knowledge of the topic.

You might also want to use a highlighter pen to emphasise key points.

Recite

The recite stage involves trying to remember all the key ideas that were contained in the part of the chapter you have been reading. Try explaining what you have just read to someone else. If you cannot remember some of the ideas, go back to the Read stage.

Review

When you have read the entire chapter, you should review the key ideas from the text and be able to combine the information from different parts of the chapter into a coherent structure. Producing a mind map of the key ideas can often help. If your mind seems a total blank you need to go back to the earlier stages in the reading process.

 Have you got any questions? Always question everything you read by saying, for example, "Does this explain my own knowledge of the world?" or "Do I understand all the words?"

EXAM HINT

In order to succeed in exams, you must be able to recall the information you need. The Recite and Review stages of the SQ3R approach are designed to achieve precisely that.

Time Management

Studying effectively involves managing your time well. Often you may have good intentions at the start of the week, but as the time flies by you realise that the two or three essential pieces of work you were going to do haven't been tackled. And yet, when you know you will be extremely busy you often manage your time more effectively because you know that if you don't do the work now, there will be no time at the end of the week.

So what do you do with the 100 hours or more at your disposal each week? You probably only have some vague idea where most of the time goes. As time is such a valuable commodity, it is a good idea to make the most efficient use of it, as you will probably be surprised at how much time you tend to waste. Here are some suggestions on how to manage your time:

- Create a timetable of the times that are available and unavailable over a week. Now indicate which subjects you can study on different days, and how much time within each day you are going to spend on any subject.
- Decide what is, for you, a reasonable span of attention (possibly 30–40 minutes). Set aside a number of periods of time during the week for study. Make a commitment to yourself to use these periods for study.
- Note that the more of a habit studying becomes, the less effortful it will be, and the less resistant you will be to making a start.
- No one has limitless concentration. After initially high levels of concentration, the level decreases until the end is in sight. So make sure that the time you commit to studying is realistic. You can probably improve your level of concentration by including short (10-minute) rest periods. Remember to avoid distractions like the television in your study area (don't kid yourself that you can watch TV *and* study—reward yourself later with an hour slumped in front of the TV).
- During these study times, there will be a tendency to find other things to do (e.g. phoning a friend). This is where the hard part begins. You must try to be firm and say to yourself that this is time you have committed to studying, and that is what you are going to do. However, you will have time available later for other things. It is hard to do to start with, but it gets easier.

One motivational strategy is to reward yourself at regular intervals. For example, after you have read 10 pages or worked for an hour, have a cup of tea, go for a brief walk, or phone or text a friend. Make sure your rewards are for easily achievable goals— but not too easy!

KEY TERM

Planning fallacy: the false belief that a plan will be completed on time even though past experience suggests it won't.

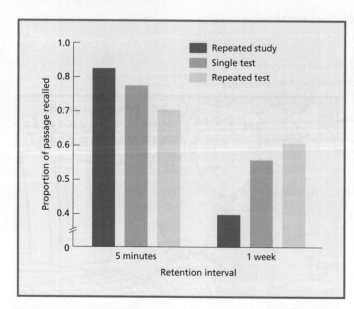

The results of Roediger and Karpicke's (2006) study on the testing effect.

Planning fallacy

Although you might have never heard of the **planning fallacy**, there is a good chance that you may have experienced it. Kahneman and Tversky (1979) defined the planning fallacy as "a tendency to hold a confident belief that one's own project will proceed as planned, even while knowing that the vast majority of similar projects have run late". In other words, we all kid ourselves that it will be easy despite knowing that, on previous occasions, we and other people have not managed to fulfil our planned intentions.

As we are psychologists, we might be interested to know if there is evidence to support this planning fallacy, and indeed there is. Buehler et al. (1994) found that, on average, students submitted a major piece of work 22 days later than they had predicted, even when they were specifically told that the purpose of the study was to examine the accuracy of people's predictions. Buehler et al. found that students were much better at predicting completion times for other students than for themselves. The reason for this is that they were more likely to use what is called "distributional" information (which comes from knowledge about similar tasks completed in the past) when making predictions about other students, whereas with themselves they tended to use "singular" information (related to the current task).

The testing effect

When students are revising for an exam, they often skim through their notes, discovering to their delight (or even surprise) that most of the material seems familiar. What this means is that they have reasonable recognition memory for the material. However, there is a large difference between *recognising* information as familiar and being able to produce it at will during an anxiety-inducing exam. To succeed in written exams, you must *recall* the information you need. As generations of students have discovered to their cost, good recognition memory for the information relevant to an exam is no guarantee at all that recall will be equally good.

This leads us neatly into the *testing effect*, which describes the best way to revise—by repeated testing rather than repeated study, the method used by many students. The testing effect was demonstrated by Roediger and Karpicke (2006). They gave students some text on a general scientific topic and asked them to memorise it, but they had to do this in a specific way.

- Group 1 (repeated study) were told to memorise the text by reading it through four times.
- Group 2 (single test) were told to memorise the text by reading it through three times and then trying to recall as much as they could (self test).
- Group 3 (repeated test) were told to memorise the text by reading it once and then giving themselves three self tests.

What did they find? Look at the graph on the left. It shows that repeated study works in the short term, but in the long term (after one week) repeated test proved a much more effective strategy. Most students "believe" in repeated study and in fact, in this experiment, the students in Group 1 (repeated *study* method) predicted they would do better than Group 3. In fact they did 50% worse than Group 3 (the repeated *test* method). So it would seem that repeated testing is better than repeated study.

How can we explain the testing effect? Bjork and Bjork (1992) argued that an excellent way to improve long-term memory is via effortful retrieval, as happened in the repeated test condition. "Effortful retrieval" means that your effort is focused on *recalling* the information rather than just repeatedly trying to remember it. The take-home message is that if you make the effort to recall information several times as you study it, this will make the information in question much more memorable in the long term.

 Why do many people fail to achieve work targets, despite the fact that they really should know better?

SECTION 2
HOW CAN I DO WELL IN THE EXAM?

Very few students like exams, but there are a lot of strategies that you can use to make them less stressful, so that on the day of the exams you will be very keen to let the examiner know what you have learned about psychology.

Four key factors will help you do well in an exam:

1. Knowing how you learn.
2. Knowing what you will be examined on (*i.e. knowing the specification*).
3. Knowing how you will be assessed and what form the questions will take.
4. Knowing how to prepare for the exam and what to do in the examination room.

Knowing How You Learn

Think about the strategies that work for you. Some students like summarising their notes onto cards. Others devise posters or put "post-its" around their room. Others find it much easier to learn information by discussing their ideas with a friend.

Try the quiz below to help you think about how you learn.

Look at the following questions and answer yes or no	YES	NO
1. I often see my notes in my head when I sit an exam.		
2. I can never seem to start my work.		
3. When I explain my ideas to someone else, they often become clearer to me.		
4. I find it easy to remember conversations word for word.		
5. If a friend phones me I'll stop working and chat for hours.		
6. I often say what I am writing down to myself.		
7. I find it easier to remember my notes when I highlight key points.		
8. I can remember my notes by repeating them over and over again to myself.		
9. I often look at my book, but nothing ever goes in.		
10. I like it when people ask me questions about psychology and I can explain things to them.		
11. I like using different coloured pens when making revision notes.		
12. I find it hard to work on my own.		
13. I can always find something else to do when I am meant to be studying.		
14. I can remember where things are on a page.		
15. I enjoy talking about psychology to my friends.		
16. I often hear my teacher's voice when I read through my notes.		

- If you answered yes to questions 1, 7, 11, and 14, you enjoy learning using a visual approach. Making posters, using "post-its" and coloured pens and highlighters will help you for the exam.
- If you answered yes to questions 2, 5, 9, and 13, you are easily distracted and find it hard to start work. You need to remove all distractions (e.g. mobile phone) and realise that it might take you 5–10 minutes to settle into doing the work. Focus on the task you have set yourself for a certain amount of time (e.g. 30 minutes) and then take a break.
- If you answered yes to questions 3, 10, 12, and 15, you enjoy learning in a social way. Working with a friend as you revise and discussing ideas will help you for the exam.
- If you answered yes to questions 4, 6, 8, and 16, you enjoy learning information using sound. Some students make recordings of the key points they need to remember, and then listen to them before they go to sleep.
- If you answered yes to a range of questions, you don't have a preferred method of learning information and may use a range of strategies to help you.

Knowing What You Will be Examined on

EXAM HINT

Read the specification—this will help you reduce the amount you need to revise!

The AS psychology exam is divided into *two* units but it is essential to know which topics are assessed in each unit.

- UNIT 1: Explores cognitive psychology, developmental psychology, and research methods.
- UNIT 2: Explores biological psychology, social psychology, and individual differences.

Each exam paper lasts 1 hour 30 minutes and consists of a number of compulsory questions. Questions may be subdivided into more than one part.

There are a variety of question styles, which are described on pages 11 and 12. All questions are based directly on the specification so make sure you know the specific terms in the specification.

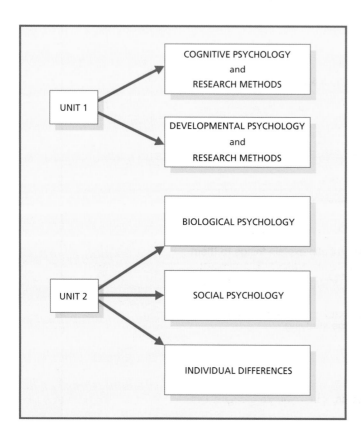

Knowing How You Will be Assessed

There are two exams in AS Psychology and each lasts for 1 hour and 30 minutes. Each exam is worth 50% of the AS result (but 25% of the overall A level).

There are three main assessment objectives in the exams. These are assessment objectives 1, 2, and 3, which are described in detail on the next page. Basically, AO1 is description, AO2 is evaluation and application of knowledge, and AO3 is a consideration of how science works.

In total on each exam there are 72 marks. On Unit 1 these marks are divided equally between the three assessment objectives—so 24 marks each for AO1 and AO2 and AO3. On Unit 2 there are fewer marks for AO3 (just 12 marks) so there are more for AO1 and AO2 (30 marks each).

In general you don't have to know what assessment objective a question is testing, you should just answer the question, as in the questions below:

Outline ***two*** *behaviours that are characteristic of a securely attached infant. (2 marks)*
Describe the multi-store model of memory. (6 marks)
Explain ***one*** *strength and* ***one*** *limitation of the working memory model. (4 marks)*

AO1 Knowledge and understanding of science and how science works

Where the examiners will be looking to see whether students can:

a) recognise, recall, and show understanding of scientific knowledge;
b) select, organise, and communicate relevant information in a variety of forms.

AO2 Application of knowledge and understanding of science and how science works

Where candidates should be able to:

a) analyse and evaluate scientific knowledge and processes;
b) apply scientific knowledge and processes to unfamiliar situations including those related to issues;
c) assess the validity, reliability, and credibility of scientific information.

AO3 How science works—psychology

Where candidates should be able to:

a) describe ethical, safe, and skilful practical techniques and processes, selecting appropriate qualitative and quantitative methods;
b) know how to make, record, and communicate reliable and valid observations and measurement with appropriate precision and accuracy, through using primary and secondary sources;
c) analyse, interpret, explain, and evaluate the methodology, results, and impact of their own and others' experimental and investigative activities in a variety of ways.

EXAM HINT
You might want to return to this page as you read through the book so you get a better understanding of what the examiner is looking for as you progress through the course.

Outline the main features of the sympathomedullary pathway. (3 marks)
Describe personality factors that have been shown to influence the way people respond to stress.
(4 marks)

However, there are some other questions where it isn't always clear what is expected of you unless they have been explained to you. Consider the following:

Evaluate the behavioural approach to psychopathology. (6 marks)

The question above is an AO2 question. Credit would only be given to an evaluation of the approach. The word *evaluate* tells you this.

The following question is also an AO2 question:

James is afraid of flying. Just thinking of flying causes him distress and even going to the airport is a problem. In order to overcome this fear he consults a behavioural psychologist who feels that he may benefit from systematic desensitisation.
Describe how this therapy might be carried out to overcome James's fear of flying. (4 marks)

This also an AO2 question because it involves the application of knowledge. You must make sure that this is what you do—many students make the mistake, in such questions, of simply supplying the facts. For example, in the example above just *describing* the process of systematic desensitisation would gain limited marks. For full marks you must apply the process to the specific situation—James's fear of flying.

There are other "tricks" to be aware of. What would you do with the questions below?

Outline what is involved in the cognitive interview. (3 marks)
Outline what is involved with psychoanalysis. (3 marks)

Such questions require a description of what happens, for example, when you do a cognitive interview or psychoanalysis.

EXAM HINT

If there is a question asking for a comparison (e.g. give two differences between ...) make sure you draw the comparison, rather than describing each separately and expecting the examiner to identify the comparison, as this would receive no marks! So make sure you've used WHEREAS or IN COMPARISON.

What about these questions?

*Describe **one** study related to stress and the immune system. (6 marks)*
Describe how research has investigated stress and the immune system. (6 marks)
Describe what research has shown about stress and the immune system. (6 marks)

Questions on research or research studies may come in one of the three forms above—a general question on one study, a question on procedures only (how), or a question on findings/conclusions (show). If a question says "show" then procedures would not be creditworthy.

Finally, we have the extended writing questions:

Outline and evaluate Bowlby's theory of attachment. (8 marks)
*Discuss **one or more** biological methods of stress management. (10 marks)*
Outline and evaluate research related to conformity (majority influence). (12 marks)
Some people regard the biological approach to psychopathology as the dominant approach. Discuss the biological approach to psychopathology. (12 marks)

On each exam there will be one extended writing question worth 12 marks. On Unit 2 there may be more than one, and on both exams there may also be extended writing questions worth 8 or 10 marks. These questions all involve 50% AO1 and 50% AO2. You will need to think carefully about exactly what you are describing or outlining (AO1) and then how you are going to evaluate or comment on this (AO2).

Strategies to Improve Your Evaluation (AO2)

Kinds of AO2

One way to think about how you can improve your marks for AO2 questions is to consider how you can evaluate the research studies and theories you have studied. Focus on:

EXAM HINT

Avoid "common-sense" answers: you must convince the examiner that your answer is drawn from what you have learned, not from everyday knowledge.

- *Application.* Can the research or theories be applied to everyday life? Does the research benefit humanity?
- *Methodology.* How was the research done? Can you comment on the validity, reliability, or credibility of the research or information? What sampling technique was used, and can we generalise from this sample? Did the participants simply do what they thought the researcher wanted them to do? Could the researcher have been biased?
- *Culture/gender.* How universal are the findings? Do the findings have any relevance for non-Western societies and are the findings gender specific?
- *Commentary.* Use evidence to support your answer. Consider the strengths and weaknesses of the evidence. Explore how psychologists have challenged different theories. Discuss how effective these challenges have been.

AO2 trigger phrases

Don't expect the examiner to read your mind. Unless it is written down, they cannot know what you intended to say. Spell out the points to the examiners. Use phrases like:

EXAM HINT

When in doubt, try writing a sentence that starts "This suggests that ..." or "Therefore, one can conclude ...".

- "This research on eyewitness testimony clearly has applications to everyday life where mistaken identity has led to the wrong person being imprisoned ..."
- "One major problem with this research was that the sample was male and hence it is unclear whether these findings can be generalised to females ..."
- "It is important to recognise the limitations of this definition in that what may be seen as normal in one culture (e.g. having three wives) might be seen as abnormal in other cultures."

Constructing coherent arguments

Constructing coherent arguments takes practice. One way to construct your argument is by thinking about your conclusion, and then working backwards. For example, if you were given the question:

Discuss research into the effects of day care on children's social development. (12 marks)

Your conclusion might be that day care can have a beneficial effect on social development. Working backwards your answer would need to include:

- The evidence that might support your view.
- The strengths and weaknesses of this evidence.
- Other factors that need to be taken into consideration such as:
  - The type of day care being offered.
  - Individual differences.
  - The alternative care provided at home.

Making sure you have enough AO2

Some examiners suggest that answers to 12-mark questions can be broken down into two paragraphs. Using the knowledge that you can only get 6 marks for AO1 and that 6 marks are given for AO2, the first paragraph can be predominantly an AO1 response while the second paragraph would be AO2. For example if you were given the question:

Discuss explanations of why people obey. (12 marks)

- *Paragraph 1* would describe one or more explanations for why people obey, such as the agentic state and/or buffers. In total this paragraph should be about 150 words.
- *Paragraph 2* would evaluate these explanations. This may involve research evidence that supports the explanations, or research evidence that challenges it. This paragraph should again be 150 words.
- An alternative approach would be to use six paragraphs, each of about 50 words:
  - *Paragraph 1* Describe one explanation.
  - *Paragraph 2* Evaluate this explanation.
  - *Paragraph 3* Describe one explanation.
  - *Paragraph 4* Evaluate this explanation.
  - *Paragraph 5* Describe one explanation.
  - *Paragraph 6* Evaluate this explanation.

Assessment Objective 3: How Science Works

So far we have just looked at questions that relate to AO1 and AO2. Questions that assess AO3 come in two forms:

1. On Unit 1 there will be two or more structured questions, one related to cognitive psychology and one related to developmental psychology. For example:

A psychologist wishes to investigate the effects of day care on early child development. She decides to compare social behaviours in children who enter day care before the age of 2 years with children who start day care after the age of 2 years.
(a) Identify the independent variable in this study. (1 mark)
(b) Write a suitable hypothesis for this study. (2 marks)
(c) Suggest a suitable sampling method and explain how you would use it. (3 marks)

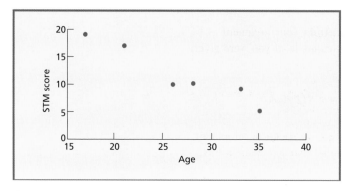

STM = short-term memory.

2. On Units 1 and 2 there will be questions on the research methods themselves as well as ethics, validity, and the interpretation of graphs and tables. For example:

(a) *Explain one limitation of using an interview to collect data. (2 marks)*

(b) *Describe one ethical issue raised by research into conformity. (3 marks)*

(c) *Explain a way of dealing with the ethical issue described in (b). (2 marks)*

(d) *What does the scattergraph on the left show about memory? (3 marks)*

(e) *Explain difficulties in drawing conclusions from this data. (2 marks)*

How the Exams are Marked

Examiners are given mark schemes to enable them to work out how many marks to award to an answer. Questions that are worth 2 or 3 marks tend to be marked in terms of a simple formula, such as:

- 1 mark for each strength and a further mark for explaining why it is a strength.
- 1 mark for a brief answer and a further 2 marks for elaboration.
- Up to 2 marks for factors and 2 further marks for elaboration of factors.

For questions worth 4 or more marks the mark schemes on this and the next page are either used singly or they are both used if the question involves both description and evaluation.

EXAM HINT

The number of marks for each question is variable but you can judge how much to write by writing approximately 1 minute per mark on these short-answer questions. Be careful not to write too much or too little. Your answers may be correct but just lacking in detail/elaboration. Use research evidence and examples to increase the content.

Description — knowledge and understanding (AO1)			
4-mark question	6-mark question		
4 marks	6 marks	**Accurate and reasonably detailed**	Accurate and reasonably detailed description that demonstrates sound knowledge and understanding. There is appropriate selection of material to address the question.
3 marks	5–4 marks	**Less detailed but generally accurate**	Less detailed but generally accurate description that demonstrates relevant knowledge and understanding. There is some evidence of selection of material to address the question.
2 marks	3–2 marks	**Basic**	Basic description that demonstrates some relevant knowledge and understanding but lacks detail and may be muddled. There is little evidence of selection of material to address the question.
1 mark	1 mark	**Very brief/ flawed**	Very brief or flawed description that demonstrates very little knowledge or understanding. Selection of information is largely inappropriate.
0 marks	0 marks		No creditworthy material

4-mark question	6-mark question		
Evaluation—application of knowledge and understanding (AO2)			
4 marks	6 marks	**Effective evaluation**	Effective use of material to address the question and provide informed evaluation. Effective use of research evidence. Broad range of issues and/or evidence in reasonable depth, or a narrower range in greater depth. Clear expression of ideas, good range of specialist terms, few errors of grammar, punctuation, and spelling.
3 marks	5–4 marks	**Reasonable evaluation**	Material is not always used effectively but produces a reasonable evaluation. Reasonable use of research evidence. A range of issues and/or evidence in limited depth, or a narrower range in greater depth. Reasonable expression of ideas, a range of specialist terms, some errors of grammar, punctuation, and spelling.
2 marks	3–2 marks	**Basic evaluation**	The use of material provides only a basic evaluation. Basic use of research evidence. Superficial consideration of a restricted range of issues and/or evidence. Expression of ideas lacks clarity; some specialist terms used; errors of grammar, punctuation, and spelling detract from clarity.
1 mark	1 mark	**Rudimentary evaluation**	The use of material provides only a rudimentary evaluation. Use of research evidence is just discernible or absent. Expression of ideas poor; few specialist terms used; errors of grammar, punctuation, and spelling often obscure the meaning.
0 marks	0 marks		No creditworthy material

Some ideas of how examiners use these mark schemes can be seen by looking at the following questions and examiners' comments.

Question: Describe one study of duration of short-term memory. (6 marks)

Candidate's answer: Peterson and Peterson did a study on the capacity of short-term memory. Participants were shown three-letter consonants, such as RTG. Then they were asked to recall them either after 3, 12, 15, or 18 seconds. The longer the interval, the worse their recall was.

Examiner's comment: The candidate has included some information, such as who did the study and what they did, but there is minimal detail. The findings have been treated rather briefly and certain other details were omitted (such as what the participants did while they were waiting to recall the digits). Therefore this answer would be described as "limited", close to "basic", and would get 3 out of 6 marks.

Question: "People who witness a crime want to be able to provide useful information to the police to help them catch the criminal." Outline and evaluate psychological research into the accuracy of eyewitness testimony. (12 marks)

Candidate's answer: Psychological research has investigated many areas of memory that are relevant to eyewitness testimony. The first area I will consider is Loftus's research on the way the language used in questioning the eyewitness will affect recall. In her experiment it was found that, if people were asked "About how fast were the cars going when they smashed into each other?", they estimated the cars' speed as being faster than if the word "hit" was used in the question. Questions that suggest a particular answer are known as leading questions.

Another line of evidence has looked at the effect of age of the witnesses on accuracy. Bronfenbrenner compared the memories of young children and older children and adults. They heard about an incident and two days later their memory of it was tested. Some of the participants had been given misleading information at the time of the incident. Bronfenbrenner found that in general there were few age differences except where there had been misleading information. The younger children were much more affected by this.

There are other factors which might reduce accuracy of eyewitness memory. Loftus showed that anxiety, especially when there was a physical threat such as a gun or knife at the incident, focused the eyewitness's attention on the weapon and not the culprit, and so their memory of the culprit was poor. This is called the weapon focus.

One criticism of this research is that these studies were laboratory experiments and so we cannot be sure the findings would be generalisable to everyday behaviour because of the artificial nature of the tasks. This criticism is supported by other studies, such as Valentine et al., which found no weapon effect on accuracy of eyewitnesses.

The evidence about age raises some real-life concerns. Adults such as jurors seem to readily accept children's testimony as they are seen as having no reason to lie, and also they seem confident. However, because of the reasons discussed above it is clear that children's testimony is as likely to be as, or more, flawed and inaccurate compared to adults'.

This is not to say that adults' memories are always correct. Several research studies, e.g. Brewer et al., have shown that older adults are as likely to have reconstructed memories as children, much more so than younger adults. Older adults also seem very suggestible, which makes their testimony less accurate. This could be explained by the young and the old being concerned to please the questioners and not wanting to cause trouble.

Examiner's comment: The candidate has presented a well-structured answer to the question, following a variation of the six-paragraph rule described on page 9. The AO1 material (description of psychological research) is accurate and generally detailed though the third paragraph lacks specific details of the research, so 5 out of 6 marks. The AO2 material (commentary on the research) displays depth—each point has been explained. The range is reasonable but not broad so again 5 out of 6 marks. This gives a total of 10 marks, which would be equivalent to a Grade A.

EXAM HINT

Remember: There is rarely a single right answer. Instead, obtaining high marks involves producing answers that are well-informed, well-constructed, well-argued, and in which the material used is well-selected.

So now you know what each unit is about and how you will be assessed. The last aspect of doing well in exams is to focus on exam technique.

Knowing How to Prepare for the Exam

Revise the topics you know you will be tested on:

• Make a glossary of key terms or concepts for each topic.

- Make sure you can describe and evaluate all theories, models, and research areas identified in the specification.
- Make sure you can apply your knowledge to real-life examples.
- Make sure you can evaluate psychological theories and research in terms of:
  - APPLICATION
  - METHODOLOGY
  - ETHICS
  - GENDER AND CULTURAL FACTORS
- Make sure you know how you will be assessed.

Proper preparation for the exam, and an understanding of how to gain marks, will increase your chances of getting a good grade.

Methodology

Whenever you read about research ask yourself the following questions:

- What research method did they use?
- How did they select the sample?
- Was the sample biased in any way?
- Were there any other biases in the study?
- How were the data collected?
- How were the data analysed?
- What did they conclude from the study?
- What other conclusions could they have drawn?
- How ethical was the study?

In the Examination Room

- Read all the questions carefully BEFORE YOU START WRITING. Remember you have to answer all questions, so you need to plan your time wisely.
- Underline the key words in the question, so that if you are asked to describe the *limitation* of a certain method you don't describe its *strength*.
- Before you start writing, quickly jot down the key points you want to include in your answer, so you don't forget your points as you start answering the question.
- Keep focused on the question set so that you don't fall into the trap of:
  - writing down everything you know about the topic, whether it is relevant or not;
  - repeating the same point over and over again;
  - drifting away from the question.
- In extended writing questions make sure each paragraph relates back to the question.
- Use the marks by the side of the question to help you plan your time. You should aim to spend approximately just over a minute per mark. If the question is worth 12 marks you need to spend three times as long answering this question as a 4-mark question.
- Be careful about how you express yourself:
  - Avoid making sweeping, inaccurate, ill-informed, or judgemental statements.
  - Avoid expressing personal opinions such as "I really don't like this study." Instead use phrases like "This study has been criticised for causing the participants stress."
  - Always back up your views with evidence.
  - Avoid one-word criticisms like "this study was unethical". Instead expand on your answer by stating why the study was unethical.
- And above all else, DON'T PANIC. Even if the examination questions aren't the ones you wanted, if you have prepared for the exam and understand how you can gain marks, you will be able to write an answer.

EXAM HINT

Remember that quantity doesn't equal quality. Stick to the point and organise your answer clearly so that the examiner can follow your argument.

Coping with stress in exams

If you know what to expect in an exam it removes the element of surprise and allows you to be prepared. This preparation will involve:

- organising your information;
- learning the information;
- understanding how the information can be used to answer questions in the exam.

But studying psychology also helps. Chapter 5 looks at stress management, so reading that before the exam will give you some ideas about how to lessen stress.

Here is some advice from that chapter:

- THINK POSITIVELY: This will increase your sense of control: "I can only do my best."
- AVOID DEFENCE MECHANISMS SUCH AS DENIAL: Recognise the feeling of stress and intellectualise your problem.
- RELAX: At intervals during the exam have a break and think positive thoughts unrelated to the exam.
- SOCIAL SUPPORT: Think about comforting people or things.
- PHYSICAL EXERCISE AND EMOTIONAL DISCHARGE: Go for a run before the exam, stretch your legs, find some means of discharging tension during the exam (that doesn't disturb anyone else).

Revision Questions

At the end of each chapter you will find sample exam-style questions. These will give you an idea of the type of question you might be asked in the exam. You could also use them to practise writing answers under timed conditions and can then check your work against the sample answers we provide online.

What you need to know

Section 3: Models of memory p. 17

■ The multi-store model including the concepts of encoding, capacity, and duration.
Strengths and limitations of the model.

■ The working memory model, including its strengths and limitations.

Short-term memory (STM) is the part of the memory system in which information is initially stored. Information that we remember is held in long-term memory (LTM). What causes information to be moved from STM to LTM? Some answers to that question are considered. There is also consideration of the nature of short-term memory and whether it is best regarded as a system consisting of various components. The working memory model is an example of a theoretical approach based on the assumption that short-term memory is complex and consists of several components.

Section 4: Memory in everyday life p. 38

■ Eyewitness testimony (EWT). Factors affecting the accuracy of EWT, including misleading information, anxiety, age of witness.

■ Improving accuracy of EWT, including the use of the cognitive interview.

■ Strategies for memory improvement.

This section looks at practical applications of memory research. Eyewitness reports involve identifying suspects or describing what happened when a crime was committed. How reliable are eyewitnesses when they try to recall what happened? In our everyday lives we often find it frustrating or embarrassing when we simply forget something that is really important (e.g. a close friend's birthday). Ways in which we can all improve our memories are discussed.

Memory

2

You may think that in an ideal world we would remember every detail of things that happen, especially when they are important. However, if we remembered *everything* our memories would be very full. As a result, we would find it hard to think because of the enormous wealth of detail we would always be remembering. In fact, of course, we actually forget lots of things, many of them (alas!) things we didn't want to forget. What makes some things memorable and others forgettable?

This chapter explores one topic in cognitive psychology—human memory. How important is memory? Imagine if we were without it. We would not recognise anyone or anything as familiar. We would not be able to talk, read, or write, because we would remember nothing about language. In many ways we would be like newborn babies.

We use memory for numerous purposes—to keep track of conversations, to remember telephone numbers while we dial them, to write essays in exams, to make sense of what we read, and to recognise people's faces. There are many different kinds of memory, suggesting we have a number of memory systems. This chapter explores in detail the sub-divisions of human memory, the accuracy of eyewitness testimony, and ways in which you can improve your memory.

SECTION 3
MODELS OF MEMORY

Memory is the process of retaining information for some time after it was learned. Thus, there are close links between **learning** and **memory**. Something that is learned is lodged in memory, and we can only remember things learned in the past.

Memory and learning can most clearly be demonstrated by good performance on a memory test. For example, we could give someone a list of words for a specified period of time and then some time later ask them to recall the list. When learning and memorising the words in the list, there are three stages:

1. **Encoding**: When the person is given the list, they encode the words. They place the words in memory. "Encoding" means to put something into a code, in this case the code used to store it in memory—some kind of memory trace. For example, if you hear the word "chair", you might encode it in terms of your favourite chair you normally sit in at home. In other words, your encoding of the word "chair" involves converting or changing the word you hear into a meaningful form.

Are learning and memory different? If so, what is the difference?

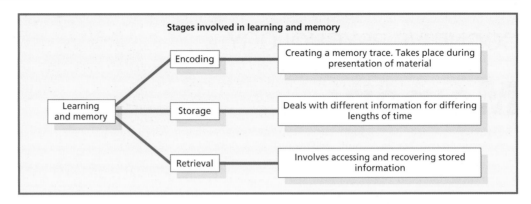

2. Storage: As a result of encoding, the information is stored within the memory system. As we will see, some information remains stored in memory for decades or even an entire lifetime.

3. Retrieval: Recovering stored information from the memory system. This involves recall or "remembering".

Psychologists interested in learning focus on encoding and storage. In contrast, those interested in memory concentrate most on retrieval. Note that all these processes depend on each other—we only know that an individual has learned something if they remember it, and memory depends on previous learning.

Testing memory

Psychologists use various methods to test recall or learning.

- Free recall. Give participants some words to learn and then ask them to recall the words in any order.
- Cued recall. After presenting the material to be learned, provide cues to help recall. For example, saying that some of the items are minerals.
- Recognition. Giving a list of words which includes some of those in the initial presentation. Participants are asked to identify those in the original list.
- Paired-associate learning. Participants are given word pairs to learn and then tested by presenting the first word in each pair and asking them to recall the second word.
- Nonsense syllables. Participants are asked to memorise meaningless sets of letters. These may be trigrams (three letters).

Multi-Store Model of Memory

There is an important distinction between two kinds of memory: short-term memory and long-term memory. Information in short-term memory lasts for only a short time (a few seconds). In contrast, information in long-term memory can theoretically last forever or at least for a very long time.

Trying to remember a telephone number for a few seconds is sometimes used as an example of the use of **short-term memory**. This example illustrates two of the key features of short-term memory: a very limited capacity and a very limited duration. **Long-term memory**, on the other hand, has unlimited capacity and lasts (potentially) forever. As an example, you might think of some of your most vivid childhood memories.

The model of memory put forward by Atkinson and Shiffrin (1968) is the most important theoretical approach based on the notion that there are separate short-term and long-term memory stores. In fact, they actually argued there are three kinds of memory stores. This explains why their approach

KEY TERMS

Storage: storing a memory for a period of time so that it can be used later.

Retrieval: the process of recovering information stored in long-term memory. If retrieval is successful, the individual remembers the information in question.

Short-term memory: a temporary place for storing information during which it receives limited processing (e.g. verbal rehearsal). Short-term memory has a very limited capacity and short duration, unless the information in it is maintained through rehearsal.

Long-term memory: a relatively permanent memory store with an unlimited capacity and duration, containing different components such as episodic (personal events), semantic (facts and information), and procedural (actions and skills) memory.

is known as the **multi-store model** of memory. Here are the crucial assumptions built into this model:

1. Human memory consists of three kinds of memory stores.
2. Information from the environment is initially received by the **sensory stores**. There is one sensory store for each sense modality—a store for what we see, one for what we hear, and so on. Information lasts for a very short period of time (fractions of a second, or a second or two) in these sensory stores.
3. Some of the information in the sensory stores is attended to (and processed further) within the short-term store. The main feature of the short-term store is that it has limited capacity—we can only keep about *seven* items in this store at any one time.
4. Some of the information processed in the short-term store is transferred to the long-term store. How does information get into the long-term store? We need to rehearse or repeat verbally information in the short-term store to put it into the long-term store. The more something is rehearsed, the stronger the memory trace in long-term memory.
5. The key feature of the long-term store is that information in it can often last for a long time. As I have already mentioned, in some cases information in the long-term store remains there for our entire lifetime.
6. There are important differences between short-term and long-term memory in forgetting. When information is forgotten from the short-term store, it simply disappears from the memory system. In contrast, most information that is forgotten from the long-term store is still in the memory system but can't be accessed (e.g. because of interference from other information).

Even if we don't pay attention when we're spoken to, we are often able to repeat the last few things said. This is because that information is held for a few seconds in a sensory memory store, before entering short-term memory.

In what follows, we will be looking mainly at the short-term and long-term memory stores. However, we will start by briefly considering the sensory stores.

Sensory stores

Our sense organs are constantly bombarded with information. At this very moment, you are receiving visual information from this book, there is probably auditory information in the form of human voices or traffic noise, and you can feel something from that part of you in contact with the chair on which you are sitting. There is a separate sensory store for each type of information—the iconic store is used for visual information, the echoic store for auditory information, the haptic store concerned with touching and feeling, and so on. There has been far more research on the iconic store than any of the others, and so I will focus on that store.

Sperling (1960) carried out the classic research on this store. He presented a visual array containing three rows of four letters each for 50 milliseconds (1/20 of a second). Participants

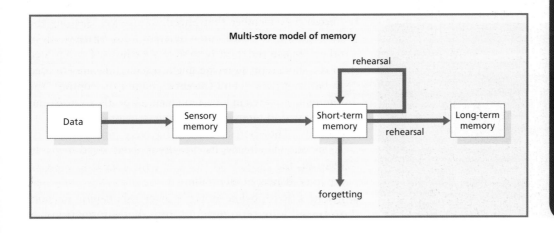

Multi-store model of memory

could only report four or five letters when asked to provide full recall but claimed to have seen many more. Sperling assumed this happened because visual information had faded before most of it could be reported.

Sperling (1960) tested the above hypothesis by telling participants to recall only *part* of the information presented. Sperling's results supported his assumption—part recall was very good and suggested that the iconic store had held nine or ten items. Full recall was much poorer because information in the iconic store decays within about 0.5 seconds.

Why is the iconic store useful? One reason is that the processes involved in visual perception *always* operate on the information in the iconic store rather than directly on the visual environment. The iconic store is also useful when it comes to watching movies. Movies are often presented at 24 frames per second with each frame differing slightly from the previous and next ones. We perceive smooth motion rather than jerky motion because the iconic store allows us to integrate information from successive frames in a way that wouldn't be possible in its absence.

Short-term vs long-term memory: Brain damage

We all know certain kinds of information disappear rapidly from memory whereas others last for years and years. Accordingly, you may think it is obvious that there are separate short-term and long-term stores. I will shortly be discussing the main differences between these two stores. Before that, however, I want to discuss the strongest evidence for separate memory stores. Strangely enough, it consists of research on brain-damaged patients. If short-term and long-term memory are really separate, we might expect to find some brain-damaged patients with impaired long-term memory but intact short-term memory. Others should have impaired short-term memory but intact long-term memory.

In **amnesia**, a person loses much of their long-term memory. This is often due to an accident that has caused brain damage or it can be due to chronic alcoholism. In spite of their brain damage, amnesic patients typically have intact short-term memory. This was shown convincingly by Spiers et al. (2001) in a review of 147 amnesic patients with serious long-term memory problems. *None* of these patients had a significant problem with short-term memory.

The opposite pattern (good long-term memory but poor short-term memory) has also been found occasionally. Consider, KF, who suffered brain damage after a motorcycle accident. He had no problem with long-term learning and recall, but his digit span was greatly impaired (Shallice & Warrington, 1970).

Short-term vs long-term memory: Capacity, duration, and encoding

However, to prove the point (or get as close to proof as we can), we need to start by listing all the likely differences between the short-term and long-term memory stores.

When we have listed the differences, we can consider the relevant research evidence. Finally, we will evaluate that evidence and decide how accurately the multi-store model actually accounts for human memory. Here are possible (or probable!) differences between the short-term and long-term memory stores:

1. *Encoding*: Remember that encoding involves *changing* the information presented into a different form. Since words or other items in the short-term store are rehearsed or repeated in the short-term store, we might assume they are encoded in terms of their sound (acoustic coding). In contrast, the information stored in long-term memory nearly always seems to be stored in terms of its meaning (semantic coding).

2. *Capacity*: The short-term store has very limited capacity. As mentioned already, its capacity is about seven items. In contrast, the capacity of the long-term store is so large we are in no danger at all of filling it.

3. *Duration*: It is obvious from the names short-term memory store and long-term memory store that information has

---

KEY TERM

Amnesia: a severe loss of some kinds of long-term memory, usually as a result of brain damage.

EXAM HINT

The specification requires you to study the concepts of encoding, capacity and duration. You may be set questions on each of these topics, including questions that ask you to explain the terms and, also, questions on research studies. For example,

- "Explain how psychologists have investigated the capacity of human memory. (4 marks)"
- "Explain how research has investigated duration in short-term human memory. (4 marks)"
- "Explain what research has shown about encoding in human memory. (4 marks)"

Be prepared.

greater duration (i.e. lasts longer) in the long-term store than in the short-term store! As we will see, information in the short-term store, if not rehearsed, disappears within about 18–20 seconds. In contrast, elderly people can recognise the names of fellow students from 48 years previously (Bahrick et al., 1975). Thus, we have proof that long-term memory can last virtually 50 years at least.

Now we will look at the evidence relating to these various assumptions about the short-term and long-term memory stores. After that, we will evaluate the multi-store model, trying to identify its main strengths and limitations.

Short-term memory: Capacity
It is harder than you might imagine to estimate the capacity of short-term memory. Psychologists have devised two main strategies: span measures and the recency effect in free recall.

Span measures
In 1887, Joseph Jacobs used memory span as a measure of how much can be stored in short-term memory. Jacobs presented his participants with a random sequence of digits or letters, and then asked them to repeat the items back in the same order. **Memory span** was the longest sequence of items recalled accurately at least 50% of the time. The average number of items recalled was between five and nine, and digits were recalled better (9.3 items) than letters (7.3 items).

Jacobs' approach was limited. First, his research lacked **mundane realism**, because his span tasks were not representative of everyday memory demands. Second, if we could only remember a few letters, we would be unable to remember the following sequence of 10 letters: P S Y C H O L O G Y! In fact, of course, we can remember that sequence because it's easy to organise the information in memory.

Miller (1956) took account of the above point, and argued that the span of immediate memory is "seven, plus or minus two", whether the units are numbers, letters, or words. He claimed we should focus on **chunks** (integrated pieces or units of information). About seven chunks of information can be held in short-term memory at any time. The question of what constitutes a "chunk" depends on your personal experience. For example, "IBM" would be one chunk if you know about International Business Machines, but it would be three if you didn't know what IBM stood for.

Simon (1974) tested Miller's ideas on **chunking**. In his research, he studied memory span for words, two-word phrases, and eight-word phrases. The number of words in the span increased from seven words to nine with two-word phrases and 22 with eight-word phrases. At the level

> **?** To what extent can we apply the findings of Jacobs to everyday life?

> **?** Are there any problems with using letter or digit span as a measure of the capacity of short-term memory?

HOW SCIENCE WORKS: Chunking

Scientific method involves observing what occurs and seeing if there is a pattern. For example, you know that Miller found most people have an STM capacity of 7 plus or minus 2, which we call Miller's magic number. But you can test the idea that we can store far more than 9 items in STM by chunking them. This means we group similar things together in one category, for example: mug+spoon+teabag+sugar+milk. Ask whoever does the main shopping at home how they remember what's needed—do they chunk their list?

From such observations you could construct a prediction, called a hypothesis, and then you could test it. You could predict that people will recall more things, or recall them faster, if they chunk items rather than trying to remember them randomly.

You could try compiling and printing out a random shopping list for the supermarket, mixing up about 25 items from all around the store. Then make a second list of 25 different items but this time chunk them, i.e. group together similar items (like fresh vegetables; tinned goods; but don't use headings!). Test someone—not the main shopper—on the first list: give them 1 minute to read and learn, then 2 minutes to recall by writing items down. Then do the same for the second list. They will probably do better or faster on the second list, and you can explain why to them.

In science it is important to test the hypothesis, and find out whether it is correct or wrong. This is the way we increase scientific knowledge.

KEY TERMS

Memory span: an assessment of how much can be stored in short-term memory (STM) at any time.

Mundane realism: the use of an artificial situation that closely resembles a natural situation.

Chunks: integrated units of information.

Chunking: the process of combining individual items (e.g. letters; numbers) into larger, meaningful units.

of chunks, Simon argued that an entire phrase forms a single chunk. The number of chunks recalled varied less over conditions than the number of words—it fell from six or seven with unrelated words to four with two-word phrases and three with eight-word phrases. As with Jacobs' earlier research, the study by Simon (1974) lacks mundane realism in that the demands on the participants were very different from those of our everyday lives.

Cowan et al. (2005) argued that the capacity of short-term memory is often exaggerated. For example, people may recall some of the information from long-term memory rather than short-term memory. Cowan et al. (2005) reduced the involvement of long-term memory by using the running memory task—a series of digits ended at an unpredictable point, with the participants' task being to recall the items from the end of the list. The average number of items recalled was 3.87, suggesting that the true capacity of short-term memory is about four items.

The recency effect

A familiar example of the **recency effect** is the observation that a pop group is only as good as their last hit song. People generally have a good memory for most-recent things (e.g. the movie they saw last). In relation to short-term memory, the recency effect can be measured using free recall—participants see a list of words or syllables, and immediately recall them in any order. The recency effect is demonstrated by the fact that the last two or three items in a list are usually much better remembered than items from the middle of the list. These last few items are well remembered because they are in the short-term store when the list presentation comes to an end.

Glanzer and Cunitz (1966) introduced an interference task involving counting backwards by threes for 10 seconds between the end of the list and the start of recall. This eliminated the recency effect but had no effect on recall of the rest of the list. The two or three words at the end of the list were in a fragile state in short-term memory, and so were easily wiped out by the task of counting backwards. In contrast, the other list items were in the long-term store and so were unaffected.

> **?** If you were shown these ten words: cat, butter, car, house, carpet, tomato, beer, river, pool, tennis; and then asked to recall them immediately in any order, what words are likely to be best remembered?

ACTIVITY: Memory span

Read quickly through the following list of digits once. Cover the list and try to write the digits down in the correct order.

7 3 5 1 5 6 9 8 2 7 4

How many did you remember in the correct order? This is one way of measuring your memory span. Now try the following digits:

1 9 3 9 1 0 6 6 1 8 0 5 1 2 1 5

More digits, but if you recognised the "chunks" you should have remembered them all:

1939 Start of Second World War
1066 Battle of Hastings
1805 Battle of Trafalgar
1215 Signing of the Magna Carta

Did you find any recency effects when you tried to recall the list of digits? Try the test again (with different data) with this in mind.

KEY TERM

Recency effect: better free recall of the last few items in a list, where higher performance is due to the information being in the short-term store.

Long-term memory: Capacity

As already mentioned, long-term memory has essentially unlimited capacity. There is much evidence that our ability to store information in long-term memory is surprisingly good.

Standing et al. (1970) presented their participants with 2560 pictures over a number of days. Approximately 90% of these pictures were identified correctly on a subsequent memory test.

Konkle et al. (2010) extended the findings of Standing et al. (1970). They presented participants with 2912 pictures of scenes at 3 seconds per scene followed by a test of recognition memory. The scenes belonged to a total of 128 different general categories. Long-term memory for these scenes was very good. When participants had to choose between a previously presented scene and a new scene from a category not used during presentation, they were correct 96% of the time. Memory performance remained above 75% even when the previously presented scene and the new scene both came from the same category. The finding that participants could discriminate among rather similar scenes suggests that the information stored in long-term memory is reasonably detailed.

Short-term memory: Duration

We have seen that the capacity of short-term memory is very limited. However, this leaves open another important issue—how long does information last in short-term memory? This is a crucial question. If information is lost rapidly from short-term memory, this must limit our ability to think about several things at once.

KEY STUDY

Peterson and Peterson (1959): Duration of short-term memory

Peterson and Peterson (1959) assessed the duration of short-term memory using what became known as the Brown–Peterson technique. They aimed to test the hypothesis that information that is not rehearsed is lost rapidly from short-term memory. They used the experimental method under laboratory conditions to test this hypothesis.

On each trial, participants were presented with a trigram consisting of three consonants (e.g. BVM, CTG), which they knew they would be asked to recall in the correct order. Recall was required after a delay of 3, 6, 9, 12, 15, or 18 seconds. Thus, the length of the delay period was the independent variable.

The participants had to count backwards in threes from a random three-digit number (e.g. 866, 863, 860, and so on) between the initial presentation of the trigram and the time when they were asked to recall it. This was done to prevent **rehearsal** of the trigram, because rehearsal would have improved performance by keeping information in short-term memory.

Recall had to be 100% accurate and in the correct order (serial recall) to be regarded as correct. Thus, the percentage correct serial recall was the dependent variable. The participants were tested repeatedly with the various time delays. Thus, the design involved repeated measures. The experimenters varied the time delay, and the effect of time delay on memory was assessed in terms of the number of trigrams recalled.

Findings

What did Peterson and Peterson (1959) find? There was a rapid increase in forgetting from short-term memory as the time delay increased (see Figure overleaf). After 3 seconds, 80% of the trigrams were recalled, after 6 seconds 50% were recalled, and after 18 seconds fewer than 10% were recalled.

One conclusion is that information in short-term memory is fragile and easily forgotten. Another conclusion is that short-term memory is distinct from long-term memory in that forgetting is enormously faster from short-term memory.

Limitations

We could make some criticisms of this study. First, Peterson and Peterson (1959) used very artificial stimuli (i.e. trigrams) essentially lacking in meaning. Thus, the study lacks mundane realism and external validity. For example, short-term memory is likely to be better in everyday life than for the stimuli used in this study.

continued overleaf

[?] Was the approach taken by Peterson and Peterson (1959) too artificial to tell us much about short-term forgetting in everyday life?

[?] Why was information in short-term memory forgotten so quickly?

KEY TERM

Rehearsal: the verbal repetition of information (often words), which typically has the effect of increasing our long-term memory for the rehearsed information.

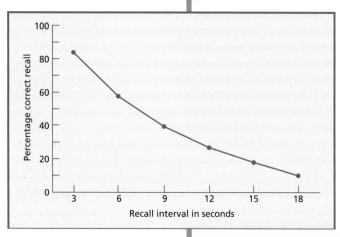

The graph shows a steady decline in short-term memory recall after longer retention intervals (from Peterson & Peterson, 1959).

Second, the participants were given many trials with different trigrams and may have become confused. Keppel and Underwood (1962) used the same task as Peterson and Peterson (1959) but observed *no* forgetting over time on the very first trial. Why was this? Forgetting is caused in part by proactive interference (disruption of current learning and memory by previous learning), and only the first trigram presented is free from proactive interference.

Third, Peterson and Peterson (1959) only considered short-term memory duration for one type of stimulus. Their study did not provide information about the duration of short-term memory for other kinds of stimuli (e.g. pictures; melodies; smells).

Long-term memory: Duration

How can one assess how long a memory lasts? This is difficult. Even if you can't remember something, it is hard to prove it's not in memory somewhere but you simply can't bring it to mind. If you can remember something, it might be an *inaccurate* memory you have constructed.

KEY STUDY

Bahrick et al. (1975): Very-long-term memory (VLTM)

In spite of the problems involved, psychologists have successfully conducted research into "very-long-term memory" (VLTM). It is said the elderly don't lose their childhood memories, and many skills (e.g. riding a bicycle) are never forgotten.

Bahrick et al. (1975) aimed to study the duration of very-long-term memory using photographs from high-school yearbooks (an annual publication where everyone's picture is shown with their name and other details). They used an opportunity sample of 392 American ex-high-school students aged from 17 to 74. Age was the variable of interest in an independent groups design.

Participants' memory was tested in various ways:

(1) Free recall of the names of as many their former classmates as possible.
(2) A photo recognition test where they identified former classmates from 50 photos, only some of which showed their classmates.
(3) A name recognition test.
(4) A name and photo matching test.

Thus, there were four dependent variables (types of behaviour assessed) in this study.

Findings
What did Bahrick et al. (1975) find? There was 90% accuracy in face and name recognition even for those participants who had left high school 34 years previously. After 48 years, this declined to 80% for name recognition and 40% for face recognition. Thus, people do have genuine very-long-term memories. However, free recall was much less accurate: 60% accurate after 15 years and only 30% accurate after 48 years. These findings mean that very long-term memory is much better when suitable cues (e.g. photographs) are available than when they aren't.

Limitations

Compared to the vast majority of laboratory-based research, Bahrick et al.'s research has high mundane realism. Asking participants to recall their classmates tests real-life memory. Thus, the research is more representative of natural behaviour and so has high external validity (i.e. the findings are likely to generalise to other situations).

Classmates' faces are a very specific type of information. They might have emotional significance and there will have been much opportunity for rehearsal given the daily contact involved. The same is not true of other types of information and so these findings can't be generalised to other types of information. For example, wishful thinking plays a part in very-long-term memory for academic grades. Bahrick et al. (2008) found that American ex-college students had reasonable recall of their academic grades over intervals of up to 54 years. However, the great majority of errors involved inflating the actual grade.

Some memories never fade. Can you remember the names of your primary school classmates?

A serious limitation with the study is that there were different individuals in each age group. *Why* does that matter? An important reason why today's older adults have poorer memory than today's young adults is because on average they received fewer years of education—additional years of education enhance people's memories (Rönnlund et al., 2005). That means there are several possible explanations for the finding that older adults in the study had poorer memory for their classmates than did younger adults:

(1) It could be due to the greater length of time since they were at school.
(2) It could be due to the negative effects of age on memory ability.
(3) It could be due to the fact that older adults in Bahrick et al.'s study received less education than the younger ones and so had had poorer memory throughout their adult lives.

It is entirely possible that all three factors were jointly responsible for the age difference in memory for classmates.

Encoding in short-term vs long-term memory

When psychologists talk about encoding, they refer to the way in which information is stored in memory. For example, encoding can be in terms of acoustic (sound) or semantic (meaning) coding. The words "cap" and "can" are acoustically similar; "cap" and "hat" are semantically similar. We can remember words by the way they sound or by their meaning.

It seems that short-term and long-term memory differ in the way information is coded. If you have to remember something for a short while (e.g. a phone number), you probably repeat it to yourself (rehearsal). People do this whether they heard the number or saw it, suggesting that short-term memory may encode information acoustically. Conrad (1964) studied this by comparing performance with acoustically and visually presented information. Participants were presented with six letters for 0.75 seconds each and asked to recall them in the same order. When the letters *sounded* alike (even though they were presented *visually*), errors were made in terms of sound confusions (for example, S being recalled instead of X). This showed that short-term memory can involve **acoustic coding**.

Baddeley (1966) extended Conrad's research. He found that if participants recalled words from short-term memory, they didn't confuse words having the same meaning (e.g. "big" and "large"). However, they often confused words that sounded similar (e.g. remembering "cat" instead of "cap"). The opposite was true for long-term memory. This suggests that short-term memory largely uses an acoustic code, whereas long-term memory depends mostly on

KEY TERM

Acoustic coding: encoding words in terms of their sound using information stored in long-term memory.

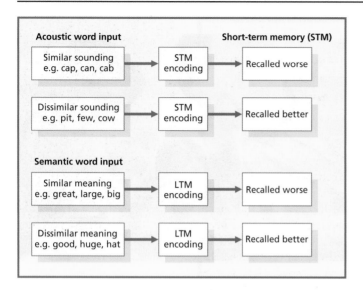

semantic coding based the meaning of words. These findings convinced many psychologists that the distinction between short-term and long-term memory is both genuine and important.

Baddeley's (1966) approach was limited in that he didn't consider the possibility of **visual coding** existing in short-term memory. Posner (1969) found evidence that visual codes are used. For example, when "A" was followed by "A", people were faster to decide that it was the same letter than when "A" was followed by "a". The visual code for the second letter differed from that of the first letter when "A" was followed by "a" and that slowed people down.

EVALUATION

There is some validity in the notion that encoding in short-term memory tends to involve rehearsal and acoustic coding. That is clearly not the whole story. As we saw earlier, Simon (1974) found that people can organise phrases into chunks in long-term memory—such chunking clearly involves semantic processing. In addition, encoding in short-term memory can involve visual coding (Posner, 1969).

There is also some validity in the notion that information in long-term memory is often encoded semantically. However, it can also be encoded in many other ways including acoustically, visually, or by taste or smell. If you don't believe me, then try to think of memories of someone's voice (acoustic encoding), the taste and smell of your favourite food or drink, or the feel of snow on your hands.

In sum, the types of information found in short-term memory and in long-term memory are much greater than used to be thought. Thus, we can't use encoding differences as a way of showing clearly that there are separate short-term and long-term memory stores.

ACTIVITY: Semantic and acoustic recall

You could test the effects of semantic and acoustic recall by using Baddeley's word lists and asking for immediate or delayed recall. Construct four word lists:

Acoustically similar: man, cap, can, cab, mad, mat, map
Acoustically dissimilar: pit, few, cow, pen, sup, bar, day
Semantically similar: great, large, big, huge, broad, fat, high
Semantically dissimilar: good, safe, thin, deep, strong, foul, hot

Divide participants into two groups—immediate recall (short-term memory) and longer-term recall. Participants should be randomly allocated to conditions to ensure that both groups of participants are equivalent.

For each group, which lists are they best at recalling and which lists do they perform least well on?

KEY TERMS

Semantic coding: encoding or processing words in terms of their meaning based on information stored in long-term memory.

Visual coding: encoding letters or words in terms of their visual shape.

EXAM HINT

In an exam it is very important to be able to distinguish between STM and LTM. To make sure you can do this learn the table on the next page.

This is quite easy, as it's mainly common sense. The clue is to make sure you understand the terminology:

Capacity = How much does it hold?
Duration = How long can it hold information?
Encoding = In what form is it "registered" in the memory store?

Comparing STM and LTM	Short-term memory	Long-term memory
Duration (how long it lasts)	Short (seconds)	Long, potentially forever
Capacity (how much it holds)	Limited by duration	Unlimited
Encoding differences	Acoustic	Semantic

Is there more than one long-term memory store?

According to Atkinson and Shiffrin's (1968) multi-store model, there is only *one* long-term memory store. As soon as you start thinking about it, that seems unlikely. We have an enormous variety of information stored in long-term memory, including, for example, the knowledge that Keira Knightley is a film star, how to ride a bicycle, that we had fish and chips for lunch yesterday, and the meaning of the word "bling". It seems improbable that all this knowledge is stored within a *single* long-term memory store.

Cohen and Squire (1980) argued that long-term memory is divided into two memory systems: **declarative knowledge** and **procedural knowledge**. Declarative knowledge is concerned with "knowing that". For example, we know we had roast pork for Sunday lunch and that Paris is the capital of France. In contrast, procedural knowledge is concerned with "knowing how". For example, we know how to play various sports, play the piano, and so on.

If declarative knowledge and procedural knowledge belong to separate systems in different brain regions, some brain-damaged patients might suffer problems with only one of the two systems. This is exactly what has been found. There was a famous **case study** (detailed investigation of a single individual) involving a man known as HM. He received brain surgery because he suffered from frequent epileptic seizures. After the operation, his memory for declarative knowledge was very poor—he couldn't remember most of the events and experiences he had after the operation. However, he could still acquire and remember procedural knowledge. For example, he learned mirror drawing (tracing a figure seen only in mirror image) almost as rapidly as non-brain-damaged individuals.

Spiers et al. (2001) reviewed 147 cases of amnesia (severe problems with long-term memory). Every one of them had poor declarative knowledge, but *none* of them had any problems with procedural knowledge. The procedural skills the amnesic patients had acquired included learning to play the piano and mirror drawing. This is convincing evidence that declarative knowledge and procedural knowledge are separate forms of long-term memory.

ACTIVITY: Procedural and declarative knowledge

State whether the following involve procedural or declarative knowledge.

- Your name
- Driving a car
- The capital city of Japan
- The value of m^2 when $m = 6$
- Balancing on one leg

Think of some other examples of procedural and declarative knowledge.

 Which type of memory (procedural or declarative) is likely to be tested in a memory experiment?

CASE STUDY: The man who never got older

In the 1950s a man known as "HM" sought medical help for his epileptic seizures. He had been forced to give up his job because the seizures had become so frequent and severe, and it was not possible to control them with drugs. In desperation the doctors decided to remove a structure called the hippocampus from both hemispheres of his brain because this was the seat of his seizures. No one quite knew what the outcome would be. The operation did reduce his epilepsy but it also had a dramatic effect on his memory.

His personality and intellect remained the same, but his memory was severely affected. Some aspects of his memory were fairly intact: he could still talk and recall the skills he knew previously (semantic memory), he continued to be able to form short-term memories, but was unable to form any new long-term ones. For example, given the task of memorising a number he could recall it 15 minutes later but, after being distracted, he had no recollection. He could read the same magazine over and over again without realising that he had read it before.

HM moved house after his operation and had great difficulty learning his new route home. After 6 years he was finally able to at least find his way around the house. This shows that he did have some memory capacity and, intellectually, he was quite "intact" so he did have some awareness of his predicament.

For many years he reported that the year was 1953 and he was 27 years old. As time went on he clearly realised this could not be true and he started to guess a more appropriate answer. In other words he tried to reconstruct his memories, although not very successfully.

Explicit memory is memory based on conscious recollection whereas implicit memory is memory that does not involve conscious recollection.

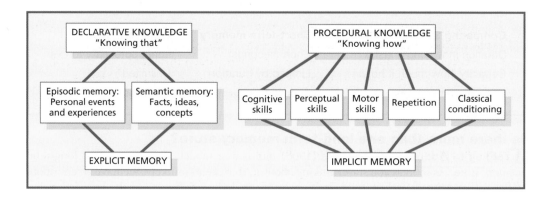

EVALUATION OF THE MULTI-STORE MODEL

We have considered the evidence concerned with short-term and long-term memory. It is now time to draw up a balance sheet of the strengths and limitations of the multi-store model:

- Strength: There is strong support for the basic distinction between short-term and long-term memory stores from studies on brain-damaged patients. Patients with amnesia have severe problems with long-term memory but not with short-term memory. In addition, some patients have problems with short-term memory but not with long-term memory (Shallice & Warrington, 1970).
- Strength: The multi-store has been very influential. Many subsequent theories of memory used the multi-store model as their inspiration.
- Strength: The capacity of the two stores is radically different. The capacity of the short-term store is about seven items (Jacobs, 1887; Simon, 1974). In contrast, there are no known limits on the capacity of the long-term store. For example, Standing et al. (1970) found that 90% of 2560 pictures presented once were remembered on a test of long-term memory.
- Strength: There are huge differences in the duration of information in short-term and long-term memory. Unrehearsed information in short-term memory vanishes within about 20 seconds (Peterson & Peterson, 1959). In contrast, some information in long-term memory is still there 48 years after learning (Bahrick et al., 1975).
- Limitation: The model argues that the transfer of information from short-term to long-term memory is through *rehearsal*. However, in daily life most people devote very little time to rehearsal, although they are constantly storing away new information in long-term memory. Rehearsal may describe what happens when psychologists conduct experiments on word lists in laboratories but this isn't true to life.
- Limitation: It is assumed that information in the short-term store is encoded in terms of its sound (acoustic coding) whereas information in the long-term store is encoded in terms of its meaning (semantic coding). I don't want to seem frivolous, but it seems to me like magic for information to change from sound to meaning as it proceeds along an arrow from the short-term to the long-term store!
- Limitation: Atkinson and Shiffrin (1968) argued that information is processed in short-term memory *before* proceeding to long-term memory. Matters can't be that simple. Suppose you use short-term memory to rehearse "IBM" as a single chunk. This is *only* possible after you have contacted long-term memory to work out the meaning of IBM! Most information in short-term memory must have made contact with information in long-term memory before being rehearsed.
- Limitation: The model is oversimplified in its assumption that there is a *single* long-term memory store. In fact, there are a number of long-term memory stores. Atkinson

and Shiffrin (1968) focused almost exclusively on declarative knowledge and had practically nothing to say about procedural knowledge (e.g. the learning of skills).

- Limitation: The model is oversimplified in its assumption that there is a *single* short-term store. Evidence that there is more than one short-term store comes from work on the working memory model, to which we now turn.

The Working Memory Model

What is the point of short-term memory in everyday life? Textbook writers sometimes argue it allows us to remember a telephone number for the few seconds taken to dial it. However, that isn't of much use now everyone has a mobile phone that stores numerous phone numbers.

In 1974, two British psychologists, Alan Baddeley and Graham Hitch, came up with a convincing answer to the above question. They pointed out that we use short-term memory when we work on a complex problem (e.g. in arithmetic) and need to keep track of where we have got to in the problem.

Suppose you were given the addition problem 13 + 18 + 24. You would add 13 and 18 and keep the answer (31) in short-term memory. You would then add 24 to 31 and produce the correct answer of 55. Baddeley and Hitch used the term working memory to refer to a system involving processing and short-term memory in combination, and theirs was a **working memory model**.

Baddeley and Hitch's (1974) working memory model differed from previous ideas about short-term memory not only in emphasising its general usefulness in everyday life but also by arguing (very reasonably) that rehearsal is only one of several processes occurring in short-term memory.

It is now time to consider in more detail the **working memory system** put forward by Baddeley and Hitch (1974) and developed by Baddeley (2001). It has *four* components, each having limited capacity:

- **Central executive**: A modality-free component, meaning it can process information from *any* sensory modality (e.g. visual, auditory). It is like attention.
- **Phonological loop** (originally called the articulatory loop): This is a temporary storage system holding verbal information in a phonological (speech-based) form. It is involved in verbal rehearsal and in speech perception. The phonological loop consists of an articulatory process involving rehearsal and a phonological store that holds phonological information briefly.
- **Visuo-spatial sketchpad** (sometimes called a scratch pad): This is specialised for the rehearsal and temporary storage of visual and spatial information. It consists of an inner scribe that processes spatial and movement information and a visual cache that stores information about visual form and colour.
- **Episodic buffer**: This is a storage system that can briefly hold information from all the other three components of the working memory system.

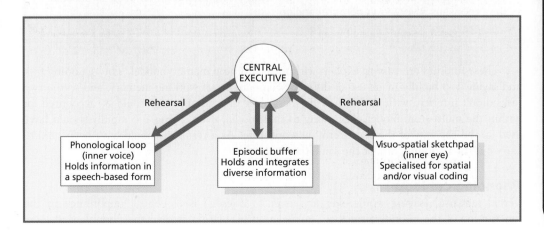

KEY TERMS

Working memory model: the model of short-term memory proposed to replace the multi-store model. It consists of a central executive plus slave systems that deal with different sensory modalities.

Working memory system: the concept that short-term (or working) memory can be subdivided into other stores that handle different modalities (sound and visual data).

Central executive: the key component of working memory. It is a modality-free system (i.e. not visual or auditory) of limited capacity and is similar to "paying attention" to something.

Phonological loop: a component of the working memory system concerned with speech perception and production.

Visuo-spatial sketchpad: a component within the working memory system designed for spatial and/or visual coding.

Episodic buffer: a component of working memory used to integrate and store briefly information from the phonological loop, the visuo-spatial sketchpad and long-term memory.

If you add up two items in your head—real life mental arithmetic!—when out shopping, which parts of your working memory are you using?

How can we tell which component or components are being used when people perform a given task? According to the model, every component has limited capacity and is relatively independent of the other components in its functioning. Two predictions follow:

1. If two tasks use the *same* component, they cannot be performed together successfully.
2. If two tasks use *different* components, it should be possible to perform them as well together as separately.

Here is a simple example showing the correctness of the second prediction. Your ability to make sense of the material in this book mainly involves focusing on visual information (using the visuo-spatial sketchpad) and attending to it (using the central executive). If you said "the" over and over again (using the phonological loop) while reading this book, it would have little effect on your comprehension. At any rate, that is what I would predict!

Here is an example of how the working memory system operates. Hitch and Baddeley (1976) asked participants to carry out a verbal reasoning task to decide whether each in a set of sentences provided a true or false description of the letter pair that followed it (e.g. A is followed by B: BA). At the same time, the participants had to do a task where little thought or attention was involved (only using the phonological loop by saying 1 2 3 4 5 6 rapidly) or a task that involved the central executive as well as the phonological or articulatory loop (remembering six random digits). As predicted, reasoning performance was slowed down by the additional task when it involved using the central executive but not when it involved only the phonological loop.

ACTIVITY: Processes in comprehension

You can investigate some of the processes involved in comprehension by using an approach similar to the one used by Hitch and Baddeley (1976). Start by selecting a fairly short text (250–300 words) that could be taken from a book or newspaper. There are three groups of participants who are assigned at random to the conditions. In the first condition, participants read the text and at the same time count backwards by threes, a task that involves the central executive and the phonological loop. In the second condition, participants read the text and at the same time say the numbers 1 2 3 4 5 6 rapidly over and over again, a task that involves only the phonological loop. In the third condition, participants only read the text and do not perform a second task at the same time. A few seconds after the text has been read, participants in all three conditions are given the same comprehension test to assess how much information they have extracted from it. You should find that participants in the first condition have the lowest level of comprehension and that there is little difference between the second and third conditions. These findings would indicate that the central executive (including attention) is important for comprehension, whereas the phonological loop is not. This experiment shows how the working memory approach can be used to assess the processes involved in comprehension.

These findings are easy to explain within the working memory model. The reasoning task and saying 1–6 rapidly made use of different components of working memory, and so the two tasks didn't interfere with each other. It is less clear how the findings could be accounted for within the multi-store model. According to that model, even saying 1–6 rapidly should have used up the capacity of the short-term memory store. As a result, it should have been hard to carry out the reasoning task at the same time.

Phonological loop
Verbal rehearsal (saying words over and over to oneself) is of central importance in the functioning of the phonological loop. Baddeley et al. (1975) studied the phonological loop.

KEY STUDY

Robbins et al. (1996): Dual-task performance and working memory

Robbins et al. (1996) carried out an experiment to show how the working memory model works in practice. The participants consisted of 12 moderately good and very good chess players, who were given the task of selecting moves from various chess positions while performing a second task at the same time. This second task involved the central executive, the visuo-spatial sketchpad, the phonological loop, or none of the components of the working memory system (control condition). The independent variable manipulated by the researchers was the nature of the second task. Since all participants performed in all four conditions, it was a repeated measures design. The dependent variable (behavioural measure of interest) was the quality of the chess moves selected.

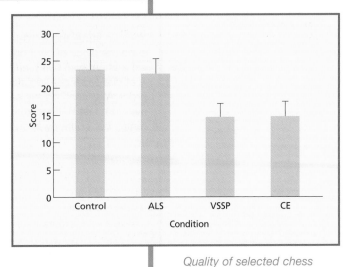

Quality of selected chess moves for participants with no secondary task (control), with a secondary task involving the phonological loop (ALS: articulatory suppression), with a secondary task involving the visuo-spatial sketchpad (VSSP), and with a secondary task involving the central executive (CE).

Findings

The findings are shown in the Figure. As can be seen, the quality of the moves selected was reduced when the second task involved the central executive or the visuo-spatial sketchpad. However, there was no negative effect when the second task involved the phonological loop.

What do these findings mean? They indicate that selecting good chess moves requires use of the central executive and the visuo-spatial sketchpad. We know this because chess performance suffered when these components weren't fully available. However, selecting good moves does not involve the phonological loop. We know this because chess performance did not suffer when this component was being used for the second task. Thus, this experiment shows the working memory model can be used to clarify which processes people use when performing complex tasks such as selecting chess moves.

Limitations

This is an important study because it shows clearly which components of the working memory system are and are not involved in playing chess. What are its limitations? First, it could be argued that outstanding chess players (e.g. grandmasters) have so much expertise that their chess performance wouldn't be affected by having to perform a second task at the same, time. In other words, the findings may be limited to players below grandmaster standard.

According to Robbins et al. (1996), selecting good chess moves requires use of the central executive and the visuo-spatial sketchpad but not of the phonological loop.

Second, Robbins et al. (1996) were interested in the effects of the second task on chess performance. However, they also found that chess performance made performance worse on the second tasks involving the visuo-spatial sketchpad and the central executive. This complicates the interpretation of the findings.

Third, all the chess positions used were well into the game when several pieces had already been taken. It is possible that the involvement of the working memory system would differ early in the game when nearly all the pieces remain.

They asked participants to recall sets of five words immediately in the correct order. Participants' ability to do this was better with short words than with long ones. Further investigation of this **word-length effect** showed that participants could recall as many words as they could read out loud in 2 seconds. This suggests the capacity of the phonological or articulatory loop is determined by how long it takes to rehearse verbal information.

ACTIVITY: Mueller et al. (2003): Word-length effect

You can study the word-length effect for yourself. Write each of the words below on a separate piece of card and make two piles, one for each list. Then carry out the following experiment with five friends tested one at a time. Present four words at random from List A at one word per second to one friend and ask them to recall the words in the correct order. After that, do the same with List B. Next, present five words from List A and then five from List B. Keep going to work out the maximum number of words each friend can remember correctly in order from each list.

List A	List B
cult	advantage
dare	behaviour
fate	circumstance
guess	defiance
hint	fantasy
mood	interim
oath	misery
plea	narrowness
rush	occasion
truce	protocol
verb	ridicule
zeal	upheaval

The above words were taken from an article by Mueller et al. (2003). Their participants had an average span of 6.72 with List A words and of 5.09 with List B words. Mueller et al. found that the words in List A took an average of 418 milliseconds to say compared to 672 for those in List B. Thus, the number of items that can be stored in short-term memory depends in part on the time required to pronounce each one.

Baddeley and Hitch (1974) assumed the phonological loop is generally used when people remember visually presented words in the correct order. It follows that it should be harder to remember words having similar sounds than words having dissimilar sounds—there would be much confusion and interference among the words having similar sounds.

The above prediction was tested by Larsen et al. (2000). Here is one of their lists of words with similar sounds: FEE, HE, KNEE, LEE, ME, and SHE, and here is a list with dissimilar sounds: BAY, HOE, IT, ODD, SHY, and UP. As predicted, the ability to recall the words in order was 25% worse with the words having similar sounds. This is the **phonological similarity effect**. It indicates that speech-based rehearsal processes within the phonological loop were used in remembering these words.

Real world

What is the value of the phonological loop in everyday life? Children with a deficient phonological loop generally have problems with reading. For example, Gathercole and Baddeley (1990) found that children with reading problems had an impaired memory span and found it difficult to decide whether words rhymed, suggesting they had a phonological loop deficit. The phonological loop is also useful when learning *new* words. In a study by Papagno et al. (1991), native Italian speakers learned pairs of Italian words and pairs of Italian–Russian words. In one condition, participants performed an articulatory suppression task (saying something meaningless over and over again) during the learning task. Articulatory suppression (which prevented use of

KEY TERM

Phonological similarity effect: the finding that immediate recall of a word list in the correct order is impaired when the words sound similar to each other.

the phonological loop on the learning task) greatly slowed down the learning of foreign vocabulary.

Visuo-spatial sketchpad

The visuo-spatial sketchpad is used for the temporary storage and manipulation of visual patterns and spatial movement. Note that there are significant differences between visual and spatial processing. Consider individuals blind since birth. They can find their way around a familiar environment (e.g. their own living room) without knocking into the furniture—this is achieved by using spatial processing since they can't use visual processing.

The visuo-spatial sketchpad is used in many situations in everyday life, such as finding the route when walking, or playing computer games. Logie et al. (1989) used a complex computer game called Space Fortress, which involves manoeuvring a spaceship around a computer screen. Performance on Space Fortress was worse when participants performed an additional visuo-spatial task at the same time. Thus, the visuo-spatial sketchpad was needed for effective computer-game performance.

Spatial vs visual processing

What is the visuo-spatial sketchpad like? It might be a *single* system combining visual and spatial processing. Alternatively, there might be partially or completely separate visual and spatial systems. Klauer and Zhao (2004) tried to find out. They used two main tasks: (1) a spatial task involving memory for dot locations; and (2) a visual task involving memory for Chinese ideographs (symbols). Participants sometimes performed a second task at the same time as the main task. This second task involved spatial interference or visual interference.

What would we predict if there are separate spatial and visual components? First, the spatial interference task should disrupt performance more on the spatial main task than on the visual main task. Second, the visual interference task should disrupt performance more on the visual main task than on the spatial main task. As shown in the Figure, both predictions were confirmed. If the visuo-spatial sketchpad consisted of a single system, this pattern of results would not be expected.

Additional evidence supporting the notion of separate visual and spatial systems within the visuo-spatial sketchpad was reported by Smith and Jonides (1997) in an ingenious study. Two visual stimuli were presented together, followed by a probe stimulus. Participants decided whether the probe was in the same location as one of the initial stimuli (spatial task) or they decided whether it had the same form or shape (visual task).

Even though the stimuli were identical in the two tasks, there were clear differences in patterns of brain activation. There was more activity in the *right* hemisphere during the spatial task than the visual task. However, there was more activity in the *left* hemisphere during the visual task than the spatial one. These findings suggest there is a visual processing system based mainly in the left hemisphere and a spatial processing system based mostly in the right hemisphere.

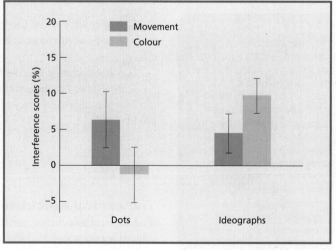

Amount of interference on a spatial task (dots) and a visual task (symbols) as a function of secondary task (spatial: movement distribution vs visual: colour discrimination). From Klauer and Zhao (2004).

KEY TERM

Mental rotation: a type of task in which participants imagine rotating two- or three-dimensional objects in order to perform some task.

Gender difference

It has sometimes been argued that males are slightly better on average than females at spatial processing and navigation. This has been studied using tasks involving **mental rotation**. With such tasks, you have to imagine rotating a shape or object. In one of the most-used mental rotation tasks, participants are presented with a letter in its normal form or in reversed mirror-image form and have to decide which form it is in. The further from its upright form the letter is presented, the longer it takes participants to make the decision because mental rotation to the upright position takes longer (Cooper & Shepard, 1973).

Lippa et al. (2010) carried out a large-scale study of mental rotation in 53 countries. Males significantly outperformed females on mental rotation in every country, although the gender difference was often fairly small. One possible reason why males have slightly superior spatial ability is because they spend much more time than females playing video games. Spence et al. (2009) studied males and females who had rarely, if ever, played video games. The male and female participants reached the same level of performance on a video game following training.

EVALUATION

➕ The visuo-spatial sketchpad is of major importance in our everyday lives.

➕ We engage in visual and/or spatial processing most of the time and such processing involves the visuo-spatial sketchpad.

➕ The systems involved in visual and spatial processing are different.

➕ There are interesting gender differences in spatial processing within the visuo-spatial sketchpad.

➖ We don't know much about the interconnections between visual and spatial processing—for example, how we combine visual and spatial information when walking.

➖ We don't know the limits on the amount of visual or spatial processing that can be done at any moment.

➖ If we engage in complex visual or spatial processing, the central executive will be involved as well as the visuo-spatial sketchpad. However, we don't know how much complexity is needed before the visuo-spatial sketchpad is unable to cope on its own.

EXAM HINT

Questions on evaluation will either ask you to describe **one** limitation of the model (or **one** strength) or will simply ask you to evaluate the model.

In both cases it is quality rather than quantity that counts. Always *explain* your criticism. For example, don't just say "one weakness is that little is known about the working memory model". To attract marks you must go on to explain that it hasn't been measured with precision and that the details of functioning are unclear.

The maximum number of marks for any evaluation question will be 6. You will gain more marks by explaining three criticisms fully rather than just listing six of them.

The central executive

The central executive, which resembles an attentional system, is the most important and versatile component of the working memory system. Indeed, it is so important it is always used when we perform any kind of complex task (e.g. understanding a psychology textbook; listening to a talk). In the original working memory model (Baddeley & Hitch, 1974), it was suggested that the central executive was *unitary*, meaning it functioned as a single unit. However, it is now clear that the central executive is more complex than that.

What is the central executive used for? One of the most influential suggestions stems from the research of Miyake et al. (2000), who gave their participants several tasks requiring the central executive. These tasks varied in terms of which of the following three functions they used:

1. *Inhibition function*: this is used when you need to prevent yourself from attending to task-irrelevant stimuli or responses. Thus, it reduces *distraction* effects. Consider the **Stroop task**, on which participants name the colours in which words are printed. In the most difficult condition, the words are conflicting colour words (e.g. the word BLUE printed in red). In this condition, performance is slowed down and there are often many errors. The inhibition function is needed to minimise the distraction effect created by the conflicting colour word.

2. *Shifting function*: this is used when you shift attention from one task to another. Suppose you are presented with a series of trials, on each of which two numbers are presented. In one condition there is task switching: on some trials you have to multiply the two numbers and on other trials you have to divide one by the other. In the other condition there are long blocks of trials on which you always multiply the two numbers and there are other long blocks of trials on which you divide one number by the other. Performance is slower in the task-switching condition, because attention has to be switched backwards and forwards between the tasks. Task switching involves the shifting function.

3. *Updating function*: this is used when you need to update the information you remember to take account of changes in the world. For example, motorists need to update their stored information when the speed limit changes from 30 mph to 20 mph or vice versa. In the laboratory, the updating function is required when participants are presented with members of various categories and have to keep track of the most recently presented member of each category.

Dysexecutive syndrome

We can understand the importance of the central executive by studying brain-damaged individuals whose central executive is impaired. Such individuals suffer from **dysexecutive syndrome**, which involves problems with planning, organising, monitoring behaviour, and initiating behaviour. They typically have damage within the frontal lobes, which occupy the front region of the brain. Individuals with dysexecutive syndrome typically have great problems in holding down a job and functioning adequately in everyday life.

The notion of a dysexecutive syndrome suggests that brain damage to the frontal lobes typically impairs *all* central executive functions. That is often the case with patients having widespread damage to the frontal lobes but isn't true of patients with more specific brain damage. Stuss and Alexander (2007) identified *three* different executive functions involving the frontal lobes: task setting (planning); monitoring (checking one's own performance, or "quality control"); and energisation (sustained attention or concentration).

Stuss and Alexander (2007) found many patients had major problems with only *one* of these central executive functions. Thus, rather than thinking in terms of a *single* global dysexecutive syndrome, we need to identify *three* more specific dysexecutive syndromes.

EVALUATION

➕ The central executive is the most important component of working memory.

➕ The central executive is involved in complex tasks such as selecting chess moves (Robbins et al., 1996) and verbal reasoning (Hitch & Baddeley, 1976).

➕ We use the central executive whenever tasks involve attentional processes and/or planning, task shifting, organising, and monitoring.

➕ Brain-damaged patients with dysexecutive syndrome show the problems encountered by anyone whose central executive is impaired.

➖ A major issue is to work out the number and nature of functions carried out by the central executive. Miyake et al. (2000) and Stuss and Alexander (2007) argued there are three major functions. Unfortunately, however, their two lists of functions only overlap in part.

The Stroop effect

RED

BLUE

RED

BLUE

KEY TERMS

Stroop task: a task that involves naming the colours in which words are printed. Performance is slowed when the words are conflicting colour words (e.g. the word RED printed in green).

Dysexecutive syndrome: a condition caused by brain damage (typically in the frontal lobes) in which there is severe impairment of the functioning of the central executive component of working memory.

Episodic buffer

As mentioned earlier, the episodic buffer is used for the integration and brief storage of information from the other components and from long-term memory. Chincotta et al. (1999) provided evidence in support of the existence of an episodic buffer. They studied memory span for Arabic numerals and digit words, finding that participants used both verbal and visual encoding while performing the task. This suggests information was combined from both the visuo-spatial sketchpad (Arabic numerals) and the phonological loop (digit words) within the episodic buffer.

How important is working memory?

Working memory is of fundamental importance in information processing and thinking. This has been shown in research stemming from the work of Daneman and Carpenter (1980), who argued that the essence of a working memory system is that it is used for storage and processing at the same time. They used a task in which participants read several sentences for comprehension (a processing task) and then recalled the final word of each sentence (storage task). The largest number of sentences from which a participant could recall all the final words more than 50% of the time was his/her **reading span**. This reading span was taken as a measure of working memory capacity.

Why did Daneman and Carpenter (1980) argue that reading span assessed working memory capacity? They assumed the processes involved in comprehending the sentences require a smaller proportion of the available working memory capacity of those with a large capacity. As a result, they have more capacity available for retaining the last words of the sentences.

Working memory capacity as measured by reading span is fairly closely associated with intelligence. For example, Conway et al. (2003) reviewed research on working memory capacity and general intelligence. The typical correlation was about +0.6, indicating that the two constructs (while by no means identical) are nevertheless similar.

EVALUATION OF THE WORKING MEMORY MODEL

- Strength: The working memory model is an advance on the account of short-term memory provided by the short-term store because it is concerned with both active processing *and* the brief storage of information. As a result, it is relevant to activities such as mental arithmetic, verbal reasoning, and comprehension, as well as to traditional short-term memory tasks. Thus, it is much more than just a theory of memory.

- Strength: The working memory model views verbal rehearsal as an *optional* process occurring within the phonological or articulatory loop. Information in working memory can be processed without involving rehearsal. This view is more realistic than the central importance of verbal rehearsal in the multi-store model.

- Strength: Performance on tasks of any complexity depends on some combination of the four components of the working memory model, indicating they are particularly important parts of the human cognitive processing system. For example, we saw that choosing moves at chess depends very much on the central executive and visuo-spatial sketchpad (Robbins et al., 1996).

- Strength: All components of the working memory model are important in everyday life. This is especially true of the central executive—brain-damaged individuals with dysexecutive syndrome have enormous difficulties in coping with other people and the environment. It is also noteworthy that working memory capacity correlates moderately highly with intelligence.

- Strength: Knowledge of the functioning of the working memory system can benefit brain-damaged individuals. They can be taught how to make the best use of those components of the working memory system still functioning reasonably well.

- Limitation: Relatively little is known about the central executive. It has limited capacity, but this capacity has not been measured with precision. It is argued that the central executive is "modality-free" (i.e. it does not rely on any specific way

KEY TERM

Reading span: the largest number of sentences read for comprehension from which an individual can recall all the final words more than 50% of the time; it is used as a measure of working memory capacity.

of receiving information, such as sound or vision) and is used in many different processing operations. However, the details of its functioning remain unclear.

- Limitation: It was originally proposed that the central executive was unitary in the sense that it "spoke with one voice". However, it now appears that it fulfils at least three functions (Miyake et al., 2000; Stuss & Alexander, 2007). As yet, the number and nature of its functions are unclear.
- Limitation: The four components of the working memory model *interact* with each other in the performance of many tasks. However, it is unclear *how* this happens in practice.
- Limitation: The model is concerned with memory. However, it tells us very little about long-term memory and how processing in the working memory system relates to the long-term storage of information. In this respect, the working memory model is less informative than the multi-store model.

Section Summary

What is memory?
- Learning and memory involve the retention of information, but the study of memory focuses on cognitive processes and retrieval.
- Memory tests assess learning.
- Psychologists distinguish between short-term and long-term memory in terms of:
  - capacity;
  - duration;
  - encoding.

Nature of short-term memory
- The short-term store is described as:
  - having limited capacity of 7 plus or minus 2 chunks;
  - having limited duration;
  - using mainly acoustic coding.
- Capacity: Span measures indicate an STM capacity of about 7 items but this can be increased by chunking. Capacity for STM can also be seen in the recency effect (higher recall for the last few items in a list).
- Duration: The Brown–Peterson technique is a means of showing STM duration. If rehearsal is prevented, there is little recall beyond 18 seconds.
- Encoding: This differs from long-term memory, which is more semantically coded.
- Evidence about different kinds of short-term memory comes from the study of brain-damaged individuals, which also supports a distinction between short-term and long-term memory. However, it is hard to generalise from case studies.

Nature of long-term memory
- The long-term memory store is described as:
  - having an unlimited capacity;
  - lasting forever;
  - using mainly semantic coding.
- Capacity: Unlike in STM, we never reach the upper limit of the LTM store capacity.
- Duration: Its duration has been shown in studies of VLTMs (very-long-term memories).
- Encoding: This differs from long-term memory, which is more acoustically coded.
- Long-term memory can be divided into:
  - declarative knowledge: knowing that certain things are the case;
  - procedural knowledge: knowing how to do certain things (e.g. play the piano).

Multi-store model

- The multi-store model of memory supports the distinction between three separate stores and proposes that information is transferred from the short-term memory store to the long-term memory store by rehearsal.
- This model has been criticised in that:
  - Rehearsal is much less important in forming long-term memories than is assumed within the model.
  - It is not correct that information always goes into short-term memory before long-term memory.
  - The model is oversimplified in assuming there is only one short-term store and one long-term store.

Working memory model

- The working memory model consists of a central executive, a phonological loop, a visuo-spatial sketchpad, and an episodic buffer.
- Two tasks can be performed together without disruption if they use different components of working memory, but not if they use the same ones.
- The phonological loop is used when learning new words, the visuo-spatial sketchpad when finding a route or playing computer games, the central executive for complex thinking and reasoning, and the episodic buffer for integrating information from other components.
- Three of the functions of the central executive are as follows:
  - inhibition function: this is used to reduce distraction effects;
  - shifting function: this is used to shift attention from one task to another;
  - updating function: this is used to update the information in working memory.
- Working memory is of fundamental importance in information processing and thinking, and working memory capacity is closely associated with intelligence.
- The working memory model has been criticised in that:
  - The number and nature of the functions of the central executive remain unclear.
  - We don't know in detail how the components of working memory interact with each other.
  - The model is concerned with memory but tells us very little about long-term memory.

SECTION 4
MEMORY IN EVERYDAY LIFE

Eyewitness Testimony

In this section, we focus on a major practical application of human memory research—**eyewitness testimony**. As Brown (1986, p. 258) pointed out, "Judges, defence attorneys and psychologists believe it to be just about the least trustworthy kind of evidence of guilt, whereas jurors have always found it *more* persuasive than any other sort of evidence."

DNA tests can often establish whether someone was responsible (or not responsible) for certain crimes. In the United States, 200 people have been shown to be innocent by DNA tests, and more than 75% had been found guilty on the basis of mistaken eyewitness identification. In early 2008, DNA testing led to the release of Charles Chatman, who had spent nearly 20 years in prison in Texas. He was 20 years old when a young woman who had been raped picked him out from a line-up. As a result, he was sentenced to 99 years in prison. On his last night in prison, Chatman said to the press: "I'm bitter, I'm angry. But I'm not angry or bitter to the point where I want to hurt anyone or get revenge."

KEY TERM

Eyewitness testimony: an account or evidence provided by people who witnessed an event such as a crime, reporting from their memory. Research suggests that this evidence may not be factually accurate.

The accuracy of eyewitness testimony depends on various factors. For example, eyewitness memory is likely to be less accurate if eyewitnesses are presented with **misleading information**. In addition, we might expect children and older adults would tend to have less accurate memories than young adults. It also seems reasonable to assume that very anxious eyewitnesses might find it more difficult to remember what they have witnessed. We will consider these (and other) factors in our subsequent discussion.

Misleading information

One reason eyewitness testimony is so unreliable is because the events witnessed are typically unexpected. As a result, eyewitnesses may not pay close attention to what is going on. A less obvious reason is that the memories eyewitnesses have of an event are *fragile*, and so can easily be distorted and made inaccurate by the questions they are asked.

Eyewitness testimony has been found by psychologists to be extremely unreliable, yet jurors tend to find such testimony highly believable.

KEY STUDY

Loftus and Palmer (1974): Effects of misleading information

Loftus and Palmer (1974) carried out two laboratory experiments. In the first one, participants saw a short film of a multiple-car accident. After viewing the film, they described what had happened and then answered specific questions. Some were asked, "About how fast were the cars going when they hit each other?" whereas for other participants the word "hit" was replaced by "smashed into", "collided", "bumped", or "contacted". In this experiment, the independent variable involved manipulating the verb used in the question.

The dependent variable was the estimate of speed. Speed estimates were higher (40.8 mph) when the word "smashed" was used, lower with "collided" (39.3 mph), and lower still with "bumped" (38.1 mph) and "hit" (34.0 mph).

In the second laboratory experiment, participants watched a film of a multiple-car accident. Some were asked how fast the cars were going when they "smashed into" or "hit" each other. There was also a control condition in which there was no question about speed.

One week later, all participants were asked, "Did you see any glass?" There wasn't actually any glass in the film. However, 32% of those previously asked about speed using the verb "smashed" said they had seen broken glass (see Figure). In contrast, only 14% of the participants previously questioned with the verb "hit" said they had seen broken glass, and the figure was 12% for the control participants.

One of the main strengths of these experiments is that they showed that our memory for events is so fragile it can be distorted by changing *one* word in *one* question! As we will see, this has had a major influence on the ways in which detectives question eyewitnesses. One limitation of these experiments is that they were laboratory-based and so were unlikely to engage the eyewitnesses emotionally. As a result, the eyewitnesses may not have done their utmost to produce accurate answers.

Loftus and Palmer (1974) found that assessment of the speed of a videotaped car crash and recollection of whether there was broken glass present were affected by the verb used to ask the question. The verbs "hit" and "smash" have different implications as shown in (a) and (b).

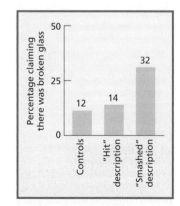

Results from Loftus and Palmer's (1974) study showing how the verb used in the initial description of a car accident affected recall of the incident after 1 week.

KEY TERM

Misleading information: incorrect information that may be given in good faith or deliberately (also known as misinformation).

EXAM HINT

With regard to eyewitness testimony, be ready to discuss several different essay questions:

- The accuracy of eyewitness testimony (EWT).
- The effects of age of witness on accuracy of EWT.
- The effects of anxiety on accuracy of EWT (see below).
- The effects of misleading information on accuracy of EWT (see page 39).
- The use of the cognitive interview to improve accuracy of EWT (see page 46).

The tendency for eyewitness memory to be influenced by misleading information provided after the event is very strong. Eakin et al. (2003) showed participants slides of a maintenance man stealing money and a calculator. Eyewitness memory was impaired by misleading post-event information. More surprisingly, memory was impaired even when the eyewitnesses were warned immediately about the presence of misleading information and told to disregard it.

How worried should we be that eyewitnesses' memory can be distorted by information presented after observing a crime? Note that most research has focused on distortions for *minor* details (e.g. presence of broken glass) rather than *central* features. Dalton and Daneman (2006) presented eyewitnesses with misinformation about central and minor features. Memory distortions were much more common following misinformation about minor features. Thus, misinformation has only a modest effect on the memory for crucial features.

We have seen that misleading information presented *after* an incident can disrupt eyewitness memory. What about misleading information presented *before* an incident? Lindsay et al. (2004) showed eyewitnesses a video of a museum burglary. Those who had listened to a similar narrative about a burglary the day before made many more errors when recalling information from the video than did those who had listened to a dissimilar narrative. This is worrying because we can't control what eyewitnesses are exposed to before seeing a crime or other incident.

Explanations

Why does misleading information distort eyewitnesses' memory? Perhaps eyewitnesses in **experiments** respond to social pressures (e.g. to please the experimenter). However, that seems unlikely. If that were the main reason, then eyewitnesses would presumably be less influenced by misleading information if offered money for being accurate in their recollections. In fact, Loftus (1979) found participants offered $25 for accurate memory were just as influenced by misleading information as those offered no reward. Misinformation acceptance is more likely (Loftus, 1992). Eyewitnesses "accept" misleading information presented to them after an event and subsequently regard it as forming part of their memory for that event.

Another explanation is based on **source misattribution** (Johnson et al., 1993). The basic idea is that a question may activate memories from various sources. The individual decides on the source of any activated memory on the basis of the information it contains. Source misattribution (remembering incorrectly the source of a memory) is likely when the memories from two sources (e.g. events) are rather similar.

Allen and Lindsay (1998) reported evidence of source misattribution. Eyewitnesses saw two slide shows describing two events with different people in different settings. However, some details in the two events were similar (e.g. a can of Pepsi vs a can of Coke). When the eyewitnesses recalled the first event, some details from the second event were mistakenly recalled.

Other factors also contribute to the effects of misleading information (Wright & Loftus, 2008). Misinformation is likely to be accepted when related information from the original event wasn't stored in memory. Another possibility is that the misinformation and information from the original event are combined together in memory.

Anxiety

Eyewitnesses (especially if they are also victims) are often very anxious and stressed during the witnessing of a crime because of the potential danger to themselves. Before discussing the effects of **anxiety** on eyewitness memory, consider two points:

1. Eyewitnesses remember attended aspects of the crime situation much better than non-attended aspects. Since the precise details of the crime situation determine what an eyewitness is likely to attend to, we must beware of simple generalisations.
2. While the threat or danger in which the eyewitness is placed is the main factor determining his/her level of anxiety, it is not the only one. Eyewitnesses with an anxious personality are likely to experience more anxiety in a given crime situation than those with a non-anxious personality.

KEY TERMS

Experiment: a procedure undertaken to make a discovery about causal relationships. The experimenter manipulates one variable to see its effect on another variable.

Source misattribution: errors in long-term memory that occur when the rememberer is mistaken about the source or origin of a retrieved memory.

Anxiety: a normal emotion similar to nervousness, worry, or apprehension, but if excessive it can interfere with everyday life and might then be judged an anxiety disorder.

Weapon focus

We might assume that eyewitnesses exposed to a violent crime attend mainly to those aspects of the situation posing a *direct* threat. This assumption lies behind research on **weapon focus**—high levels of attention to (and good memory for) the criminal's weapon but *not* other information. Loftus (1979) discussed a study in which some participants overheard a hostile and aggressive argument between two people followed by one of them emerging holding a letter opener covered with blood.

Other participants overheard a harmless conversation between two people followed by one of them emerging holding a pen. When participants tried to identify the culprit from photographs, only 33% of those in the weapon condition did so compared to 49% in the other condition. This shows weapon focus.

Loftus et al. (1987) asked participants to watch one of two sequences:

1. A person pointing a gun at a cashier and receiving some cash.
2. A person passing a cheque to the cashier and receiving some cash.

Eyewitnesses looked more at the gun than at the cheque (weapon focus). As a result, memory for details unrelated to the gun/cheque was poorer in the weapon condition.

We must be cautious about accepting findings on weapon focus at face value for two reasons. First, a weapon may attract attention because it is unusual (or unexpected) in most of the contexts in which it is seen by eyewitnesses as well as because it poses a threat. Pickel (1999) found *no* evidence of weapon focus when eyewitnesses saw someone pointing a gun in a situation (a shooting range) where guns are expected. Second, most research has been laboratory based. Valentine et al. (2003) considered the evidence from over 300 line-ups. The presence of a weapon had no effect on the probability of an eyewitness identifying the suspect.

Stress

Deffenbacher et al. (2004) carried out meta-analyses combining findings from numerous studies on the effects of anxiety and stress on eyewitness memory. In the first one, they considered the effects of anxiety and stress on accuracy of face identification. Average correct identifications were 54% for low anxiety or stress conditions compared to 42% for high anxiety or stress conditions. Thus, heightened anxiety and stress reduce eyewitness identification accuracy.

In their second meta-analysis, Deffenbacher et al. considered the effects of anxiety and stress on recall of culprit details, crime scene details, and actions of central characters. The average percentage of details correctly recalled was 64% in low anxiety or stress conditions compared to 52% in high anxiety or stress conditions. Thus, high anxiety or stress reduces the ability of eyewitnesses to remember details of a crime.

Bothwell et al. (1987) showed the importance of **individual differences** in anxiety. They compared groups low and high in the personality dimension of neuroticism (high scorers are very anxious). When the stress level was *low*, 68% of those high in neuroticism and 50% of those low in neuroticism correctly identified the culprit. In contrast, when the stress level was *high*, only 32% of those high in neuroticism identified the culprit, much lower than the figure of 75% for those low in neuroticism. Thus, individuals who were extremely anxious (high neuroticism + high stress condition) had easily the worst memory.

Eyewitness memory can be impaired by misleading post-event information. However, important information, such as the weapon used in a crime, is less likely to be distorted than trivial information.

EVALUATION

➕ Weapon focus is an important phenomenon with eyewitness memory.

➕ Stress and anxiety generally have negative effects on the memory of eyewitnesses.

➖ The weapon focus effect may occur either because the weapon is dangerous or because it is unexpected in the current situation.

➖ Weapon focus is a more reliable effect in the laboratory than in real life.

➖ Individual differences in susceptibility to anxiety and stress are often overlooked.

KEY TERMS

Weapon focus: the finding that eyewitnesses pay so much attention to a weapon that they ignore other details and so can't remember them.

Individual differences: the characteristics that vary from one individual to another; intelligence and personality are major ways in which individuals differ.

Age of witness

Do you think an eyewitness's age is relevant when deciding whether his/her memory for an event is likely to be accurate? I would guess that your answer is "Yes", and that you believe young children and older people have greater memory problems than young and middle-aged adults. As we will see, the evidence supports those beliefs.

Children vs adults

Pozzulo and Lindsay (1998) carried out a **meta-analysis** combining the data from numerous studies on children and adults. They reported three main findings. First, young children up to the age of 5 were less likely than older children and adults to make correct identifications when the culprit was present in the line-up. Second, children over the age of 5 performed as well as adults at correct identifications when the culprit was present. Third, children up to the age of 13 were much more likely than adults to make a choice when the culprit was *not* present in the line-up—children are more sensitive than adults to the social demands to make a choice.

Younger children are more suggestible than older ones. Bronfenbrenner (1988) compared memory for an incident in young children (3 or 4 years old), older children (10, 11, or 12 years old), and adults. Two days after hearing about the incident, all participants performed a memory test. Memory performance was only slightly affected by age when no misleading information had been presented. In contrast, memory accuracy was much lower in younger than in older children when misleading information had been given.

> **HOW SCIENCE WORKS: Memory and age**
>
> Do your parents remember what you tell them? Do your friends remember what you tell them? Is memory an age thing?
>
> You could do a correlational analysis of memory and age, starting by constructing a simple STM memory game—perhaps a picture that could be looked at for 1 minute and then replaced by 20 questions about it. Careful planning of research is really important. For example, you need to write standardised instructions (and either read them out yourself or give them to each participant to read) so that every participant receives exactly the same information, in order to minimise investigator effects and extraneous variables. Ethical issues are also important, as outlined in the BPS Guidelines. You should test only participants aged over 16, as you would need written informed consent from parents if you used younger participants, an important ethical consideration in the UK. Another practical and ethical point is that you could state at the beginning of your instructions that you will need to know the participant's age in years—then if anyone doesn't want to tell you this personal information they can withdraw from your study and not waste their or your time, or feel obliged or stressed. If you have about 10 participants spread through four or five decades in age you could then present, analyse, and interpret the data by plotting a scattergram, with age in years on the horizontal axis and STM game score on the vertical axis. Then you could draw a line of best fit and see what correlation you get.
>
> You will also recall that even a strong correlation does not infer a causal link—it might be a causal relationship between your two co-variables, or it might not. You could present your scattergram and conclusion to your class or group, and ask for non-causal explanations of your findings.

Explanations

Why do young children produce distorted reports of events when exposed to suggestive influences? One reason is that young children yield to social pressure and a lack of social support even when their own recollection is accurate (Bruck & Melnyk, 2004). This is especially likely when they are interviewed by an older person.

Another reason is cognitive incompetence. Young children may come to believe their own distorted memory reports because of limitations in processing, attention, or language. Evidence for this comes from studies in which children continued to produce false memories after having been warned the interviewer may have been mistaken in his/her suggestions (Bruck & Melnyk, 2004).

KEY TERM

Meta-analysis: a form of analysis in which the data from several related studies are combined to obtain an overall estimate.

Keast et al. (2007) confirmed that children are much more likely than adults to choose someone when shown a line-up not containing the culprit. In addition, children were much more overconfident than adults in their ability to make correct memory decisions. This overconfidence could lead jurors to accept too readily what children claim to remember.

Memory enhancement

How can we enhance the memory accuracy of very young eyewitnesses? Some of the information they store in memory after witnessing an event is in visual form rather than language. Accordingly, Gross and Hayne (1999) argued we could improve matters by asking children to *draw* what they can remember about an event before asking them to report verbally. Children aged 5 and 6 were taken to Cadbury's chocolate factory by a woman wearing a purple suit who called herself "Charlie Chocolate". Memory for the event was tested 1 day and 6 months later. Children who had produced drawings recalled 30% more information in their verbal reports than children who hadn't produced a drawing.

Older vs younger adults

Brewer et al. (2005) reviewed research on eyewitness identification in older people (60- to 80-year-olds). Older people are more likely than younger adults to choose someone from a line-up even when the culprit is not present. In addition, older people are strongly influenced by misleading suggestions. In one study (Mueller-Johnson & Ceci, 2004), older adults (average age 76) and young adults (average age 20) underwent relaxation techniques including body massage. Several weeks later, the participants were given misleading information (e.g. they had been massaged on parts of their body that hadn't been touched). The misleading information distorted the memories of the older adults much more than those of the young adults.

Dodson and Krueger (2006) showed a video to younger and older adults, who later completed a **questionnaire** that misleadingly referred to events *not* shown on the video. The older adults were more likely than the younger ones to produce false memories triggered by the misleading suggestions. Worryingly, the older adults were very confident about the correctness of their false memories (the younger adults were much less confident about the accuracy of their false memories).

Own-age bias

Wright and Stroud (2002) considered differences between younger and older adults identifying the culprits after being presented with crime videos. They found an **own-age bias**, with both groups being more accurate at identification when the culprit was of a similar age to themselves.

What causes own-age bias? Harrison and Hole (2009) found it was due to the greater *exposure* most people have to people of their own age. Teachers (who spend hours a day exposed to children's faces) showed no evidence of own-age bias: they recognised children's faces as well as those of people of their own age.

Memory enhancement

How can we enhance the memory of older adults? A central problem is that their memories are very easily distorted by misleading or interfering information. Jacoby et al. (2005) presented

"Well I know he was wearing tights."

misleading information to younger and older adults. On a subsequent recall test, older adults had a 43% chance of producing false memories compared to only 4% for the younger adults. Much of this occurred because of source misattribution by the older adults.

Two recommendations follow from Jacoby et al.'s (2005) findings:

1. It is very important to ensure that older adults aren't exposed to any misleading information that might distort their memory.
2. Older adults often produce genuine memories in that they are based on information or events to which they have been exposed. The problem is that older adults often misremember the context or circumstances in which the information was encountered. Thus, it is essential to engage in detailed questioning with older adults to decide whether remembered events actually occurred at the time of the crime or other incident.

OVERALL EVALUATION

➕ There is much evidence that children and older adults generally have worse memory than young adults.

➕ An important reason why younger children's memory is poor is because they are highly suggestible. This suggestibility occurs because they are responsive to social pressure and are cognitively incompetent.

➕ An important reason why older adults' memory is poor is because they are prone to source misattribution.

- The memory abilities of young children are often underestimated because they can't express all they remember in language.

- The memory performance of older adults is closer to that of young adults when they are trying to identify an older culprit—own-age bias.

Reconstructive nature of memory

An influential way of understanding the unreliability of eyewitness memory is based on the ideas of Bartlett (1932). One of his central ideas was the notion of **schema** (an organised package of information containing certain knowledge about the world). Schemas are stored in long-term memory and help us to make sense of the world.

According to Bartlett (1932), memory does *not* simply involve remembering presented information. Our prior knowledge in the form of schemas influences what we remember and how we remember it. According to Bartlett, what we remember depends on the information we were exposed to at the time of learning *and* our relevant schematic knowledge. The impact of schematic knowledge means that what we recall is sometimes in error—it is consistent with one of our schemas but does not correspond precisely to what we learned. Thus, we fill in the gaps in our memory on the basis of what we *think* might have happened.

Can you imagine elderly ladies like these committing a robbery? Our stereotypical schemas may influence expectations of what a person is likely to wear, say, do, and so on.

Tuckey and Brewer (2003a, 2003b) showed how Bartlett's views could account for memory errors by eyewitnesses. Tuckey and Brewer (2003a) obtained information about people's bank robbery schema. It typically included the following aspects: robbers are male; they wear disguises; they wear dark clothes; they make demands for money; and they have a getaway car with a driver in it.

Tuckey and Brewer (2003b) asked eyewitnesses to recall the details of a simulated crime. As predicted, eyewitnesses interpreted ambiguous information as being consistent with their crime schema. This led them to make memory errors based on information contained in the crime schema but not in the actual crime.

Relevance of laboratory findings

Do laboratory findings on eyewitness testimony apply to the real world? Doubts have been raised because there are several important differences between eyewitnesses' typical laboratory experiences and when observing a real-life crime. First, eyewitnesses are much more likely to be the victims in real life than in the laboratory. Second, it is much less stressful and anxiety-provoking to watch a video of a violent crime than to experience a real-life violent crime (especially from the perspective of the victim). Third, in laboratory research, the consequences of an eyewitness making a mistake are trivial. In contrast, they can literally be a matter of life or death in an American court of law.

What is crucially important is whether the above differences have large effects on the accuracy of eyewitness memory. Evidence they may not was reported by Ihlebaek et al. (2003). They used a staged robbery involving two robbers armed with handguns. In the live condition, the eyewitnesses were ordered repeatedly to "Stay down!" A video taken during the live condition was presented to eyewitnesses in the video condition. Participants in both conditions exaggerated the duration of the event, and showed similar patterns in what was well and poorly remembered. However, eyewitnesses in the video condition recalled more information. These findings suggest the inaccuracies and distortions in eyewitness memory obtained under laboratory conditions *underestimate* eyewitnesses' memory deficiencies for real-life events and are not simply artificial errors.

KEY TERM

Schema: an "organised" packet of information about the world, events, or people that is stored in long-term memory. For example, most people have a schema containing information about the normal sequence of events when having a meal in a restaurant.

? Why do people still believe eyewitnesses when we know memory is faulty?

Tollestrup et al. (1994) analysed police records on identifications by eyewitnesses to crimes involving fraud and robbery. Factors shown to be important in laboratory studies (e.g. weapon focus; poorer memory at longer time intervals) were also important in real-life crimes.

Limitations

Although most laboratory studies show eyewitness memory is unreliable and can be distorted, some studies show that real-life recall can be very accurate. One such study was by Yuille and Cutshall (1986). They interviewed people who had witnessed a crime where one person was shot dead and another person seriously injured. These interviews (given some months later) were analysed, along with interviews given to the police immediately after the incident. The eyewitness accounts were very accurate, and the accuracy and amount of information recalled didn't diminish over time. The eyewitnesses' accounts were also not distorted by leading questions. Yuille and Cutshall concluded that laboratory studies such as those outlined above are not always generalisable to real life (i.e. Yuille and Cutshall's study has more **external validity**) and that more field research is needed.

There is another limitation with research on the effects of post-event information on eyewitness memory. It has typically been found that such information can distort memory of relatively minor details (e.g. broken glass; Dalton & Daneman, 2006). This may limit the practical importance of this line of research.

Improving Accuracy of Eyewitness Testimony Including the Use of the Cognitive Interview

Many innocent people have been imprisoned purely on the basis of eyewitness testimony. Mistakes by eyewitnesses may occur because of what happens at the time of the crime or incident, or because of what happens afterwards. It follows from our previous discussion about misleading information that the questions asked during a police interview may distort an eyewitness's memory, and thus reduce its reliability.

What used to happen in the United Kingdom was that an eyewitness's account was often repeatedly interrupted. The interruptions made it hard for the eyewitness to focus fully on recalling the event, and thus reduced recall. As a result of psychological research, the Home Office issued guidelines recommending that police interviews should proceed from free recall (i.e. spontaneous reporting of what was remembered) to general open-ended questions, concluding with more specific questions. That reduces the chances of eyewitness memory being distorted by misleading information. However, psychologists have gone further and developed even more effective interview techniques.

Geiselman et al. (1985) argued that interview techniques should take account of basic characteristics of human memory:

- Memory traces are complex, and contain various features and/or kinds of information.
- The effectiveness of a retrieval cue depends on the extent to which the information it contains is *similar* to information stored in the memory trace. For example, if you wanted to remember the events of your early childhood, visiting where you lived as a child would probably provide good retrieval cues.
- Various retrieval cues may permit access to any given memory trace. For example, an eyewitness may remember additional information if they imagine themselves viewing the crime or incident from the perspective of another eyewitness who was also present.

Geiselman et al. (1985) used the above considerations to develop the basic **cognitive interview**, which is based on four general retrieval rules:

1. Mental reinstatement of the environment and any personal contact experienced during the crime.
2. Encouraging the reporting of every detail including fragmentary and apparently minor ones.
3. Describing the incident in several different orders.
4. Reporting the incident from different viewpoints, including those of other eyewitnesses.

KEY TERMS

External validity: the validity of an experiment outside the research situation itself; the extent to which the findings of a research study are applicable to other situations, especially "everyday" situations.

Cognitive interview: an interview technique that is based on our knowledge about the way human memory works; paying attention, for example, to the use of retrieval cues.

Geiselman et al. (1985) compared the effectiveness of the basic cognitive interview and the standard police interview. The average number of correct statements was 41.1 using the basic cognitive interview compared to only 29.4 using the standard police interview.

Fisher et al. (1987) devised the enhanced cognitive interview. This is based on the following recommendations (Roy, 1991, p. 399):

Investigations should minimise distractions, induce the eyewitness to speak slowly, allow a pause between the response and next question, tailor language to suit the individual eyewitness, follow up with interpretive comment, try to reduce eyewitness anxiety, avoid judgmental and personal comments, and always review the eyewitness's description of events or people under investigation.

Findings

Fisher et al. (1987) found the enhanced cognitive interview was more effective than the basic cognitive interview. Eyewitnesses produced an average of 57.5 correct statements when given the enhanced interview compared to 39.6 with the basic cognitive interview. However, there were 28% more incorrect statements with the enhanced interview. Fisher et al.'s findings were obtained under artificial laboratory conditions.

Fisher et al. (1990) trained detectives in the Robbery Division of Metro-Dade Police Department in Miami in the enhanced cognitive interview. Training produced an average increase of 46% in the number of pieces of information elicited from eyewitnesses at interview. Where confirmation was possible, over 90% of these pieces of information were shown to be accurate.

Evidence the enhanced cognitive interview is generally very effective was reported by Köhnken et al. (1999) in a review of over 50 studies. The enhanced cognitive interview consistently elicited more correct information than standard police interviews. Indeed, the average eyewitness given an enhanced cognitive interview produced more correct items of information than 81% of eyewitnesses given a standard interview. However, there was a small cost in terms of reduced accuracy. The average eyewitness given an enhanced cognitive interview produced more errors than 61% of those given a standard interview.

Does the cognitive interview reduce the negative effects of misleading information on eyewitness memory? Centofanti and Reece (2006) addressed that question. Eyewitnesses watched a video of a bank robbery followed by neutral or misleading information. Overall, 35% more correct details were recalled with the cognitive interview than with a structured interview. However, the negative effects of misleading information on eyewitness memory were as great with the cognitive interview as with the structured interview.

> **?** Have you had the experience of not being able to remember something until you found a clue to cue that memory, like running upstairs to get something and then being unable to remember what it was until you were back in the kitchen again? What was the memory cue in your own example?

EVALUATION

➕ The cognitive interview has proved to be very successful in increasing the amount of information about crimes that can be obtained from eyewitnesses.

➕ The enhanced cognitive interview is even more effective than the cognitive interview in enhancing eyewitness memory.

➖ It is worrying that there is a small increase in the amount of incorrect information provided by witnesses when the cognitive interview is used.

➖ The cognitive interview is generally less effective at enhancing recall when used at longer intervals of time after the crime or incident (Geiselman & Fisher, 1997). Thus, eyewitnesses should be interviewed as soon as possible after the crime or incident.

➖ The cognitive interview contains several components, and it isn't clear whether all contribute to the success of the technique. However, Milne and Bull (2002) found four components (context reinstatement; change perspective; change order; and report everything) all had roughly equal beneficial effects on eyewitness recall by children and young adults.

 The cognitive interview doesn't reduce the negative effects of misleading information on eyewitness memory (Centofanti & Reece, 2006).

Additional factors

The cognitive interview includes many of the factors that improve the accuracy of eyewitness memory. However, other factors are also important, and we will consider two here. First, Perfect et al. (2008) compared recall when eyewitnesses closed their eyes or kept them open. Eyewitnesses recalled more visual and auditory details when their eyes were closed and there was no increase in false recall.

Why was this simple technique effective? In essence, it reduced distraction from the immediate environment and so allowed eyewitnesses to focus exclusively on their memory for the event.

Second, eyewitnesses are often presented with a line-up consisting of the suspect plus various other individuals and are asked to decide whether the culprit is present. There is a real danger of an innocent person being selected, especially when the actual culprit isn't in the line-up. Steblay (1997) reviewed studies in which eyewitnesses were warned that the culprit might not be in the line-up. This reduced mistaken identification rates in culprit-absent line-ups by 42% while reducing accurate identification in culprit-present line-ups by only 2%.

Strategies for Memory Improvement

Nearly everyone complains about their memory. In spite of the power and elegance of the human memory system, it is not infallible and we have to learn to live with that fallibility. However, we can improve our memory, and several ways are discussed here. Hopefully, you will find the material of interest not only as a topic in psychology but also as a source of practical tips about improving your memory to cope more effectively with exams!

Organisation

The single most important principle if you want to improve your memory is to make full use of your pre-existing knowledge when learning something new. This makes it much easier to *organise* the information you are learning. "Organisation" is a vague notion, but here is Mandler's (1967, p. 330) definition of it: "A set of objects or events are said to be organised when a consistent relation among the members of the set can be specified and, specifically, when membership of the objects or events in subsets (groups, concepts, categories, chunks) is stable and identifiable."

Organisation is *not* the only factor important in improving memory. Relating what you want to learn to what you already know is also very important. In addition, as we saw in Chapter 1 (page 4) with the findings of Roediger and Karpicke (2006), simply practising recall of to-be-remembered material can improve memory by up to 50%.

Psychologists have studied the role of organisation in memory in many different ways. We will start by considering studies in which the material itself is arranged so it is generally fairly easy for the learner to organise it. After that, we discuss research showing that even random words can be organised in memory. Finally, we consider studies in which learners are provided with special strategies or methods allowing them to organise even random information very efficiently.

Organisation in the learning material

We can see the importance of organisation and knowledge in studies carried out using categorised word lists (see Activity). For example, a categorised word list might consist of four

---

ACTIVITY: Organisation aids memory

You can demonstrate that organisation aids memory by constructing two lists of the same words. List 1 will be a categorised word list containing a number of words belonging to each of several categories (e.g. four-footed animals; sports; flowers; articles of furniture). List 2 will consist of the same words but presented in a random order (e.g. golf, rose, cat, tennis, carnation, and so on). To avoid bias, you should allocate participants to conditions (list 1 or list 2) on a random basis. Give them a set time to study the list. After an interval (during which they should count backwards in threes to prevent rehearsal and to prevent recall from short-term memory), give them a test of free recall. You should find that participants given list 1 recall more words than those given list 2, and that they are much more likely to recall the words category by category. The conclusion is that organisation benefits memory.

---

words belonging to each of six categories (e.g. four-footed animals; articles of furniture; girls' names; birds; sports; and cities). One group is presented with the words neatly organised into their categories, whereas another group is presented with the words in random order. After the list has been presented, all participants recall as many words as possible in any order (free recall).

There are three key findings (Shuell, 1969). First, recall is much higher when the words are presented in an organised way. Second, participants given the organised list typically recall the words category by category (**categorical clustering**), and those given the random list also show evidence of categorical clustering. Third, participants showing the greatest categorical clustering recall more words than those with the least categorical clustering whether they received the list in an organised or random order.

How do people use their knowledge of categories to enhance recall of categorised word lists? One possibility is that organisation is used at the time of learning or storage. Another possibility is that organisation is used at the time of retrieval and recall (e.g. using category names to generate recall of category members). As we will see, organisation benefits learning *and* retrieval.

Direct evidence that organisational processes occur during learning was obtained by Weist (1972). He presented a categorised word list in a random order followed by a test of free recall (recall in any order). In addition, he introduced the novel twist of asking participants to rehearse out loud during learning, and he took a tape recording of their rehearsal. Rehearsal showed clear evidence that organisation into categories occurs during learning. The more organised the rehearsal was, the better the participant's subsequent recall.

Bower et al. (1969) provided a very clear illustration of the importance of organisation in memory. All participants were given four trials to learn and remember 112 words belonging to four hierarchies each with four levels. For one group, the words were presented in an organised way reflecting participants' knowledge (see Figure overleaf). In the other condition, the same 112 words were presented in a random order.

Memory performance was strikingly different in the two conditions (see Figure overleaf), being three and a half times greater in the organised condition than the random one on the first trial. Indeed, participants in the random condition recalled fewer words after *four* trials than those in the organised condition did after just *one* trial!

Bower et al. (1969) obtained strong evidence that the participants given the list of words in an organised way used the hierarchical structure in their recall. First, a higher-level category was almost always recalled *before* the members of that category. Second, participants who failed to recall a higher-level category typically had poor (or no) recall of category members.

Organising random words

We have seen that people are generally very good at organising categorised or hierarchical lists of words. What happens if we ask people to learn a list of *random* words? Mandler (1967)

One of the hierarchies used by Bower et al. (1969).

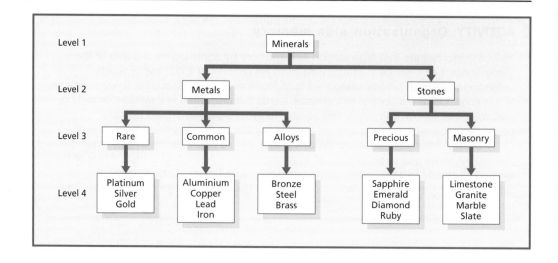

addressed this question. Participants were given a pack of 52 cards, each with a random word on it. They sorted the cards into between two and seven categories according to any system they wanted. They continued with the sorting task until they sorted the words consistently. At this point, they were given a test of free recall.

Recall was poorest for participants who used only two categories and best for those using seven categories. There was an average increase of 3.9 words recalled per additional category used in sorting. According to Mandler, those participants using several categories in sorting imposed more *organisation* on the list. This led Mandler (1967, p. 328) to conclude that "Memory and organisation are not only correlated, but organisation is a necessary condition for memory."

Does organisation always enhance memory?

Organisation doesn't *always* improve memory. Consider the ideas of Bartlett (1932; discussed on page 45). He focused on the notion of schema (an organised collection of knowledge about certain aspects of the world). According to Bartlett, what we remember is influenced by our relevant schematic knowledge. This schematic knowledge provides a retrieval plan that assists us to remember. However, we may "remember" information that fits our schematic knowledge but wasn't actually presented.

Sulin and Dooling (1974) obtained evidence that schematic organisation can produce errors in memory. They presented participants with a story about an evil dictator. One group was told the story was about Adolf Hitler, whereas the other group was told it was about Gerald Martin. One week later, all the participants were given a recognition test involving sentences. They had to decide whether each sentence had been presented in the story. The crucial sentence was as follows: "He hated the Jews particularly and so persecuted them." Participants in the group told the story was about Adolf Hitler were much more likely to indicate (mistakenly) that the sentence had been in the story. This happened because those participants used their schematic knowledge of Hitler.

Mnemonic techniques

The world is full of books promising to improve your memory dramatically. As you might imagine, the authors of these books often exaggerate the effectiveness of the techniques they describe. However, many memory techniques *are* extremely effective. The term **mnemonic techniques** refers to methods or systems devised to improve people's memory. There are more such techniques than you can shake a stick at, but we will focus on the most important ones. We will divide them up into those relying mainly on visual imagery and

---

ACTIVITY: Schemas

In small groups, write your own schemas for the following:

- Catching a train
- Buying a newspaper
- Starting school

How easy was it to agree on a uniform pattern of events? Were any of the themes easier to agree on than the others? Why might this be?

KEY TERM

Mnemonic techniques: artificial systems or methods that are used to enhance people's memory. The techniques all involve providing a structure so that even random material can be organised effectively at the time of learning, and they provide a retrieval structure (typically through the use of cues) that makes it easy to recall learned material.

those mostly word-based. While these techniques typically increase the organisation of the material to be learned, they depend mainly on using previous knowledge to facilitate the learning process.

Visual imagery mnemonic: Method of loci

One of the most popular mnemonic techniques is the **method of loci**. What happens is that the to-be-remembered items of information are associated with well-known locations (e.g. places along a walk) (see Activity).

The method of loci is very effective. Bower (1973) compared recall of five lists of 20 nouns each for groups using or not using the method of loci. The former group recalled 72% of the nouns against only 28% for the latter group. The method of loci is effective because it provides a way of organising random material so as to make use of pre-existing knowledge about sequences of locations. It makes it much easier to *recall* the information, because you have a convenient cue (i.e. given location) for every to-be-remembered word.

The method of loci is clearly very useful if you try to remember a list of random words in order. However, it has been argued that it is of little use when learning complex material in the real world. This issue was studied by De Beni et al. (1997). They presented a text orally or in written form to students, who used either the method of loci or rehearsal to remember the text. Memory was tested shortly after presentation and 1 week later.

With oral presentation, the method of loci led to greatly increased recall at both retention intervals, indicating it was very effective with a lecture-style presentation. However, there was no effect of learning method when the text was presented in written form. The method of loci was ineffective with written presentation because the visual nature of the presentation *interfered* with the use of visual imagery.

In Sulin and Dooling's (1974) study, participants used their schematic knowledge of Hitler to incorrectly organise the information about the story they had been told. The study revealed how schematic organisation can lead to errors in long-term memory and recall.

EVALUATION

➕ The method of loci provides a way of using previous knowledge and organising information that can be very effective in improving memory (especially with lists of unrelated words).

➕ The method of loci is also effective when people are trying to learn and remember an extended text presented orally (De Beni et al., 1997).

➕ The method is so effective because it provides a very detailed set of retrieval cues (i.e. the locations) to assist the rememberer.

➖ It is harder to use the method when the material to be remembered is abstract rather than concrete because abstract material doesn't lend itself to visual imagery.

➖ If the to-be-learned material is presented visually, there is a danger that it will interfere with the use of visual imagery that is needed with the method of loci (De Beni et al., 1997). Why doesn't visual presentation seem to cause a problem when learners use the method of loci with word lists? Learners don't have to engage in continuous visual processing of the words, thus permitting visual imagery to be used. In contrast, reading an extended text as in the De Beni et al. study requires almost constant visual processing.

KEY TERM

Method of loci: a mnemonic technique in which various items of information are remembered by associating them with successive locations (e.g. along a favourite walk).

- The method of loci involves treating each item to be learned (e.g. words; facts) separately from the others. This is fine if you want to learn a list of unrelated words, but would be less effective if you wanted to *integrate* the to-be-learned information.

- You need reasonable visual imagery ability to use the method of loci, it is hard to recall any given item without working through the list, and it is hard to use if the information to be learned is presented rapidly.

EXAM HINT

When you discuss ways of improving memory in an exam it is useful to have a simple example at your fingertips, such as mnemonics that use the first letter, e.g. "My Very Energetic Monkey Jumps Superbly Unless Nervous" for the order of the planets.

However, questions are likely to ask you to *apply* your knowledge to a particular situation (such as a teacher trying to remember her students' names) rather than asking you to just describe a technique. So make sure you do as required and *use* your knowledge rather than describe it. It may help you to practise doing this.

ACTIVITY: Method of loci

Think of 10 locations in your home, choosing them so that the sequence of moving from one to the next is obvious: for example, from front door to entrance hall to kitchen to bedroom. Check that you can imagine moving through your 10 locations in a consistent order without difficulty. Now think of 10 items and imagine them in those locations. If your first item is a *pipe*, you might imagine it poking out of the letterbox in your front door with great clouds of smoke billowing into the street. If the second item is a *cabbage*, you might imagine your hall obstructed by an enormous cabbage, and so on. When it comes to recall, walk mentally the route around your house.

Now try to create similarly striking images associating your 10 chosen locations with the words below:

shirt eagle paperclip rose camera mushroom crocodile handkerchief sausage mayor

Try to recall the 10 items listed above. No, don't look! Rely on the images you created.

Visual imagery mnemonic: Pegword method

The **pegword method** resembles the method of loci in that it relies on visual imagery and allows you to remember sequences of 10 unrelated items in the correct order—the method can be extended for longer sequences. As with the method of loci, it works because it makes use of your pre-existing knowledge.

Here's what is involved in the pegword method. First, you have to memorise 10 pegwords. Since each pegword rhymes with a number from one to ten, this is fairly easy. Try it for yourself.

One = *bun*	Two = *shoe*	Three = *tree*	Four = *door*
Five = *hive*	Six = *sticks*	Seven = *heaven*	Eight = *gate*
Nine = *wine*	Ten = *hen*		

Having mastered this, you are ready to memorise 10 unrelated words. Suppose these are as follows: *battleship, pig, chair, sheep, castle, rug, grass, beach, milkmaid, binoculars*. Take the first pegword, bun (rhyming with one), and form an image of a *bun* interacting with *battleship*. You might, for example, imagine a battleship sailing into an enormous floating bun. Now take the second pegword, *shoe*, and imagine it interacting with *pig*, perhaps a large shoe with a pig sitting in it. Pegword three is *tree*, and the third word on the list is *chair*—you might imagine a chair wedged in the branches of a tree. Work through the rest of the items, forming an appropriate interactive image in each case. I am confident that when you have completed the task, you will be able to recall all 10 items in the correct order. Was I right?

ACTIVITY: The pegword method

You can show that the pegword method is effective by comparing two groups of participants with *random* allocation to the two groups. One group receives training in the pegword method and the other group does not. Everyone is then presented with the same list of 10 unrelated concrete nouns (nouns referring to things you can see). The list needs to be presented fairly slowly so that those in the pegword method group have time to form interactive images. When the list is finished, you could ask everyone to count backwards by threes for 10 seconds to prevent recall from short-term memory. Finally, everyone writes down as many words as possible IN THE CORRECT ORDER. You should find that the pegword method group does much better at this serial recall task. The conclusion is that the pegword method enhances memory because it provides an effective way of organising the material at learning and it also facilitates retrieval.

Findings

The pegword method is very effective. Morris and Reid (1970) found twice as many words were recalled when the system was used than when it was not. It is effective because strong visual images are formed and because the pegwords themselves provide powerful retrieval cues when people are trying to remember the list. Wang and Thomas (2000) found the pegword method was as effective as the method of loci.

However, there are limitations with the pegword method. First, it requires fairly extensive training for it to be effective, especially if the words are presented rapidly. Second, the method is easier to use with concrete than with abstract material. The reason is that it is very hard to form interactive images with abstract words. Third, the method can be very useful if you want to remember 10 random words in the correct order. However, that isn't a very useful skill in everyday life! Fourth, interference has sometimes been found when people use the pegword method to learn a list of words and then re-learn the same list with the words re-assigned to different pegwords (Bellezza, 1982).

Verbal mnemonic: Story method

The **story method** is one of the most effective verbal mnemonics. It is used to remember a series of unrelated words in the correct order by linking them together within a story. One of the main reasons it is effective is that it imposes *meaning* on the material—a series of unrelated words doesn't naturally convey much meaning! I will show this method at work with the 10 words I used to illustrate use of the pegword method:

> *In the kitchen of the BATTLESHIP, there was a PIG that sat in a CHAIR. There was also a SHEEP that had previously lived in a CASTLE. In port, the sailors took a RUG and sat on the GRASS close to the BEACH. While there, they saw a MILKMAID watching them through her BINOCULARS.*

Bower and Clark (1969) showed that the story method can be extremely effective. They gave their participants the task of recalling 12 lists of 10 nouns each in the correct order when given the first word of each list as cues. Those who had constructed narrative stories recalled 93% of the words compared to only 13% for those who didn't do so. This is one of the largest differences in long-term memory between groups I have ever come across—learners using the story method recalled *seven* times as many words as the controls!

The story method has some limitations. First, it requires fairly extensive training—it took me a few minutes to construct the story given above! Second, it is hard to use if the information

KEY TERM

Story method: a mnemonic technique in which a list of words is learned by linking them together within the context of a story.

is presented rapidly. Third, you generally have to work your way through the list if you want to find a given item (e.g. the seventh one). Fourth, the ability to recall unrelated words in the correct order is of little general value.

Verbal mnemonics

Two verbal mnemonics that have been in existence for a long time are **acronyms** and **acrostics**. An acronym is a word formed by taking the initial letters of other words in turn. For example, the acronym ROY G BIV can be used to remember the colours of the rainbow in order: Red Orange Yellow Green Blue Indigo Violet. Here is another example. The acronym HOMES allows you to remember the names of the Great Lakes in North America: Huron Ontario Michigan Erie Superior.

An acrostic is generally an entire sentence formed with the first letter of each word acting as a prompt for the to-be-remembered information. For example, you could remember the planets in order from the sun by using the sentence "My Very Educated Mother Just Sent Us Nine Pizzas". If you consider the first letters, you should produce the correct order: Mercury, Venus, Earth, Mars, Jupiter, Saturn, Uranus, Neptune, Pluto.

Acronyms and acrostics are effective because they impose some structure or organisation on the information we are trying to remember.

Why do mnemonic techniques work?

Why are mnemonic techniques so effective? An important part of the answer is that they allow us to make use of our knowledge of the world around us. However, the full story is more complicated. Suppose we asked taxi drivers and students to recall lists of streets in the city in which they lived. We would expect that the taxi drivers (with their superb knowledge of the spatial layout of the city's streets) would always outperform the students. In fact, that is *not* the case.

Kalakoski and Saariluoma (2001) asked Helsinki taxi drivers and students to recall lists of 15 Helsinki street names in the order presented. In one condition, the streets were connected and were presented in an order forming a spatially continuous route through the city. In this condition, the taxi drivers recalled 87% of the street names correctly against only 45% by the students. In another condition, non-adjacent street names taken from all over Helsinki were presented in a random order. Now there was no difference in recall between the taxi drivers and the students.

What can we conclude from the above findings? It is obvious that the taxi drivers knew considerably more than the students about the spatial structure of Helsinki's streets. This knowledge could be used effectively to facilitate learning and retrieval when all the streets were close together in that spatial structure. However, the taxi drivers couldn't use their special knowledge effectively to organise the to-be-remembered information when the street names were distributed randomly around the city.

Why are techniques such as the method of loci, the pegword method, and the story method so effective? Ericsson (1988) argued there are three requirements if we are to achieve very high memory skills:

1. *Meaningful encoding*: the information should be processed meaningfully, relating it to preexisting knowledge. This is clearly the case when you use known locations (the method of loci) or the number sequence (pegword method), or when taxi drivers use their knowledge of their own town or city. This is the encoding principle.
2. *Retrieval structure*: cues should be stored with the information to aid subsequent retrieval. The connected series of locations or the number sequence both provide an immediately available retrieval structure, as does the knowledge of spatial layout possessed by taxi drivers. This is the retrieval structure principle.
3. *Speed-up*: extensive practice allows the processes involved in encoding and retrieval to function faster and faster. The importance of extensive practice can be seen in the generally superior memory for street names shown by taxi drivers compared to students in Kalakoski and Saariluoma's (2001) study. The importance of practice was shown by Ericsson and Chase (1982). They paid a student, SF, to practise the digit-span task for 1 hour a day for 2 years. The normal digit span (number of random digits that can be repeated back in the

In Kalakoski and Saariluoma's (2001) study, taxi drivers exhibited a superior recall ability for a list of street names only when the street names were presented as a spatially continuous route through the city.

correct order) is 6 or 7. SF eventually attained a span of 80 items! This is the speed-up principle.

Overview of organisation, knowledge, and memory

We have discussed several ways in which the effects of organisation and pre-existing knowledge on learning and long-term memory have been studied. In spite of the diversity of the experimental approaches adopted, there are important common themes (see Figure). First, in every case, people use pre-existing knowledge to organise the to-be-learned material at the time of learning. This knowledge can take many different forms—it may be knowledge nearly everyone possesses, it may be idiosyncratic knowledge, or it may be knowledge specifically acquired to enhance memory (e.g. pegword method).

Second, organisation provides a systematic retrieval plan assisting in the recall of the relevant information. The retrieval cues associated with the retrieval plan can be general or specific. General retrieval cues are relevant for several possible words. For example, the cue "four-footed animals" may lead us to think of dozens of four-footed animals. In contrast, specific retrieval cues are relevant for only one word. For example, using the pegword method, you may have formed an association between "bun" and "battleship". The cue "bun" *only* cues "battleship".

Organisation at learning	Organisational cue at retrieval
• Knowledge of categories: catagorised word lists	Category names: general
• Knowledge of hierarchies: hierarchical word lists	Levels within hierarchy: general
• Schematic knowledge	Schema-relevant cues: general
• Idiosyncratic knowledge: subjective organisation, Mandler's (1967) approach	Idiosyncratic cues: general
• Knowledge of locations	Location cues: specific
• Specially acquired knowledge, pegword method	Pegword cues: specific

Different approaches to studying organisation and memory. General cues are ones that cue several words, whereas specific cues are ones that cue only a single word.

EVALUATION

Here are the strengths and limitations of research on organisation and on the use of pre-existing knowledge in memory:

- Strength: All the methods and techniques we have discussed are effective (or very effective) in improving memory in part because they make use of our previous knowledge.
- Strength: The effects that are observed occur in part because organisation enhances learning (meaningful encoding). That is perhaps especially the case with the story method.
- Strength: Use of mnemonic techniques such as the method of loci and the pegword method has the advantage that we can identify precisely the pre-existing knowledge learners are using to enhance memory.
- Strength: The effects also occur because organisation provides a retrieval plan to assist recall.
- Strength: One of the key reasons why organisation benefits memory is because we have a limited ability to chunk information into more than about seven chunks (Mandler, 1967).
- Strength: Some of the techniques have fairly broad applicability in the real world. For example, the method of loci has been found to enhance memory for a 2000-word text presented orally (De Beni et al., 1997).
- Limitation: The notion of "organisation" is somewhat vague. For example, it is not very clear whether the same organisational principles explain all of the findings we have discussed.
- Limitation: We assume that learners use their pre-existing knowledge to organise lists of random words, but we really don't know *what* knowledge they are using or *why* they selected that particular knowledge.
- Limitation: Some mnemonic techniques (e.g. method of loci; pegword method) are limited in that they can only readily be used with concrete material (nouns referring to visible objects) and when information at retrieval is accessed in a rigid order.

- Limitation: Many of the methods are of limited applicability. For example, they typically don't allow for much integration of the to-be-learned material, and they are hard to apply to complex learning (e.g. mastering AS Psychology!).
- Limitation: We know people are good at organising random words (e.g. Mandler's approach), but we don't know in detail how this is achieved.
- Limitation: Organisation generally enhances memory. However, when the retrieval cues are general, there is a danger of an increase in the number of errors (e.g. Sulin & Dooling, 1974).

Mind maps

In recent years, there has been a substantial increase in the use of mind maps (Buzan & Buzan, 1993). A **mind map** is "a diagram used to represent words, ideas, tasks or other items linked to and arranged radially around a central key word or idea" (Wikipedia). A concrete example of a mind map is shown in the Figure. As you can see, information is presented very flexibly. However, the most important concepts and words are typically written in large letters fairly close to the central concept and the less important ones are written in smaller letters farther away from the central concept.

Several factors determine the effectiveness of mind maps. However, one of the main ones is that mind maps serve to organise and integrate the information that needs to be learned.

Findings

The available evidence suggests mind maps are effective. Farrand et al. (2002) presented medical students with a 600-word text to learn. Half had been trained in the mind-map technique and the others were simply instructed to use study techniques learned previously. One week after learning, students in the mind-map group recalled 10% more factual knowledge from the text than those using ordinary study techniques.

KEY TERM

Mind map: a complex diagram in which several ideas are organised via links around some central idea or theme.

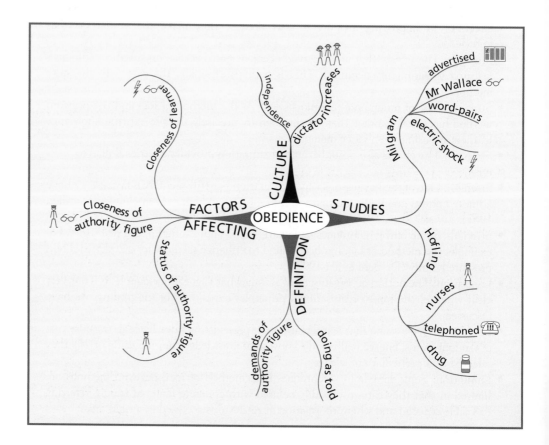

The beginnings of a mind map for obedience.

Ismail et al. (2010) studied computer science students who were learning computer programming. Students who used mind maps showed better memory for what they had learned than did students who didn't use mind maps. This was the case for students low and high in logical-thinking ability.

Nesbit and Adescope (2006) carried out a meta-analysis combining the findings from 55 studies. The use of mind maps was consistently associated with increased knowledge retention among students of all ages studying various subjects including psychology, science, statistics, and nursing.

Budd (2004) pointed out that many students don't seem very motivated when using mind maps. Those favouring a "doing" learning style felt they learned a lot from using mind maps, and rated the use of mind maps as highly as lectures. In contrast, students preferring a "thinking" learning style were less sure about the value of mind maps, and rated lectures much more favourably than the use of mind maps.

Try making a mind map of the multi-store model, and then another of eyewitness testimony research and look to see where you have used categories?

EVALUATION

Mind maps possess various advantages compared to the traditional approach based on note taking. First, students need to be actively involved in the learning process to produce satisfactory mind maps, whereas note taking often mainly involves writing down word for word phrases or sentences read in a textbook or spoken by the teacher.

Second, the concepts contained within mind maps are shown as having several links or associations to each other. This makes it easier for the learner to organise the material effectively, and is more realistic and useful than the linear presentation of information in texts or conventional notes. It is interesting that a study on nursing students found their initial mind maps consisted of a linear sequence of concepts but their later ones involved more complex patterns (Hsu & Hsieh, 2005).

Third, each concept is typically reduced to one or two words within mind maps, thus reducing ideas to their essence. Note takers often include lots of trivial details. Fourth, mind maps provide striking visual images that may be easier to remember than conventional notes.

Section Summary

Reliability of eyewitness testimony
* Eyewitness testimony is often inaccurate but is generally believed by jurors.

Factors affecting the accuracy of eyewitness testimony
* Misleading information presented before or after an incident can cause distorted memory.
* There is some evidence that misleading information has less of a negative impact with real-life crimes, and that memory distortions occur mainly to minor details rather than to information of central importance.
* Age is an important factor influencing the accuracy of eyewitness testimony—young children and older adults are generally less accurate than young adults.
* High anxiety or stress leads to reduced ability of eyewitnesses to make accurate face identifications and to remember details of a crime.
* Most people possess a bank robbery schema. This can assist eyewitness memory, but can also cause eyewitnesses to make memory errors based on information consistent with that schema.

Relevance of laboratory findings

- Doubts have been expressed about the value of laboratory findings for eyewitness testimony in the real world. However, most factors found to be important in the laboratory are also important in the real world.
- If anything, eyewitness inaccuracies and distortions observed in the laboratory *underestimate* the memory problems experienced by eyewitnesses to real crimes.

Misleading information and the use of the cognitive interview

- The cognitive interview is used to enhance eyewitness memory. It involves mental recreation of the context at the time of the crime, reporting of all details, and recall in various orders and from different perspectives.
- The cognitive interview is an effective technique, but the enhanced cognitive interview (including minimising of distractions, avoidance of personal comments, and review of what the eyewitness says) is even more effective.
- There are some limitations with the cognitive interview:
  - it produces an increase in the amount of incorrect information recalled compared to standard techniques;
  - it is less effective when used at long intervals after a crime;
  - it is not very clear which components of the cognitive interview contribute most to its success.

Strategies for memory improvement

- It is very important for learners to make full use of their pre-existing knowledge when learning something new, because this makes it much easier to organise the information.
- There are various forms of organisation, including organisation by categories and hierarchical organisation.
- Organisation is often used at the time of learning *and* at the time of retrieval.
- Mandler (1967) found learners who sorted a list of words into several categories recalled much more than those who used only a few.
- Organisation is not always effective—it can sometimes lead to an increase in memory errors.
- The method of loci is one of the best known visual imagery techniques. It is very effective when the to-be-learned information is presented orally but not always when presented visually. It capitalises on the learner's pre-existing knowledge.
- There are limitations with the method of loci:
  - it is hard to use with abstract material;
  - it doesn't produce integration of the to-be-learned material;
  - it is hard to recall any given item without working through the list.
- The pegword method is another visual imagery mnemonic that provides learners with the knowledge needed to memorise successfully. It is also very effective but suffers from similar limitations to the method of loci.
- The various mnemonic techniques work because they involve:
  - meaningful encoding;
  - retrieval structure;
  - speed-up.
- Mind maps can be very effective at enhancing memory, in part because they help to organise and integrate the information to be learned. In addition, the learner is actively involved in the learning process.

You have reached the end of the chapter on cognitive psychology. Cognitive psychology is an approach or perspective in psychology. The material in this chapter has exemplified the way that cognitive psychologists explain behaviour. They look at behaviour in terms of the way that it can be explained by reference to mental (cognitive) processes. This is sometimes regarded as a rather "mechanistic" approach to the study of behaviour because it focuses on machine-like processes and can tend to minimise the influence of social or emotional factors.

Further Reading

- Most of the topics discussed in this chapter are dealt with in detail in M.W. Eysenck (2012) *Fundamentals of cognition (2nd Edn)* (Hove, UK: Psychology Press).

- The same is true of A. Baddeley, M.W. Eysenck, and M.C. Anderson (2009) *Memory* (Hove, UK: Psychology Press).

- There is a good account of the main factors influencing the accuracy of eyewitness testimony in G.L. Wells and E.A. Olson (2003) Eyewitness testimony. *Annual Review of Psychology, 54,* 277–295.

- Some of the reasons why eyewitness testimony is fallible are discussed by E.F. Loftus (2004) Memories of things unseen. *Current Directions in Psychological Science, 13,* 145–147.

- Useful memory techniques are discussed by M.W. Eysenck (2011) How to improve your memory. *Psychology Review, 17,* 11–13.

Revision Questions

The examination questions aim to sample the material in this whole chapter. For advice on how to answer such questions refer to Chapter 1, Section 2.

1. a. Outline the main features of the multi-store model of memory. (6 marks)

    b. Explain **one** limitation of the multi-store model of memory. (4 marks)

2. a. Explain what is meant by encoding, capacity and duration. (6 marks)

    b. Outline what research has shown about the duration of short-term memory. (4 marks)

3. Describe and evaluate the working memory model of memory. (12 marks)

4. a. Explain **one** way that the accuracy of eyewitness testimony can be improved. (2 marks)

    b. Outline how psychologists have investigated the accuracy of eyewitness testimony. (4 marks)

    c. Explain why studies of eyewitness testimony have been criticised as lacking validity. (5 marks)

5. Discuss the use of the cognitive interview. (10 marks)

6. Tom is preparing to take his driving theory test. He needs to memorise all sorts of facts such as using headlights when you cannot see for more than 100m (328 feet) and you should allow at least a 2s gap between you and the vehicle in front on roads carrying faster-moving traffic.

    Explain **one** strategy that Tom could use to help him remember this information, and explain why this might improve his memory for this task. (4 marks)

EXAM HINT

Some examination questions require you to apply your knowledge. They start with a "stem" describing a scenario (as in question 6 on this page). Whilst you probably have not seen the scenario before, if you have revised everything you will have the knowledge needed to answer the question. Just remember to apply your knowledge. You might briefly outline a theory or research study but then must use this to explain the scenario.

What you need to know

Section 5: Attachment p. 61

- Explanations of attachment, including learning theory and Bowlby's theory.
- Types of attachment: secure attachment, insecure-avoidant, and insecure-resistant.
- Use of the "Strange Situation" in attachment research.
- Cultural variations in attachment.
- The effects of disruption of attachment, failure to form attachment (privation), and institutional care.

When do infants first become attached? What is the sequence of attachment development, and are there individual differences and cultural variations? Are there theories that can account for why children form attachments, and why they become attached to one person rather than another? What happens when children have disrupted attachment with their caregiver(s)? In the short term, infants become anxious. We will consider how this subsequently influences the child's development. We will also explore the important distinction between disruption of attachment (separation from caregivers) and privation (a lack of attachment).

Section 6: Attachment in everyday life p. 95

- The impact of different forms of day care on children's social development, including the effects on aggression and peer relations.
- How research into attachment and day care has influenced child-care practices.

What are the effects (beneficial and adverse) of day care on children? Does the type of day care matter? We will focus on day care's effects on social development, including those on aggression and peer relations. We will also consider the ways in which child-care practices have been influenced by psychological research into attachment and day care.

Early Social Development

3

People develop attachments to all sorts of things—footwear, favourite restaurants, friends, lovers, and parents. You form attachments throughout your life, but among the most important ones are those formed early in development.

Attachment is like a piece of invisible string that binds individuals to permit healthy development. The tie is reciprocal—parents are as attached to their children as the children are to their parents. Attachment is a central topic in developmental psychology. In this chapter, we will consider how attachment develops and why it happens at all, as well as other related issues. One of these other issues is disruption of attachment, which happens when children are separated from their parent or caregiver. Such separation can involve deprivation and privation, and is found among children in institutional care.

Finally, we move on to the issue of day care and its effects on social development. This is an important issue because literally millions of young children in the United Kingdom and numerous other countries are placed into day care several days a week. The research carried out by psychologists on day care has important implications for child-care practices, and these are considered in detail.

SECTION 5
ATTACHMENT

What is Attachment?

According to Shaffer (1993), an attachment is "a close emotional relationship between two persons, characterised by mutual affection and a desire to maintain proximity [closeness]". It is an emotional relationship experienced throughout the lifespan. When you are attached to someone, it makes you feel good to be in that person's company and also makes you feel anxious when they aren't there. You may also experience a longing to be reunited. This is the "desire to maintain proximity".

> **KEY TERM**
>
> **Attachment:** a strong, emotional bond between an infant and his or her caregiver(s) that is characterised by a desire to maintain proximity. Such bonds may be secure or insecure.

There are certain behaviours that characterise attachment: distress on separation, pleasure when reunited, seeking out the attachment figure, and general orientation to each other.

Maccoby (1980) identified *four* key behaviours associated with attachment:

- *Seeking proximity to primary caregiver.* The infant tries to stay close to its "attachment figure".
- *Distress on separation.* When caregiver and infant are separated, *both* experience feelings of distress.
- *Pleasure when reunited.* Obvious pleasure is shown when the child is reunited with his/her caregiver.
- *General orientation of behaviour towards primary caregiver.* The infant is aware of his/her caregiver at all times and may frequently make contact for reassurance.

In sum, attachment has a very strong emotional component. In addition, however, it also has a behavioural component (e.g. staying close to the other person). Finally, attachment has a cognitive component—for example, we have numerous happy memories of those to whom we are attached.

Explanations of Attachment: Learning Theory and Bowlby's Theory

The great majority of infants (about 75% in many cultures) form **secure attachments** with their mother or principal caregiver. As we will see later, forming secure attachments is of great value in ensuring infants' happiness and healthy social development. There are more theories to explain how and why attachments are formed and maintained than you can shake a stick at. However, we will focus on two major theories: learning theory and Bowlby's theory.

Learning theory

The most basic principle of **learning theory** is that all behaviour has been learned. That means behaviour isn't **innate** and doesn't depend on genetic factors. Learning theorists (also called "behaviourists") argued that learning is the result of **conditioning**, which is a form of learning. According to learning theorists (or "behaviourists"), there are two main forms of conditioning— **classical conditioning** and **operant conditioning** (see the box).

Classical conditioning

- Unconditioned stimulus (US) e.g. food → causes → reflex response, e.g. salivation.
- Neutral stimulus (NS) e.g. bell → causes → no response.
- NS and US are paired in time (they co-occur).
- NS (e.g. bell) is now a conditioned stimulus (CS) → which produces → a conditioned response (CR) (a new stimulus-response link is learned, the bell causes salivation).

Operant conditioning

- A behaviour that has a positive effect is more likely to be repeated.
- Negative reinforcement (escape from aversive stimulus) is agreeable.
- Punishment is disagreeable.

Classical conditioning

How can infant attachment behaviour be explained by classical conditioning? The stimulus of food (an unconditioned stimulus) produces a sense of pleasure (an unconditioned response). The person providing the food (usually the mother) becomes *associated* with this pleasure. As a result, the provider of food becomes a conditioned stimulus that independently produces the unconditioned stimulus (pleasure). The food-giver thus becomes a source of pleasure to the infant. According to classical conditioning theory, this is the basis of the attachment bond.

What are the limitations of the classical conditioning account? First, it strongly implies that infants will form their major attachment with the mother or other food-giver. In fact, however, this was found to be the case for only 61% of infants (Schaffer & Emerson, 1964).

Second, it isn't clear why infants would form attachments with adults other than the food-giver. In fact, however, over 80% of infants have more than one strong attachment at the age of 18 months (Schaffer & Emerson, 1964).

Third, the attachments formed by infants are emotionally rich and complex. The classical conditioning account doesn't account for this richness and complexity nor for the great importance of attachment to infants.

Operant conditioning: Basic theory

According to the operant conditioning approach (e.g. Skinner, 1938), any response followed by **positive reinforcement** (reward such as food or praise) will be strengthened. All such responses are more likely to be produced in the future when the individual is in the same situation. Dollard and Miller (1950) put forward a simple account of the development of attachments based on operant conditioning. Their focus was on motivation, i.e. the forces driving behaviour:

- All humans possess various primary motives or drives, such as those of hunger, thirst, and sex. Stimuli satisfying these primary drives are **primary reinforcers**.
- A person will be "driven" to seek food to satisfy his/her hunger.
- Eating food results in drive reduction and is positively reinforcing or rewarding.
- According to the principles of operant conditioning, anything that is rewarded is likely to be repeated and so this behaviour is learned.
- The mother or other caregiver provides the food that reduces the drive, and so becomes a **secondary reinforcer**—he/she becomes a reinforcer by association with a primary reinforcer.
- From then on, the infant seeks to be with the person who has become a secondary reinforcer, because he/she is now a source of reward. The infant has become attached.

Mothers can also learn to be attached to their infants because of positive reinforcement. For example, mothers are rewarded when they make their child smile or stop crying.

Findings

We must be careful when assuming the findings obtained from other species apply to humans. However, Harlow carried out important studies on infant monkeys that seem of real relevance to human infants and that cast doubt on the learning theory approach. To test whether monkeys prefer the activity of feeding to bodily comfort, Harlow (1959) had very young rhesus monkeys taken from their mothers and placed in cages with two surrogate [substitute] mothers as shown in the picture. One "mother" was made of wire and the other was covered in soft cloth. Milk was provided by the wire mother for some of the monkeys, whereas it was provided by the cloth mother for the others.

What did Harlow (1959) find? The monkeys spent most of their time clinging to the cloth mother even when she didn't supply milk—this is NOT as predicted by learning theory. The reason was that the cloth mother provided "contact comfort", which the monkeys regarded as more important than food. If the monkeys were frightened by a teddy-bear drummer, they ran to their cloth mother.

Unfortunately, the monkeys didn't develop normally. Later in life they were indifferent or abusive to other monkeys, and had difficulty with mating and parenting. Thus, contact comfort is preferable (but not sufficient) for healthy development.

This theoretical approach is very limited in several ways. First, it predicts all infants would be attached to the food-giver. However, Schaffer and Emerson (1964) found 39% of infants had their main attachment to an adult other than the one who mostly fed and looked after them.

Second, this approach implies that infants would generally form only *one* strong attachment (i.e. with the food-giver). In fact, over 80% of infants at the age of 18 months have attached to more than one adult (Schaffer & Emerson, 1964).

? How do classical and operant conditioning differ?

The monkeys in Harlow's study appeared to be more attached to a cloth-covered artificial "mother" than to a wire version.

Although the wire mother on the left is where the baby monkey receives his food, he runs to the cloth mother for comfort when he is frightened by the teddy bear drummer (Harlow, 1959).

Operant conditioning: Gewirtz

Gewirtz (e.g. 1991) put forward a more complex and realistic operant conditioning theory of infant attachment. He argued that the mother is *always* a very important source of positive reinforcement or reward for her child, not just in the context of feeding. Mothers who are sensitive and responsive to their child monitor his/her behaviour carefully and use positive reinforcement to strengthen the attachment. For example, sensitive mothers provide reward to soothe the infant or to encourage him/her to respond to her.

There is much evidence (discussed later) that maternal sensitivity is associated with attachment—sensitive mothers are more likely than non-sensitive ones to have securely attached infants. It follows from Gewirtz's theory that aspects of maternal sensitivity that involve providing positive reinforcement when the infant really needs it should be most associated with infant attachment. That is what Dunst and Kassow (2008) found. These findings make sense—we would expect infants to be better adjusted if their mother is responsive to their needs.

What are the limitations of Gewirtz's theory? First, if securely attached infants are rewarded for interacting with their mother, it isn't very clear why such infants often voluntarily separate themselves from their mother. Second, the theory focuses too much on the notion that attachment is merely a form of behaviour. In reality, attachment is a complex mixture of emotional, cognitive, and behavioural components.

Social learning theory

Social learning theory is a more sophisticated version of the learning theory approaches discussed so far. Learning theory claims that learning takes place *directly* with no intervening mental process or processes. In other words, direct associations are formed between stimuli and responses. For example, a rat sees a lever and presses it to receive food reward.

Within social learning theory, on the other hand, it is argued that we also learn more *indirectly*. Much of what we learn is based on observing the behaviour of others (**observational learning**). Of most relevance here is vicarious reinforcement—we learn to produce a new behaviour by seeing someone else perform that behaviour and being **reinforced** or rewarded for performing it. According to social learning theorists, the kind of imitation involved in vicarious reinforcement is very important.

Hay and Vespo (1988) used social learning theory to explain attachment. They suggested attachment occurs because parents "deliberately teach their children to love them and to understand human relationships" (p. 82). Some of the techniques involved are:

* *Modelling*: Learning based on observing and imitating a model's behaviour.
* *Direct instruction*: Providing reward or reinforcement when the child behaves in the required way.

KEY TERMS

Social learning theory: the view that behaviour can be explained in terms of direct and indirect reinforcement, through imitation, identification, and modelling.

Observational learning: learning through imitating or copying the behaviour of others (especially when that behaviour is rewarded or reinforced).

Reinforced: a behaviour is likely to re-occur because the response was rewarded.

- *Social facilitation*: Using the presence of others to encourage the child to understand positive relationships between people.

Social learning theory emphasises the notion that infants' attachment to their mother or other caregiver involves learning certain responses (e.g. seeking closeness to the mother). All the techniques discussed by Hay and Vespo (1988) (i.e. modelling; direct instruction; and social facilitation) undoubtedly influence infants' attachment behaviour.

However, social learning theory focuses on only part of what is involved in attachment. For example, consider **oxytocin** (sometimes known as the "cuddle hormone"). Infants' attachment to their mother is greater when the mother has relatively high levels of oxytocin (Galbally et al., 2011). Such findings suggest we need to consider *internal* factors (e.g. mother's oxytocin level) as well as *external* ones (e.g. mother's behaviour; infant's behaviour) when understanding mother–infant attachment.

Some psychologists think of attachment behaviour as something that is learned because it is reinforced. Young children may learn about human relationships by imitating the affectionate behaviours of their parents.

EVALUATION

➕ An infant's attachment to its mother probably occurs in part because he/she learns to associate food with the food-giver (classical conditioning). It also occurs in part because the mother rewards the infant and the infant rewards the mother (e.g. by smiling).

➕ There is some evidence (e.g. Hay & Vespo, 1988) that children can acquire attachment behaviour via social learning.

➕ It is likely that young children start to imitate aspects of the loving behaviour of their caregiver or caregivers as a result of observational learning.

➕ Research on social learning theory has practical applications. Parents or other caregivers need to be aware that their children use observation and imitation when developing attachments. Thus, it is very important for parents to act as positive role models.

➖ Harlow's evidence indicates that young monkeys preferred a cloth mother that didn't provide milk to a wire mother that did. This is the *opposite* of the prediction from learning theory, which claims infants form attachments to the person who feeds them. However, research on monkeys may not apply to humans. Against that, human infants often become attached to adults *not* involved in feeding or basic caregiving (Schaffer & Emerson, 1964).

➖ Learning theory is criticised for being **reductionist**, "reducing" the complexities of human behaviour to over-simple ideas such as stimulus, response, and reinforcement. These ideas are too simple to explain attachment.

➖ Social learning theory describes some processes involved in parent–child attachments. However, the strong emotional intensity of many parent–child attachments isn't really *explained* by social learning theorists.

➖ There is some evidence (discussed later) that genetic differences between infants help to explain why they differ in attachment type. However, genetic factors are ignored within the learning theory approach.

KEY TERMS

Oxytocin: this hormone promotes feelings of well-being and calm in mothers as part of the attachment process; it is sometimes referred to as the "cuddle hormone".

Reductionist: an argument or theory that reduces complex factors to a set of simple principles.

Bowlby's theory

John Bowlby (1907–1990) was a child psychoanalyst whose main interest was in the relationship between caregiver and child. He realised that Freud's views of the importance of maternal care could be combined with key ideas of the ethologists to produce a major new theory. **Ethologists** study animals in their natural surroundings. They emphasised the notion of **imprinting**. This is the tendency for the young of some species of birds to follow the first moving object they see and to continue to follow it after that.

Bowlby's idea was that infants would show imprinting to their own mother, which would explain the strong attachment most infants have for their mother. This theory has had a profound effect on the way psychologists think about attachment and infant development.

The fundamental principle of Bowlby's theory is that attachment is an innate and **adaptive** process for both infant and parent. Attachment behaviour has evolved and endured because it promotes survival. Attachment promotes survival in several ways:

The attachment between a child and his or her caregiver serves many important functions. According to Bowlby, it maintains proximity for safety, the caregiver acts as a secure base for exploration, and the attachment relationship acts as a template (pattern) for all future relationships.

1. *Safety*: Attachment results in a desire to maintain proximity and thus ensure safety. Both infant and caregiver experience anxious feelings when separated, which creates a proximity-seeking drive (striving to be close to the other person).

2. *Emotional relationships*: Attachment enables the infant to learn how to form and conduct healthy emotional relationships. Bowlby used the concept of the internal working model—a set of conscious and/or unconscious rules and expectations regarding our relationships with others—to explain how this happens. This model develops out of the primary attachment relationship and is used as a template or pattern for future relationships.

3. A *secure base for exploration*: Attachment also provides a secure base for exploration, a process of fundamental importance for cognitive and social development. The child often returns periodically to "touch base" with its attachment figure. An insecurely attached child is less willing to wander. Exploration is very important for cognitive development, as was shown by Bus and van IJzendoorn (1988). They assessed the attachment types of children aged 2 years old. Three years later, the securely attached children showed more interest in written material than the insecurely attached children.

Role of social releasers

According to Bowlby, attachment must be innate or the infant and parent might *not* show it. The infant and the mother/caregiver must both be actively involved for the attachment to be secure and lasting. Bowlby argued that the infant innately elicits caregiving from its mother-figure by means of social releasers. **Social releasers** are behaviours such as smiling or crying that encourage a response—humans are innately programmed to respond to these social releasers.

Most people feel uncomfortable when they hear an infant or adult crying, which helps to ensure someone will respond. It is a mechanism that maximises the chances of survival by

KEY TERMS

Ethologists: individuals who study animal behaviour in its natural environment, focusing on the importance of innate capacities and the functions of behaviours.

Imprinting: a restricted form of learning that takes place rapidly and has both short-term effects (e.g. a following response) and long-lasting effects (e.g. choice of reproductive partner).

Adaptive: the extent to which a behaviour increases the reproductive potential of an individual and survival of its genes.

Social releasers: a social behaviour or characteristic that elicits a caregiving reaction. Bowlby suggested that these were innate and critical in the process of forming attachments.

keeping the caregiver close. These innate behaviours and innate responses are a fundamental part of the process of forming an attachment.

Bowlby's theoretical approach also provides an explanation for the notion (discussed later) that children separated from parent or caregiver show three successive stages of reaction (Robertson & Bowlby, 1952): protest; despair; and detachment. The protest stage increases the probability that the mother will find the infant. The following despair stage conserves energy and allows the defenceless infant to survive as long as possible in a dangerous environment.

The features of a baby face are very appealing. They act as a "social releaser", a social stimulus that "releases" a desire to offer caregiving.

KEY STUDY

Bowlby's proposed phases in the development of attachment

Bowlby proposed that an infant is born with a set of behavioural systems that are ready to be activated, for example crying, sucking, and clinging (all called "social releasers"), and an ability to respond to the "stimuli that commonly emanate from a human being"—sounds, faces, and touch. Shortly thereafter other behaviours appear, which are equally innate though not present at birth, such as smiling and crawling. From these small beginnings, sophisticated systems soon develop.

In the table below, four phases in the development of attachments are described, with very approximate ages.

Phase 1 Birth–8 weeks	Orientation and signals towards people without discrimination of one special person	Infants behave in characteristic and friendly ways towards other people but their ability to discriminate between them is very limited, e.g. they may just recognise familiar voices
Phase 2 About 8/10 weeks–6 months	Orientation and signals directed towards one or more special people	Infants continue to be generally friendly but there is beginning to be a marked difference of behaviour towards one mother figure or primary caregiver
Phase 3 6 months through to 1–2 years old	Maintenance of proximity to a special person by means of locomotion (movement) as well as signals to that person	The infant starts to follow his or her mother-figure, greet her (him) when she (he) returns, and use her (him) as a base from which to explore. The infant selects other people as subsidiary attachment figures. At the same time the infant's friendly responses to other people decrease and the infant treats strangers with increasing caution
Phase 4 Starts around the age of 2	Formation of a goal-correct partnership in which the child takes account of the caregiver's emotional goals	The child develops insight into the mother-figure's behaviour and this opens up a whole new relationship where the infant can consciously influence what she (or he) does. This is the beginning of a real partnership

Adapted from J. Bowlby (1969), *Attachment and love, Vol. 1: Attachment.* London: Hogarth.

Critical period

I mentioned earlier that Bowlby was influenced by the ethologists, who study species in their natural environment. The ethologists emphasise the concept of a **critical period**. In the case of biological characteristics, development must occur during a set period, otherwise it won't take place. Ethologists suggested this principle of a critical period might also apply to attachment. The ethologist Konrad Lorenz found the young of some bird species followed the first moving

Lorenz hatched some goslings and arranged it so that he would be the first thing that they saw. From then on they followed him everywhere and showed no recognition of their actual mother. The goslings formed a picture (imprint) of the object they were to follow.

? **Do you think that there are problems with generalising from the behaviour of one species to another?**

object they saw on hatching, and continued to follow it from then on. This is imprinting, the main characteristics of which are:

1. It occurs during a short critical period. If the infant isn't exposed to a "mother" within a critical time window, imprinting won't take place.
2. It is irreversible—once imprinting to an object has occurred, it can't be changed.
3. It has lasting outcomes. It results in the formation of a bond between the caregiver and its young and so has consequences in the short term for safety and food. It also affects the individual in the long term because it acts as a template or pattern for reproductive partners. For example, Immelmann (1972) arranged for zebra finches to be raised by Bengalese finches and vice versa. In later years, when the finches were given a free choice, they preferred to mate with the species on which they had been imprinted.

Like attachment, this **bonding** process is desirable. It means the offspring are more likely to survive and so the parents' genes are passed on to the next generation.

Imprinting

You may be thinking (totally understandably!) that human infants are much more complex than young birds, and so the findings of ethologists have limited application to humans. That is absolutely right. In addition, however, there has been controversy concerning notions such as imprinting and critical periods, even in birds.

Guiton (1966) found he could reverse imprinting in chickens. Guiton's chickens were initially imprinted on yellow rubber gloves. When the chickens matured, this early imprint acted as a mate template or pattern and the chickens tried to mate with the rubber gloves. This appears to support the claims made for imprinting. However, after the chickens had spent some time with their own species, they engaged in normal sexual behaviour with their own kind.

The idea of a critical period is too strong. It would be more appropriate to describe it as a *sensitive period*. Thus, although imprinting is *less* likely to occur outside a given time window, it *can* occur at other times. The notion of a sensitive period is that imprinting takes place most easily at a certain time but may still happen at any time.

KEY TERM

Bonding: the process of forming close ties with another.

CASE STUDY: Amorous turkeys

Some psychologists were conducting research on the effects of hormones on turkeys. In one room there were 35 full-grown male turkeys. If you walked into the room, the turkeys fled to the furthest corner and if you walked towards them, the turkeys slid along the wall to maintain a maximum distance between you and them. This is fairly normal behaviour for wild turkeys. However, in another room, there was a group of turkeys who behaved in a very different manner. These turkeys greeted you by stopping dead in their tracks, fixing their eyes on you, spreading their tail into a full courtship fan, putting their heads down and ponderously walking towards you, all at the same time. Their intention was clearly one of mating. (Fortunately turkeys in mid-courtship are famously slow so it is easy to avoid their advances.)

What was the difference between these two groups? The first set were raised away from humans, whereas the second group had received an injection of the male hormone, testosterone, when they were younger. The hormone created an artificial sensitive period during which the turkeys imprinted on their companion at the time—a male experimenter. Subsequently, these turkeys showed little interest in female turkeys; however, they were aroused whenever they saw a male human—displaying their tail feathers and strutting their stuff.

It has been suggested that the reason this learning was so strong and apparently irreversible was because it took place at a time of high arousal—when hormones were administered. In real life, hormones may be involved as well. Perhaps, for these birds, a moving object creates a sense of pleasure and this pleasure triggers the production of endorphins, opiate-like biochemicals produced by the body, which in turn create a state of arousal that is optimal for learning.

(From Howard S. Hoffman, 1996, *Amorous turkeys and addicted ducklings: A search for the causes of social attachment*. Boston, MA: Author's Cooperative.)

Bowlby (1969) claimed that something like imprinting occurs in infants. He proposed that infants have an innate tendency to orient towards one individual. This attachment is innate, and like all biological mechanisms should have a critical period for its development. Bowlby argued that this critical period ends at some point at about 3 or 4 years of age, after which it would be impossible to establish a powerful attachment to the caregiver.

Klaus and Kennell (1976) argued there is a *sensitive period* immediately after birth in which bonding (part of attachment) can occur through skin-to-skin contact. They compared two groups of infants. One group had much more contact with their mother during the first three days of life. One month later, more bonding had occurred in the extended-contact group than the routine contact group. During feeding, the extended-contact mothers cuddled and comforted their babies more, and also maintained more eye contact with them.

Some later research failed to repeat the findings of Klaus and Kennell (1976). For example, Lozoff (1983) reported that mothers were no more affectionate towards their babies in cultures encouraging early bodily contact between mother and baby. However, there is some support for the skin-to-skin hypothesis. Bystrova et al. (2009) compared the effects of skin-to-skin contact for 25–120 minutes after birth, early suckling, and initial separation of mother and infant. Mother–infant interaction one year later was better following in the skin-to-skin and suckling conditions than in the separation condition, suggesting there is a very early sensitive period for bonding.

Klaus and Kennell suggested that prolonged skin-to-skin contact between baby and mother gave rise to greater bonding. However, recent research, including cross-cultural studies, indicates that other forms of attention also promote bonding.

In sum, the relationship between mother and baby develops and changes over time rather than being fixed shortly after birth. However, early bonding experiences may well be helpful.

Monotropy or multiple attachments?

There has been much debate about whether infants become attached to only one person or to several. Attachment to one person is called "monotropy" (leaning towards one thing). Bowlby (1953) claimed infants have a hierarchy of attachments, at the top of which is one central caregiver—this is the **monotropy hypothesis**. This one person is generally (but not invariably) the mother. Thus, the terms "maternal" and "mothering" don't have to refer to a woman. Bowlby (1969) said, "It is because of this marked tendency to monotropy that we are capable of deep feelings."

The special significance of monotropy is that it alone provides the experience of an intense emotional relationship that forms the basis of the internal working model—the schema the child has for forming future relationships. However, Bowlby's notion that young children typically only have one very close attachment is exaggerated. Schaffer and Emerson (1964) found 31% of infants had five or more attachments and only 13% were attached to only one person.

Do early attachments affect future relationships?

According to Bowlby, infants construct an internal working model consisting of rules and expectations concerning their relationships and attachments with other people. This model influences their subsequent relationships including adulthood ones. Supporting evidence was reported by Hazan and Shaver (1987). They classified their adult participants as secure, ambivalent (opposing emotions), or avoidant attachment types based on their description of their childhood experiences.

Secure types described their adult love experiences as happy and trusting, and they accepted their partners regardless of any faults. Ambivalent types experienced love as involving obsession, desire for reciprocation, intensity, and jealousy, and worry that their partners might abandon them. Avoidant lovers typically feared intimacy, emotional highs and lows, and jealousy. They believed they didn't need to be loved to be happy. These findings suggest childhood attachment type influences adult romantic experiences.

A major problem with Hazan and Shaver's (1987) study is that the data concerning childhood attachments were collected several years later. As a result, what was recalled may have been inaccurate. Another issue is that Hazan and Shaver assumed that attachment type is *consistent* and determines the style of love. However, reality is more complex. In subsequent research, Shaver and Hazan (1993) found 22% of their adult sample changed their attachment style over a 12-month period, often as a result of relationship experiences. Thus, attachment style can influence style of love, but actual experiences of love can also influence attachment style.

Parenting is one of the most important relationships in adult life. A person's attachment to their own parents will influence their subsequent relationship with their own child.

EVALUATION OF BOWLBY'S THEORY

➕ Bowlby rightly emphasised the importance of attachment in infants and children. Indeed, nothing matters more for healthy infant development than having one or more secure attachments.

➕ Bowlby put forward the first ever systematic and comprehensive theory of attachment, and most subsequent theorists have used his main ideas.

⊕ The notion that the infant's attachment to the caregiver is typically strong and robust has been shown to be correct.

⊕ According to Bowlby, the infant's attachment to the mother is typically so strong and important that it persists even when he/she is maltreated by the mother. This is generally the case.

⊕ Bowlby's theorising strongly influenced the development of the Strange Situation (discussed later), easily the most popular way of studying attachment behaviour in infants.

⊕ Bowlby's claim that there is a critical period for the infant to form a strong attachment with its caregiver is partially correct.

⊖ Most of the theory's assumptions are too strong and dogmatic. In other words, many of Bowlby's views are exaggerations.

⊖ There is little support for the monotropy hypothesis with its emphasis on a *single* main attachment. Schaffer and Emerson (1964) found 31% of 18-month-old infants had five or more attachments. Most infants form two or more strong attachments at a relatively early age.

⊖ Healthy psychological development isn't always served by having only one primary attachment. It may be better to have a network of close attachments to sustain the needs of a growing infant (Thomas, 1998). This is certainly true in Caribbean countries. Even in European countries, infants probably benefit from the differences among their attachments. For example, fathers' style of play is more often physically stimulating and unpredictable whereas mothers are more likely to hold their infants, soothe them, attend to their needs, and read them stories (Parke, 1981). In Bowlby's defence, there is a *hierarchy* among an infant's attachments. For example, the Efe from the Democratic Republic of the Congo live in extended family groups. The infants are looked after and even breastfed by different women but usually sleep with their own mother at night. By the age of 6 months, the infants still prefer their mothers (Tronick et al., 1992).

⊖ Bowlby's view of attachment as a template (pattern) for future relationships leads us to expect any given child to form similar relationships with others. However, the similarities among a child's various relationships are quite low (Main & Weston, 1981). Evidence links attachment style to later relationships (e.g. Hazan & Shaver, 1987, discussed earlier), but this is not a universal finding. Howes et al. (1994) found parent–child relationships weren't always positively correlated with child–peer relationships. Even when there are positive correlations between the main attachment relationship and later relationships, other explanations are possible. Children who are appealing to their parents tend to be appealing to other people, so a child who does well in one relationship is likely to do well in others (Jacobson & Wille, 1986).

⊖ There is very little direct evidence that infant attachment involves processes resembling imprinting, and it is preferable to focus on sensitive periods rather than critical periods. As we will see later, some children kept in isolation or severely deprived circumstances for the first several years of their lives nevertheless form strong attachments following adoption. Thus, it is NOT absolutely essential for children to form a strong attachment when very young.

Types of Attachment: Secure Attachment, Insecure-Avoidant, and Insecure-Resistant

Many psychological theories seem to assume everyone is the same. However, as I am sure you will agree, we are all different and that is certainly true of infants' attachment behaviour. Schaffer and Emerson (1964) found that at 18 months very few (13%) infants were attached to only one person. Indeed, 31% had five or more attachments such as to the father, grandparent, or older sibling. In 65% of the children the first specific attachment was to the mother, and in a further 30% the mother was the first joint object of attachment.

Finally, Schaffer and Emerson (1964) found that in 39% of cases the person who usually fed, bathed, and changed the infant was *not* his/her primary attachment object. Thus, many of the mothers (and some of the fathers) were not the person who performed these tasks yet they were the main attachment object.

Numerous studies have been designed to establish whether infants are securely or insecurely attached. Most of those studies have used the "Strange Situation", which is described in detail in the next section. The links between this section and the next one are so close that it is best to consider them together.

Secure attachment, insecure-avoidant attachment, and insecure-resistant attachment

It might seem natural to divide infants into those who are securely attached and those who are insecurely attached. However, Ainsworth and Bell (1970) argued that this is too simple on the basis of a study using the "Strange Situation"—have a look at the description on p. 76. What is of interest in this situation is to see how the infant responds to a series of stressors (an unfamiliar room; presence of a stranger; separation from the mother).

Ainsworth and Bell (1970) identified three patterns of attachment based on the behaviour of infants in the "Strange Situation". Subsequently, Ainsworth et al. (1978) reported the findings from several studies using the Strange Situation in the United States. They confirmed the notion there are three main attachment types and provided a detailed account:

- *Secure attachment*: the infant is distressed by the caregiver's absence. However, he/she rapidly returns to a state of contentment after the caregiver's return, immediately seeking contact with the caregiver. There is a clear difference in the infant's reaction to the caregiver and to the stranger. Ainsworth et al. reported that 70% of American infants show secure attachment.
- *Insecure-resistant attachment*: the infant is insecure in the presence of the caregiver, and becomes very distressed when the caregiver leaves. He/she resists contact with the caregiver upon return, and is wary of the stranger. About 10% of American infants were found to be resistant.

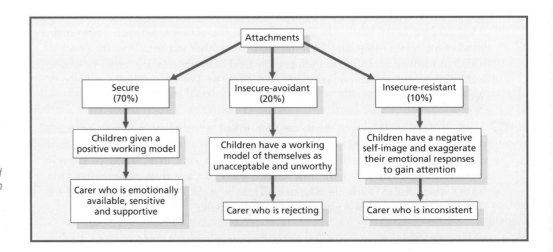

Ainsworth and Bell proposed three attachment types. Main and Solomon proposed a fourth category, which they described as "disorganised attachment".

- *Insecure-avoidant attachment*: the infant doesn't seek contact with the caregiver, and shows little distress when separated. The infant avoids contact with the caregiver upon return, showing limited distress and maintaining distance (physical and/or psychological) from the mother. The infant treats the stranger in a similar way to the caregiver, often avoiding him/her. About 20% of American infants show insecure-avoidant attachment.

Insecure-avoidant vs insecure-resistant attachment

What was novel about Ainsworth's approach was the distinction between two types of **insecure attachment**. What is the essence of this distinction? Insecure-avoidant infants *inhibit* their attachment needs because they have a fear of rejection that is often based on having received insensitive maternal care. In contrast, insecure-resistant infants tend to *exaggerate* their attachment needs because they have been exposed to inconsistent care from the mother.

McNamara et al. (2003) compared sleep problems in insecure-resistant and insecure-avoidant infants. They predicted that insecure-resistant infants would be more likely to wake up repeatedly during the night and have greater difficulty in falling asleep again—both of these effects were predicted on the basis that these infants exaggerate their attachment needs. Both predictions were supported.

In spite of these differences, there are important similarities between insecure-avoidant and insecure-resistant infants. As we will see, both groups of infants are more likely to have behaviour problems, display social and play incompetence, and so on later in childhood than securely attached infants. Thus, insecure-avoidant and insecure-resistant infants experience similar problems and difficulties relative to securely attached children.

Consistency over time

There is now a considerable amount of evidence indicating that these three types of attachment can be identified in infants. The value of categorising infant attachment in this way is much greater if attachment type in infancy *predicts* attachment type later in childhood than if it does not. If there is consistency in type of attachment over time, that is likely to be of great significance in each child's development. Conversely, if early attachment type doesn't predict later attachment type, then early attachment type is unlikely to predict subsequent development.

Wartner et al. (1994) assessed infants' attachment patterns to their mother at the age of 12 months using the categories of secure attachment, insecure-avoidant, insecure-resistant, and disorganised (inconsistent behaviour within the Strange Situation). They then re-assessed attachment at the age of 6. Strikingly, 82% of the children remained in the same category over the 5-year period—this indicates great consistency of attachment type over time.

Similar findings have been reported in most other research. However, consistency of attachment type hasn't always been found. Weinfield et al. (2004) carried out a **longitudinal** study on children considered to be at high risk at birth because of poverty. Attachment type was assessed at 12 and 18 months, and again at the age of 19. There was very little overall consistency in attachment type in this high-risk group. Reasons for this included changes in maternal life stress, family functioning during childhood, and child maltreatment.

Mothers who remember their attachment experience with their own mother as being secure are more likely to have securely attached children (reviewed by Thompson, 2000). Young children also start to form an **internal working model** based on their expectations about important attachments in their lives. When changes occur in the lives of mothers and/or their children that alter their internal working models, the result is often changes in the child's attachment type (Thompson, 2000).

How valuable is secure attachment?

There are many advantages for infants to be securely rather than insecurely attached. For example, Wartner et al. (1994) observed the preschool behaviour of securely and insecurely attached children. The securely attached ones showed more competence in their play, were better at conflict resolution, and had fewer behaviour problems.

KEY TERMS

Insecure attachment: a weak emotional bond between child and caregiver(s) leading to an anxious and insecure relationship, which can have a negative effect on development.

Longitudinal: over an extended period of time, especially with reference to studies.

Internal working model: a mental model of the world that enables individuals to predict, control, and manipulate their environment. The infant has many of them, some of which will be related to relationships.

Szewczyk-Sokolowski et al. (2005) found that securely attached preschool children were more accepted by their peers.

Fearon et al. (2010) carried out a meta-analysis of studies looking at the relationship between attachment type and aggressive or antisocial behaviour. Insecure-avoidant and insecure-resistant children were more likely than securely attached ones to have problems with aggression. However, the risk of problems with aggression was greatest in disorganised children lacking a consistent type of attachment.

One of the most thorough studies on the relationship between child attachment type and subsequent development was reported by Belsky and Fearon (2002). Attachment type was assessed at the age of 15 months and then five developmental outcomes were recorded at the age of 3. Infants categorised as securely attached had greater social competence, school readiness, expressive language (speaking), and receptive language (language comprehension) than insecurely attached ones. They also had fewer behaviour problems.

Most of the research has indicated that insecure attachment in infancy is associated with subsequent problems in high-risk groups (e.g. maltreated children; extreme poverty). What about low-risk groups? The NICHD Early Child Care Research Network (2006) found in low-risk children that insecure attachment at 15 months was associated with several behaviour problems at the age of 6.

Nearly all the findings discussed in this section are basically correlational—there are associations between security of attachment and various measures such as peer acceptance, fewer behaviour problems, and higher social competence. Since there wasn't **random allocation** of children to secure and insecure attachment groups, we can't be confident these desirable outcomes were *caused* by secure attachment. For example, children who have a temperament making them sociable and non-anxious may find it easier to be securely attached, to gain peer acceptance, and to become socially competent.

Attachment in monkeys

Secure attachment is important not only in humans but also in numerous other species. Compelling evidence of what happens to monkeys lacking any secure attachment (indeed, lacking any kind of attachment) was reported by Harlow and Harlow (1962). They raised monkeys for long periods of time in total isolation. When the monkeys were placed with other monkeys, they remained withdrawn and extremely fearful. In comparison, monkeys raised with a cloth "mother" were much more able to engage in social activity. Thus, the cloth mother (even though not providing secure attachment) was better than nothing.

In another **experiment**, four young monkeys were raised on their own without even a cloth or wire "mother". These monkeys spent the first few months huddled together, but gradually developed more independence and finally seemed to have suffered no ill effects. These findings suggest that secure attachment based on the infant–infant affectional bond can be just as effective as secure attachment based on the mother–infant bond. (See Freud and Dann's study on page 88 for more effects of infant–infant bonding.)

Are there advantages in being insecurely attached?

We have seen there are many advantages to being securely attached. Are there any advantages associated with being insecurely attached (insecure-avoidant or insecure-resistant)? Ein-Dor et al. (2010) provided an interesting answer. They argued that individuals who are insecure-resistant are extremely vigilant to threats—this can be a substantial advantage in dangerous environments. Individuals who are insecure-avoidant focus more than others on self-preservation and are likely to be good at finding escape routes when danger looms.

In contrast, securely attached individuals may be so emotionally stable and non-anxious that they underestimate the seriousness of a threat to their well-being. The take-home message is that being insecurely attached is a disadvantage most of the time but may be advantageous when the situation is dangerous or threatening.

Three attachment types?

So far we have identified three main attachment types based mainly on research using the "Strange Situation" (discussed in detail shortly). However, this approach has its limitations.

Studies that look at the association between two variables have the drawback that they appear to demonstrate cause and effect, whereas all they really show is whether a correlation exists.

? Why should one be cautious in using results from animal studies to explain human behaviour?

KEY TERMS

Random allocation: placing participants in different experimental conditions using random methods to ensure no differences between the groups.

Experiment: a procedure undertaken to make a discovery about causal relationships. The experimenter manipulates one variable to see its effect on another variable.

First, there is evidence for a fourth attachment type. Second, there are doubts as to whether it is a good idea to *pigeonhole* infants by categorising them as having a given attachment type.

Main and Solomon (1986) used the "Strange Situation". As most researchers have done, they found evidence for secure attachment, insecure-avoidant attachment, and insecure-resistant attachment. In addition, however, a few infants displayed **disorganised attachment**—their behaviour was inconsistent and fitted none of the three main attachment types. Infants with disorganised attachment are more likely than other infants to have mothers who maltreat them or suffer from alcohol or drug problems (van IJzendoorn et al., 1999). Disorganised attachment is associated with subsequent aggressive behaviour and abnormality.

Placing infants into three categories based on attachment type is neat and tidy. However, it oversimplifies matters. Why is that? One reason is because infants *within* any given category differ in their attachment behaviour. For example, two children might both be classified as showing avoidant attachment, but one might display much more avoidant behaviour than the other. More generally, the boundary between just falling into an attachment category and just not falling into it is arbitrary.

We can take more account of **individual differences** in attachment by using *dimensions* (going from very low to very high) instead of categories. Fraley and Spieker (2003) identified *two* attachment dimensions:

1. *Avoidant/withdrawal vs proximity-seeking strategies*: This is concerned with the extent to which the child tries to maintain physical closeness to his/her mother.
2. *Angry and resistant strategies vs emotional confidence*: This is concerned with the child's emotional reactions to the attachment figure's behaviour.

As can be seen in the Figure, secure, insecure-resistant, and insecure-avoidant attachment all fit neatly into this two-dimensional framework. The dimensional approach is preferable to the categorical one of Ainsworth because it takes more account of small individual differences in attachment behaviour.

KEY TERMS

Disorganised attachment: a type of attachment in which the child's attachment behaviour is inconsistent and hard to classify.

Individual differences: the characteristics that vary from one individual to another; intelligence and personality are major ways in which individuals differ.

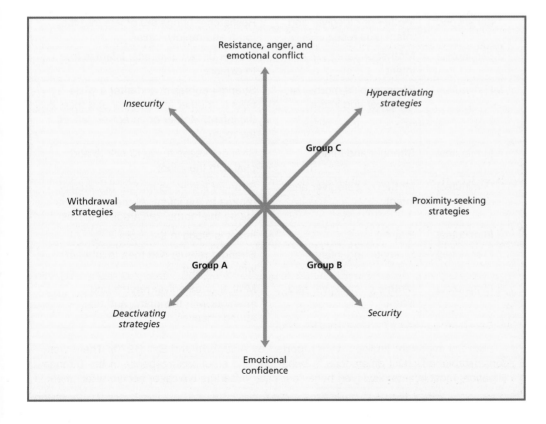

A two-dimensional model of individual differences in attachment. Group A has avoidant attachment, Group B has secure attachment, and Group C has resistant attachment. From Fraley and Spieker (2003).

Use of the "Strange Situation" in Attachment Research

In order to understand the importance of infants' attachment behaviour, it is important to have a good method for assessing that behaviour. Several methods could be used. One approach would involve observational studies in which the experimenter simply observes the natural interactions between the infant and its caregiver (usually mother) in the home environment. However, that would have the disadvantage that the experimenter would have very little control over what happened—he or she wouldn't be in a position to manipulate aspects of the situation.

Mary Ainsworth was an American psychologist who spent some time in the 1950s working in London with John Bowlby at the Tavistock Clinic in London. This led her to adopt an approach to assessing infant attachment based in part on Bowlby's theoretical views (see Box).

KEY STUDY

Ainsworth and Bell (1970): "Strange Situation" study

Mary Ainsworth devised the **Strange Situation** as a short but effective way of assessing the quality of an infant's attachment to its caregiver (typically the mother). Here we discuss the important study by Ainsworth and Bell (1970) on infants' attachments, based on the Strange Situation, which aimed to investigate individual variation in infant attachments, especially differences between secure and insecure attachments. Ainsworth and Bell hoped their method of assessing attachments (the Strange Situation test) would prove to be a reliable and valid measure of attachments.

The Strange Situation test lasts for just over 20 minutes and was used on American infants aged between 12 and 18 months. It takes place in the laboratory and the method used is controlled observation. The Strange Situation consists of *eight* stages or episodes as follows:

Stage	People in the room	Procedure
1 (30 seconds)	Mother or caregiver and infant plus researcher	Researcher brings the others into the room and rapidly leaves
2 (3 minutes)	Mother or caregiver and infant	Mother or caregiver sits; infant is free to explore
3 (3 minutes)	Stranger plus mother or caregiver and infant	Stranger comes in and after a while talks to mother or caregiver and then to the infant. Mother or caregiver leaves the room
4 (3 minutes)	Stranger and infant	Stranger keeps trying to talk to and play with the infant
5 (3 minutes)	Mother or caregiver and infant	Stranger leaves as mother or caregiver returns to the infant. At the end of this stage, the mother or caregiver leaves
6 (3 minutes)	Infant	Infant is alone in the room
7 (3 minutes)	Stranger and infant	Stranger returns and tries to interact with the infant
8 (3 minutes)	Mother or caregiver and infant	Mother or caregiver returns and interacts with the infant, and the stranger leaves

Several important findings were reported by Ainsworth and Bell (1970). There were considerable individual differences in behaviour and emotional response in the Strange Situation. Most infants displayed behaviour categorised as typical or secure attachment,

---

while a few were insecure-resistant or insecure-avoidant. As discussed earlier, the securely attached infants were distressed when separated from the caregiver and sought contact and soothing on reunion. Insecure-resistant attachment was characterised by ambivalence (conflicting emotions) and inconsistency as the infants were very distressed at separation but resisted the caregiver on reunion. Insecure-avoidant attachment was characterised by detachment as the infants didn't seek contact with the caregiver and showed little distress at separation.

Evaluation
The "Strange Situation" has been used numerous times in research. Indeed, it is easily the most popular method to assess infant attachment. It has the advantage of systematically placing the infant in various common situations in which its behaviour is carefully recorded.

Another advantage of the "Strange Situation" is that it is a straightforward method to use. In addition, numerous studies have reported similar findings to those of Ainsworth and Bell (1970); in other words their findings can readily be replicated. Finally, as we have seen, the type of attachment behaviour displayed by infants in the "Strange Situation" predicts their future level of psychological adjustment.

What are the limitations of this study? First, the Strange Situation was developed in the United States and this study was carried out in that country. As a result, the "Strange Situation" may be culturally biased and the findings not applicable to other parts of the world. Attachment behaviour regarded as healthy in the United States may not be so regarded elsewhere in the world, and the same may be true of attachment behaviour regarded as unhealthy in the United States. This issue is discussed in detail in the section on cultural variations in attachment.

Second, the Strange Situation is artificial in ways that may distort behaviour. For example, some mothers or caregivers are likely to behave differently towards their child when they know they are being observed than they would do at home when alone with their child.

Third, the study was carried out in an unfamiliar playroom. As a result, the infants' behaviour may have been rather different from how it would have been in the comfort of their own home. This issue was addressed by Vaughn and Waters (1990) who compared the behaviour of one-year-olds in the Strange Situation and at home. Securely attached infants in the Strange Situation had higher security and sociability scores based on their home behaviour than did insecurely attached infants. However, the differences in home behaviour between insecure-avoidant and insecure-resistant infants were small and non-significant.

Fourth, it could be argued that this study raises ethical issues. The Strange Situation is stressful for many infants. It often makes them distressed, which is clearly undesirable.

What conclusions can we draw from Ainsworth and Bell's (1970) approach? First, the Strange Situation provides a good measure of attachment because it allows us to discriminate between attachment types. Remember, however, that they failed to identify disorganised attachment which has emerged as an important attachment type.

Second, secure attachment is the preferred type of attachment, and is linked to healthy emotional and social development (see previous section). However, as we have seen, it has been argued (Ein-Dor et al., 2010) that insecure attachment may sometimes be an advantage when individuals are faced with major threats and dangers.

Third, as we will see, the Strange Situation has been used successfully to explore cultural variations in infants' attachments. Cross-cultural research has revealed some interested differences in the meaning of attachment across societies.

Why are there individual differences in attachment?

Why do some infants have a secure attachment to their mother, whereas others don't? Several answers to that question have been proposed. In essence, however, what are likely to be most important are aspects of the mother's or caregiver's behaviour (e.g. their sensitivity) and aspects of the infant's temperament or personality. It is also possible that the effects of maternal sensitivity depend on the infant's temperament. We will discuss these three possibilities in turn.

[?] What are the strengths of the experimental approach used by Ainsworth and Bell?

[?] Are there problems with using the Strange Situation in very different cultures?

[?] What factors determine infants' attachment style?

Remember that the term "maternal" means mothering, which could be done by anyone, not just the infant's mother.

Maternal sensitivity hypothesis

Ainsworth et al. (1978, p. 152) explained individual differences in infant attachment in their **maternal sensitivity hypothesis**: "The most important aspect of maternal behaviour commonly associated with the security-anxiety dimension of infant attachment is … sensitive responsiveness to infant signals and communications".

Ainsworth et al. (1978) reported that most of the caregivers of securely attached infants were very sensitive to their needs, and responded to their infants in an emotionally expressive way. In contrast, the caregivers of insecure-resistant infants were interested in them but often misunderstood their infants' behaviour. Of particular importance, these caregivers varied in the way they treated their infants, and so the infant couldn't rely on the caregiver's emotional support.

Finally, there were the caregivers of avoidant infants. Ainsworth et al. (1978) reported that many of these caregivers were uninterested in their infants. The caregivers often rejected their infants and were self-centred and rigid in their behaviour. However, some caregivers of avoidant infants behaved rather differently. These caregivers acted in a suffocating way, always interacting with their infants even when the infants didn't want any interaction. What these types of caregivers had in common was that they weren't sensitive to the needs of their infants.

The maternal sensitivity hypothesis has received much support. De Wolff and van IJzendoorn (1997) carried out a meta-analysis across many studies and obtained a correlation of +0.24 between maternal sensitivity and security of infant attachment. This indicates a positive (but fairly weak) association. De Wolff and van IJzendoorn also found that aspects of mothers' behaviour only partly related to sensitivity were also important. These aspects included stimulation (any action of the mother directed at her baby) and attitude (mother's expression of positive emotion to her baby).

Most research on the maternal sensitivity hypothesis is correlational and has involved finding associations between maternal sensitivity and secure attachment. As a result, it doesn't prove that differences in maternal sensitivity *cause* differences in security of attachment. Clearer evidence can be obtained by looking at the effects of interventions designed to increase maternal sensitivity. A meta-analysis of relevant studies indicated that such interventions made infants more securely attached (Bakermans-Kranenburg et al., 2003).

Video-based interventions in which the mother can see in detail how she interacts with her child have proved effective. They have been found to increase the mother's parenting sensitivity, to increase secure attachment, and to reduce aggression.

Limitations

The maternal sensitivity hypothesis exaggerates the role of the mother. Lucassen et al. (2011) carried out a meta-analysis of studies in which *paternal* sensitivity had been assessed. There was a correlation of +0.12 between the father's sensitivity and infant–father attachment, indicating that paternal sensitivity is modestly associated with the infant's security of attachment to the father. However, the association is smaller than that between maternal sensitivity and security of infant–mother attachment. This suggests that *paternal* sensitivity is less important than *maternal* sensitivity.

There is another weakness with the maternal sensitivity hypothesis: it ignores the role played by the infant himself/herself. This issue is discussed next.

Temperament hypothesis

We could try to account for individual differences in infant attachment by using the **temperament hypothesis**. According to this hypothesis (initially proposed by Kagan, 1984), an infant's relationships with primary caregivers (and those later in life) can be explained by the infant's innate temperament (the character it inherits through its genes). Some infants' temperaments are better suited at forming attachments than those of others.

KEY TERMS

Maternal sensitivity hypothesis: the notion that individual differences in infant attachment are due mainly to the sensitivity (or otherwise) of the mother.

Temperament hypothesis: the view that a child's temperament is responsible for the quality of attachment between the child and its caregiver, as opposed to the view that experience is more important.

There is limited support for the temperament hypothesis. For example, Belsky and Rovine (1987) reported that newborns showing signs of behavioural instability (e.g. tremors or shaking) were less likely than others to become securely attached to their mother. This finding suggests their innate personality was of importance in attachment formation.

It is assumed by the temperament hypothesis that genetic factors influence temperament and that temperament influences infant attachment. We can broaden the temperament hypothesis by focusing on the role of genetic factors within the child on attachment type. The most effective way of doing that is to study pairs of identical twins (sharing 100% of their genes) and fraternal twins (sharing 50% of their genes). If the infant's temperamental characteristics influence his/her attachment style, then identical twins should show more agreement than fraternal twins with respect to attachment style.

O'Connor and Croft (2001) found modest support for the above hypothesis, suggesting that genetic factors probably influence young children's attachment type to a small extent. However, more negative findings were reported by Bokhorst et al. (2003) in a study on identical and fraternal twins. First, the role of genetic factors in accounting for individual differences in infant attachment type was negligible. Second the **concordance rate** (extent of agreement on attachment type) between twins within a pair wasn't influenced by similarities or differences in temperamental reactivity.

There are various reasons why we must be careful not to exaggerate the role played by the infant's genetic make-up and personality in determining its attachment style. First, infants' temperament as assessed by their parents is not usually associated with their attachment type as determined by the Strange Situation assessment (Durkin, 1995).

Second, there is only a modest tendency for infants' attachment type with their father to be the same as their attachment type with their mother (de Wolff & van IJzendoorn, 1997). This suggests an infant's attachment to his/her mother depends mainly on the parents' characteristics rather than on its temperament.

Third, it should be noted that the child's temperament influences maternal sensitivity and maternal sensitivity influences the child's temperament (Therriault et al., 2011). That makes it very hard to disentangle the impact of child temperament on attachment type.

Maternal sensitivity + temperament

As we have seen, neither maternal sensitivity nor infant temperament is wholly responsible for the development of attachment. Is the mother or the infant more important in determining the quality of the infant–mother attachment? van IJzendoorn et al. (1992) answered this question by comparing groups in which the mother had problems (e.g. mental illness) and in which the child had problems (e.g. deafness). The key finding was that there were far more insecurely attached children in the mother problem group than in the child problem group. Thus, the mother influences infant–mother attachment more than the child.

Increasing evidence indicates that there is an *interaction* between maternal sensitivity and infant temperament in determining child adjustment and attachment. What that means is that *both* factors make a contribution in *combination*. Supporting evidence was reported by Spangler (1990) in a study of German mothers. Their responsiveness to their infants was influenced by their perceptions of the infants' temperament.

Additional supporting evidence was reported by Stright et al. (2008). They assessed maternal parenting style (including sensitivity) and temperament (e.g. adaptability; negative moods) in early childhood. The impact of maternal parenting style on the child's psychological adjustment at the age of 6 was much greater in children with a difficult temperament. Those with an easy temperament mostly had good psychological adjustment regardless of the mother's parenting style.

Cultural Variations in Attachment

If attachment is an innate behaviour, we would expect attachment behaviours to be very similar around the world. On the other hand, it is possible that mother–infant attachment behaviour depends heavily on cultural expectations concerning what is regarded as appropriate. If that is the case, we would expect large differences in attachment behaviour from culture to culture.

ACTIVITY: Theories of attachment

List all the theories of attachment covered in this section. For each of them, suggest how the following questions would be answered: Why do attachments form? With whom are attachments formed? What is the major drawback of this explanation?

KEY TERM

Concordance rate: in twin studies, the probability that if one twin has a given characteristic or disorder the other twin also has the same disorder.

How do cultures differ from each other? There is an important distinction between **individualistic cultures** and **collectivistic cultures**. Individualistic cultures are ones in which individuals take responsibility for their own lives and in which the emphasis is on independence. Examples of individualistic cultures are the UK and the USA. In contrast, collectivistic cultures are ones in which the group is more important than the individual and in which the emphasis is on interdependence. Examples of collectivistic cultures are Japan, China, and Israel.

What differences in attachment might we expect to find in the two kinds of cultures? Here is one example. Consider infants' exploratory behaviour in the Strange Situation (discussed

KEY STUDY

Cross-cultural study by van IJzendoorn and Kroonenberg (1988)

Van IJzendoorn and Kroonenberg (1988) studied cultural variations in attachment types through a meta-analysis of research (combining findings from many studies) on attachment behaviour in several countries. They compared only the findings of observational studies using the Strange Situation to draw inferences about its external validity as a measure of attachment in other populations and other settings.

Van IJzendoorn and Kroonenberg (1988) compared the findings from 32 studies that had used the Strange Situation to measure attachment and to classify the attachment relationship between mother and infant. None of the children was older than 24 months of age. Research from eight different countries was compared, including Western cultures (USA, Great Britain, Germany, Sweden, and the Netherlands) and non-Western cultures (Japan, China, Israel). Van IJzendoorn and Kroonenberg researched various databases for studies on attachment.

Considerable consistency in the overall distribution of attachment types was found across all the cultures studied. Secure attachment was the most common type of attachment in all eight countries. However, significant differences were found in the distributions of insecure attachments. In Western cultures, the dominant insecure type is avoidant. In contrast, the dominant insecure type in non-Western cultures is resistant, with China being the only exception (insecure-avoidant and insecure-resistant were equally common). A key finding was that the variation in attachment type *within* cultures was one and a half times as great as variation *between* cultures.

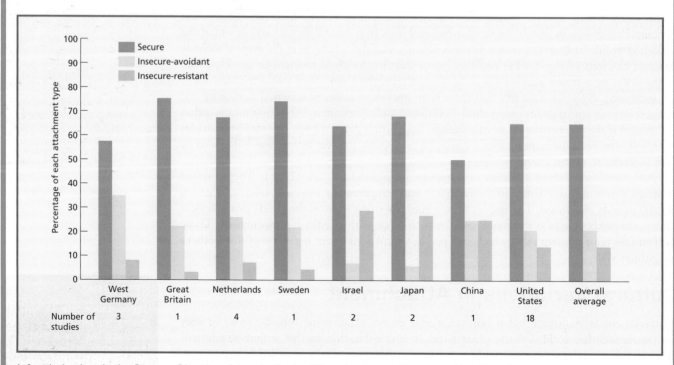

Infant behaviour in the Strange Situation, from studies in different cultures. (Data from Van IJzendoorn & Kroonenberg, 1988.)

above). Mothers in individualistic cultures might regard such behaviour as indicating that their child is securely attached and so is starting to become independent. Mothers in collectivistic cultures might be less positive about their child's exploratory behaviour because it suggests a weakening of interdependence (and so security) between mother and child.

Rothbaum et al. (2007) found that American and Japanese mothers both felt positively about their child's exploratory behaviour. However, as predicted, the perceived association between exploratory behaviour and secure attachment was greater for American mothers (from an individualistic culture) than for Japanese mothers (from a collectivistic culture).

? How similar is attachment behaviour in different cultures?

EVALUATION

➕ Van IJzendoorn and Kroonenberg reported a thorough meta-analysis to consider numerous findings on cultural variations using the Strange Situation.

➕ Their findings show it is wrong to think of any given culture as consisting of the same practices. The notion there is a *single* British or American culture is a gross oversimplification. In fact, there are several sub-cultures within most large countries differing considerably in their child-rearing practices.

➕ The findings of van IJzendoorn and Kroonenberg suggest that the idea of focusing on cultural variations is important and has some validity.

➖ The study doesn't tell us *why* patterns of attachment vary so much *within* cultures. Perhaps variations in child-rearing practices are important. However, the study didn't provide any concrete evidence to support this speculation.

➖ It is very hard to know whether participants in the different countries were comparable. For example, the researchers failed to show that the percentage of middle-class mothers was the same in all eight countries. This limits the conclusions that can validly be drawn.

➖ The Strange Situation was created and tested in the United States, so it may be culturally biased (ethnocentric). In other words, the Strange Situation may reflect the norms and values of American culture. Thus, the Strange Situation lacks external validity, meaning the findings and insights based on it may be less meaningful than used to be thought. The research discussed by van IJzendoorn and Kroonenberg (1988) involves an **imposed etic**—the use of a technique developed in one culture to study another culture.

➖ The various findings were based exclusively on children aged no more than 24 months. Thus, the study doesn't tell us anything directly about children's attachments from the third year of life onwards.

EXAM HINT

You may be asked an essay question on this topic. For example "Describe and evaluate cultural variations in attachment. (12 marks)".

This means you need to consider 6 marks' worth of material describing such variations and 6 marks' worth evaluating the variations. The evaluation is likely to focus on the weaknesses of the research methods used in the studies described.

Findings

Sagi et al. (1991) studied cultural variations in the Strange Situation in the United States, Israel, Japan, and Germany. The findings for the American infants were very similar to those reported by Ainsworth et al. (1978): 71% showed secure attachment, 12% showed resistant attachment, and 17% were avoidant.

The Israeli infants behaved rather differently. Secure attachment was shown by 62% of the Israeli infants, 33% were resistant, and only 5% were avoidant. These infants lived on a kibbutz, which is a communal settlement in which children are looked after much of the time by adults not part of their family. However, since they mostly had a close relationship with their mothers, they tended not to be avoidant.

Japanese mothers practically never leave their infants alone with a stranger. However, in spite of the differences in child-rearing practices in Japan and in Israel, the Japanese infants

KEY TERM

Imposed etic: the use of a technique developed in one culture to study another culture.

Children from different countries vary in their attachment types. The graph summarises research from Sagi et al. (1991) and Ainsworth and Bell (1970).

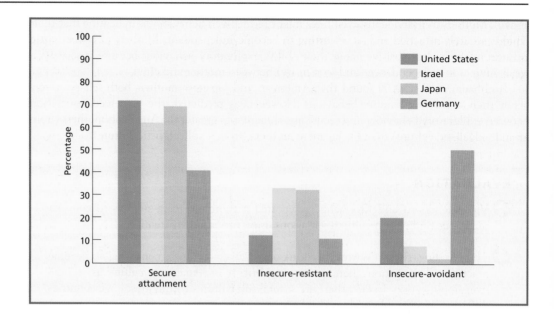

showed similar attachment styles to the Israeli ones. Two-thirds (68%) had a secure attachment, 32% were insecure-resistant, and none was insecure-avoidant. It is not surprising that none of the Japanese infants treated a stranger similarly to their mother given that most have rarely if ever been on their own with a stranger.

Striking evidence that Japanese infants find it hard to cope with being alone with a stranger was reported by Takahashi (1990) using the Strange Situation. The majority of the infants became so distressed when in the presence of the stranger that it was necessary to stop their involvement in the study on ethical grounds. In contrast, Durrett et al. (1984) studied Japanese families in which the mothers were pursuing careers and so left their children in the care of others. Their children showed a similar pattern of attachment styles to those in the United States.

Finally, the German infants showed a different pattern of attachment from the other three groups. Only 40% of them were securely attached, 49% were avoidant, and 11% were resistant. Why was that? German parents regard some aspects of securely attached behaviour as indicating that infants are spoiled (Sagi & Lewkowicz, 1987). In addition, Grossmann et al. (1985, p. 253) argued that German culture requires distance between parents and children: "The ideal is an independent, non-clinging infant who does not make demands on the parents but rather unquestioningly obeys their commands".

Posada et al. (1995) carried out a study in seven countries (China, Colombia, Germany, Israel, Japan, Norway, and the USA). Most infants in all of the countries were securely attached and showed clear evidence of regarding their mother as a secure base. However, the details of secure-base behaviour varied both within and between cultures. Of most importance, Posada et al. asked experts in all seven countries to rate infants' behaviour in terms of the extent to which it indicates that they have a secure base. There was a high measure of agreement among these experts. Thus, the notion of a secure base is very similar across cultures even though the ways in which it is displayed varies cross-culturally.

Rothbaum et al. (2007) explored how American and Japanese mothers regard mother–child attachment. There were important similarities. As discussed earlier, mothers in both cultures regarded exploratory behaviour in the Strange Situation as desirable. They also associated secure attachment with desirable characteristics and insecure attachment with undesirable characteristics.

However, Rothbaum et al. (2007) also found there were important differences. For example, the mothers were asked how they would interpret it if their child called for its mother during naptime. American mothers regarded this behaviour negatively (e.g. the child was testing the limits of what it was allowed to do). In contrast, Japanese mothers regarded it positively as a sign of secure attachment. This difference reflects the greater emphasis on interdependence within collectivistic cultures.

? Thinking of your own area, your town or village, what sub-cultures are you aware of? Could any of these have different ideas on child-rearing?

How important are cultural variations in attachment?

There are various cross-cultural *similarities* in attachment behaviour. For example, a clear majority of infants in most cultures are securely attached to their mother or caregiver. This suggests that secure mother–infant attachment is of great value at a universal level. In addition, maternal sensitivity predicts the child's attachment security in most countries and attachment security in turn is associated with various long-term benefits.

There are also various cross-cultural *differences* in attachment behaviour. For example, Sagi et al. (1991) found that 41% of German infants had insecure-avoidant attachment compared to 0% in Japan. This large difference seems to reflect the emphasis on independence in Germany (an individualistic culture) versus the emphasis on interdependence in Japan (a collectivistic culture). As we have seen, Rothbaum et al. (2007) found differences in the way secure attachment was regarded in individualistic and collectivistic cultures.

Rothbaum et al. (2000, p. 1101) argued as follows: "Assumptions ... such as that children are the logical focus of attention and that behaviour in reunions best captures the dynamics of close relationships, are based in Western thought". These assumptions underlie most cross-cultural theory and research and are claimed to invalidate the findings obtained. For example, the Strange Situation was devised by Western psychologists and may have limited relevance in other cultures. In the same way, intelligence tests devised in the West may provide poor assessment of intelligence in other parts of the world.

Rothbaum et al. (2000) went on to contrast the Western notion of security or secure attachment with the Japanese word *amae* (a-mah-yeh), which means emotional dependence (literally "indulgent dependence"). Infants showing **amae** exhibit much clinging behaviour and need for attention. These forms of behaviour are regarded as indicating insecure attachment by Western psychologists but indicate good adjustment in Japan.

It can be argued that Rothbaum et al. (2000) overstated the matter. It is true that there are important differences in attachment behaviour between individualistic and collectivistic cultures. However, that doesn't necessarily mean that the entire notion of security or secure attachment has radically different meanings in different cultures. Of importance here is the study by Posada et al. (1995). They found that ideas about the nature of security and a safe base were very similar across seven very different cultures.

In sum, it is likely that having infants securely attached to their mother is very advantageous in virtually all cultures. It is also likely to be true universally that children whose mothers or caregivers are sensitive to their needs are more likely to be securely attached than children whose mothers are less sensitive. These are deep and profound cross-cultural similarities. The precise forms of behaviour shown by children who are securely attached undoubtedly vary from culture to culture. However, these differences in behaviour are less important than the underlying similarities.

? Do you think we all tend to judge other social groups or cultures from our own point of view? Do you ever comment on another type of behaviour, different from your own? How do you do this? Could it be a type of cultural relativism?

Cross-cultural research

There are several reasons for conducting cross-cultural research; that is, research that looks at the customs and practices of different countries and makes comparisons with our own cultural norms. First of all, such research can tell us about what might be universal in human behaviour. If the same behaviours are observed in many different cultures, all of which have different ways of socialising children, then the behaviour may be due to innate (universal) factors rather than learning. The second reason for conducting cross-cultural research is that it offers us insights into our own behaviour, insights that we may not otherwise be aware of. Perhaps that is the appeal of watching programmes on the television that show foreign lands and different people.

There are some major weaknesses in cross-cultural research. First of all, any sample of a group of people may well be biased and therefore we may be mistaken in thinking that the observations made of one group of people are representative of that culture. Second, where the observations are made by an outsider, that person's own culture will bias how they interpret the data they observe. Finally, the psychological tools that are used to measure people, such as IQ tests and the Strange Situation, are designed in one particular culture and based on assumptions of that culture. They may not have much meaning in another culture.

Therefore, cross-cultural research does have the potential to be highly informative about human behaviour but also has many important weaknesses.

KEY TERM

Amae: a Japanese word referring to a positive form of attachment that involves emotional dependence, clinging, and attention-seeking behaviour. Such behaviour is regarded more negatively in Western countries.

Disruption of Attachment, Failure to Form Attachment (Privation), and Effects of Institutional Care

In the real world, circumstances such as divorce between parents or the death of a parent can disrupt the child's attachments or even prevent them from being formed. If attachment is critical to healthy psychological development, then Bowlby's theory would predict that any disruption to this process should result in the opposite effect—unhealthy psychological development. One way of determining the validity of Bowlby's theory is to consider the effects of such disruption.

In this section, we discuss the effects on the young child of being separated from one or more of the most important adults in his/her life. Most studies have focused on the long-term effects of disruption of attachment. However, we will first consider short-term effects.

Short-term effects of disruption of attachment

Even fairly brief disruption of attachment with a primary caregiver can have severe emotional effects on the child. Short-term disruption of attachment can be distinguished from long-term disruption of attachment. **Short-term disruption of attachment** involves distress when a child is separated for a fairly short time period from a person to whom there is an attachment bond. In contrast, **long-term disruption of attachment** occurs when a bond has been formed and is then broken for what are generally fairly long periods of time.

According to Bowlby's theory, even short-term disruption of attachment with their primary caregiver can cause severe emotional effects to young children. In the early 1950s, this view was controversial, and the necessary evidence wasn't available. However, relevant evidence was published in 1952.

Separation from the mother can have severe emotional effects on a child. The first stage of the child's response to the separation is known as protest: an intense period during which the child cries for much of the time.

Robertson and Bowlby (1952) studied young children who experienced disruption of attachment with their mother for some time, often because she had gone into hospital. They observed *three* stages in the child's response to this short-term disruption of attachment, leading them to produce the protest–despair–detachment (PDD) model:

1. *Protest*, which is often very intense. The child cries often, and sometimes seems panic-stricken. Anger and fear are present.
2. *Despair*, involving a total loss of hope. The child is often apathetic, and shows little interest in its surroundings. The child often engages in self-comforting behaviour (e.g. thumb-sucking; rocking).
3. *Detachment*, during which the child seems less distressed. If the mother or caregiver re-appears during this stage, she is not responded to with any great interest.

It used to be thought that children in the third stage of detachment had adjusted fairly well to short-term disruption of attachment with their mother. However, the calm behaviour shown by the child when its mother re-appears probably disguises its true feelings. Fortunately, most children do re-establish an attachment to the mother over a period of time.

EVALUATION OF THE PDD MODEL

Is it inevitable that short-term disruption of attachment produces the various negative effects predicted by the PDD model? Robertson and Robertson (1971) suggested it isn't. They looked after several young children in their own home who had experienced short-term disruption of attachment with their mothers. They ensured the children became familiar with their new surroundings beforehand to minimise any distress. They also provided the children with a similar daily routine and discussed the children's mothers with them. This approach proved successful, with the children showing much less distress than most children experiencing short-term disruption of attachment.

The Robertsons also studied other children experiencing short-term disruption of attachment with their mothers who spent their time in a residential nursery. These children didn't cope well—they received good physical care but lacked emotional care. The Robertsons said the nursery children experienced **bond disruption**, whereas the others didn't because they were offered substitute mothering. Therefore, we might conclude that short-term disruption of attachment need not lead to deprivation, but may do so if accompanied by bond disruption.

Barrett (1997) was much more critical of the PDD model, pointing out the lack of convincing evidence for the proposed sequence of protest, despair, and detachment. Of importance, the model doesn't take individual differences into account. For example, a securely attached child may show little initial protest and cope relatively well, whereas an insecure-resistant child would be plunged more immediately into protest and despair.

Barrett (1997) also argued that the PDD model is flawed because it assumes very young children are much less socially competent than is actually the case. Thus, many young children have a greater ability to cope with short-term disruption of attachment than assumed by Robertson and Bowlby (1952).

Long-term effects of disruption of attachment: Maternal deprivation

Prior to the development of his theory of attachment, John Bowlby proposed the **maternal deprivation hypothesis** (1953), which focused on the effects of long-term disruption of attachment. According to this hypothesis, breaking the maternal bond with the child during the early years of its life is likely to have serious effects on its intellectual, social, and emotional development.

Bowlby (1953) also claimed that many of these negative effects could be permanent and irreversible. Contrary to popular belief, however, Bowlby argued that 25% (rather than 100%) of children suffer long-term damage from maternal deprivation involving long-term disruption of attachment (Di Dwyer, personal communication). Finally, Bowlby endorsed monotropy. This is the notion (discussed earlier) that human infants have an innate tendency to form strong bonds with one particular individual (typically the mother).

When Bowlby put forward his maternal deprivation hypothesis in the early 1950s, it was regarded as revolutionary. Most professionals at that time felt that adequate physical provision was most important for healthy development. In spite of that, it was accepted by the early 1940s that children could suffer to some extent if they experienced long-term disruption of attachment with their mother. However, the full extent of such suffering hadn't been clearly established.

Findings

In the context of the time, Bowlby's (1944) classic study of juvenile thieves had a major impact. He carried out his well-known study on clients from the child guidance clinic where he worked. He interviewed the children and their families, and gradually built up a record of their early life experiences. Some children had experienced "early and prolonged separation from their mothers", and some were emotionally maladjusted. In particular, he diagnosed the condition of affectionless psychopathy in some of the children, a disorder involving a lack of guilt and remorse. Could there be a link between this form of emotional maladjustment and early disruption of attachment?

Bowlby focused on children referred to the clinic because of stealing (these were the juvenile thieves). He compared them with control children referred to the clinic because of emotional problems but who hadn't committed any crimes. He found 32% of the thieves were affectionless psychopaths lacking a social conscience, whereas none of the control children was. Of the thieves diagnosed as affectionless psychopaths, 86% had experienced early disruption of attachment (even if only for a week before the age of 5). In contrast, only 17% of the thieves without affectionless psychopathy had suffered disruption of attachment in the form of maternal deprivation.

This study by Bowlby is important for various reasons. First, the findings seemed to show long-term disruption of attachment can have very severe effects, including a lack of emotional development (affectionless psychopathy). Second, Bowlby's results suggested that early long-term disruption of attachment could have long-lasting negative effects still present several years later. Third, the findings of this study led many other researchers to examine the relationship between children's early experience and their subsequent emotional development.

Bowlby (1951, 1953) supported his hypothesis with the research of Spitz (1945) and Goldfarb (1947). Spitz visited several very poor orphanages and other institutions in South America. Children in those orphanages received very little warmth or attention from the staff and had become apathetic. Many suffered from **anaclitic depression** (resigned helplessness and loss of appetite). This was attributed to their lack of emotional care and long-term disruption of attachment with their mothers. Spitz and Wolf (1946) studied 100 apparently normal children who became seriously depressed after staying in hospital—the children generally recovered well only if the separation lasted less than 3 months.

Goldfarb (1947) compared two groups of infants who before fostering spent only the first few months or 3 years at a poor and inadequately staffed orphanage. Both groups were tested up to the age of 12. Those children who had spent 3 years at the orphanage did less well than the others on intelligence tests, were less socially mature, and more likely to be aggressive.

In the 1950s, orphanages in the UK gradually began to disappear and so research into the negative effects of living in such institutions was limited. Since then, however, there has been a new opportunity to study orphans—children from Romania. Findings on these children are discussed later.

EVALUATION

Bowlby was correct in emphasising the importance of the relationship between mother or other caregiver and the child. However, his approach was oversimplified in various ways:

1. The emotional problems shown by children in orphanages and other institutions may be due to the poor quality of those institutions rather than to disruption of attachment in the form of maternal deprivation.
2. As we will see, many of the adverse effects of maternal deprivation are more reversible than Bowlby assumed.
3. Bowlby didn't distinguish clearly between disruption of attachment (the child is separated from a major attachment) and privation (the child has never had a close attachment) (see below).

Distinguishing disruption of attachment, failure to form attachment (privation), and institutional care

Rutter (1972) pointed out that Bowlby assumed *all* experiences of disruption of attachment were the same. In fact, however, there are some very important differences. Children may experience short-term disruption of attachment, as in the Robertsons' studies, or they may have repeated and prolonged disruptions of attachment. Children may experience disruption of attachment with the mother without bond disruption, or they may have no adequate substitute care. Finally, children may experience a lack of attachment as a result of never having formed any close attachments.

Rutter (1972) argued there is a crucial difference between disruption of attachment and privation, a distinction *not* made by Bowlby. Disruption of attachment occurs when a child has formed an important attachment from which it is then separated. In contrast, **privation** (failure to form an attachment) occurs when a child has *never* formed a close relationship with anyone.

Many of Bowlby's juvenile delinquents had experienced several changes of home/principal caregiver during their early childhood. This indicated to Rutter (1981) that their later problems were due to failure to form attachment (privation) rather than disruption of attachment. Rutter argued that the effects of privation are much more severe and long-lasting than those of disruption of attachment. Research directly focusing on privation is discussed next.

As discussed earlier, it is hard to interpret the research of Spitz (1945) and Goldfarb (1947) based on children in orphanages and other institutions. The reason is that the experiences of these children differed in two important ways from those of most other children. First, these children had experienced privation. Second, these children had spent long periods of time in an institution, and the quality of most of these institutions was generally very poor. As a result, it is

KEY TERMS

Anaclitic depression: a severe form of depression in infants who experience prolonged separations from their mothers. The term "anaclitic" means "arising from emotional dependency on another".

Privation: an absence of attachments, as opposed to the loss of attachments, due to the lack of an appropriate attachment figure. Privation is likely to lead to permanent emotional damage.

hard to know the relative importance of these factors. However, in recent decades there has been an increasing interest in studying the effects on children of living in an institution. Researchers in this area focus on **institutional care**—the negative effects on speed of social and/or cognitive development that occur when children are placed in institutions (e.g. hospitals; orphanages) for short or long periods of time. We will discuss studies on institutionalisation shortly.

Long-term effects of privation (failure to form attachment)

KEY STUDY

Hodges and Tizard (1989): Effects of privation and institutional care

Hodges and Tizard (1989) studied the effects of privation but their study also tells us about the effects of institutional care. They investigated the permanence (or otherwise) of the effects of privation considering both emotional and social effects in adolescence. Sixty-five children taken into care and put into one institution before the age of 4 months formed an opportunity sample. This was a natural experiment using a matched pairs design, because the institutionalised children were compared with a control group raised at home. It was a longitudinal study (age on entering care to 16 years).

Each child had been looked after on average by 24 different caregivers by the age of 2. By the age of 4 years, 24 had been adopted, 15 restored to their natural home, and the rest remained in the institution. The children were assessed at the ages 4, 8, and 16 on emotional and social competence through interview and self-report questionnaires.

? How does a natural experiment differ from a laboratory experiment?

Findings
What did Hodges and Tizard (1989) find? At the age of 4, the children hadn't formed attachments. By the age of 8, significant differences existed between the adopted and restored children. At the age of 8 and 16, most of the adopted children had formed close relationships with their caregiver. This was less true of the children who had returned to their own families, because their parents were often unsure they wanted their children back. However, negative social effects were evident in both the adopted and restored children at school—they were attention seeking and had difficulty in forming peer relationships.

At the age of 16, the family relationships of the adopted children were as good as those of families in which none of the children had been removed from the family home. However, children who had returned to their families showed little affection for their parents, and their parents weren't very affectionate towards them. Both groups of adolescents were less likely than adolescents in ordinary families to have a special friend or to regard other adolescents as sources of emotional support. Overall, however, the adopted children were better adjusted than would have been predicted by Bowlby.

? How might we account for the different patterns of behaviour shown by adopted children and children who returned to their families?

Conclusions
What conclusions can we draw? The above findings show that some effects of privation (and institutionalisation) can be reversed, because the children were able to form attachments in spite of their privation (and experience of institutionalisation). However, some privation effects are long-lasting, as shown by the difficulties the institutionalised children faced at school. What seems to be especially important is for children who have been institutionalised to move to a loving environment. That was more likely to be the case for children who were adopted than those who returned to their own families.

Limitations
In spite of the strengths of this study, it has some limitations. First, the decision as to whether any given child should return to its own family or be adopted depended on complex issues to do with family dynamics and the child's wishes. As a result, it is hard to know precisely why adopted children suffered fewer long-term negative effects of institutionalisation than those restored to their families. Second, the interview and self-report data may provide a somewhat distorted perspective—perhaps some of the adolescents exaggerated or minimised the problems they were having with their lives.

? How has the research of Hodges and Tizard added to our knowledge of the effects of deprivation?

? What ethical issues might be involved in the case study of Genie? Do these outweigh any understandings gained from this study?

Extreme privation

A few researchers have considered the effects of very extreme privation and isolation on children. The really surprising finding is the *resilience* of many of these children. Koluchová (1976) studied identical Czech twin boys (Andrei and Vanya) who had spent most of their first 7 years locked in a cellar. They had been treated very badly and were often beaten. They were barely able to talk and relied mainly on gestures rather than speech. The twins were fostered at about the age of 9 by a pair of loving sisters. By the time they were 14, their behaviour was essentially normal. By the age of 20, they were of above average intelligence and had excellent relationships with members of their foster family (Koluchová, 1991).

Curtiss (1989) and Rymer (1993) reported a case study (detailed investigation of a single individual) of Genie (not her real name). She spent most of her childhood locked on her own in a room at her home in Temple City, Los Angeles. She was found on 4 November 1970 when 13½ years old. She hadn't been fed properly, couldn't stand erect, and had no social skills. At that time, she didn't understand language and couldn't speak. One reason she didn't speak was because she had been beaten many times for making a noise.

After she was found, Genie was put in the Children's Hospital in Los Angeles and received help from a team of scientists (the Genie Team). Within a few months, Genie could understand more than 100 words even though her "talking" at that time was limited to short high-pitched squeaks. A few months later, Genie was placed in a foster home. She showed a great interest in learning and her vocabulary increased dramatically. However, she was very poor at putting words together to form meaningful sentences. This was *not* due to low intelligence—Genie showed very good spatial ability. Brain imaging revealed that Genie had practically no left-brain activity, the side of the brain dominant in language processing.

Later on, Genie's story became tragic again. She went back to live with her mother, who proved unable to look after her. As a result, she went to several foster homes. In one of these homes, she was abused. She began to deteriorate physically and mentally, and moved to a home for retarded adults.

Not all children experiencing privation experience permanent emotional damage. Freud and Dann (1951) found that young children who form strong attachments with other young children can avoid severe damage. They studied six war orphans whose parents had been murdered in a concentration camp when the children were very young. The infants lived together in a deportation camp for about 2 years until the age of 3, and had very distressing experiences such as watching people being hanged. In this camp, they had very limited contact with anyone other than each other.

When the camp was liberated after the Second World War, the children came to England. When freed from the camp, the children hadn't yet developed speech properly, they were underweight, and they expressed hostility towards adults. However, they were greatly attached to each other. According to Freud and Dann (1951, p. 131), "The children's positive feelings were centred exclusively in their own group ... They had no other wish than to be together and became upset when they were separated from each other, even for short moments."

Case studies

Some of the studies of privation described in this chapter are case studies (see also Chapter 4). The advantage of such research is that it produces rich data that can be used by a researcher to develop new theoretical ideas. Case studies can provide information about exceptional types of behaviour or performance that had been thought to be impossible.

However, we need to be very careful when interpreting the evidence from a case study. The greatest limitation is the typically low reliability. The findings that are obtained from one unusual or exceptional individual are unlikely to be repeated in detail when another individual is studied. Thus, it is often very hard to generalise from a single case study. Second, many case studies involve the use of lengthy, fairly unstructured interviews that may produce subjective information. Third, researchers generally only report some of the data they obtained from their interviews with the participant. They may be unduly selective in terms of what they choose to report or to omit.

Children in concentration camps experienced terrible early privation. The children in this picture are awaiting release from Auschwitz in January 1945. Freud and Dann studied six such children who only had each other for companions throughout their early lives.

As time went by, the six children became attached to their adult carers. In addition, they developed rapidly at a social level and in their use of language. It is hard to say whether their early experiences had any lasting adverse effects. One (Leah) received psychiatric assistance and another (Jack) sometimes felt very alone and isolated (Moskovitz, 1983). However, it wouldn't be exceptional to find similar problems in six adults selected at random.

EVALUATION OF STUDIES OF DISRUPTION OF ATTACHMENT AND PRIVATION (FAILURE TO FORM ATTACHMENT)

➕ Most adverse effects of maternal disruption of attachment and of privation can be reversed, and children are more resilient than Bowlby believed.

➕ The evidence doesn't support Bowlby's (1951) argument that the negative effects of disruption of attachment in the form of maternal deprivation can't be reversed. Indeed, even privation doesn't always have permanent effects. For most people, early experience is very much related to what happens later on. Bad experiences are often followed by more of the same. However, where severely bad experiences are followed by much better ones, the outcome is often good (e.g. the Czech twins).

➕ In spite of the many positive findings, there is one set of children for whom the outcome is typically very discouraging. These are children with reactive attachment disorder (described in the box below) most of whom have experienced privation (failure to form attachment).

➕ Clearer evidence comes from Hodges and Tizard's (1989) longitudinal research that focused on privation. At one level, this study supports our conclusion that even privation can be recovered from being given good subsequent care. However, Hodges and Tizard's research also suggests a rather different conclusion, which is that recovery is only possible within the context of a loving relationship. Hodges and Tizard found that those children who went on to have good relationships at home coped well at home but found relationships outside the home difficult. In some way, they lacked an adequate model for future relationships. This would seem to support Bowlby's attachment theory.

⊖ It is not always clear whether children have experienced disruption of attachment or privation. Suppose a child spends the first few months of its life with its biological parents and is then sent to an institution. Most children in that situation have probably experienced privation (never having had a loving attachment) but a few may have developed an attachment to their mother prior to going to the institution (disruption of attachment).

⊖ Most studies on privation (failure to form attachment) involve very small samples, which makes it hard to generalise from them.

⊖ In some cases, it is possible the children suffering privation were abnormal from birth—we can only look back at their experiences and abilities. The fact that Genie had very little activity in the left half of her brain may indicate some inborn problem. However, it is probably more likely to reflect her almost total lack of language experience for the first several years of her life.

⊖ In the study by Hodges and Tizard (1989), the children weren't randomly allocated to return home or to be adopted. This makes it hard to know precisely why the two groups differed in their development.

Reactive attachment disorder

Consider a child in the early months of life. The child is hungry, or wet. What does the child do? He or she screams out for attention, and in the rage expressed, the mother comes to the child's aid and feeds or changes the child. Day after day, week after week, the closeness of eye contact, touch, movements, and smiles creates a bond of trust between the child and its mother.

But what happens if this cycle is broken? What if the mother doesn't want to respond to the demanding needs of the child? What if there is an undiagnosed condition in the child that is never appropriately responded to and so the child is never comforted? In these instances, the child does not learn to trust, does not learn to bond, and proceeds on with the next lesson to learn in life.

This leads to a condition called "reactive detachment disorder". Children with attachment disorders have trouble trusting others. Trusting means to love, and loving hurts. They attempt to control everyone and everything in their world. Lack of a conscience appears to be caused by their lacking trust in anyone. They become so dependent on themselves that they ignore the needs of others to the point that they will steal, damage, and destroy anything that they feel hinders their control. In short, they do not trust any caregiver or person in authority.

As a relatively new diagnosis to the DSM-IV manual, reactive attachment disorder is often misunderstood, and relatively unknown. All too often these individuals grow up untreated and become sociopaths without conscience and without concern for anyone but themselves. This condition was made popular by the academy award-winning movie *Good Will Hunting*. But unlike the movie, the hero or heroine rarely drives off into the sunset to have a happy-ever-after life. More realistically, parental dreams are lost, and the children grow up uncaring and without social conscience.

(Adapted from http://members.tripod.com/~radclass/index.html)

Long-term effects of institutional care

As mentioned earlier, much recent research has focused on Romanian children who spent their early lives in orphanages. The study of such children provides information about the effects of institutional care. Most of this research has been carried out by Michael Rutter and his colleagues in a very large longitudinal research project known as the English and Romanian Adoptee (ERA) Study. The Romanian children in this study spent the first few months or years in a Romanian institution before coming to the UK for adoption.

Rutter and the ERA Study Team (1998) followed 111 Romanian orphans adopted in the UK before the age of 2. When the orphans arrived in the UK they were physically and mentally underdeveloped. By the age of 4, however, all of them had improved as a result of improved care. Those adopted the latest showed the slowest improvements educationally and in emotional development. However, reasonable recovery occurred given good subsequent care.

O'Connor et al. (2000) studied Romanian children exposed to very severe privation and neglect in Romania before being adopted by caring British families. They compared those children adopted between 24 and 42 months (late-placed adoptees) and those adopted between 6 and 24 months (early-placed adoptees). Both groups showed significant recovery from their ordeal in Romania. However, the late-placed adoptees had greater difficulty in achieving good cognitive and social development than early-placed adoptees.

News reports in the 1980s highlighted deprivation in Romanian orphanages, with many children demonstrating anaclitic depression, having received basic sustenance but little human warmth or contact.

Smyke et al. (2007) studied young children raised in institutions in Romania. Compared to young children of the same age raised at home by their parents, those in institutional care showed severe delays in cognitive development, had poorer physical growth, and had much inferior social competence. Smyke et al. (2007) considered the factors responsible for the low levels of cognitive development and social competence in the institutionalised children. Two factors are likely to be important:

1. The percentage of their lives these children had spent in an institution.
2. The quality of caregiving the children received (assessed by analysing videotapes of child–caregiver interaction).

What Smyke et al. (2007) found was that the institutionalised children's cognitive development and social competence depended far more on the quality of caregiving than on the percentage of their lives they had spent in an institution. Thus, being brought up in an institution doesn't inevitably cause major problems provided caregiver quality is high.

HOW SCIENCE WORKS: Failure to form attachments (privation)

Attachments and the issue of day care are personal subjects and scientists have to be sensitive when investigating them, as researchers are obliged to consider possible psychological (as well as physical) risks to participants such as becoming upset, anxious, or stressed about their personal behaviour and/or history. This means that questionnaires and surveys must be constructed sensitively and participants told that they do not have to take part if they would prefer not to.

Find and print out a short piece about the Romanian orphans studied by Rutter and others, or one of the case studies of children who have failed to form attachments. Survey a few participants by asking them to read this and then say what they think were the four most important factors missing in these children's early lives. You could then look at your findings and see if there is much agreement, and get a snapshot of our cultural beliefs.

Deprivation-specific psychological patterns

It is possible that the negative effects of institutionalisation are very *similar* to the negative effects on children of experiencing any kind of psychosocial stress and adversity. These negative effects include various emotional and behavioural problems. Another possibility is that many of the negative effects of institutionalisation are specific to institutional deprivation and are *different* from the effects of other kinds of stressful environment (e.g. sexual abuse).

Kumsta et al. (2010) addressed the above issue as part of the ERA study. They were surprised to discover that institutionalisation was *not* associated with the emotional and behavioural problems that typically follow psychosocial stress. Instead, the negative effects were mostly specific to institutionalisation. This led them to identify four **deprivation-specific patterns** associated with institutional deprivation that emerged by the age of 6 and were still present several years later:

1. *Quasi-autism*: this pattern involves symptoms resembling those found in autism; these symptoms include social deficits and communication problems; poor understanding of the meanings of social contexts; and obsessive preoccupations (e.g. with watches; with the details of plumbing systems).
2. *Disinhibited attachment*: this pattern involves a lack of wariness of strangers; inappropriate affectionate behaviour; and a willingness to leave the caregiver to walk off with a stranger.
3. *Cognitive impairment*: this pattern involves a low IQ, and very general negative effects on cognition including poor performance on GCSEs. However, even 12 years after leaving institutional care, there is some evidence of continuing cognitive gains (Beckett et al., 2010).
4. *Inattention/overactivity*: this pattern involves problems with concentration and focusing on the task in hand.

Kumsta et al. (2010) pointed out that many children who had been institutionalised did *not* show the deprivation-specific patterns discussed above. However, it is of concern that many previously institutionalised children show one or more of these patterns several years after being adopted.

CASE STUDY: The Riley family

Jean Riley (54) and her husband Peter (58) adopted two children from Romania who are now aged 17 and 9. Cezarina, when they first saw her, was cross-eyed, filthy, and about four years behind in her physical development. First, Cezarina's physical problems had to be sorted out, but from then on she made good progress. However, Cezarina is "laid back" about things that seem important to Jean and Peter. Jean understands this attitude, though, because clearly examinations seem less important when a child has had to struggle to survive.

According to Jean, Cezarina is bright, but needs to have information reinforced over and over again. She has also struggled to understand jokes and sarcasm, although this may be due to difficulties with learning the language. Jean sees Cezarina as naive and emotionally immature. Cezarina says herself that initially she was frustrated because she couldn't communicate. She does see herself as being different from other girls, although she likes the same things, such as fashion and pop music. Jean runs The Parent Network for the Institutionalised Child, a group for people who have adopted such children. Cezarina has partly recovered from her poor early experiences.

(Account based on an article in *Woman*, 21 September 1998.)

Very long-term effects

Are there very long-term effects of institutional care? Sigal et al. (2003) addressed this issue in a study of middle-aged adults placed in an institution at birth or early childhood. These adults were far more likely never to have married than a randomly selected control group (45% vs 17%), they reported fewer social contacts, and more psychological distress including depression.

Sigal et al. (2003) found that the very long-term effects were not limited to psychological factors. In addition, the adults who had been institutionalised were much more likely to suffer from various physical illnesses (e.g. migraine; stomach ulcers; and arthritis). Thus, adults institutionalised several decades earlier seem to suffer very long-term consequences psychologically and physically.

EXAM HINT

This part of the specification is concerned with three topics:

1. Disruption of attachment
2. Failure to form attachment (privation)
3. Institutional care

You need to be very clear about which studies go with which topics.

Disruption of care is largely concerned with the work of Robertson and Robertson (see page 84) and also Bowlby's "44 juvenile thieves study" (page 85).

Failure to form attachment could include Hodges and Tizard (1989), as well as case studies such as Genie (Curtiss, 1989). Remember to discuss the limitations of such case studies (page 88).

Institutional care would exclude the case studies (because these children were not in institutions) but would include Hodges and Tizard as well as other studies on this page.

Section Summary

Explanations of attachment: Learning theory and Bowlby's theory

- According to learning theorists, infant attachment behaviour can be explained in terms of classical and/or operant conditioning. The basic assumption is that the mother is rewarding for the infant because she provides a source of food.
- According to Gewirtz, securely attached infants are rewarded or reinforced by interacting with their mother.
- According to social learning theorists, infant attachment to the caregiver occurs through modelling, direct instruction, and social facilitation.
- The learning theory approach exaggerates the importance of food in infant attachment, and it is reductionist and oversimplified.
- Another limitation with learning theory is that it exaggerates the importance of behaviour in attachment and de-emphasises the strong emotional bond between infant and caregiver.
- According to Bowlby, attachment is an innate and adaptive process for both infant and parent. There is a critical period early in life during which bonding or attachment needs to take place. This resembles imprinting in some species of birds. In fact, it is preferable to think in terms of sensitive periods rather than critical periods.
- There is some support for Bowlby's assumption that early attachments influence subsequent relationships.
- According to Bowlby's monotropy hypothesis, infants have a hierarchy of attachments at the top of which is one caregiver (typically the mother). In fact, many secure infants have strong attachments to two or more adults.

Types of attachment: Secure attachment, insecure-avoidant, and insecure-resistant

- There is an important distinction between secure and insecure attachment. Maltreated children are more likely than other children to be insecurely attached.
- Ainsworth argued that there are two forms of insecure attachment: insecure-avoidant and insecure-resistant. Insecure-avoidant children inhibit their attachment needs, whereas insecure-resistant children exaggerate their attachment needs.
- There is also a fourth attachment style: disorganised.
- Most children show consistency of attachment style over time.
- Secure attachment is associated with greater social competence and language skills.
- Individuals who are insecure-avoidant have the advantage of focusing on self-preservation and those who are insecure-resistant have the advantage of high vigilance in threatening situations.
- Considering attachment types within a two-dimensional framework (avoidant-withdrawal vs proximity-seeking and angry and resistant strategies vs emotional confidence) permits a more fine-grained account of individual differences in attachment.
- Studies on monkeys show that infant–infant affectional bonds can be as effective as mother–infant bonds.

Use of the "Strange Situation" in attachment research

- The "Strange Situation" provides a thorough assessment of infants' attachment type and is easily the most commonly used technique for measuring attachment.
- Ainsworth found using the Strange Situation that about 70% of infants show secure attachment, 20% avoidant attachment, and 10% resistant attachment.
- Research based on the Strange Situation has the following weaknesses:
  – it is culturally biased;
  – it is artificial because caregivers know they are being observed;
  – it involves an unfamiliar room rather than the infant's home; however, attachment behaviour is similar in both environments.

- Maternal sensitivity is positively associated with secure infant attachment, and there is a small positive association between paternal sensitivity and secure attachment.
- According to the temperament hypothesis, infants' attachment style depends on their innate temperament. This hypothesis doesn't explain why there is only a modest tendency for infants' attachment type with their father to be the same as that with their mother.
- Attachment type in infants generally depends more on the mother than on the infant's characteristics.

Cultural variations in attachment

- Van IJzendoorn and Kroonenberg (1988) found that secure attachment was the most common type of infant attachment in eight different countries. The dominant insecure attachment type was avoidant in Western cultures but resistant in non-Western cultures.
- In spite of cultural differences in attachment, van IJzendoorn and Kroonenberg (1988) found that the variation in attachment types within cultures was greater than the variation between cultures.
- There are various weaknesses with the research of van IJzendoorn and Kroonenberg (1988):
  - It doesn't tell us why patterns of attachment vary so much within any given culture.
  - It is misleading to focus on cultures rather than sub-cultures. The research involved the Strange Situation test, which was created and tested in the United States and so may be culturally biased.
  - It considered only children aged no more than 24 months, and so tells us nothing about children's attachments at older ages.
- The Japanese regard amae (emotional dependence) as indicating that an infant is securely attached to its mother. In Western countries, however, such clinging behaviour is regarded as indicating insecure attachment.

Effects of disruption of attachment, failure to form attachment (privation), and institutional care

- According to Robertson and Bowlby (1952), young children experiencing short-term disruption of attachment with their mother go through three stages: protest; despair, and detachment. There is no strong evidence for this sequence of stages, and this approach doesn't take account of individual differences among children.
- According to Bowlby's maternal deprivation hypothesis, breaking the maternal bond with a young child (long-term disruption of attachment) often causes serious effects to its social, intellectual, and emotional development.
- Studies by Bowlby and others seem to indicate that long-term disruption of attachment in the form of maternal deprivation can produce negative effects that are still evident several years later.
- There are various weaknesses with the maternal deprivation hypothesis:
  - Bowlby failed to distinguish clearly between disruption of attachment and privation, in which the child has never formed a close relationship.
  - It is often unclear whether the adverse effects observed in children who have experienced privation or disruption of attachment are due to that or to poor quality care they receive afterwards.
  - The effects of privation and disruption of attachment are often more reversible than was assumed by Bowlby.
- It is important to distinguish among disruption of attachment, privation (never having had a close attachment), and institutionalisation (adverse effects of living in an institution).
- Hodges and Tizard (1989) found that some of the negative effects of privation (lack of attachment) and institutional care can be reversed, with the children concerned

forming strong attachments. What was most important was for children who had been institutionalised to move to a loving environment.

- Some children have shown reasonable recovery from extreme privation. This is especially likely when such children form strong attachments with other children.
- Many of the studies on extreme privation are limited because they involve very small samples and so it is hard to generalise the findings.
- Children brought up in institutions in Romania generally have poor social and cognitive skills. However, those who received a high quality of caregiving did much better than other institutionalised children.
- Romanian children who had been institutionalised and then adopted by British families often suffer from one or more deprivation-specific patterns: quasi-autism; disinhibited attachment; cognitive impairment; and inattention/overactivity.
- Middle-aged adults who had been institutionalised in early childhood were found to have long-term negative psychological and physical effects.

SECTION 6
ATTACHMENT IN EVERYDAY LIFE

Some people interpreted Bowlby's maternal deprivation hypothesis as meaning that **day care** was a bad thing. Separation would harm the child's emotional development if he/she spent time away from a primary caregiver. However, this is only an interpretation put on Bowlby's views. Bowlby himself didn't specifically suggest that women should stay at home with their children. However, it seems logical that if absent mothers create unhappy children, then mothers need to be present full-time. It is even possible that Bowlby's views were popularised by post-war governments to encourage women to stay at home—a cheaper alternative than providing universal child-care facilities.

There were those who argued for the *benefits* of day care, at least for certain children. In America in the 1960s there was a move towards providing preschool care for disadvantaged children to enable them to start school on a par with their middle-class peers. For example, there was Headstart, which involved half a million children in its first year. Kagan et al. (1980) asked whether there wasn't some kind of dual standard: lower-class children might benefit from day care as a source of intellectual enrichment, whereas middle-class children would be harmed because of maternal deprivation.

Many parents have to work for economic reasons, and others want to because they enjoy their work or would otherwise feel trapped at home. In several countries, very large numbers of young children are put into day care for several days a week while their mothers are at work. In the United States, 80% of children under the age of 6 spend an average of 40 hours a week in non-parental care. Until the 1960s, this happened only rarely.

There are many different forms of day care. For example, young children can be looked after at home by a relative, they can go to a day nursery, they can be looked after at home by a childminder, and so on. As we will see, the precise effects of day care often vary depending on what kind of day care a child experiences.

In view of the millions of children involved, the effects of day care are of great practical concern. We have seen there are arguments for and against it. We will now consider how much day care affects the social development of children. After that, we consider the implications of research into attachment and day care for child-care policy and practices, including the availability of quality day care.

KEY TERM

Day care: care that is provided by people other than the parent of the infant, for example, nurseries, childminders, play groups, relatives, etc. A temporary alternative to the caregiver, day care is distinct from institutionalised care, which provides permanent substitute care.

? Did you or one of your siblings have day care? What can be recalled about that experience?

Impact of Different Forms of Day Care on Children's Social Development, Including the Effects on Aggression and Peer Relations

We will very shortly discuss research concerned with the effects of day care on children's social development, focusing especially on peer relations and aggression. Before that, however, it is important to emphasise that much early research in this area was limited. For example, we should distinguish between the effects on children of the *quantity* of day care (e.g. number of hours per week) and its *quality* (e.g. does it provide for children's needs?). It is likely that quantity and quality are both important.

We can see some of the complexities by considering a study by Campbell et al. (2000). They focused on children who received family-based day care (often by childminders) or went to a day nursery between the ages of 1½ and 3 years. Children's social development was lower if they had spent long hours each day in day care, suggesting high quantity of day care is a bad thing. However, social development among children who had been in day care for only a few hours a day was higher in those who had this day care several days a week. This suggests that high quantity of day care is a good thing! Thus, we need to consider the timing pattern of day care as well as the sheer quantity.

We should also distinguish between different types of day care—there is no reason to assume that day care provided by grandparents will have precisely the same effects as day care provided in a group setting (e.g. preschool nursery). However, these (and other) distinctions have often been ignored.

Childminding

An important type of day care is childminding (including what are called child-care home and in-home care in the National Institute of Child Health and Human Development (NICHD) research). It involves the child being looked after in the home of a paid childminder. Many parents prefer this form of day care to some others because it appears more similar to the care a child might get in its own home.

Mayall and Petrie (1983) studied a group of London children aged under 2 and their mothers and childminders. The quality of care offered to these children varied considerably. Some childminders were excellent. However, others provided an unstimulating environment and the children didn't thrive.

Bryant et al. (1980) also studied childminding. They found some children were disturbed. Many minders felt they didn't have to form emotional bonds with the children or to stimulate them. They often rewarded quiet behaviour, and this encouraged the children to be passive and under-stimulated.

Day nurseries

? Why do you think that it might be significant that the staff at the Boston school had responsibility for a small number of children, and maintained close emotional contact with them?

Kagan et al. (1980) set up their own nursery school in Boston. The school had a mixed intake from middle- and lower-class families and from various ethnic groups. The staff at the school each had special responsibility for a small group of children, thus ensuring close emotional contact. The study focused on 33 infants who attended the nursery full-time from the age of 3½ months who were compared with a matched home control group. Kagan et al. assessed the children throughout the 2 years they were at the nursery school, measuring attachment, cognitive achievements, and general sociability, finding no consistently large differences between the nursery and home children.

Day nurseries sometimes have adverse effects on children. For example, consider a study by Vandell and Corasaniti (1990) in Texas. Children with extensive child-care experiences from infancy were rated by parents and teachers as having poorer peer relationships and emotional health. At that time, Texas had very low official requirements for child-care facilities. As a result, most carers weren't highly trained and the child-to-caregiver ratios were high. Thus, it is quality of care that should concern us rather than whether day care is a good thing.

National Institute of Child Health and Human Development (NICHD): Potential Research Problems

? How might you use this evidence to advise parents on which form of child care to use?

Much research investigating the effects of day care is limited and hard to interpret. However, large-scale, high-quality research has been carried out by the National Institute of Child Health and Human Development (NICHD) since the early 1990s. Details of the research findings will be provided in what follows. First of all I want to indicate why the NICHD research on day care is outstanding. That will prove useful when it comes to identifying limitations in other research.

What are the strengths of the NICHD approach? First, it is important to distinguish among effects due to the quality of care, the quantity or amount of care, and the type of care. Before the NICHD research there had been very few attempts to examine all three features.

Second, in order to have a fairly complete picture of the effects of day care, it is essential to carry out *longitudinal* studies in which children are followed up over a long period. In the NICHD research, information on the children was collected frequently from early infancy through to 54 months. Subsequent research funded by the NICHD considered possible long-term consequences of day care through to 12 years (Belsky et al., 2007).

Third, children's development depends very much on the quality of parenting they receive as well as possible effects of day care. However, children aren't randomly assigned to receive (or not to receive) day care—the decision is influenced by the specific conditions within each family in which each family finds itself. Thus, a major issue in research designed to compare development in children exposed and not exposed to day care is that of selection bias. **Selection bias** occurs when two groups (e.g. children receiving vs not receiving day care) consist of different types of individuals.

Borge et al. (2004) found major selection bias—50% of children in their study looked after full-time by their mothers had very socially disadvantaged backgrounds compared to only 25% in the day-care group. In the NICHD research, detailed information about family backgrounds was obtained and taken fully into account when working out the effects of day care on children's development.

Fourth, as mentioned earlier, most early researchers didn't think it was important to distinguish clearly among different types of day care. In contrast, the NICHD research involved comparing the effects of five different types of day care. These were as follows: (1) father care; (2) grandparent care; (3) child-care home: home-based care outside the child's home excluding care by grandparents; (4) in-home care: any caregiver in the child's home except the father or grandparent; (5) centre care: group care (e.g. at a day nursery).

Social development: Effects on attachment

The effects of day care on **social development** can be significant. Bowlby said there could be irrevocable harm if infants were separated from a primary caregiver, and there is limited support for this. For example, Belsky and Rovine (1988) found there was an increased risk of children developing insecure attachments if they were in day care for at least 4 months and if this had begun before their first birthday.

In fact, however, day care typically doesn't affect emotional development. Clarke-Stewart et al. (1994) studied the relationship between time spent in day care and quality of attachment in over 500 children. Fifteen-month-old children experiencing "high-intensity" child care (30 hours or more a week from 3 months of age) were no more distressed when separated from their mothers in the Strange Situation than "low-intensity" children (fewer than 10 hours a week).

Roggman et al. (1994) also found no ill-effects from early day care when they looked at behaviour in the Strange Situation. They compared infants cared for at home with those who attended day care before the age of 1. Both groups were equally securely attached to their mothers.

A very thorough attempt to assess day care's effects on social development was reported by Erel et al. (2000). They carried out several meta-analyses based on numerous studies in which they related day care to six measures of child social development:

1. Secure vs insecure attachment to the mother.
2. Attachment behaviours: avoidance and resistance (reflecting insecure attachment) and exploration (reflecting secure attachment).
3. Mother–child interaction: responsiveness to the mother, smiling at mother, obeying mother, and so on.

KEY TERMS

Selection bias: when different types of individuals are assigned to groups that are to be compared, differences in behaviour between the two groups may be due to this bias rather than to differences in the ways in which the groups are treated.

Social development: the development of a child's social skills, such as the ability to relate to and empathise with others, which is the result of interaction between the child's genes and their environment.

4.   Adjustment: self-esteem, lack of behaviour problems, and so on.
5.   Social interaction with peers.
6.   Social interaction with non-parental adults.

Erel et al. (2000) found day care had non-significant effects on all six measures described above for girls and boys. The effects remained non-significant even for children who had spent a long time in day care several days a week. Erel et al. also found that day care had no effects on cognitive development (e.g. school performance; IQ). In spite of these findings, it is still possible that children exposed to certain forms of day care suffer negative effects on their social development.

Why did Belsky and Rovine (1988) find negative effects of day care on attachment whereas most subsequent research has not found this? Two likely reasons are the increasing quality of child care and reduced parental guilt about day care (Shpancer, 2006).

Social development: Effects on peer relations

The effects of group day care on young children can be variable. There may be some negative consequences of children (especially very young ones) being away from their mothers for many hours a week, there may also be positive consequences. Spending many hours a week with other children (as in centre care) might help children to develop social skills and to interact happily with other children of the same age (their **peers**).

Children who go more often to a day nursery become more active, outgoing, and playful. Shea (1981) videotaped 3- and 4-year-old children during their first 10 weeks at nursery school. **Sociability** (seeking out and enjoying others' company) increased over time. There was a decrease in the distance from the nearest child and an increase in frequency of peer interaction (interaction with children of the same age).

The above increases in sociability were greater in children attending the nursery school 5 days a week than in those attending for only 2 days. Thus, it was the experience of nursery school rather than maturation or some other factor that produced the changes.

Clarke-Stewart et al. (1994) also found that peer relationships were more advanced in day-care children. This study looked at 150 children from Chicago aged between 2 and 3 and from various social backgrounds. The children in day care had more advanced peer relationships probably due to their extensive experience coping with peers in the day-care setting. They learned earlier how to cope in social situations and how to negotiate with peers.

However, day care doesn't have beneficial effects on the peer relations of *all* children. When children are shy and unsociable, the nursery experience can be threatening. This can have a negative effect on their school career (Pennebaker et al., 1981).

Earlier we discussed the work of Erel et al. (2000), which included various meta-analyses to assess the effects of day care. Erel et al. found that day care had no effect overall on children's social interactions with peers regardless of the amount of day care per week, the number of months the child had had in day care, and the child's gender.

Clarke-Stewart et al. (1994) found that children attending nursery school had more advanced peer relationships, learning how to cope in social situations and negotiate with peers earlier than children not in day care.

NICHD study

Finding an *association* between day-care quality and children's social development is not sufficient to show it has a causal effect on children's social development. The reason is that children experiencing high-quality day care tend to have parents who are better educated and more responsive than those experiencing low-quality care (Marshall, 2004). Thus, it is hard to determine whether parenting or the day care is responsible for the association between day-care quality and children's development.

This issue was addressed in a large National Institute of Child Health and Human Development Study (NICHD study) in which over 1000 children were studied from birth. When the effects of family environment were controlled, the influence of day-care quality during the first 4½ years of life on social development including peer relations was modest (NICHD, 2003a). However, higher-quality child care was associated with higher levels of cognitive skills and language performance.

The NICHD study (2003b) focused on the effects of amount of time spent in child care on children's development. When the effects of family environment were controlled, increased time in non-maternal care during the first 4½ years of life was associated with less social competence at 54 months of age. However, the effect was small.

Love et al. (2003) wondered whether quantity of care would have similar negative effects in other cultures (i.e. Australia; Israel). Child outcomes in both those cultures depended more on quality of care (e.g. regulated vs unregulated care) than on quantity. Indeed, quantity of care had few effects on the children.

Why did Love et al.'s (2003) findings differ from those of NICHD (2003b)? The range of quality of child care was much greater in Love et al.'s study, thus making quality more important than quantity in influencing children's development.

Effects on aggression

There is increasing interest in the possibility that group day care may affect children's aggression. There are two main reasons for this. First, children in group day care spend much of their time with their peers. This provides many more opportunities for physical aggression than does home care. We could also look at this more positively—perhaps children in group day care learn more effective ways of resolving interpersonal conflict without resorting to physical aggression.

Second, physical aggression peaks in the preschool years (the years during which the great majority of day care takes place). It is known such behaviour is an important risk factor for subsequent anti-social behaviour.

Much research has focused on **externalising problems** (problem behaviours including aggression, disobedience, and some kinds of assertiveness). Different externalising problems are found together. However, when researchers find that day care is associated with externalising problems it isn't always clear whether the level of aggression increased.

Bates et al. (1994) found that children who spent more time receiving day care during their first 5 years of life exhibited more behavioural problems such as peer-directed aggression.

Any negative effects of day care on aggression would probably be more obvious over fairly long time periods. Accordingly, Vandell and Corasaniti (1990) studied 8-year-olds. Children who received full-time day care starting in their first year of life and continuing until they started school were rated as being more non-compliant than other children. Bates et al. (1994) found children who spent more time receiving any type of day care during their first 5 years of life had more behaviour problems, peer-rated aggression, and observed aggression than those receiving less day care.

Borge et al. (2004) compared physical aggression in large numbers of 2- and 3-year-old Canadian children attending group day care or being looked after full-time by their own mothers. In contrast to other research, more children looked after by their own mothers showed high levels of physical aggression (7.4% vs 5.2%). This remained the case when the focus was only on children from very socially disadvantaged families. However, the two groups of children didn't differ in physical aggression when the focus was on children who didn't come from very disadvantaged families.

Clarke-Stewart (1989) argued that researchers often fail to distinguish between aggressive and disobedient behaviour on the one hand and assertive behaviour on the other hand. Day care may be associated with assertive behaviour (often regarded as positive) rather than with aggressive behaviour (typically regarded as negative). Precisely this issue was addressed in the NICHD research on day care (NICHD, 2003a, 2003b). Levels of aggression (e.g. cruelty to others; involved in many fights) and assertiveness (e.g. bragging or boasting; demands attention) at 54 months were higher in children who had spent more time in day care.

Van IJzendoorn et al. (2004) re-analysed the above data from the NICHD research programme and reported some additional findings. First, the effects of spending a long time in day care on externalising problems mainly occurred when day care involved non-relatives (i.e. nannies, babysitters, day-care homes, and centres) than when it did not. Second, centre-based care (involving much time in groups) was especially associated with externalising problems.

Belsky et al. (2007) considered the long-term effects of day care on the children in the NICHD programme through to 12 years. The amount of time spent in day care in early childhood predicted externalising problems less well at the age of 12 years than 54 months. Problem behaviours at 12 years were associated with large amounts of time in centres involving large groups of peers but were NOT associated with amount of day care in other settings.

EVALUATION

It looks as if young children spending large amounts of time in group day care have an increased risk of displaying physical aggression. However, children aren't assigned *randomly* to receive group day care or be looked after continuously by their mothers. As a result, children receiving group day care may show more physical aggression because of factors (e.g. problems within the family) having nothing to do with the group day care itself. For example, Borge et al. (2004) found the families of children looked after full-time by their mothers were twice as likely as those of children in day care to be very socially disadvantaged.

It would be useful to compare children's physical aggression *before* they receive group day care and *during* the period when they receive such day care. However, that is generally not feasible, because children mostly start to receive group day care at a very early age.

It is also important to distinguish between aggression and assertiveness. The finding that day care can increase assertiveness would be generally be regarded as a positive outcome.

Effects of different forms of day care

Little research has directly considered the effects on children of receiving different forms of day care. One exception is research by Moss and Melhuish (1991). They studied children in London who received day care starting before 12 months of age. Some of these children were cared for by relatives, others by childminders, and still others attended a day nursery.

The three conditions of day care didn't differ only in terms of the person looking after the children. In addition, the ratio of adults to children was highest for those children looked after by relatives and lowest for those in day nurseries. The other side of the coin was that there was the most contact with other children in the nursery and the least with relatives.

How did the three day-care conditions differ in their effects? At the age of 18 months, children receiving day care from relatives showed the best language development whereas those in the nursery performed worst. This remained the case (but the gap was smaller) at 3 years. At 3 years, children attending nursery did best in terms of cooperation, sharing, and having a good understanding of their peers. Thus, there were advantages and disadvantages associated with nursery care. However, it is important to note that the differences in the effects across the three groups were fairly small.

Leach et al. (2008) compared the quality of several forms of day care: childminders; grandparents; nannies; and nurseries. The quality of child care was very similar for childminders, grandparents, and nannies, but was lower for nurseries. However, grandparents offered children fewer activities than did childminders or nannies. In general, the more infants any given adult had to care for, the lower the quality of care provided.

Statham (2011) reviewed research specifically on day care provided by grandparents. There is some evidence that children cared for by grandparents have relatively good vocabularies but perform less well than other children on tests of literacy and numeracy. In addition, such children sometimes have higher levels of peer difficulties and are more likely to be hyperactive.

In sum, most differences among different forms of day care are fairly small. However, it is hard to interpret the findings because children aren't allocated at random to receive the various types of day care. For example, families from relatively disadvantaged groups are the ones most likely to use grandparent child care. Adverse effects associated with grandparent care may reflect the family's disadvantaged position rather than the care itself.

 What special ethical considerations should be taken into account when conducting work with young children?

How Research into Attachment and Day Care has influenced Child-Care Practices

What are the implications of the research we have discussed for child-care practices? To anticipate, the major conclusion is that most adverse effects of day care on children occur because of the poor *quality* of care rather than simply because of separation. That is an optimistic conclusion, because it means nearly all children would suffer few or no adverse effects if they received day care of sufficient quality.

The above conclusion fits with the views of many authorities. Bowlby's arguments could be interpreted as favouring *improved* child care. He suggested that separation could be compensated for by adequate bond substitution in which the children's emotional needs are emphasised. For many parents, there is little choice about day care—it is an economic necessity.

There is one important issue to address before we discuss factors associated with day care having beneficial or adverse effects on children. Suppose researchers compare young children receiving day care in two different kinds of settings: in one the child–staff ratio is low and in the other it is high. Suppose also we find the social development of children in the former setting is greater than that of children in the latter setting.

Could we conclude that the difference in child–staff ratio is responsible for the findings? The short answer is "No". All we have is correlational evidence—there is an association between child–staff ratio and social development. Perhaps the child–staff ratio genuinely makes a difference. However, there are other possibilities. If it costs more for parents to place their children in day care with a favourable child–staff ratio, it may simply be that children in day care with a high child–staff ratio come from more socially disadvantaged homes than those in day care with a low child–staff ratio.

HOW SCIENCE WORKS: Day care

Our government has promoted day care for as many preschool children as possible, but opinions about day care are varied and strongly held. In this sort of case, scientific research is particularly important as it is evidence-based and not anecdote-based. You could produce a short questionnaire asking participants to rate various factors (which have been identified in real research) as important in determining the quality of day care on a scale of 1 to 5, with 1 = not important and 5 = very important. In this way you could compare a sample of people's opinions with actual research, and see whether or not the two match. You could then interpret what your comparison means, and decide what conclusion you would draw from your findings.

Features of high-quality day care

We have discussed much research on day care, and we will be discussing more such research shortly. Before considering implications for child-care practices, it will be useful to list the features of high-quality day care. This then provides the goal towards which practices should be aimed.

- The caregiver or caregivers should provide sensitive emotional care and shouldn't be emotionally detached.
- Caregivers should have numerous interactions with the children in their care, and should ensure the children are actively engaged with their environment.
- Consistency of care (minimal change of caregivers) is associated with high-quality day care.

Caregivers should ensure the children in their care are actively engaged with their environment.

- Day care provided by relatives is associated with less aggression by children than day care provided by non-relatives.
- Day care provision in which there is a low child-to-caregiver ratio is of higher quality than where there is a high ratio.
- Day care provided by well-trained caregivers is typically of higher quality than day care provided by poorly trained or untrained caregivers.
- Research on attachment indicates that insecurely attached children have poorer peer relations and more behaviour problems, so it is especially important that they receive high-quality care.

Implications for child-care practices

The research on day care carried out by psychologists has several implications for child-care practices. In this section, we will discuss the major implications that seem justified in the light of the evidence.

Consistency of care

Several studies point to the importance of consistency of care. For example, in Hodges and Tizard's study of institutional care (1989; see page 87), one reason the children didn't form attachments was because they had an average of 50 caregivers before the age of 4. In contrast, in Kagan et al.'s (1980) study of day care, a key criterion was that the children received consistent emotional support.

The NICHD study (1997) reported that the highest infant-to-caregiver ratio should be 3:1 to ensure infants had sensitive and positive interactions. In order to improve consistency, a day-care facility needs to ensure minimal turnover of staff, and to arrange that each child is assigned to *one* specific individual who is more or less constantly available and feels responsible for the child. It may also be important to establish consistent routines and physical environments.

Love et al. (2003) reported additional support for the importance of consistency of care. Australian children who had experienced the most changes in their care arrangements had more behaviour problems and less effective social skills than other children.

Quality of care

High-quality care is of fundamental importance if children in day care are to show good social development. Schaffer and Emerson (1964) note it is very hard to define "quality of care" although we can identify some features of day care that contribute to it. One important feature is the amount of verbal interaction between caregiver and child. Related to that, Ridley et al. (2000) found in child-care classrooms that *observed engagement* (the extent to which children

actively interacted with each other or with a task) was positively related to the quality of the day care. Tizard (1979) found that mothers had more complex conversations with their children than teachers did, because teachers have to divide their attention.

A second way to improve the quality of day care is by increasing the availability of suitable toys, books, and other playthings. Sufficient stimulation is clearly important for development.

Third, and perhaps most important, is the issue of providing sensitive emotional care. The NICHD study found a quarter of the infant care providers gave highly sensitive infant care, and half provided moderately sensitive care. Worryingly, one-fifth of the caregivers were "emotionally detached" from the infants under their care—infant development suffers when day care lacks emotional involvement.

Quality of day care can be improved with the provision of sufficient toys and books to stimulate learning and development.

Why are caregiver-to-child ratios and caregiver training important? NICHD Early Child Care Research Network (2002, p. 206) came up with an interesting answer: "More caregiver training may lead to better interactions between children and adults, while lower ratios may lead to more interactions."

Quality of care: Attachment

What are the implications of research on attachment for quality of care? High-quality care is even more important for insecurely attached children than securely attached ones for two reasons. First, securely attached children are more accepted by their peers (Szewczyk-Sokolowski et al., 2005), and so cope better with day care. Belsky and Fearon (2002) found that children securely attached at 15 months showed more social competence than those insecurely attached at 15 months. Insecurely attached children are less likely than securely attached ones to form good peer relations during day care, and so are more in need of high-quality day care to enhance their social skills.

Second, securely attached children have fewer behaviour problems (Belsky & Fearon, 2002; Wartner et al., 1994) and are also better at conflict resolution (Wartner et al., 1994). Thus, insecurely attached children are more likely than securely attached ones to be disruptive and aggressive in day care, and so excellent quality day care is needed to reduce these problems.

There is another important implication of research into attachment. Wartner et al. (1994) found that the type of attachment young children showed at the age of 12 months predicted reasonably well their type of attachment at 6 years. The finding that early attachments have long-lasting effects on children makes it all the more important that those providing day care provide high-quality and sensitive care.

Stressfulness of care

It has often been argued that day care can be somewhat stressful for young children. Support for this argument was reported by Vermeer and van IJzendoorn (2006). They reviewed nine studies in which the level of cortisol (known as the "stress hormone") was assessed in young children at home and at day-care centres. Cortisol levels increased during the day at day-care centres but not at home, suggesting that day care was associated with increased stress. The effects were greater in children younger than 36 months and those who weren't securely attached.

The various ways these findings should influence child-care practices are clear. First, it may be preferable for young, insecurely attached children to receive less stressful day care (e.g. provided by grandparents). Second, young children are more likely to be stressed if they spend many hours per day in day care. This suggests it is best if the time young children spend in day care is distributed across the week with only a few hours per day. We have already discussed evidence showing this is effective in promoting children's social development (Campbell et al., 2000). Third, it is desirable to take special steps to minimise the stress and maximise the contentment of children in day care.

Key persons

An influential approach to improving day care is based on the notion of key persons (Jackson & Goldschmied, 2004). The key person is at the centre of the child's experience at day nursery. He/she is in overall charge of the child's initial settling in to day nursery (e.g. reducing any stress associated with separation from the mother). In addition, the key person provides a warm and reassuring presence for the child, acting in some ways as an attachment figure. Finally, the key person discusses all major decisions with the mother, and even makes home visits to achieve a greater understanding of the child's needs.

The "key person" approach has been shown to improve day care by creating a family atmosphere that allows the child to relax and achieve good social and cognitive development.

Jackson and Goldschmied (2004) discuss much evidence showing the effectiveness of their key person approach. In general, this approach has proved effective in creating a family atmosphere in which young children (even insecurely attached ones) can relax and achieve good social and cognitive development.

Child–environment fit

Parents often have little choice but to place their child in day care for several days every week, and financial issues may limit their options in terms of type of day care. However, wherever feasible, it would make sense for parents or other caregivers to relate their decisions with respect to day care to the needs and personality of their child. Here are three examples:

- First, externalising problems including aggression are greater in centre-based care than when the child is in a child-care home or receives in-home care. If a child is displaying aggressive tendencies, it may be advantageous for him/her to be in a child-care home or to receive in-home care rather than to receive centre-based care.
- Second, Borge et al. (2004) found only very socially disadvantaged children were less aggressive in group day care than when looked after full-time by their mother. Thus, group day care may be more beneficial than being looked after all the time by their mother for children from very socially disadvantaged backgrounds but not those from less disadvantaged backgrounds.
- Third, children attending group day care have more advanced peer relationships (Clarke-Stewart et al., 1994) than those who do not. It would seem likely that the beneficial effects on peer relationships would depend on other aspects of the child's background. For example, young children with no siblings and very limited opportunities otherwise to play with their peers might gain more from attending group day care than other young children.

According to Clarke-Stewart (1989) the adverse effects of day care on a child's development may not be "that 40 hours of day care is hard on infants but that 40 hours of work is hard on mothers".

Effects of separation on parents

As Clarke-Stewart (1989, p. 270) pointed out, the reason for adverse effects of day care on children's development may not be "that 40 hours of day care is hard on infants but that 40 hours of work is hard on mothers". Harrison and Ungerer (2002) considered the mother's position in families when she returned to paid employment during the infant's first year. Infants were less likely to be securely attached to their mother if she wasn't committed to work and had anxieties about using child care. To reduce mothers' feelings of **anxiety** or guilt, it is helpful to provide more interlinking between home and day care (e.g. workplace nurseries).

It might also help to relieve some of the guilt experienced by mothers to recognise that day care is *not* necessarily associated with negative effects. For some children, there are actually benefits of having parents who work. Brown and Harris (1978) found that women who didn't work and had several young children to care for were more likely to become seriously depressed. Shaffer (1993) reported that children of working mothers tend to be more confident in social settings. Going out to work enables some women to be *better* mothers.

KEY TERM

Anxiety: a normal emotion similar to nervousness, worry, or apprehension, but if excessive it can interfere with everyday life and might then be judged an anxiety disorder.

Section Summary

Different forms of day care

- Some childminders don't feel the need to form emotional bonds with the child they are looking after.
- Day nurseries in areas in which the official requirements for child-care facilities are low often have adverse effects on children.

- Many children are looked after by members of their family (e.g. grandparents). Such day care is mostly as good as other forms. However, care by grandparents is associated with hyperactivity in young children and problems with peers.
- There is selection bias in terms of which form of day care is received by young children. This makes it hard to interpret the findings.

Social development and peer relations

- Erel et al. (2000) reported that day care on average had no effects on attachment to the mother, adjustment, and social interaction.
- Children in day care often show more advanced peer relationships than other children. However, the effects tend to be small or even negative when the effects of family environment are controlled.

Effects on aggression

- Research shows that levels of aggression and assertiveness are higher in children who have been in day care. These effects are greater in children who have spent the most time in day care.
- Increased aggression and other externalising problems occur mainly when children are in centres with large groups of peers rather than being looked after by relatives.

How research into attachment and day care has influenced child-care practices

- High-quality day care possesses various features:
  - sensitive emotional care by caregivers;
  - numerous interactions between caregivers and children;
  - consistency of care and minimal change of caregivers;
  - day care provided by relatives is associated with less aggression by children;
  - a low child-to-caregiver ratio;
  - well-trained caregivers;
  - special attention to the needs of insecurely attached children.
- It is important that each child is assigned to one specific individual rather than to different individuals at different times. Consistency of care is very important.
- Of great importance is the provision of sensitive emotional care and the avoidance of emotional detachment.
- Insecurely attached children are in special need of high-quality day care. They tend to have poorer peer relations and behave more disruptively than securely attached children, and so caregiver sensitivity and emotional engagement are of particular importance.
- Another reason why it is important to focus on insecurely attached young children in day care is that type of attachment tends to be consistent over a period of years. Accordingly, it is important for children to become securely attached at the youngest age possible.
- Day care can be stressful for some young children. This stress can be reduced by placing young children in day care for only a few hours a day and by using a system involving key persons.
- Account needs to be taken of child–environment fit. For example, children with aggressive tendencies should probably not receive centre-based care, which may encourage those tendencies.
- Mothers' feelings of anxiety or guilt can be reduced by providing more interlinking between home and day care (e.g. workplace nurseries).

You have reached the end of the chapter on developmental psychology. Developmental psychology is an approach or perspective in psychology. The material in this chapter has exemplified the way that developmental psychologists explain behaviour. They look at behaviour in terms of the way that people change as they grow older, and the forces that create this change. Many of the changes, as we have seen, are due to inherited factors (nature). However, a major contribution also comes from the influence of other people and the physical environment (nurture). Development doesn't stop when you leave childhood, it continues through the lifespan. If you go on to study psychology further, you will consider this wider area of developmental, or lifespan, psychology.

Further Reading

- There is accessible and up-to-date coverage of the topics discussed in this chapter in L.E. Berk (2008) *Child development (8th Edn)* (New York: Pearson).

- All you might ever want to know about attachment is to be found in J. Mercer (2006) Attachment theory and its vicissitudes: Toward an updated theory. *Theory & Psychology, 21,* 25–45.

- The effects of privation and what can be done to reverse those effects are discussed in M. Rutter, C. Beckett, J. Castle, J. Kreppner, S. Stevens, and E. Sonuga-Burke (2009). *Policy and practice implications from the English and Romanian Adoptees (ERA) Study: Forty-five key questions* (London: BAAF).

Revision Questions

EXAM HINT

See the Exam hint on page 59 regarding questions that ask you to apply your knowledge.

The examination questions aim to sample the material in this whole chapter. For advice on how to answer such questions refer to Chapter 1, Section 2.

1. a. Outline **two** behaviours that are characteristic of a securely attached child. (2 marks)

   b. Outline **two** behaviours that are characteristic of a child described as 'insecure-avoidant'. (2 marks)

   c. Outline **two** behaviours that are characteristic of a child described as 'insecure-resistant'. (2 marks)

   d. Explain why the validity of research into types of attachment has been criticised. (5 marks)

2. Describe and evaluate the use of the 'Strange Situation' in attachment research. (10 marks)

3. a. Outline what research has shown about cultural variations in attachment. (6 marks)

   b. Outline how psychologists have investigated the effects of institutional care on attachment. (4 marks)

4. The manager of a day nursery is aware that many parents worry about the effects that disruption of attachment will have on their young children.

   Using your knowledge of psychology, suggest some advice that the manager might give to parents. (4 marks)

5. Describe and evaluate the effects of day care on social development. (12 marks)

What you need to know

Section 7: Methods and techniques p. 109

■ Knowledge and understanding of the following research methods, their advantages and weaknesses: experimental method, including laboratory, field and natural experiments, studies using a correlational analysis, observational techniques, self-report techniques including questionnaire and interview, case studies.

Psychologists use a wide range of research methods and techniques to shed light on human behaviour. What are the advantages and weaknesses of these methods and techniques? How are they used?

Section 8: Investigation design p. 129

■ The following features of investigation design: aims, hypotheses including directional and non-directional, experimental design (independent groups, repeated measures, and matched pairs), design of naturalistic observations including the development and use of behavioural categories, design of questionnaires and interviews, operationalisation of variables including independent and dependent variables, pilot studies, control of extraneous variables, reliability and validity, awareness of the BPS Code of Ethics, ethical issues and the ways in which psychologists deal with them, selection of participants and sampling techniques, selection of participants and sampling techniques including random, opportunity, and volunteer sampling, demand characteristics and investigator effects.

There are numerous aspects of investigation design that need to be adhered to in order to ensure that the findings obtained are valid and can be replicated. The main aspects (including a consideration of ethical issues) are discussed.

Section 9: Data analysis and presentation p. 153

■ The following features of data analysis, presentation, and interpretation: presentation and interpretation of quantitative data including graphs, scattergrams, and tables, analysis and interpretation of quantitative data, measures of central tendency including ranges and standard deviations, analysis and interpretation of correlational data, positive and negative correlations and the interpretation of correlation coefficients, presentation of qualitative data, processes involved in content analysis.

A key aspect of the research process is the final interpretation of the results. What statistical methods enable us to interpret research findings and draw conclusions?

Research Methods

4

In a sense, we are all "armchair psychologists"—everyone has opinions about human behaviour. Psychologists don't just present theories about why people behave as they do, but they also seek to support or challenge these theories with **research**—systematic study of a problem—including experiments, interviews, and case studies. Throughout this book we rely on such evidence as a means of analysing theories. In this chapter we will consider the different methods used to conduct research, as well as other important features of the research process.

SECTION 7
METHODS AND TECHNIQUES

The Scientific Approach

Like any other **science**, psychology is concerned with theories and data. All sciences share one fundamental feature: they aim to discover facts about the world by using systematic and objective methods of investigation. The research process starts with casual observations about one feature of the world, for example, that people imitate the violence they see on television or that there are concerns about how the Nazis so easily made ordinary people obey them (see page 245). These observations collectively form a **theory** (a general explanation or account of certain findings or data). For example, someone might put forward a theory in which it is assumed that genetic factors play a role in all mental disorders.

Theories invariably produce a number of further expectations, which can be stated as a **research hypothesis**—a formal and unambiguous statement about what you believe to be true. Here is an example of a hypothesis: Schizophrenia is a condition that depends in part on genetic factors (see page 265). A hypothesis is stated with the purpose of trying to prove or disprove it. And that is why scientists conduct research—to prove or disprove their hypotheses. If it is disproved, then the theory has to be adjusted, and a new hypothesis produced, and tested, and so on. This process is shown in the Figure overleaf.

What is the relationship between theories and hypotheses? In essence, theories provide rather general accounts of a range of findings. The various assumptions built into a theory will typically generate several hypotheses—thus, hypotheses are specific predictions that follow from some theory.

Psychologists spend a lot of their time collecting data in order to test various hypotheses. In addition to **laboratory experiments**, they make use of many different methods of investigation, each of which can provide useful information about human behaviour.

When a researcher has decided which hypothesis he/she wants to test, the next crucial issue is to decide which research method is the one that is most appropriate. It may seem natural to ask which of the various research methods (discussed in detail below) is the best. This question is too simple, a given research method may be the best way to test certain hypotheses but may

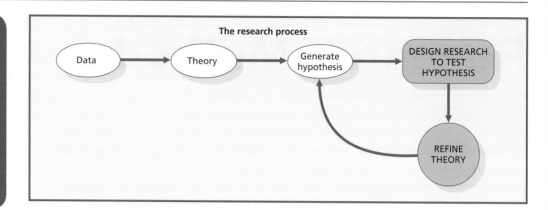

The research process

be less suitable or even impossible to use to test other hypotheses. In what follows, we will consider the advantages and weaknesses of each research method in turn.

Experimental Methods: Laboratory Experiments

There are various experimental methods including laboratory, field, and natural experiments. Most studies using experimental methods are laboratory experiments. This method is not the *only* scientific method, but it is the *most* scientific because it is highly objective and systematic. As we will see, experimental methods have the great advantage of permitting us to work out cause-and-effect relationships. We will start by focusing mostly on laboratory experiments, and then consider the three main types of experiments using experimental methods.

A variable is something that varies! How long you sleep each night is a variable, whereas the number of days in a week is a fixed quantity.

Dependent and independent variables

In order to understand what is involved in the experimental method, we will consider a concrete example. Put yourself in the position of the British psychologist Alan Baddeley (1966), who thought that acoustic coding was important in short-term memory, with people tending to confuse similar-sounding words when they tried to recall them in the right order. This led him to test the following hypothesis: More errors will be made in recalling acoustically similar word lists in the correct order than in recalling acoustically dissimilar word lists (see page 25).

In order to test this hypothesis, Baddeley compared the numbers of errors in short-term memory with lists of words that were acoustically similar and others that were acoustically dissimilar. This hypothesis refers to two **variables**—whether the list words were acoustically similar or dissimilar and the performance of the people learning the lists (errors made).

The variable directly manipulated by the experimenter is called the **independent variable (IV)**, i.e. acoustic similarity vs dissimilarity. The other variable, the one affected by the IV, is called the **dependent variable (DV)**, i.e. how many errors are made on each type of list. (It is called *dependent* because it depends on something the experimenter controls.) The DV is some aspect of behaviour that is going to be measured or assessed, to decide whether or not the IV caused a change in behaviour.

The experimental process can be summarised thus:

- Experimenter acts on IV
- Changes in IV lead to changes in DV
- Changes in DV measured by experimenter

KEY TERMS

Variables: things that vary or change.

Independent variable (IV): some aspect of the research situation that is manipulated by the researcher in order to observe whether a change occurs in another variable.

Dependent variable (DV): an aspect of the participant's behaviour that is measured in the study.

ACTIVITY: The experimental process

To apply what you have learnt about the experimental process, refer to one of the experiments into short-term memory processing (e.g. Baddeley, 1966; Jacobs, 1887; Peterson & Peterson, 1959) and operationalise the IV and DV.

Experimental control

We come now to the most important principle of the experimental method: control. The IV is manipulated and the DV is free to vary. However, all other variables *must* be *controlled*, i.e. kept constant, so we can assume that the only variable causing any subsequent change in the DV *must* be the IV. In our example, we would control all aspects of the situation (extraneous variables) other than acoustic similarity by making sure both types of word lists had words of the same length, frequency of occurrence in the language, and so on. Other factors we may need to control when using the experimental method are always using the same room for the experiment, keeping the temperature the same, and having the same lighting.

Extraneous variables

Variables that are *not* controlled may become **extraneous variables**. Such variables are not of interest to the researcher, but may get in the way of the link between the independent and dependent variable. For example, suppose the words used in the acoustically similar lists were much longer words than those used in the acoustically dissimilar lists.

We wouldn't know whether the higher number of errors with acoustically similar lists than with acoustically dissimilar lists was due to the independent variable (acoustic similarity vs dissimilarity) or to the extraneous variable of word length. The presence of any extraneous variables is really serious, because it prevents us from being able to interpret our findings. Other kinds of extraneous variables are discussed on page 139.

Participants and settings

Proper use of the experimental method requires careful consideration of how participants are allocated to the various conditions. Suppose we found that participants learning in a quiet setting performed better than those learning in a noisy setting, but, by mistake, all the most intelligent participants were in the quiet condition and the least intelligent ones in the noise condition. We then wouldn't know whether the good performance in the quiet condition was due to quiet or to the cleverness of the participants. The main way of guarding against this possibility is by means of **randomisation**, in which participants are allocated at random. That helps to ensure that there are no systematic differences between the participants in the various conditions.

Numerous studies are carried out using students as participants, raising the issue of whether students are representative of society as a whole. For example, students tend to be more intelligent and much younger than most people. However, they are representative in the sense that about half of all students are male and half are female.

Advantages of the experimental method applied to laboratory experiments

The greatest advantage of the experimental method is that it allows us to establish causal (or cause-and-effect) relationships. The independent variable in an experiment is often regarded as a cause, and the dependent variable is the effect. We assume that, if *y* (e.g. many errors in recall) follows *x* (e.g. acoustically similar word list), then it is reasonable to infer that *x* caused *y*.

However, findings from studies based on the experimental method do *not* necessarily establish causality. For example, consider an imaginary study carried out in a hot country. Half the participants sleep in bedrooms with the windows open, and the other half sleep in bedrooms with the windows closed. Those sleeping in bedrooms with the windows open are more likely to catch malaria. Having the window open or closed is *relevant* to catching the disease, but it tells us nothing direct about the major causal factor in malaria (infected mosquitoes).

The other major advantage of the experimental method is known as **replicability**. If an experiment has been conducted in a carefully controlled way, other researchers should be able to repeat or replicate the findings.

Replication is important to confirm an experimental result. If the result is "real", it should be possible to obtain the same result when you repeat the experiment. However, if it was a fluke, it isn't likely to be repeatable. Therefore, it is highly desirable in research to replicate a study using precisely the same techniques and conditions. If the conditions aren't the same, it could explain why the results are not the same. This may allow us to make sense of the inconsistent findings from studies following up on Hofling et al.'s (1966) study on nurses obeying doctors when they shouldn't (see page 230).

Then there is the issue of objectivity. The experimental method applied to laboratory experiments is more objective than other methods. However, total objectivity is impossible

? What are the main obstacles to replication in research using human participants?

KEY TERMS

Extraneous variables: variables other than the independent variable that are not controlled and may affect the dependent variable (measure of behaviour) and so prevent us from interpreting our findings.

Randomisation: the allocation of participants to conditions on a random basis, i.e. totally unbiased distribution.

Replicability: the ability to repeat the methods used in a study and achieve the same findings.

KEY TERMS

Ecological validity: the extent to which research findings can be generalised to naturally occurring situations.

Mundane realism: the use of an artificial situation that closely resembles a natural situation.

Experimental realism: the use of an artificial situation in which participants become so involved that they are fooled into thinking the set-up is real rather than artificial.

Demand characteristics: features of an experiment that help participants to work out what is expected of them, and lead them to behave in certain predictable ways.

since the experimenter's interests, values, and judgements will always have some influence, and the control of all extraneous variables is impossible. Nevertheless, the experimental method offers the best chance of objectivity.

Weaknesses of the experimental method applied to laboratory experiments

The experimental method applied to laboratory experiments often lacks **ecological validity**, which is the extent to which experimental findings are applicable to everyday settings. The problem here was expressed in somewhat exaggerated terms by Heather (1976), who claimed the only thing learned from laboratory experiments is how people behave in laboratory experiments!

Carlsmith et al. (1976) drew a distinction between **mundane realism** and **experimental realism** (see Chapter 6). Experimental realism (where participants are fooled that an artificial set-up is real) may be more important than mundane realism (where an artificial situation closely resembles a real-life situation) in producing findings that generalise to real-life situations. In practice, laboratory experiments often lack mundane realism and experimental realism.

ACTIVITY: Mundane realism

Asch's famous line-matching experiment had experimental realism (see p. 215). Discuss with a partner or in a small group how you could adapt the experiment to increase its mundane realism, and produce a list of your recommendations.

Participants in psychological experiments usually try to perform the task set by the experimenter as well as they can in order to gain his or her approval.

An important reason why laboratory experiments are more artificial than other research methods is because the participants in laboratory experiments know their behaviour is being observed. One consequence of being observed is that the participants try to work out the experimenter's hypothesis, and then act accordingly. In this connection, Orne (1962) emphasised the importance of **demand characteristics**—the features of an experiment that "invite" participants to behave in certain predictable ways. Demand characteristics may help us to explain why Milgram (1963, 1974) found higher levels of obedience in his experiments at Yale University than in a run-down office building (65% vs 48%, respectively). Demand characteristics were also probably involved in Zimbardo's Stanford Prison Experiment, where the prison-like environment suggests that certain forms of behaviour were expected.

A LABORATORY EXPERIMENT: Eyewitness testimony

Loftus has run a large number of laboratory experiments looking at the factual accuracy of eyewitnesses' memory. Several of these involved participants looking at slides or film of car crashes. In one such experiment there were two conditions. Some of the participants were asked if they had seen any broken glass after the accident whereas others were asked if they had seen the broken glass. The only difference between the two groups was the wording, "any" or "the", with the latter suggesting the glass was there, thus being a leading question.

This type of experiment has been criticised as having low external/ecological validity and low mundane realism. Can you explain why this was a *laboratory* experiment, and exactly why it has those criticisms?

Another consequence of participants in laboratory experiments knowing they are being observed is **evaluation apprehension**, a term used by Rosenberg (1965). The basic idea is that most people are anxious about being observed by the experimenter, and want him/her to evaluate them favourably. This may lead them to behave in ways they wouldn't normally.

> In what way have you altered your own natural behaviour when you were aware of being observed? Was this because of evaluation apprehension or some other reason?

Laboratory experiments

Advantages:

- Establish cause-and-effect relationships
- Allow for replication
- Good control of extraneous variables

Weaknesses:

- Artificial
- Participants know they are being observed (demand characteristics and evaluation apprehension)
- Low in external validity
- Lack ecological validity

ACTIVITY: Laboratory experiments

To apply what you have learnt, find a study to illustrate each of the advantages and weaknesses of laboratory experiments (e.g. Asch's 1951, 1956 experiment has been replicated many times, thus showing it is reliable).

Field Experiments

Field experiments are carried out in natural settings such as in the street, in a school, or at work. Some field experiments (e.g. Hofling et al., 1966) have focused on obedience to authority (see p. 230). Another example is a study by Shotland and Straw (1976). They arranged for a man and a woman to stage an argument and a fight fairly close to a number of bystanders. In one condition, the woman screamed, "I don't know you!" In a second condition, she screamed, "I don't know why I ever married you!" When the bystanders thought the fight involved strangers, 65% of them intervened, against only 19% when they thought it involved a married couple. Thus, the experiment showed that people were less likely to lend a helping hand when it was a "lovers' quarrel" than when it was not.

Field experiments, like laboratory experiments, involve direct control of the independent variable by the experimenter and also direct allocation of participants to conditions. Thus, causal relationships can be determined (provided the experiment is carried out carefully and extraneous variables are avoided!). Field experiments are also reasonably well controlled, which means they can be replicated.

Advantages of field experiments

What are the advantages of field experiments? First, the behaviour of the participants is often more *typical* of their normal behaviour and less artificial than in laboratory experiments. In other words, field experiments tend to have high ecological validity. These advantages occur because the participants aren't aware they are taking part in an experiment.

Second, it is often possible to establish cause-and-effect relations. This is the case because the researcher is able to control the independent variable.

Third, there is a low risk of problems such as demand characteristics and evaluation apprehension. This advantage stems from the participants' lack of awareness that their behaviour is being measured by the researcher.

Weaknesses of field experiments

What are the weaknesses of field experiments? First, it is hard to eliminate extraneous variables in the field, because the researcher has much less control over the situation than is the case

KEY TERMS

Evaluation apprehension: concern felt by research participants that their performance is being judged.

Field experiment: a study in which the experimental method is used in a more naturalistic situation.

> **A FIELD EXPERIMENT: Prejudice**
>
> A study in 2001 found that people were less likely to help gays and lesbians compared to heterosexuals. How was this done? Researchers telephoned over 200 British men and women at home and said it was a wrong number, but asked if the participant would make a call on to the caller's partner. This partner was of course a confederate, and was either same-sex or opposite-sex, to give the impression of a gay/lesbian or heterosexual partnership. The apparently heterosexual callers were most likely to receive the requested help, and the apparently gay men the least likely, with the apparently lesbian women in between.
>
> Can you think what extraneous variables might have had an effect here in producing these findings?

under laboratory conditions. This can be a serious weakness that prevents the researcher from establishing cause-and-effect relations.

Second, it is often hard (or impossible) to ensure that participants are allocated at random to the various condition.

Third, it is hard to obtain large amounts of very detailed information from participants. Field experiments are limited in this way because (1) it is generally not possible to introduce bulky equipment into a natural setting, and (2) the participants in a field experiment are likely to realise they are taking part in an experiment if attempts are made to obtain a lot of information from them.

Fourth, field experiments pose ethical issues. Most field experiments don't lend themselves to obtaining informed consent from the participants. For example, the study by Shotland and Straw (1976) would have been rendered meaningless if the participants had been asked beforehand to give their consent to witnessing a staged quarrel! In addition, it isn't possible to offer the **right to withdraw**—participants who don't know they are taking part in an experiment can't be given the right to withdraw from it!

Field experiments

Advantages:

- Behaviour of participants more typical than in a laboratory experiment, high ecological validity
- Establishes cause-and-effect relationships
- Participants not aware they are being observed so low risk of demand characteristics and evaluation apprehension

Weaknesses:

- Ethical issues, such as a lack of voluntary informed consent
- Low in internal validity, poor control

> **ACTIVITY: Field experiments**
>
> To apply your knowledge of field experiments, describe a field study and clearly identify its advantages and disadvantages (e.g. Hofling et al., 1966).

Natural Experiments

Another form of experimental method involves using a naturally occurring event for research purposes. Such **natural experiments** don't qualify as genuine experiments. Use of the experimental method requires that the independent variable is *manipulated* by the experimenter.

An example of a natural experiment is a study reported by Charlton (1998). It was based on the introduction of television to the island of St. Helena, and was designed to see whether television causes violence. Its inhabitants received television for the first time in 1995 (the naturally occurring event), but there was no evidence of any negative effects on the children.

Another example of a natural experiment is the study by Hodges and Tizard (1989; see page 87) on the long-term effects of privation in children taken into care when very young. Some

> **KEY TERMS**
>
> **Right to withdraw:** the basic right of participants in a research study to stop their involvement at any point, and to withdraw their results if they wish to do so.
>
> **Natural experiment:** a type of experiment where use is made of some naturally occurring variable(s).

of the children were adopted whereas others returned to their natural home. The decision about whether each child should be adopted or restored to his/her home was the naturally occurring event outside the control of the researchers. Contrary to what might have been expected, the adopted children on average showed better emotional adjustment than the restored children.

> **A NATURAL EXPERIMENT: Exam stress**
>
> So do you think exams are stressful? How would we test this? A natural experiment could ask for student volunteers to give blood samples 8 weeks before exams and again after the first exam. Analysis would give levels of the stress hormones adrenaline, noradrenaline, and cortisol.
>
> - What would you expect to see happen? Can you write this as a hypothesis?
> - Can you identify the IV, the variable that was changing naturally (because this would be a natural experiment)?
> - And what would be the DV, the variable that the research team measured?

What might be the practical uses of results such as those from the Mount St Helens study?

Advantages of natural experiments

What are the advantages of natural experiments? First, the participants in natural experiments are often not aware they are taking part in an experiment (even though they often know their behaviour is being observed), so they behave fairly naturally.

Second, natural experiments allow us to study the effects on behaviour of independent variables it would be unethical for the experimenter to manipulate. For example, consider the study by Hodges and Tizard (1989). No ethical committee would have allowed children to be taken into care and then either adopted or restored to their natural home to satisfy the researchers' requirements.

Third, natural experiments are generally high in ecological validity. This is the case because natural experiments involve observing behaviour under real-life conditions.

Natural experiments are such a good way of doing research, so why are there so few actually done?

Weaknesses of natural experiments

What are the weaknesses of natural experiments? First, the participants aren't assigned at random to conditions. As a result, observed differences in behaviour between groups may be due to differences in the types of participants in the groups rather than to the effects of the independent variable. For example, in the study by Hodges and Tizard (1989), the children who were adopted were *initially* better adjusted than the children who were restored to their natural home. Thus, the finding that the adopted children subsequently showed better emotional adjustment than the restored children may be due to their personality or early experiences rather than to the fact that they were adopted.

Second, the researcher doesn't have control over the situation. As a result, there may be extraneous variables that make it hard or impossible to decide whether the natural event was responsible for the findings. For example, the introduction of television into St. Helena may have coincided with other changes in that society that helped to prevent television from having negative effects on the children.

Third, and linked to the second point, the lack of control over the situation often means that it isn't possible to establish cause-and-effect relations.

Natural experiments

Advantages	Weaknesses
• Participants behave naturally	• IV not directly manipulated
• Investigate the effects of independent variables that it would be unethical to manipulate	• Participants not allocated at random to conditions
• High in ecological validity	• Difficult to identify what aspects of the independent variable have caused the effects on behaviour
	• Not possible to establish cause and effect

? When would one have to use a correlational design?

Studies Using a Correlational Analysis

The essence of the correlational approach is that it involves the assessment of the relationship between two variables (known as **co-variables**) obtained from the same individuals. For example, we could test the hypothesis that watching violence on television leads to aggressive behaviour by obtaining information from a number of people about: (1) the amount of violent television they watched (one variable), and (2) the extent to which they behaved aggressively in various situations (second variable).

If the above hypothesis is correct, those who have seen the most violence on television would tend to be the most aggressive. In other words, this study would be looking for a **correlation**, or association, between watching violent programmes and being aggressive. The closer the link between them, the greater would be the correlation or association.

One of the best-known uses of the correlational approach is in the study of life events and stress-related illnesses. For example, Rahe et al. (1970; see page 185) found there was a significant positive correlation between the stress of recent life events (taking account of the number and severity of these events) and physical illness. These findings support those of many other researchers.

The two examples we have discussed both involve focusing on positive correlations. In a positive correlation as scores on one variable increase so do scores on the other variable. There are also negative correlations. With negative correlations as scores on one variable increase, scores on the other variable decrease. An example is the study by Marmot et al. (1997; see page 193). They assessed job control and stress-related illness in thousands of workers. As job control increased, stress-related illness decreased.

There is more on the presentation of correlational information in the section on scattergrams (see pages 159 and 160). There you can see examples of positive and negative correlations.

> **A CORRELATIONAL ANALYSIS: Television violence and aggressive behaviour**
>
> Positive correlations between hours of television violence watched and actual aggressive behaviour for children and adolescents are shown by the majority of correlational analyses on this topic. Such research has been done in many countries including Poland, the UK, Finland, Australia, and the USA. But does this mean that watching violence on TV actually causes people to become more hostile in their behaviour? One important point is that correlations cannot be used to infer cause and effect, because they merely show a link that may, or may not, be causal. For example, it is possible that people who are naturally more aggressive prefer to watch violent programmes, as they find them more enjoyable, more exciting. And another point in this research area is that although studying in a wide range of countries seems to have allowed for cultural relativism, in fact these are all Western industrialised types of culture and so there may be cross-cultural differences that have not been demonstrated.

Advantages of correlational studies

What are the advantages of correlational methods? First, correlational methods allow us to see that there is a relationship between two variables. This doesn't prove that one variable is causing the other, but is a very useful starting point for further research.

Second, many hypotheses can't be examined directly by means of experimental designs. For example, the hypothesis that life events cause various physical diseases can't be tested by forcing some people to experience lots of negative events! All we can do is examine correlations or associations between the number and severity of negative life events and the probability of suffering from various diseases.

Third, we can obtain large amounts of data on a number of variables in a correlational study much more rapidly and efficiently than using experimental designs. For example, **questionnaires** permit researchers to study the associations between aggressive behaviour and a wide range of activities (such as watching violent films in the cinema, reading violent books, being frustrated at work or at home).

KEY TERMS

Co-variables: the variables involved in a correlational study that may vary together (co-vary).

Correlation: an association that is found between two variables.

Questionnaire: a survey requiring written answers.

Fourth, correlational research *can* produce reasonably definite information about causal relationships if there is *no* association between the two co-variables. For example, if there were no association at all between stressful life events and physical illness, this would suggest that physical illnesses are *not* caused by stressful life events.

Fifth, **correlational analysis** is used in prediction. If you find that two variables are correlated, you can predict one from another. It is also a useful method when manipulation of variables is impossible.

Weaknesses of correlational studies

What are the weaknesses of correlational studies? First, and most importantly, correlational designs make it hard (or impossible) to establish cause and effect. In our first example, the existence of an association between the amount of television violence watched and aggressive behaviour would be consistent with the hypothesis that watching violent

Correlation or causation?

programmes can *cause* aggressive behaviour. However, it could equally be that aggressive individuals may choose to watch more violent programmes than those who are less aggressive, in other words the causality operates in the other direction. Or there is a third variable accounting for the association between watching violent programmes and aggressive behaviour, e.g. people in disadvantaged families may watch more television and their deprived circumstances may also cause them to behave aggressively. If that were the case, then the number of violent television programmes watched might have no direct effect at all on aggressive behaviour.

Second, and linked to the first point, researchers don't control or manipulate any aspect of the situation with correlational studies. This is the main reason why it is so hard to interpret the findings that emerge from such studies.

Third, correlations are limited in what they tell us about the relationship between two variables. More specifically, they assess linear relationships in which there is a simple linear (straight) relationship between two variables. In the real world, however, there are often more complex relationships but these aren't identified by correlations. For example, consider the relationship between weight and physical health. Physical health is relatively poor among those who are severely underweight or overweight and highest in those of intermediate weight. This inverted-U or curvilinear relationship between weight and physical health can't be assessed using correlations.

Correlational studies

Advantages

- Allow us to see that there is a relationship between two variables
- Allow study of hypotheses that cannot be examined directly
- More data on more variables can be collected more quickly than in an experimental set-up
- Problems of interpretation are reduced when no association is found

Weaknesses

- Cause and effect cannot be established
- Interpretation of results is difficult
- Direction of causality is uncertain
- Variables other than the one of interest may be operating

ACTIVITY: Correlational studies

To apply what you have learnt, consider a correlational study that looks at the relationship between stress and the immune system, or stress and personality. With reference to this study identify the advantages and disadvantages as outlined above.

KEY TERM

Correlational analysis: testing a hypothesis using an association that is found between two variables.

Observational Techniques

Behaviour is observed in virtually every psychological study. For example, in Milgram's (1963; see Chapter 6) research on obedience to authority, a film record was made of the participants' behaviour so that their emotional states could be observed. However, we will consider studies in which **observational techniques** are of central importance.

There are several observational techniques (Coolican, 2004). However, the three most important techniques are as follows:

1. **Controlled observations** involve the researcher exercising control over the environment in which the observations are made.
2. **Naturalistic observations** involve observations of participants in natural situations without any direct intervention from the observers.
3. **Participant observations** involve natural situations in which the observer is directly involved in the interactions of the participants, who are typically group members.

General issues

We will consider each of these types of observational study shortly. However, some general issues apply to all of them. For example, how can observers avoid being overloaded in their attempts to record their observations of others' behaviour? One approach is **event sampling**, focusing only on actions or events of particular interest to the researcher. Another approach is **time sampling**, where observations are made only during specified time periods (e.g. the first 10 minutes of each hour). Yet another approach is **point sampling**, where one individual is observed in order to categorise their current behaviour, after which a second individual is observed, and so on.

Another general issue relates to the information recorded by the observer or observers. In the past, observers typically made immediate ratings of participants' behaviour using pre-determined categories. More recently, however, there has been increased use of video or film recording, so ratings can be made in a more leisurely way and re-checked if necessary.

There is a more detailed discussion of the development and use of behavioural categories in observational studies later in the chapter. Here we note that it is important for researchers to develop precise and unambiguous categories. After that, they need to ensure observers are trained in the use of the categories being used to produce high reliability or consistency of measurement. Reliability can be assessed by correlating the observational records of two or more observers, producing a measure of inter-observer reliability.

One reason why it is important to ensure the categories used are very clear is because of the dangers of observer bias. **Observer bias** occurs when an observer's record of what he/she has observed is distorted by his/her expectations. For example, the same behaviour displayed by a boy and a girl might be more likely to be categorised as aggressive when produced by a boy because of stereotypes about male aggression.

There is a final general issue. Researchers setting up an observational study must decide whether participants will be aware of being observed. The disadvantage with participants

When conducting observational studies, researchers need to decide whether participants will be aware that they are being observed, as this may affect their behaviour.

knowing they are being observed is that this knowledge may very well influence their behaviour. For example, Zegoib et al. (1975) found that mothers who knew they were observed interacted more with their children and behaved more warmly towards them than did mothers who didn't know. The main disadvantage with participants not knowing they are being observed is that it is regarded as unethical for participants not to give full informed consent to their involvement in a study.

Controlled observations

Many studies (especially in developmental psychology) involve controlled observations using situations subject to at least some experimental control. For example, Ainsworth and Bell (1970; see Chapter 3) carried out a laboratory study in which infants were observed as they responded to a carefully organised sequence of events involving the mother/caregiver leaving the infant and returning. These observations were used to categorise the infants' behaviour in terms of attachment style.

Advantages of controlled observations

What are the advantages of controlled observations? First, controlled observations are often used in the context of a laboratory experiment. In principle, this can provide the positive features of the experimental method (e.g. possibility to infer cause-and-effect relationships) together with detailed observational information.

> ? What advantages might be gained by observing children in a naturalistic environment rather than in a laboratory?

Second, if the situation is well controlled, there is less risk of unwanted extraneous variables influencing participants' behaviour than is the case with naturalistic or participant observations. This is important because it increases the researcher's ability to interpret his/her findings.

Third, richer and more complete information is often obtained from studies using controlled observations than from conventional experimental studies in which participants are only required to produce limited responses.

Weaknesses of controlled observations

The method of controlled observations has various weaknesses. First, carrying out studies in artificial situations (e.g. laboratories) can influence the participants' behaviour. This may be especially the case with young children who can become anxious in a strange environment.

Second, the artificiality of the situation may make it hard to generalise the findings to more natural situations.

Third, there can be problems with controlled observations when participants know their behaviour is being observed. These problems include investigator effects (due to experimenter expectations) and demand characteristics (due to participant expectations).

> **A CONTROLLED OBSERVATION: Attachment and cuddly toys**
>
> Toddlers' attachment to their cuddly toys was investigated in an observational study. Their mothers were asked about each child's favourite toys. Then, with their mothers nearby, the toddlers were assessed under varying levels of situational stressfulness, and the preferred toys in each situation were noted. As expected, the children's preference for familiar toys increased as the stressfulness of their situation increased.
>
> What do you think of the ethics of such experiments? What precautions would you take to make sure the participants were always well looked after?

Naturalistic observations

Naturalistic observations involve methods designed to examine behaviour in natural situations *without* the experimenter interfering. This approach was developed by ethologists such as Lorenz. They studied non-human species in their natural habitat and discovered much about the animals' behaviour.

An example of the use of naturalistic observations in human research is the attachment study by Anderson (1972). He observed children in a London park and noticed it was very unusual to see a child under the age of 3 wandering more than 200 feet from his/her mother before returning.

Naturalistic observations were also used by Schaffer and Emerson (1964), who carried out a **longitudinal** observational study on children. They found children differed considerably in their attachment behaviour. However, most children develop fairly strong attachments to one or more adults during early childhood.

> **KEY TERMS**
>
> **Longitudinal:** over an extended period of time, especially with reference to studies.

Naturalistic observation, for example, observing children's behaviour in a playground, can provide more extensive information than a laboratory study. However, the participants' behaviour may alter if they are aware that they are being observed.

KEY TERMS

Undisclosed observation: an observational study where the participants have not been informed that it is taking place.

A NATURALISTIC OBSERVATION: Social behaviour

A lot of research puts people into unusual settings or situations where we cannot be sure we are seeing real-life behaviours. This is a justification for doing naturalistic observations, seeing natural everyday behaviour. It is also a strategy for some very sensitive research areas. For example, social behaviours of preschool children who have a history of abuse can be observed and compared with those of children with no such history. The results of these observations of children at play have shown that the abused children made fewer social interactions, were more withdrawn, and when they did interact they used more negative behaviours such as aggression, compared to the other group.

How would you decide what counted as negative behaviours, as aggression? How would you set up your behavioural categories so that you could use several observers yet have reliable data?

What factors or issues might cause difficulties in observing people like this?

Advantages of naturalistic observations

Here are the main advantages of naturalistic observations. First, if the participants are unaware that they are being observed, this method provides a way of observing people behaving naturally. This removes problems from demand characteristics (guessing what the experiment is about) or evaluation apprehension (seeking the approval of the researcher).

Second, many studies based on naturalistic observations provide richer and fuller information than typical laboratory experiments. For example, Schaffer and Emerson's (1964) naturalistic observations on attachment behaviour in children can be compared with Ainsworth and Bell's (1970) structural observation research (see Chapter 3). Schaffer and Emerson's approach allowed them to show that young children often form multiple important attachments, an important finding not considered by Ainsworth and Bell.

Third, the fact that people's behaviour is being observed in real-life situations means that it is likely that the findings will have ecological validity.

Fourth, it is sometimes possible to use naturalistic observations when other methods can't be used (when participants can't be disrupted at work). Naturalistic observations may work better than other methods with children and non-human animals.

Weaknesses of naturalistic observations

Here are the most important weaknesses of naturalistic observations. First, the experimenter has essentially no control over the situation. This means that there may be extraneous variables involved, which makes it very hard (or impossible) to decide what caused the participants to behave as they did. Second, the participants are often aware they are being observed and so their behaviour isn't natural. Note, however, that this is also true of most other kinds of research.

Third, there can be problems of replication with studies of naturalistic observations. For example, consider naturalistic observations carried out in schools. There are enormous differences among schools, and this is likely to produce large differences in observational data across schools.

Fourth, naturalistic observations pose ethical issues if the participants don't realise their behaviour is being observed (**undisclosed observation**). This can happen if one-way mirrors are used or participants are observed in public places and voluntary informed consent isn't obtained.

ACTIVITY: Naturalistic observations

This could be done in small groups. People often assume that boys' play is rougher than girls' play. This is a casual observation, but you could devise a hypothesis from it, then operationalise this. How would you do your observations, and how would you ensure inter-observer reliability? What behavioural categories would you use? What might be problems in doing this naturalistic observation? One person should act as the recorder and make a list of what the group says, and this could then be shared with other groups.

Participant observations

The extent of the observer's participation in the participants' activities can vary enormously. At one extreme, the observer may not disclose his/her research role in order to be accepted as a fully-fledged member of the group. At the other extreme, the observer may fully disclose his/her role and act primarily as an observer in his/her dealing with the group.

We will discuss very briefly two studies involving participant observations. Whyte (1943) joined an Italian street gang in Chicago, and became a participant observer. He didn't indicate he was a researcher, but simply said he was writing a book about the area. The problem he encountered in interpreting his observations was that his presence in the gang influenced their behaviour. One gang member expressed this point as follows: "You've slowed me down plenty since you've been down here. Now, when I do something, I have to think what Bill Whyte would want to know about it and how I can explain it."

Try to fit in as a member of the group and remain detached as an observer.

Festinger et al. (1956) became participant observers by joining a religious sect that believed the world was about to come to an end. When the world didn't end on the day the sect members thought it would, their leader argued they had saved the world through their faith. The participants didn't reveal to the sect members that they were researchers.

A PARTICIPANT OBSERVATION: **Football**

Football fans—are they supporters or are they hooligans? Much of what is reported in the media might suggest the latter, but when Marsh (Marsh et al., 1996) joined supporters' clubs and attended games to do his participant observations he found that there was a clear social order among the fans, and an understood set of social norms about what behaviours were and were not acceptable. For example, aggressive chants and gestures were acceptable, but actual violent contact was not. These findings did not apply to a minority who attended games not for the actual football but for opportunities to fight, but Marsh focused on the vast majority of genuine supporters.

Do you think it is ethically acceptable to join an organisation in order to observe people without their consent? Why do some researchers do this, and what problems might arise if consent was sought?

Advantages of participant observations

Here are some of the main advantages of participant observations. First, studies involving such observations are generally high in ecological validity because groups are observed in real-life settings. Second, some studies using participant observations (e.g. Whyte's, 1943, study of an Italian street gang) are long-lasting, which helps to ensure that detailed and rich information is obtained.

Third, in studies such as those of Whyte (1943) and Festinger et al. (1956), it would have been extremely difficult for useful research to have been carried out by researchers who didn't join the street gang or the religious sect, respectively.

Fourth, it is often easy to interpret the participants' behaviour because it has been observed over long periods of time in various situations.

Weaknesses of participant observations

There are various weaknesses with the use of participant observations. First, there are ethical problems about researchers deceiving the members of groups in order to join them. There is an obvious failure to obtain fully informed consent from group members.

Second, the presence of a participant observer can change and distort the behaviour of group members. This is shown in the quotation above from Whyte's (1943) study.

? What ethical issues would you flag up for participant observation research? And what issue of validity could there be?

? Sometimes it is not possible to write field notes as events are happening. What does memory research tell us about the usefulness and accuracy of notes written after the event?

Third, there can be real problems concerning the accuracy and objectivity of the reports produced by participant observers. Participant observers who have not disclosed their research role generally write down what happened some time after any given event so as not to arouse suspicion. In addition, if participant observers become involved with the group they are observing, this may bias their reports.

Self-Report Techniques Including Interview and Questionnaire

Non-psychologists often think the best way to understand others' behaviour is by asking them about it. This can be done in various ways including the use of interview and questionnaire techniques. It is indisputable that much of value can be learned in this way. However, there are two major problems with **self-report techniques**:

(1) Most people want to create a favourable opinion of themselves and this may lead them to distort their answers to personal questions.
(2) Many people don't understand themselves very well, and so their self-reports may not be very informative.

Interview techniques

Interviews come in many different shapes and sizes. They differ in terms of the amount of structure built into the interview and the types of questions asked. Coolican (2004) identified several types of interview of which the following are the most important:

- *Non-directive interviews*: These possess the least structure, with the person being interviewed (the interviewee) being free to discuss almost anything he/she wants. The interviewer guides the discussion and encourages the interviewee to be more forthcoming. Such interviews are used in the treatment of mental disorders but are of less relevance to research.
- *Semi-structured or guided interviews*: These possess a moderate amount of structure. The interviewer identifies the issues to be addressed beforehand. During the interview, further decisions are made about how and when to raise these issues. All interviewees are asked similar questions, but the precise questions vary from interviewee to interviewee.
- *Clinical interviews*: These resemble guided interviews. All the interviewees are asked the same initial questions, but the choice of follow-up questions depends on the answers given. The researcher can be given the flexibility to ask questions in various ways. Such interviews are often used by clinical psychologists to assess patients with mental disorders. Clinical interviews give interviewers the flexibility to explore interesting or unexpected answers.
- *Fully structured interviews*: In this type of interview, a standard set of questions is asked in the same fixed order to all interviewees. The interviewees are only allowed to choose their answers from a restricted set of possibilities (e.g. "Yes", "No", "Don't know"). As Coolican (2004, p. 153) pointed out, "This approach is hardly an interview worth the name at all. It is a face-to-face data-gathering technique, but could be conducted by telephone or by post."

? Have you ever been interviewed while out shopping? How would you classify this interview style?

ACTIVITY: Interview technique

Divide the class into small groups and ask each group to prepare one kind of interview technique. They should present a short demonstration to the class. Which ones worked best? What problems arose? Which would be the best ways to collect data?

Advantages of interviews

The precise advantages of interviews depend on the type of interview. Unstructured or non-directive interviews can produce very rich and personal information from the person being interviewed. It could be argued that this is often the case when therapists interview clients in order to assess their experiences and emotions. Most experimental studies focus on a very narrow aspect of behaviour, but non-directive interviews can range over a large number of topics within a manageable period of time.

Structured interviews can compare the responses of different interviewees, all of whom have been asked the same questions. Another advantage is good reliability, in that two different interviewers are likely to obtain similar responses from an interviewee when they ask exactly the

KEY TERMS

Self-report techniques: participants provide their own account of themselves, usually by means of questionnaires, surveys, or interviews.

Interview: a verbal research method in which the participant answers a series of questions.

same questions in the same order. In addition, there is a reasonable chance of being able to replicate the findings in another study. Finally, it is usually fairly easy to analyse the data obtained from structured interviews because the data tend to be in numerical form.

Weaknesses of interviews

Non-directive or unstructured interviews have a problem with the unsystematic variation of information obtained from different interviewees, making the data hard to analyse. Another weakness is that what the interviewee says is determined in a complex way by the *interaction* between him/her and the interviewer. For example, the gender, age, and personality of the interviewer may influence the course of the interview, making it hard to work out which of the interviewee's contributions are affected by the interviewer. Such influences are known as **interviewer bias**. Finally, the fact that the information obtained from interviewees is influenced by the interviewer means that the data obtained can be regarded as unreliable.

In structured interviews, what the interviewee says may be somewhat constrained and artificial because of the high level of structure built into the interview. Interviewees may find this off-putting, and it may lead them to give short, formal answers. In addition, there is none of the flexibility associated with unstructured interviews.

Three weaknesses are common to all the types of interview (with the first two also being common to most questionnaires). First, there is the issue of **social desirability bias** due to the fact that most people want to convey a positive impression of themselves. For example, people are much more willing to admit they are unhappy when filling in a questionnaire anonymously than when being interviewed (Eysenck, 1990).

Second, we can only extract information of which the interviewee is consciously aware. This is a significant weakness, because people are often unaware of the reasons why they behave in certain ways (Nisbett & Wilson, 1977).

Third, many interviewers lack some of the skills necessary to conduct interviews successfully. Good interviewers can make an interview seem natural, are sensitive to non-verbal cues, and have well-developed listening skills (Coolican, 2004).

> **?** How would research results be affected by the possibility that people might decide to give the socially acceptable response to statements such as "Smacking children is an appropriate form of punishment"?

AN INTERVIEW: Gender stereotypes

We are all familiar with gender stereotypes, but when do we start learning this type of social norm? One study showed that 5-year-old children in the USA already have well-established gender stereotypes. These children were read short stories in which the main character was described by "masculine" adjectives (e.g. tough, forceful) or "female" ones (e.g. emotional, excitable). Then each child was interviewed and asked about whether the characters were male or female. Almost all of the children were clear which sex the character belonged to.

If you were going to replicate this study what would you do as a pilot study, and why would you be doing one?

People adjust what they say to fit the circumstances.

Questionnaire techniques

What happens with use of questionnaire techniques is that participants are given a set of questions together with instructions about how to record their answers. In principle, questionnaires can be used to explore an almost endless range of issues. In practice, however, most questionnaires focus on an individual's personality or his/her attitudes and beliefs.

The types of items found in questionnaires can vary considerably. At one extreme, there are fixed-choice items (sometimes known as closed questions), which require respondents to select from a small number of choices (e.g. Yes or No). At the other extreme, there are open-ended items, which give respondents great flexibility in their responses.

Most questionnaires use fixed-choice items. Such items are easier to score and tend to produce more reliable or consistent data. However, open-ended items have their own advantages. For example, they are more realistic, in that in everyday life we can generally answer questions in our own way, and they produce richer information than fixed-choice questions.

As is discussed later in the chapter, it is harder to produce good questionnaires than might be imagined. Coolican (2004) identifies the following common mistakes that plague questionnaire construction:

- *Complexity*: the item is difficult to understand.
- *Ambiguity*: the item can be interpreted in more than one way.
- *Double-barrelled items*: the item effectively contains two questions but the respondent must give an overall "Yes" or "No" response. For example, "Global warming is definitely happening and huge resources should be put into doing something about it."
- *Leading questions*: the item contains within it the implication that a certain response is expected. For example, "Don't you think that this government is discredited?"

Advantages of questionnaires

One of the main advantages of questionnaires is that large amounts of data can be collected rapidly at relatively little cost.

Second, we can explore almost any aspect of personality and any attitudes or beliefs using questionnaires. Thus, questionnaire techniques are very versatile.

Third, many questionnaires have high reliability or consistency and reasonable validity. For example, there is a fairly strong relationship between people's attitudes towards major political parties and their actual voting behaviour (Franzoi, 1996). High reliability is more common with fixed-choice or closed questions than with open-ended items.

Fourth, open-ended items have the advantage that they can be a rich source of information about the interviewee. Such items allow the interviewee to answer questions in their preferred way.

Weaknesses of questionnaires

Questionnaires possess various weaknesses. First, people may be inclined to pretend that their personalities and their attitudes are more desirable than they actually are—social desirability bias.

Second, people may lack conscious awareness of their true personality and attitudes. You must have met people who have little or no idea of the impact they have on others.

Third, many questionnaires are poorly constructed and so lack reliability or consistency and validity. Problems of reliability are especially likely with open-ended items. It is also hard with

? Think back to what you learned about eyewitness testimony. How might Loftus' work relate to researching by asking questions? What would researchers have to be very careful about in forming questions for the interview?

A QUESTIONNAIRE: Difference smells

We know that even though our sense of smell isn't good scents still are important, especially when they trigger memories. One research study looked at memories of a visit to the Jorvik Viking Centre in York where different smells, e.g. of a fish market, are part of the experience. Participants had visited the centre some years before, and were given the questionnaire about that experience either with or without a selection of bottled smells from the centre. The findings showed much better recall with the smells than without them, supporting the idea that these smells acted as memory cues.

How do you think you would find participants for this sort of investigation? What are the advantages and disadvantages of this sort of sampling method?

open-ended items to make coherent sense of the very diverse answers provided by different participants.

Fourth, the use of fixed-choice or closed questions is rather artificial. People often find it hard to answer a complex question with "yes" or "no". The limited data obtained from such questions can mean that relatively little is discovered about an individual's personality or beliefs.

Fifth, participants may need to have high literacy skills to understand the precise meaning of the items on a questionnaire.

Interviews and questionnaires

Advantages:

- Unstructured interviews can be more revealing
- Structured interviews permit comparison between interviewees and facilitate replication
- Questionnaires allow for collection of large amounts of data

Weaknesses:

- Interviewer bias
- Social desirability bias
- People don't always know what they think
- Good interviewing requires skill

ACTIVITY: Interviews and questionnaires

To apply your knowledge, consider a study that has used the interview technique to obtain data (e.g. Friedman & Rosenman's, 1959 study on Type A behaviour and heart disease—see pages 195–196). Either obtain a copy of the original journal article to see what sort of questions were asked or try to design your own questions that might have been asked.

Case Studies

Case studies differ from the methods and techniques we have discussed so far because they involve the detailed investigation of a single individual or a small number of individuals. There are sometimes good reasons why it isn't feasible to use large numbers of participants in a study. For example, a busy clinician or therapist may find the behaviour of a given patient very revealing, but he/she may have no possibility of collecting data from other patients with the same disorder.

Case studies generally involve obtaining a very full picture of a given individual. This often includes obtaining a case history in which detailed information about the most significant events of the individual's life is obtained. Studies in which the emphasis is on the individual's past life are retrospective in that they are based on his/her memories of what has happened. Alternatively, case studies can be longitudinal. Such studies involve collecting data from an individual over a period of several months or even years.

Numerous different methods can be used in case studies. Semi-structured or clinical interviews are commonly used because they permit the researcher to obtain large amounts of data from the individual concerned relatively efficiently. These interviews can involve those who know the individual well in addition to the individual himself/herself. Sometimes observational methods are used as well.

Examples of case studies

Most of the best-known case studies involve patients with mental disorders and the information obtained was primarily based on interviews. Several case studies are discussed in various chapters of this book. In Chapter 3, for example, there is detailed information on Genie, a girl who was kept locked up in isolation for the first 13 years of her life. After being rescued, she developed very good spatial ability, but struggled to learn language. Sadly, she was subsequently sent to various foster homes, and was abused. Thus, the case study of Genie suggested that extreme privation for the first several years of life can have severe and permanent adverse effects.

One of the most famous case studies of all time is that of Anna O (see Chapter 7), who was investigated by Sigmund Freud. Anna had various physical symptoms (e.g. paralysis of her right hand and leg). According to Freud, the actual problems were psychological in nature and dated back to events connected with the death of her father years earlier. This case study convinced Freud of the power of mental causes to produce psychological and physical symptoms, as well as of the key role played by early life experiences in producing mental disorder.

Case studies are often used as a way of understanding unusual behaviours. What are the advantages and limitations of using this method of research?

A CASE STUDY: A professional musician

Case studies can be fascinating as they contain in-depth information about an individual participant or very small group, and great detail is possible. In one such study, a well-known professional musician known as CW who had suffered brain damage as a result of a rare infection in his hippocampus was monitored. The brain damage had affected his memory. Post-accident his LTM was still fine for knowledge acquired before the infection, such as speech, reading and writing, and playing music, but his STM was badly affected. Its duration was negligible and he had lost the ability to move information from his STM, his immediate awareness, into LTM. This meant that he had no knowledge of what had happened in the years since his accident, and at every moment he thought he had just become conscious for the first time.

While case studies are interesting, their problem is that we cannot generalise from one or two people to the population at large, and so cannot assume we have learned something that is true for each of us. Can you think of four specific reasons or individual differences that show why we should avoid such generalisations?

Advantages of case studies

Here are the main advantages of case studies:

- They can provide far more information about a specific individual than is usually obtained from studies involving groups of individuals. For example, very detailed information about Genie's intellectual and social development was obtained over a period of several years.
- Some case studies have been very influential because they have indicated there are serious problems with some prominent theory. There is a good example of this in Chapter 2. According to Atkinson and Shiffrin's (1968) multi-store model, there is only a single long-term memory system. This model was shown to be oversimplified by a case study on HM, an epileptic who received surgery. After the surgery he had very limited ability to acquire new declarative knowledge (e.g. knowing that he had muesli for breakfast; knowing he went to a local town last week). However, his skill learning (involving procedural knowledge) remained essentially intact. These findings suggest there are separate declarative and procedural memory systems.
- Case studies (even limited ones) can nevertheless provide useful insights that influence future theoretical developments. For example, there is the case study on Little Albert (Watson & Rayner, 1920; see page 274). This case study influenced the development of behaviour therapy—it showed that fears can be classically conditioned and suggested to behaviour therapists that fears can perhaps be eliminated through conditioning as well.
- Case studies often possess high ecological validity because the information is obtained under reasonably naturalistic conditions (e.g. in conversation).

Weaknesses of case studies

Here are the main weaknesses of case studies:

- Their greatest weakness is that what is true of a given individual may well not be true of other individuals. For example, the case study of Genie suggested that extreme privation causes severe long-term effects and greatly inhibits the development of language. However, other case studies suggest different conclusions. Soutter (1995) studied Tom, who was kept in a bare room for the first 10 years of his life. After being rescued, he became more emotionally expressive, he went to university, he made friends, and his general behaviour was normal.
- Of direct relevance to the above point is the issue of generalisation and drawing general conclusions from case studies. The individual may not be *representative* of individuals of the same age and gender. For example, there was evidence that Genie had very limited brain activity in the left hemisphere, which is very unusual. This can make the findings unreliable and invalid. Little Albert was not representative in that his personality was "on the whole stolid [passive] and unemotional" (Watson & Rayner, 1920, p. 1).

- Case studies based on individuals with mental disorders often involve lengthy and intimate interviews between patient and therapist. This can provide rich and informative data, but carries with it the potential weakness of bias on the therapist's part. For example, consider the case of Anna O, who was treated by Sigmund Freud (see Chapter 7). It is entirely possible that the questions that Freud asked her and the way he interpreted her answers were influenced by his own theoretical ideas.
- Another weakness with case studies is that of subjective selection (Coolican, 1994). The therapist or experimenter often only reports a small fraction of the information obtained, and what is selected may be influenced by his/her preconceptions.

> **ACTIVITY:**
> **Qualitative and quantitative data**
>
> List all the research methods covered in this section and, for each of them, say how they might produce qualitative and quantitative data.

Section Summary

The scientific approach
- Much research is scientific. The scientific method involves:
  - making observations;
  - formulating theories that generate hypotheses;
  - testing the hypotheses by designing research, then collecting data, and finally revising the theory in line with the new data.

Experimental method
- The key principle of the experimental method is that an independent variable is manipulated (with all extraneous variables controlled) in order to observe its effect on a dependent variable.
- Participants should be randomly allocated to conditions to further rule out extraneous variables.
- Use of the experimental method often (but by no means always) allows us to infer causality, and it aims to be replicable.
- The experimental method is used in laboratory and field experiments.

Laboratory experiments
- Advantages of laboratory experiments:
  - Laboratory experiments permit greater removal of extraneous variables.
  - They also allow more detailed data collection than field experiments.
- However, they tend to be artificial (lacking **external validity** and mundane realism).
- This artificiality can be compensated for by increased experimental realism (**internal validity**).
- Other concerns include:
  - The problems arising from knowing you are being observed (demand characteristics and evaluation apprehension).
  - Ethical issues such as being obedient to authority and the right to withdraw.

Field experiments
- Advantages of field experiments:
  - Field experiments are less artificial than laboratory experiments.
  - They suffer less from factors such as demand characteristics and evaluation apprehension.
- Weaknesses of field experiments:
  - They are less controlled.
  - They create ethical problems in terms of lack of informed consent.

Natural experiments
- Natural experiments resemble experiments but involve some naturally occurring independent variable rather than an independent variable under the control of the researcher.

> **KEY TERMS**
>
> **External validity:** the validity of an experiment outside the research situation itself; the extent to which the findings of a research study are applicable to other situations, especially "everyday" situations.
>
> **Internal validity:** the validity of an experiment in terms of the context in which it is carried out; concerns events within the experiment as distinct from external validity.

- Advantages of natural experiments:
  - One advantage of natural experiments is that participants are unaware they are taking part in an experiment, which prevents demand characteristics.
  - Natural experiments also permit the study of variables that couldn't ethically be manipulated by an experimenter.
- Weaknesses of natural experiments:
  - These include problems of interpreting the findings due to a lack of randomisation.
  - There is also an ethical concern about taking advantage of people at a time of possible high stress.
  - The presence of extraneous variables limits the ability to interpret the findings and it is hard to show cause-and-effect relations.

Studies using a correlational analysis

- Advantages of correlational analysis:
  - Many issues can only be studied by assessing correlations or associations between variables.
  - Correlational studies determine the extent that co-variables vary together, and offer the possibility of obtaining large amounts of data very rapidly.
- Weaknesses of correlational analysis:
  - Investigations using correlational analysis are less useful than experimental designs, because they don't permit inferences about causality.
  - In terms of ethical concerns, we should be wary of misinterpretations of correlational evidence.

Observational techniques

- It is important in observational studies to use unambiguous behavioural categories for recording participants' behaviour.
- Participants' behaviour is more natural if they are unaware of being observed, but this raises ethical issues due to lack of informed consent.
- Controlled observations occur in studies under experimental control. Advantages of controlled observations are:
  - Use of the experimental method permits inferences about cause and effect.
  - There is a reduced risk of extraneous variables compared to other types of observational study.
- Weaknesses of controlled observations are:
  - Use of artificial situations can reduce generalisability.
  - There can be investigator effects and demand characteristics.
- Naturalistic observations occur in natural situations without any interference from the researcher. Advantages of naturalistic observations are:
  - They provide a way of observing people behaving naturally.
  - They provide rich and full information about behaviour.
- Weaknesses of naturalistic observations are:
  - The researcher has no control over the situation.
  - There can be problems of replication.
- Participant observations occur in natural situations with the observer being more or less actively involved. Advantages of participant observations are:
  - There is flexibility in terms of the observer's involvement.
  - Participant observation is the most effective way of studying the behaviour of certain groups (e.g. street gangs).
- Weaknesses of participant observations are:
  - The presence of the participant observer distorts the behaviour of the group members.
  - The reports produced by participant observers are sometimes inaccurate and lacking in objectivity.

Self-report techniques
- There are several types of interview ranging from the unstructured to the fully structured.
- Unstructured interviews:
  - These are responsive to the personality, interests, and motivations of the interviewee and so tend to produce full information.
  - However, the data obtained tend to be unreliable.
- Structured interviews:
  - Structured interviews permit comparisons among interviewees, and they tend to be fairly reliable.
  - However, what the interviewee says can be constrained and artificial, and the data tend to be more quantitative.
- Questionnaire techniques involve presenting respondents with a set of fixed-choice or open-ended items.
- Fixed-choice items are more reliable but open-ended ones are more realistic.
- Advantages of questionnaires:
  - They are inexpensive and involve the rapid collection of much data.
  - Many questionnaires have good reliability and reasonable validity.
- Weaknesses of questionnaires:
  - Questionnaires can produce problems due to social desirability bias, and those completing questionnaires can only provide information of which they are consciously aware.
- Questionnaire techniques are mostly used in correlational studies, and so causal inferences cannot be drawn.

Case studies
- Case studies involve the collection of detailed information from a single individual or from a small number of individuals. They often (but by no means always) involve the use of interviews.
- Advantages of case studies:
  - They permit the collection of unusually detailed information about a given individual.
  - Some case studies have reported findings that are inconsistent with an influential theory.
  - Case studies can provide suggestive evidence that leads to the development of new theoretical approaches.
- Weaknesses of case studies:
  - They typically do not permit generalisation to any larger group or population.
  - Many individuals studied in case studies are not representative of any population.
  - The experimenter may exhibit bias in the way he/she collects information, especially when interview techniques are used.
  - There is a danger that the fraction of the collected information reported by the experimenter will be based on subjective (and biased) selection.

SECTION 8
INVESTIGATION DESIGN

In order to carry out a study successfully, care and attention must be devoted to each stage in its design and implementation. This section is concerned with these issues. We will focus mainly on *experimental designs*, although many of the same issues also apply to non-experimental designs. As we will see, several decisions need to be made when designing an experimental study.

Common sense recommends a quiet rather than a noisy place for study—but to test the hypothesis that noise interferes with learning requires an experimental design.

? In what way are research aims and hypotheses different?

Aims and Hypotheses

The first step when designing a study is to decide on the **aims** and **hypotheses** of the study. The aims are usually more general than the hypotheses. They help to explain the reasons for the investigator deciding to test some specific hypothesis or hypotheses. In other words, the aims tell us *why* a given study is being carried out, whereas the hypotheses tell us *what* the study is designed to test.

As an example, suppose we decide to test the general theoretical notion that to-be-learned information that is easy to organise will be better remembered than information that is hard to organise. We might present our participants with the same list of nouns (24 words with 4 words belonging to each of six categories) category by category or in random order (see Chapter 2). The main aim of this experiment would be to investigate the theory that organisation enhances memory. The *hypothesis* is more specific: "Free recall from long-term memory is higher when a categorised word list is presented category-by-category than when it is presented in random order."

Hypotheses

Experimental hypothesis

Most experimental research using the experimental method starts with someone thinking of an **experimental hypothesis** so they are clear about what they aim to prove or disprove. The experimental hypothesis is a prediction (or forecast) of what the researcher thinks will happen to the dependent variable when the independent variable changes. For example, "Loud noise will have an effect on people's ability to learn the information in a chapter of an introductory psychology textbook".

We have just seen that we talk about an experimental hypothesis in the context of a proper experiment. However, there is a more general term (**alternative hypothesis**) that can be used to refer to all hypotheses that aren't null hypotheses (see below). Thus, every experimental hypothesis is also an alternative hypothesis, but *not* every alternative hypothesis is also an experimental hypothesis. For example, we might carry out a correlational study, and form the hypothesis that Type A behaviour will be associated with coronary heart disease (see Chapter 5). That is an alternative hypothesis but *not* an experimental hypothesis.

There are two types of experimental or alternative hypothesis: directional and non-directional. A **directional hypothesis** predicts the *nature* of the effect of the independent variable on the dependent variable, e.g. "Loud noise will reduce people's ability to learn the information contained in the chapter of a textbook". In other words, such hypotheses predict not only that the independent variable will affect the dependent variable but also spell out precisely the *direction* of that effect. It is also known as a one-tailed hypothesis.

In contrast, a **non-directional hypothesis** predicts the independent variable will have an effect on the dependent variable, but the *direction* of the effect is not specified, e.g. "Loud noise will have an effect on people's ability to learn the information contained in the chapter of a textbook". This latter hypothesis (also known as a two-tailed hypothesis) allows for the possibility that loud noise might actually improve learning, perhaps by making people more alert.

So, a directional or one-tailed hypothesis states that the predicted direction in which the independent variable will influence the dependent variable (i.e. increase or decrease). In contrast, a non-directional or two-tailed hypothesis just predicts a change—but not its direction.

Null hypothesis

The **null hypothesis** simply states that the independent variable will have no effect on the dependent variable. For example, "Loud noise will have no effect on people's ability to learn the information contained in the chapter of the textbook". Sometimes it is easier to state the null hypothesis in relation to group differences. For example, "There will be no significant difference between groups a and b, and any observed differences will be due to chance factors". The purpose of most studies using the experimental method is to decide between the merits of the experimental hypothesis and the null hypothesis. Why do we need a null hypothesis when what we are interested in is the experimental hypothesis? The answer is *precision* and *proof*.

Consider the null hypothesis that loud noise will have no effect on people's learning ability. This is precise, because it predicts that the single most likely outcome is that performance will be equal in the loud noise and no-noise conditions. Failing that, there will probably only be a small difference between the two conditions, with the difference being equally likely to go in either direction.

In contrast, consider the experimental hypothesis that loud noise will reduce people's learning ability. This hypothesis is very imprecise, because it doesn't indicate *how much* learning will be impaired. This lack of precision makes it impossible to decide the exact extent to which the findings support (or fail to support) the experimental hypothesis.

If every time I toss a coin it comes down heads, we might form the hypothesis that there are heads on both sides of the coin. However, we can't prove this. The more heads we see, the more likely it would appear that the hypothesis is correct. However, if on one occasion we see tails, we have disproved the hypothesis. It is possible to disprove something but not to prove it. Therefore, we propose a null hypothesis that can be disproved (or rejected) and this implies we can accept the alternative hypothesis.

Variables

Experimental hypotheses predict that some aspect of the situation (e.g. the presence of loud noise) will have an effect on the participants' behaviour (e.g. their learning of the information in the chapter). The experimental hypothesis refers to an independent variable (IV) (the aspect of the experimental situation manipulated by the experimenter), for example, the presence versus absence of loud noise. The hypothesis also refers to a dependent variable (DV) (an aspect of the participants' behaviour measured or assessed by the experiment), for example, measuring learning.

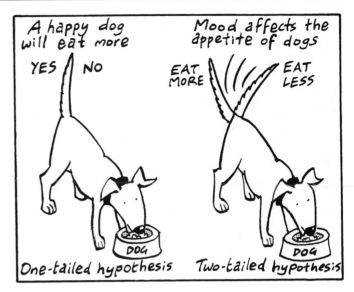

A happy dog will eat more — YES / NO — One-tailed hypothesis

Mood affects the appetite of dogs — EAT MORE / EAT LESS — Two-tailed hypothesis

ACTIVITY: Devising hypotheses

Devise suitable null and experimental hypotheses for the following:

- An investigator considers the effect of noise on students' ability to concentrate and complete a word-grid. One group only is subjected to the noise in the form of a distractor, i.e. a television programme.
- An investigator explores the view that there might be a link between the amount of television children watch and their behaviour at school.

ACTIVITY: Generating a hypothesis

1. Generate a hypothesis for each of these questions:
   - What are "football hooligans" really like?
   - Do children play differently at different ages?
   - What are the effects of caffeine on attention and concentration?
2. Identify the independent variable (IV) and dependent variable (DV) from each hypothesis.
3. Identify whether your hypotheses are one-tailed or two-tailed (remember, a one-tailed hypothesis predicts the direction of the effect of the IV on the DV, whereas a two-tailed hypothesis does not).
4. Write a null hypothesis for each of the experimental hypotheses.

KEY TERM

Null hypothesis: a hypothesis which states that any findings are due to chance factors and do not reflect a true difference, effect, or relationship.

ACTIVITY: Independent and dependent variables

In order to confirm that you do understand what independent (IV) and dependent (DV) variables are, try identifying them in the following examples.

Remember:

- The DV depends on the IV.
- The IV is manipulated by the experimenter or varies naturally.
- The DV is the one we measure.

1. Long-term separation affects emotional development more than short-term separation. (The two variables are length of separation and emotional development.)
2. Participants conform more when the model is someone they respect. (The two variables are extent of conformity and degree of respect for the model.)
3. Participants remember more words before lunch than after lunch. (The two variables are number of words remembered and whether the test is before or after lunch.)
4. Boys are better than girls at throwing a ball. (The two variables are gender and ability to throw a ball.)
5. Physical attractiveness makes a person more likeable. (The two variables are the attractiveness of a person's photograph and whether they are rated as more or less likeable.)

See page 167 for the answers.

KEY TERMS

Independent groups design: a research design in which each participant is in one condition only. Each separate group of participants experiences different levels of the IV. Sometimes referred to as an unrelated or between-subjects design.

Random allocation: placing participants in different experimental conditions using random methods to ensure no differences between the groups.

Matched pairs design: a research design that matches participants on a one-to-one basis rather than as a whole group.

Repeated measures design: a research design in which the same participants appear in both or all groups or conditions.

In a nutshell, experimental hypotheses predict that a given independent variable will have some specified effect on a given dependent variable. However, null hypotheses do *not* do this. For example, consider the longitudinal study by Friedman and Rosenman (1974; see Chapter 5) on Type A and coronary heart disease. Their null hypothesis could have been expressed as follows: "There is no relation between personality (Type A vs Type B) and coronary heart disease."

Experimental Design

The second step in the research process is to identify an appropriate design. We will consider experimental design in this section. If we wish to compare two groups with respect to a given independent variable, they must not differ in any other important way. Suppose all the least able participants in a learning experiment received the loud noise, and all the most able ones received no noise. We wouldn't know whether it was the loud noise or the low ability level that was more responsible for poor learning performance. How should we select our participants so as to avoid this problem? There are *three* main methods.

1. **Independent groups design.** Each participant is selected for only one group (e.g. no noise or loud noise), most commonly by randomisation. This could involve using a random process such as tossing a coin to allocate one of two conditions for all participants, or you could let all participants draw slips of paper numbered 1 and 2 from a hat. This **random allocation** means that in most cases the participants in the two groups end up equivalent in ability, age, and so on. An example of a study using an independent groups design is the study by Loftus and Palmer (1974, see page 39) on eyewitness testimony. Each group was asked a different question concerning the speed of the cars involved in the accident.
2. **Matched pairs design.** Each participant is selected for only one group, but the participants in the two groups are matched for some relevant factor or factors (e.g. ability, sex, age). In our example, using information about the participants' ability would ensure that the two groups were matched in terms of range of ability. For instance, a study by Kiecolt-Glaser et al. (1995) on slowing of wound healing by psychological stress involved a matched pairs design (see Chapter 5). The group of women caring for a relative with Alzheimer's disease were matched with the control women in age and family income. This helped to ensure that differences between the groups in time for wound healing could be attributed to the stress of caregiving rather than some other factor.
3. **Repeated measures design.** Each participant appears in both groups, so there are exactly the same participants in each group. In our example, this would mean that each participant learns the chapter in the loud noise condition and also in the no-noise condition. We don't need to worry about the participants in one group being cleverer than those in the other group because the *same* people appear in both groups! An example of a study using a repeated measures design is the one by Peterson and Peterson (1959; see pages 23–24) on short-term forgetting at various retention intervals, in which all participants were tested at all retention intervals.

> ### ACTIVITY: Research designs
>
> For each of the three designs mentioned (independent design, matched pairs design, and repeated measures), find at least one study that illustrates the design. With the study you have chosen for repeated measures design, identify the measures that were taken to prevent order effects and explain how counterbalancing was achieved.

Counterbalancing

The main problem with using the repeated measures design is there may be order effects. Participants may perform better when they appear in the second group because they have gained useful information about the experiment or about the task, or less well because of tiredness or boredom. It would be hard to use the repeated measures design in our earlier example—participants are almost certain to show better learning of the chapter the second time they read it regardless of whether they are exposed to loud noise.

There is a way around the problem of order effects based on **counterbalancing**. Half the participants learn the chapter first in loud noise and then in no noise, whereas the other half learn the chapter first in no noise and then in loud noise. In that way, any order effects should be balanced out.

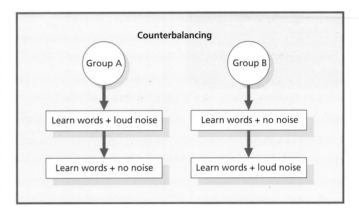

Experimental and control groups

In some experiments, one of the groups is used to provide baseline information. In our example, one group receives the **experimental treatment** (noise) whereas the other receives nothing (no noise). This latter group serves as the **control group**. Their behaviour informs us about how people behave when they aren't exposed to the experimental treatment so we can make comparisons. The group who have the noise are called the **experimental group**.

If a repeated measures design is used, then we have two different conditions: a control condition and an experimental condition.

Advantages and weaknesses of different research designs

Advantages of the independent groups design are that there are no order effects, and no participants are lost between trials. In addition, it can be used when a repeated measures design is inappropriate (e.g. when looking at gender differences). Finally, only one set of stimulus materials is required because each participant only appears in one condition.

Weaknesses of the independent groups design include the fact that there may be important **individual differences** between participants to start with (to minimise this there should be randomisation). In addition, you need more participants than with a repeated measures design.

The matched pairs design controls for some individual differences between participants and can be used when a repeated measures design is inappropriate. However, it is fairly difficult (and expensive!) to match participants in pairs. In addition, you need a large pool of participants from whom to select (more than with a repeated measures design).

Advantages of the repeated measures design are that it controls for *all* individual differences and it requires fewer participants than the other designs. The weaknesses are that it can't be used in studies in which participation in one condition has large effects on responses in the other, or in which

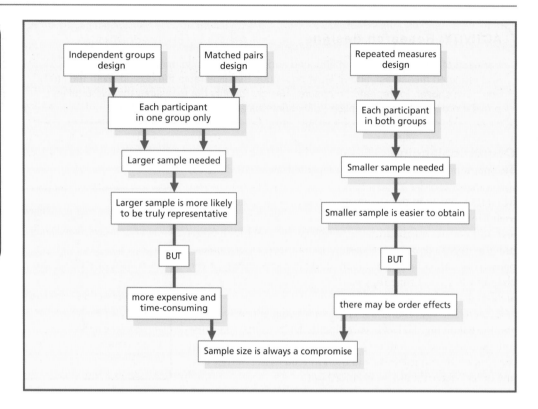

participants are likely to guess the purpose of the study, thus introducing problems with demand characteristics. There are also general problems with order effects, although counterbalancing can reduce them.

Design of Naturalistic Observations, Including the Development and Use of Behavioural Categories

Earlier in the chapter we discussed various observational techniques used in psychological research. An issue of central importance in observational research is the following: How can observers reduce the bewildering richness and variety of human behaviour to a manageable amount of information? The most common answer is that observers should use a set of behavioural categories (e.g. smiles; raises a fist; walks away), recording the frequency with which each of these types of behaviour is exhibited by each participant.

Naturalistic observations are observations that are made under natural or real-life conditions. It is important with such observations that observers should be unaware of the hypothesis or hypotheses being tested. Why is that? If observers know the hypothesis, they may see what they expect to see rather than what is actually happening. As discussed earlier, this is observer bias.

Development and use of categories

Various steps are involved in the development and use of behavioural categories. First, the researchers need to define the behavioural categories that are going to be used in the study. Decisions about which behavioural categories to use depend in part on the specific hypotheses the researcher wants to test. For example, if the researcher wants to test the hypothesis that boys are more aggressive than girls, it obviously makes sense to focus on behavioural categories relevant to verbal and non-verbal forms of aggression. The development of appropriate categories can be facilitated if the researcher spends some time observing boys and girls to see the various forms of aggressive behaviour they display.

Second, the researcher needs to decide whether the behavioural categories should be based on simple recording or on interpretation. For example, an observer may *record* that the participant has moved forwards or may *interpret* that movement as an aggressive action. In either case, what is important is that every behavioural category is unambiguously defined.

In practice, most behavioural categories used in research contain at least some interpretation. For example, Bales (1950) developed the interaction process analysis, which allows observers to categorise the interactions of members of a group. The observers record inferred meanings for the forms of behaviour shown by members of a group (e.g. "offers suggestion" or "gives information"). Categories based on simple recording are sometimes easier to use (e.g. it isn't hard to decide whether someone is moving forwards) than those based on interpretation. However, behavioural categories based on interpretation are more meaningful and are of more theoretical interest.

Third, when the behavioural categories have been decided on, the next step is to ensure the observers are properly trained in their use. It is of real importance to show that different observers use the behavioural categories in the same way. The issue here is that of reliability or consistency of measurement. Reliability can be assessed by asking two or more observers to produce observational records at the same time. When these records are correlated, we have a measure of **inter-observer reliability** (sometimes known as *inter-rater* or *inter-judge reliability*).

Reliability of measurement is very important. However, even if a system of behavioural categories is reliable, that doesn't prove it is valid in the sense of assessing what we want to assess. Validity can be shown by relating observers' records to other kinds of evidence. For example, Pepler and Craig (1995) had observers rate the aggressiveness of children's interactions using various behavioural categories. The children identified by observers as the most aggressive tended to be those rated as most aggressive by teachers, thus showing evidence for validity in the observers' records.

Design of Interviews and Questionnaires

In this section we focus on appropriate ways of designing questionnaires and interviews. We start by considering interview design and then move on to questionnaire design.

Interview design

As we saw earlier in the chapter, interviews vary in the amount of structure they possess. At one extreme, there are non-directive interviews, in which the interviewer allows the person being interviewed to discuss almost anything he/she wants. At the other extreme, there is the fully structured interview. In this type of interview, a standard set of questions is asked in the same fixed order to all interviewees, who are constrained in their possible answers to each question.

There is not much difference between a fully structured interview and a questionnaire. There are also many kinds of interviews between these two extremes—they possess some structure but lack the inflexibility of fully structured interviews.

Another difference between types of interviews concerns the nature of the questions asked. We can distinguish between closed and open questions. Closed questions require one of a small number of possible answers; example: "Do you approve of the government?" In contrast, open questions allow the interviewee considerable scope as to his/her answer; example: "What do you think about the government?" Open questions are associated with non-directive interviews and closed questions with structured interviews.

There are various types of interviews used for psychological experimentation, from non-directive interviews to fully structured designs that have a standard set of questions with restricted-choice answers.

Selecting interview and question types

How should a researcher decide which type of interview and question to choose? Non-directive interviews and open questions would be suitable in the following circumstances:

• The researcher wants to obtain a lot of rich and personal information from each interviewee.

- The researcher wants to maximise the chances that the interviewees will feel involved in the interview.
- The researcher wants to obtain a general impression of the interviewees' views rather than very specific and detailed information.
- It is not of central importance to compare the responses of different interviewees.
- The interviewer or interviewers are well trained to cope with the requirements of conducting non-directive interviews.

Structured interviews and closed questions would be suitable in the following circumstances:

- The researcher wants to obtain information that is easy to analyse.
- The researcher wants to obtain reliable data and to compare directly the answers given by different interviewees.
- The researcher has clear ideas concerning the questions he/she wants interviewees to answer.
- The interviewer(s) have limited training but can cope with the requirements of asking closed questions in a standard order.

Interviewer's characteristics

An important issue when designing an interview is to consider various characteristics of the interviewer or interviewers. Their gender, ethnicity, age, and personal qualities can all affect the interviewees' answers. For example, Wilson et al. (2002) found that Californian Latino men interviewed by women reported fewer sexual partners than men interviewed by men. In addition, men were more likely to report sex with prostitutes to an older interviewer.

There is also the possibility that the views or expectations of the interviewer will bias the responses given by interviewees—this is known as interviewer bias. Interviewer bias can be minimised by instructing interviewers to remain non-evaluative and fairly neutral regardless of whether they personally agree or disagree with what an interviewee is saying.

Questionnaire design

Questionnaires are used for many purposes (e.g. to assess personality; to assess attitudes), and how a questionnaire is designed needs to reflect fully the purpose for which it is being designed. However, some general considerations underlying questionnaire design are discussed in the box.

How can you decide how good any given questionnaire is? Three key characteristics of a good questionnaire are standardisation, reliability, and validity (reliability and validity are discussed more fully later in the chapter). **Standardised tests** are ones that have been administered to a large representative sample so an individual's score can be compared against

ACTIVITY: Construct your own questionnaire

1. Select an area of study from the work you are doing in class.
2. Research the topic to gain ideas about the possible questions to ask.
3. Develop sub-topics to investigate. It may be best to generate questions with a group of people because more varied ideas are produced (brainstorming). Each group member should put forward ideas that are received uncritically by the group. Later, the group can select the best questions.
4. Write the questions. It may help to include some irrelevant "filler" questions to mislead the respondent as to the main purpose of the survey.
5. Decide on a sequence for the questions. It is best to start with easy ones.
6. Write standardised instructions, which must include guidance regarding respondents' ethical rights.
7. Conduct a pilot run and redraft your questionnaire in response to areas of confusion or difficulty.
8. After you have conducted your questionnaire, analyse the results using descriptive data (see next section, "Data Analysis and Presentation").
9. Debrief participants and advise them of your findings.

Questionnaire construction

The first step is to generate as many ideas as possible that might be relevant to the questionnaire. Then discard those ideas that seem of little relevance, working on the basis (Dyer, 1995, p.114) that: "It is better to ask carefully designed and quite detailed questions about a few precisely defined issues than the same number on a very wide range of topics."

Closed and open questions

There is an important distinction between closed and open questions. Closed questions invite the respondent to select from various possible answers (e.g. yes or no; yes, unsure, or no; putting different answers in rank order), whereas open questions allow respondents to answer in whatever way they prefer. Most questionnaires use closed questions, because the answers are easy to score and to analyse. Open questions have the disadvantage of being much harder to analyse, but they can be more informative than closed questions.

Ambiguity and bias

Questions that are ambiguous or are likely to be interpreted in various ways should be avoided. Questions that are very long or complicated should also be avoided, because they are likely to be misunderstood. Emotive questions should be avoided because they make people defensive and result in answers that are not true. Finally, questions that are biased should be avoided. Here is an example of a biased question: "In view of the superiority of Britain, why should we consider further political integration with the rest of Europe?"

Attitude scale construction

One of the most common ways to construct an attitude scale is to use the Likert procedure. Initially various statements are collected together, and the participants' task is to indicate their level of agreement on a 5-point scale running from "strongly disagree" at one end to "strongly agree" at the other end. For positive statements (e.g. "Most Hollywood stars are outstanding actors"), strongly disagree is scored as 1 and strongly agree as 5, with intermediate points being scored 2, 3, or 4.

For negative statements (e.g. "Most Hollywood stars are not outstanding actors"), the scoring is reversed so that strongly disagree is scored as 5 and strongly agree as 1.

Question styles: A survey on chocolate

Closed question: Do you like chocolate? (tick one)

YES   NO   NOT SURE

Open question: Why do you like or dislike chocolate?

Ambiguous question: Is chocolate likely to do you more harm than a diet that consists mainly of junk food?

Biased question: Plain chocolate is a more sophisticated taste than milk chocolate. Which type do you prefer?

that of others. For example, a score of 26 out of 60 on an attitude scale measuring prejudice doesn't mean much on its own—it only becomes meaningful when we know what percentage of people score more and less than 26 on that scale.

Reliability refers to the extent to which a given questionnaire provides consistent findings. For example, if individuals who appear prejudiced on a questionnaire on one day don't appear prejudiced when re-tested on the same questionnaire the following day, the questionnaire is unreliable and of little use. The most common way of assessing reliability is the **test–retest** technique—numerous people are given the same questionnaire on two occasions and the scores are then correlated. If the correlation is high, it means that the questionnaire is reliable.

Validity refers to the extent to which a questionnaire is measuring what it is supposed to be measuring. This can be assessed by comparing scores on the questionnaire with some external criterion. For example, suppose we devise a questionnaire to assess aggression in children. This questionnaire would be valid if we showed that children obtaining high scores were rated as more aggressive by their teachers and were more likely to have been disciplined by the school.

KEY TERM

Test–retest: a technique used to establish reliability, by giving the same test to participants on two separate occasions to see if their scores remain relatively similar.

? What might be an operational definition of fatigue, or hunger?

? It might be said that the operational definition of "intelligence" is "that which is measured by intelligence tests". What is the main weakness of this definition?

Operationalisation of Variables, Including Independent and Dependent Variables

Psychologists carry out studies to test hypotheses such as "Organisation benefits memory" or "Social pressure produces majority influence". However, there is no agreement on the best way to measure psychological concepts or variables such as "organisation", "memory", "social pressure", or "majority influence". The most common approach is to make use of **operationalisation**—defining each variable of interest in terms of the operations taken to measure it. Such a definition is termed an operational definition.

Operational definitions can be used to operationalise independent variables (e.g. organisation) and dependent variables (e.g. memory). Consider the experiment by Bower et al. (1969; see Chapter 2). Bower et al. (1969) operationalised the independent variable of organisation by comparing groups in which words belonging to conceptual hierarchies were presented in an organised or random fashion. They operationalised the dependent variable of memory by measuring the number of words free recalled orally on an immediate test in about 9½ minutes.

We can see some of the weaknesses in operational definitions by focusing on the ones used by Bower et al. (1969). Manipulating the extent to which words are presented in terms of hierarchies is one way of operationalising organisation but it is clearly not the only way. Memory can be assessed by means of an immediate test of free recall. However, it could also be assessed by means of a delayed recognition test, and the findings wouldn't necessarily be the same.

Operationalisation is often used when researchers want to assess the effects of intelligence or personality on certain aspects of behaviour. For example, intelligence is generally operationalised by assuming that a given intelligence test provides an adequate measure of intelligence. In fact, however, it is improbable that any single test can capture all the richness of intelligence.

EVALUATION

Operationalisation generally provides a clear and fairly objective definition of most variables. For example, it is possible to provide operational definitions for a complex independent variable such as organisation. In the absence of operationalisation, it would simply be impossible to carry out research on most topics in psychology.

There are various weaknesses associated with the use of operational definitions. First, operational definitions are circular and arbitrary. For example, memory can be defined in many ways other than immediate free recall (Bower et al., 1969).

Second, an operational definition typically covers only *part* of the meaning of the variable or concept. For example, majority influence can reveal itself in terms of how participants feel about themselves as well as their responses on a task.

Third, we need to worry when the findings using one operational definition are very different from those using a different operational definition of the same variable. Such a difference indicates something is wrong, but it may be hard to discover exactly *what* is wrong.

Pilot Studies

An important consideration in designing good studies is to try out your planned procedures in a small-scale trial run called a **pilot study**. Such a preliminary study is a "dress rehearsal" ahead of the experiment itself. There are various advantages associated with carrying out a pilot study:

- At the most general level, pilot studies make it possible to check out standardised procedures and general design before investing time and money in the major study.
- Pilot studies provide a way of checking the details of the experiment are appropriate. For example, suppose you want your participants to learn a list of 15 words presented in categories or randomly. If you present the words very rapidly, participants may not have enough time

to learn the words. However, if you present the words very slowly, the participants may learn nearly all the words even in the condition with random presentation. A pilot study allows you to select a presentation time that produces an effect of presenting the words in categories or randomly.

- A pilot study may indicate that participants don't understand precisely what they are expected to do. For example, there may be ambiguity about some of the instructions or about some of the items on a questionnaire they have to fill in. Carrying out a pilot study can eliminate such ambiguities.
- Pilot studies can be very useful when researchers want to decide between two possible ways of carrying out their study. For example, Wilson et al. (1998) were not sure whether to use telephone or face-to-face interviews in a study on health care. The pilot study suggested they would obtain a more representative sample (and that more people would agree to participate) if they used telephone interviews.
- When carrying out research, it is important to have enough participants to obtain significant findings. However, it is wasteful of time and resources to use far more participants than is needed to achieve the purposes of the study. A pilot study can often shed light on the appropriate number of participants to include in the main study.

If an experimenter used different wording in the instructions to different participants, how might this affect the results of the study?

EXAM HINT

You might be asked to explain *what* a pilot study is—but you are more likely to be asked *how* you would do it in a particular study or *why* you would do it. If you are asked how or why make sure you do answer this question, rather than explaining what it is.

And also remember to contextualise your answer—make your answer specific to the study you are discussing by including particular details of, for example, the participants and the materials to be used.

Control of Extraneous Variables

An extraneous variable is "anything other than the independent variable that could affect the dependent variable" (Coolican, 2004, p. 112). There are many kinds of extraneous variables but they can broadly be divided up into situational variables and participant variables. Note that an important type of extraneous variable is discussed on page 111.

Extraneous situational variables that can influence performance include room temperature, the presence or absence of distracting noise, the time of day at which participants are tested and so on. Extraneous participant variables that can influence performance include intelligence, personality, gender, and age. Potential problems with participant variables can be reduced by using matched pairs designs as discussed earlier.

Concrete example
We can see the problems posed by extraneous variables with a concrete example. Consider the following study from the 1970s discussed by Coolican (2004). Coca-cola drinkers were asked to drink two glasses of cola, one containing Coke and the other containing Pepsi. The glass containing Coke was marked "Q" and the one containing Pepsi was marked "M".

The participants, who weren't told which product was in each glass, showed a preference for Pepsi. You might think that the extraneous situational variable (the letter marked on each glass) wouldn't have had any effect. However, subsequent testing indicated that people preferred the letter "M" to the letter "Q"! This problem could have been avoided by having no extraneous variables (not marking either glass). Alternatively, "M" could have been associated with Pepsi on 50% of trials and with Coke on the other 50% of trials, with the same being true of "Q".

Reliability and Validity

A central goal of any experiment or other form of study is to provide us with useful knowledge about human behaviour. If that goal is to be achieved, the study must possess reliability (i.e. consistent findings) and validity (i.e. the findings must be genuine or valid). Reliability and validity are both considered in this section.

Reliability
Reliability refers to the extent to which a given method or test provides consistent findings when repeated. Reliability can be considered in terms of internal reliability and external reliability. Internal reliability is how consistently a method measures within itself. In contrast, external reliability is how consistently a method measures over time, population, and location when repeated.

KEY TERM

Reliability: the extent to which a method of measurement or test produces consistent findings.

Internal and external reliability

Internal reliability—consistency within the method of measurement. For instance, a ruler should be measuring the same distance between 0 and 50 millimetres as between 50 and 100 millimetres.

External reliability—consistency between uses of the method of measurement. For instance, the ruler should measure the same on a Monday as it does on a Friday.

- Standardisation—comparisons can be made between studies and samples.
- Reliability—consistent and stable. For example, Milgram's study (1963, 1974; see page 227) on obedience to authority produced findings that have been repeated numerous times in many countries, and are thus reliable.
- Validity—measuring what is intended. For example, Rahe et al.'s study (1970; see page 185) showed that scores on the Social Readjustment Rating Scale were associated with physical illness. The findings suggest (but don't prove) that the Social Readjustment Rating Scale is a valid measure of the stress created by life events.

Problems relating to reliability are likely to arise when a researcher is trying to code the complex behaviour of participants using a manageable number of categories. For example, a study might require a record to be made of the number of aggressive acts performed by an individual. If only one person observes the behaviour, this would produce a rather subjective judgement, and so usually two (or more) judges provide ratings of behaviour. The ratings can then be compared to provide a measure of inter-observer reliability (see discussion in the section on naturalistic observations).

Reliability is established on psychological tests by using the test–retest method where the same test is given to participants on two separate occasions to see if their scores remain similar. The interval between testings must be long enough to prevent a **practice effect** occurring.

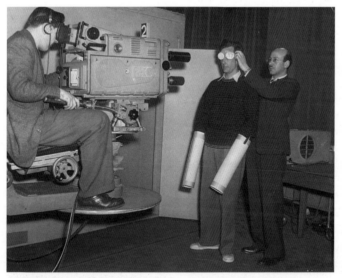

Many laboratory-based experiments in psychology (like the 1950s sensory deprivation experiment shown here) show low external validity—that is, their findings do not translate reliably to behaviour outside the laboratory.

Validity

A key requirement of research is that the findings are valid. **Validity** refers to the extent to which a study satisfies important standards in the sense that they are genuine and provide us with useful information about the phenomenon being studied. For example, if we carried out an experiment, it wouldn't be valid if we had failed to control various extraneous variables.

Campbell and Stanley (1966) drew a distinction between internal validity and external validity. Internal validity refers to the issue of whether the effects observed are genuine and caused by the independent variable. In contrast, external validity refers to the extent to which the findings of a study generalise to situations and samples other than those used in the study. This distinction is important—many experiments possess internal validity but lack external validity.

Validity is a very important issue with respect to questionnaires and other tests (e.g. intelligence tests). There are several kinds of validity and we will discuss briefly the main ones. First, there is face validity. **Face validity** is a very simple form of validity. It involves inspecting the items within a test to see whether they appear to be relevant to what the test is claimed to measure. For example, suppose a test is supposed to measure trait anxiety (a personality dimension relating to susceptibility to **anxiety**). The test would have good face validity if it contained items referring to worries about the future, tension, and feelings of unease.

ACTIVITY: Internal and external validity

Construct a brief outline for each of the following:

- An experiment that should show high internal validity.
- An experiment that will be unlikely to show high internal validity.
- An experiment that is unlikely to show high external validity.

EXAM HINT

Remember the difference between reliability and validity.

- Reliability—CONSISTENCY
- Internal validity—TRUTH
- External validity—GENERALISABILITY

If you are assessing research in a long-answer question do try to improve the quality of your evaluation by assessing reliability and validity.

Second, there is concurrent validity. **Concurrent validity** involves comparing or correlating the scores on a test with a previous test that is valid or with some relevant external criterion. For example, consider again a test designed to measure trait anxiety. A relevant external criterion might be the scores on the test obtained by patients with anxiety disorders. If the test genuinely assessed susceptibility to anxiety, we would expect anxious patients to have much higher scores than healthy individuals.

Third, there is predictive validity. **Predictive validity** refers to the extent to which scores on a given test predict future scores on a test or other criterion. For example, we could see whether trait anxiety scores obtained at one point in time predict who will develop an anxiety disorder subsequently or whether they predict scores on another test of trait anxiety known to be valid.

Awareness of the British Psychological Society (BPS) Code of Ethics

Ethics are a set of moral principles used to guide human behaviour. There are few if any absolutes in ethics, but any society or group of people develops ethics to determine what is right or wrong for that group. The need for ethical control leads to the establishment of a set of rules or **ethical guidelines** to judge the acceptability of behaviour. During the Second World War the Nazis conducted many horrific experiments on their concentration camp prisoners. At the end of the war, those responsible were tried in Nuremberg, and it became apparent a code of ethics was needed to define acceptable scientific research. As a result, the 10-point "Nuremberg code" was drawn up.

The British Psychological Society (BPS) is the major organisation for professional psychologists in the United Kingdom. In 1990, the BPS published its Ethical Principles for Conducting Research with Human Participants. The key to carrying out research in an ethical way was expressed in the following way in the Principles: "The essential principle is that the investigation should be considered from the standpoint of all participants; foreseeable threats to their psychological well-being, health, values, and dignity should be eliminated". Thus, every effort should be made to ensure participants don't experience pain, stress, or distress.

This code has been adapted by professional bodies all over the world. Within Britain, the British Psychological Society (BPS) issued a Code of Ethics and Conduct (2006; updated slightly in 2009) that should be followed by anyone involved in psychological research (see overleaf).

Below, I discuss the ways in which psychologists deal with ethical issues that are identified in the BPS Code of Ethics. Before that, however, I will briefly consider why most ethical guidelines (including those of the BPS) only have limited force. Someone who infringes the BPS Code of Ethics hasn't committed a crime, although they may be barred from the British Psychological Society.

There are other drawbacks. First, the establishment of a set of ethical guidelines enshrines its principles and may close off discussions about better solutions to a given ethical dilemma. Second, the Code makes it seem that the guidelines are ethical "truths". In fact, however, such guidelines are constantly reviewed, in part because of changing social attitudes. Third, ethical codes may take personal responsibility away from the individual researcher. It may even invite individuals to find loopholes and "play the system".

[?] Why do you think that views about the kinds of research that are ethically acceptable have changed over the years?

KEY TERMS

Concurrent validity: deciding whether a test measures what it is claimed to measure by relating the scores on the test to some other test or criterion.

Predictive validity: assessing whether a test is measuring what it is claimed to measure by seeing whether scores on the test predict some future performance (e.g. on a related test).

Ethics: a set of moral principles used to guide human behaviour.

Ethical guidelines: written codes of conduct and practice to guide and aid psychologists in planning and running research studies to an approved standard, and dealing with any issues that may arise.

BPS Code of Ethics and Conduct (2009)

The BPS Code of Ethics and Conduct (2009) applies to all psychologists and not simply those involved in research, and so is also relevant to clinical psychologists and occupational psychologists. The Code contains numerous standards and guidelines, and we will consider only the main ones here. The BPS Code of Ethics is based on four major ethical principles:

Respect

Psychologists should respect individual, cultural, and role differences. They should also avoid practices that are unfair or prejudiced, and be willing to explain the reasons for their ethical decision making.

Standard of privacy and confidentiality: Confidential information should be stored so as to avoid inadvertent disclosure and the consent of clients/participants should be obtained for disclosure of confidential information.

Standard of informed consent: "Ensure that clients, particularly children and vulnerable adults, are given ample opportunity to understand the nature, purpose, and anticipated consequences of any professional services or research participation, so that they may give informed consent to the extent that their capabilities allow" (p. 12).

Competence

Standard of ethical decision making: Psychologists should accept their responsibility to resolve ethical dilemmas with reflection, supervision, and consultation.

Responsibility

Standard of protection of research participants:

(i) Consider all research from the standpoints of research participants.
(ii) Undertake such consideration with due concern for the potential effects of factors such as age, disability, education, ethnicity, gender, language, national origin, race, religion, marital or family status and sexual orientation.
(iii) Ask research participants about individual factors that might reasonably lead to risk of harm.
(iv) Refrain from using financial compensation or other inducements for research participants to risk harm beyond that which they face in their normal lifestyles.
(v) When concluding that harm, unusual discomfort, or other negative consequences may follow from research, obtain supplemental informed consent from research participants specific to such issues.
(vi) Inform research participants from the outset that their right to withdraw at any time is not affected by the receipt or offer of any financial compensation or other inducements for participation.
(vii) Inform research participants from the outset that they may decline to answer any questions put to them.
(viii) If evidence of a psychological or physical problem is obtained then research participants should be informed, if it appears that failure to do so may endanger their present or future well-being.
(ix) Exercise particular caution when responding to requests for advice from research participants concerning psychological or other issues.
(x) When conducting research involving animals the highest standards of welfare should be observed and infliction of pain, suffering, fear distress, frustration, boredom, or lasting harm must be strictly justified.

Standard of debriefing of research participants:

(i) "Debrief research participants at the conclusion of their participation, in order to inform them of the outcomes and nature of the research, to identify any unforeseen harm, discomfort of misconceptions, and in order to arrange for assistance as needed" (p. 20).
(ii) "Take particular care when discussing outcomes with research participants, as seemingly evaluative statements may carry unintended weight" (p. 20).

Integrity

Standard of honesty and accuracy: Psychologists should "be honest and accurate in representing their professional affiliations and qualifications" (p. 21).

The full Code of Ethics and Conduct can be found at http://www.bps.org.uk

Ethical Issues and the Ways in Which Psychologists Deal With Them

The issue of ethics is critical to psychological research. The experimenter in most psychological research is in a more powerful position than the participants, and it is essential to ensure the participants aren't exploited or persuaded to behave in ways they don't want to. In addition, a professional group of people is one that "polices" itself and therefore these ethical standards are a key feature of the professionalism of psychology.

? Without ethical guidelines, how difficult would it be to express misgivings about questionable research methods?

Subjects or participants?

Until recently members of the public who took part in psychology experiments were called "subjects". This reflected the view that they were only passively involved in the research process (they did what the researcher told them) and it emphasised the power of the researcher (as the person in authority). The subject in a psychological experiment was in a rather vulnerable and exploitable position. Kelman (1972, p. 993) pointed out, "most ethical problems arising in social research can be traced to the subject's power deficiency". It follows that steps need to be taken to ensure that the participant is not placed in a powerless and vulnerable position. This is the task of an ethical code.

As a consequence of this insight it has become the practice to refer to such individuals as participants rather than subjects. Perhaps this process is analogous to the historical shift from having a political regime with "rulers and subjects" to the more modern conception of "leaders and followers". Both participants and followers have an active role to play and it would be foolish to think otherwise. The change in terminology allows for a more humane respect for individuals who participate in psychology experiments.

Ethics in psychology

Ethics are determined by a balance between means and ends, or a **cost–benefit analysis**. Certain things may be less acceptable than others. However, if the ultimate end is for the good of humankind, we may feel it is ethically justified. Most people believe that it is more acceptable to cause suffering to animals to find a cure for some serious human illness than to develop a new cosmetic.

Diener and Crandall (1978) argued there are various drawbacks with the cost–benefit approach. First, it is hard (if not impossible) to predict both costs and benefits prior to conducting a study.

Second, even after the study has been completed, it is hard to assess costs and benefits accurately. This is partly because it can depend on who is making the judgements. A participant may judge the costs differently from the researcher, and benefits may be judged differently in years to come.

Third, cost–benefit analyses tend to ignore the important rights of individuals in favour of practical considerations of possible usefulness of the findings.

There are probably more major ethical issues associated with research in psychology than any other scientific discipline. Why is this? First, all psychological experiments involve the study of living creatures. The rights of these participants to be treated in a caring and respectful way can easily be infringed by an unprincipled experimenter.

Second, the findings of psychological research may reveal unpleasant or unacceptable facts about human nature, or about certain groups within society. No matter how morally upright the experimenter may be, there is always the danger that extreme political organisations will use research findings to further their political aims. Such research is often described as "socially sensitive", and psychologists have a responsibility to consider carefully the uses to which their findings may be put.

Third, these political aims may include social control. The techniques discovered in psychological research may be exploited by dictators or others seeking to exert unjustifiable influence on society or to inflame people's prejudices.

The key ethical issues to consider are: the use of deception, informed consent, and the protection of participants from harm.

? If you recall, Watson and Rayner claimed that their experiment with Little Albert was ethical because the psychological harm inflicted was no greater than what he might experience in real life. Is this acceptable?

? How would you feel if you found out you were deliberately deceived as a participant in a research study? Would you be willing to take part in another study after knowing this?

KEY TERM

Cost–benefit analysis: a comparison between the costs of something and the related benefits, in order to decide on a course of action.

This flow chart shows ethical decisions to be taken by researchers designing a psychological study.

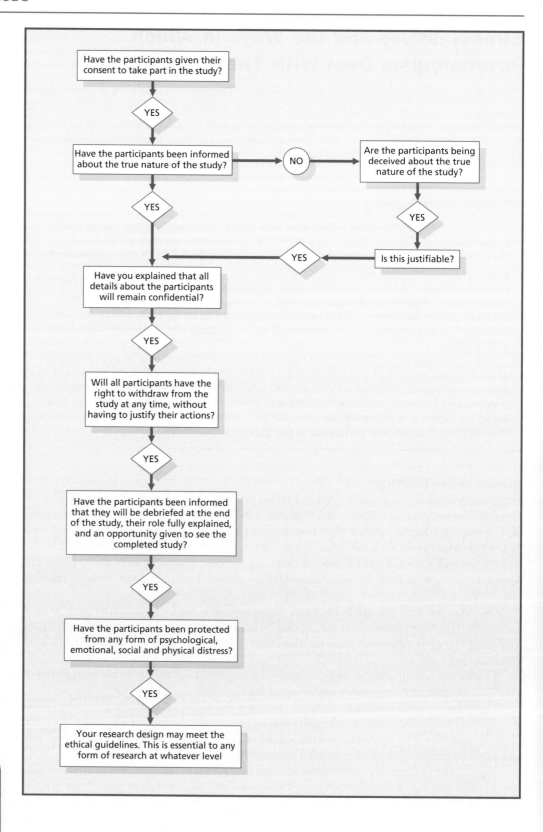

KEY TERM

Deception: in research ethics, deception refers to deliberately misleading participants, which was accepted in the past. Currently the view is that deception should be avoided wherever possible, as it could lead to psychological harm or a negative view of psychological research.

Use of deception

Honesty is a fundamental moral and ethical principle, and anyone agreeing to take part in psychological research naturally expects to be given full information beforehand. However, **deception** is sometimes necessary. A well-known example of research that had to involve deception is that of Asch (1951, 1956; see Chapter 6) on conformity. If the participants had been told the experiment was designed to study conformity to group pressure, and that all the other participants were confederates of the experimenter, this important research would have been pointless.

Deception is certainly widespread. Menges (1973) considered about 1000 experimental studies that had been carried out in the United States. Full information about what was going to happen was provided in only 3% of cases. However, full informed consent is far more common nowadays than it was over 30 years ago.

When is deception justified? First, the less potentially damaging the consequences of the deception, the more acceptable it is. Second, it is easier to justify the use of deception in studies that are important scientifically. Third, deception is more justifiable when there are no alternative, deception-free ways of studying an issue.

How can we deal with the deception issue?

One way of avoiding the ethical problems associated with deception is the use of **role-playing experiments**. Zimbardo's (1973) Stanford prison experiment (see Chapter 6) is an example of such an experiment—the participants played the role of prison guards and prisoners over a period of several days. In role-playing experiments, the participants are not deceived (e.g. they know it isn't a real prison), but try to behave as if they didn't know the true state of affairs. This approach can eliminate many of the ethical problems of deception studies.

Debriefing is an important method for dealing with deception and other ethical issues. At the end of the study, participants should be told the actual nature and purpose of the research, and asked not to tell any future participants. In addition, debriefing typically involves providing information about the experimental findings and offering participants the opportunity to have their results excluded from the study if they wish.

Debriefing can reduce any distress caused by the experimenter. According to Aronson (1988), participants should leave the research situation in "a frame of mind that is at least as sound as it was when they entered". This is *not* always the case after debriefing. Suppose you had been fully obedient in a Milgram-type experiment on obedience to authority (see Chapter 6). You might feel guilty that you had allowed yourself to give what might have been fatal electric shocks to someone with a heart condition.

Informed consent

It is the right of participants (wherever possible) to provide voluntary **informed consent**. This means several things: being informed about what will be required; being informed about the purpose of the research; being informed of their rights (e.g. the right to confidentiality, the right to leave the research at any time); and finally giving their consent. There are many situations in which this is not possible:

- Children or participants who have impairments limiting their understanding and/or communication. In such cases, the informed consent of an adult is sought.
- When deception is a necessary part of the research design as in Asch's or Milgram's research. Role-playing experiments can be used to provide informed consent, but such experiments have serious limitations.
- In field experiments when participants aren't aware they are taking part in a piece of psychological research. An example is the study by Shotland and Straw (1976) in which participants witnessed a staged quarrel between two people.

ACTIVITY: Field experiments and ethics

Find a partner and toss a coin to see who is going to support doing field experiments and who is going to oppose them on ethical grounds. Then give yourselves 5 minutes to write an argument supporting your view of why these experiments are, or are not, ethically all right. Exchange your written comments, and discuss what each of you has said.

? How would you feel if you found out you were deliberately deceived as a participant in a research study? Would you be willing to take part in another study after knowing this?

When setting up observational research it is important to consider whether the participants would normally expect to be observed by strangers in the situation. For example, making observations of the people in this picture would be acceptable, but observing them in a changing room would not.

KEY TERMS

Role-playing experiments: studies in which participants are asked to imagine how they would behave in certain situations.

Debriefing: attempts by the experimenter at the end of a study to provide detailed information for the participants about the study and to reduce any distress they might have felt.

Informed consent: relates to an ethical guideline which advises that participants should understand what they are agreeing to take part in. They should be aware of what the research involves, and their own part in this.

- There is an issue as to whether truly informed consent is possible. How easy is it for non-psychologists to understand fully what is expected of them? Prior to participation, would the "teacher" in Milgram's research have anticipated how he/she would feel when giving shocks?

Another way to obtain consent

One way of obtaining consent is to ask the opinion of members of the population from which the research participants are to be drawn. This is what Milgram did, and it is called seeking **presumptive consent**. The problem with presumptive consent is that the actual participants may find the experiment less acceptable than the non-participants whose opinions were sought beforehand.

Right to withhold data

Another means of offering informed consent is to do it afterwards. When the experiment is over, during debriefing, participants should be offered the chance to withhold their data. In essence, this gives them the same power as if they had refused to take part in the first place. However, participants who exercise their right to withhold data may nevertheless have had experiences during the experiment they wouldn't have agreed to if they had realised beforehand what was going to happen.

Protection from harm

"Harm" can mean various things. It includes both physical and psychological damage. The key test of whether a participant has been harmed is to ask whether the risk of harm was greater than in everyday life.

Physical harm

We might include excessive anxiety as physical harm because the results can be physically evident. If you consider the description of some of Milgram's participants (see Chapter 6), it is clear they experienced physical as well as psychological harm—some had seizures, and many perspired and bit their lips. Stress is a psychological state but has a physical basis (see Chapter 5).

Psychological harm

Psychological harm is harder to measure, and many studies infringe psychological "safety". Many of Milgram's participants would have felt disappointed with their own apparent willingness to obey unjust authority, which may have led to psychological harm (e.g. reduced self-esteem).

We can also consider **confidentiality** and the **right to privacy** as forms of **protection of participants from psychological harm**. Confidentiality means that no information (especially sensitive information) about any given participant should be revealed by the experimenter to anyone else. Right to privacy is a matter of concern when conducting observational research. It wouldn't be appropriate, for example, to observe a person's behaviour in their bedroom without their permission. However, it would be acceptable to observe people in a public place (e.g. a park) where public scrutiny is expected.

Selection of Participants and Sampling Techniques

Studies in psychology rarely involve more than about 100 participants. However, researchers generally want their findings to apply to a much larger group of people. In technical terms,

ACTIVITY: Target populations

Identify an appropriate target population for each project below. You would select your research sample from this population.

- To discover whether there are enough youth facilities in your community.
- To discover whether cats like dried or tinned cat food.
- To discover whether children aged between 5 and 11 watch too much violent television.
- To discover the causes of anxiety experienced by participants in research studies.

KEY TERMS

Representative sample: the notion that the sample is representative of the whole population from which it is drawn.

Sampling bias: some people have a greater or lesser chance of being selected than they should be, given their frequency in the population.

Random sampling: selecting participants on some random basis (e.g. picking numbers out of a hat). Every member of the population has an equal chance of being selected.

Systematic sampling: a modified version of random sampling in which the participants are selected in a quasi-random way (e.g. every 100th name from a population list).

the participants selected for a study form a **sample** taken from some larger **population** (called the target or sample population) consisting of all the members of the group from which the sample has been drawn.

For example, we might select a sample of 20 children aged 5 for a study. The target population would consist of all 5-year-olds living in England. Alternatively, the population might be the 5-year-olds in a particular primary school, depending on where we selected our sample.

When we carry out a study, we want the findings obtained from our sample to be true of the population from which they were drawn. In order to achieve this, we need a **representative sample**, i.e. participants who are representative or typical of the population in question. Only if we have a representative sample can we *generalise* from the behaviour of our sample to the target population in general. As in the example, we can only make statements about all 5-year-olds in the population studied, i.e. those in England or in the school, not those in the rest of the world.

Many studies have non-representative samples. For example, the participants in many published studies in psychology are undergraduate university students, who are clearly not representative of society in age or intelligence. Such studies are said to have a **sampling bias**.

The overwhelming majority of psychological research has been on people from Western, Educated, Industrialized, Rich, and Democratic (WEIRD) societies (Henrich et al., 2010). Detailed figures were provided by Arnett (2008), who considered leading psychological research. Of the participants, 96% were from WEIRD societies (68% from the United States alone). Thus, most research is not remotely representative of the world's population as a whole.

Random sampling

The best way of obtaining a representative sample from a population (e.g. students) is to use **random sampling**. This could be done by picking students' names out of a hat, or by assigning a number to everyone in the population from which the sample is to be selected. After that, a computer or random number tables could be used to generate a series of random numbers to select the sample.

If we wanted to have a representative sample of the entire adult population, we could apply one of the methods of random selection just described to the electoral roll. However, even that would be an imperfect procedure—several groups of people including children and young people, homeless people, illegal immigrants, and prisoners aren't listed.

An alternative to random sampling is what is known as **systematic sampling**. This involves selecting participants systematically from a population (e.g. by selecting every 10th or 100th person). This is less effective than random sampling, because it can't be claimed that every member of the population is equally likely to be selected.

Ideally, psychological experiments should select a random sample of the population, although true randomness can be hard to achieve.

Systematic sampling is not as effective as random sampling but it does help to overcome the biases of the researcher. If we select every hundredth name on the list, we avoid missing names that we cannot pronounce, or do not like the look of, for whatever reason.

ACTIVITY: Sampling

Find a study to illustrate volunteer sampling and another one to illustrate opportunity sampling. (Clue: most of the studies you have covered used a volunteer sample, whereas some of the studies have used opportunity samples.)

EVALUATION OF RANDOM SAMPLING

It is very hard for an experimenter to obtain a random sample for the following reasons:

1. It may not be possible to identify all of the members of the larger population from which the sample is to be selected.
2. It may not be possible to contact all those who have been selected randomly to appear in the sample—they may have moved house, or be away on holiday. You would end up with a sample that is definitely not random.
3. Some of those selected to be in the sample are likely to refuse to take part. This might not matter if those who agree to take part in research are very similar to those who don't. However, as is discussed below, volunteers typically differ in various ways from non-volunteers.

Opportunity sampling

Random sampling is often expensive and time-consuming. As a result, many researchers use **opportunity sampling**. This involves selecting participants on the basis of their availability. Opportunity sampling is often used by students carrying out experiments, and it is also very common in natural experiments.

? Psychology students often use other psychology students as the participants in their research. What problems are likely to arise, for example, in terms of evaluation apprehension and demand characteristics?

EVALUATION OF OPPORTUNITY SAMPLING

Opportunity sampling is the easiest method to use. However, it has the severe weakness that the participants may be very unrepresentative. For example, students who are friends of the student carrying out a study may be more likely to take part than students who are not. It is often hard to know whether the use of an opportunity sample has distorted the results.

Opportunity sampling gives the illusion of being drawn from a large population. However, it is generally drawn from a very small sample, such as people who shop in the town centre on a week day. Thus, the sample depends on who is available at the time. This type of group mostly constitutes a *biased sample*.

Volunteer sampling

In practice, research in psychology typically involves **volunteer sampling**. That is, the participants in a study (whether initially selected via random or opportunity sampling) nearly always consist of volunteers who have agreed to take part. It would obviously be unethical to try to force anyone to become a participant in any given study. As a result, researchers have to accept that many of those invited to participate in a study will refuse.

Do volunteer samples differ in important ways from a random sample? If so, we have **volunteer bias**. Volunteers tend to be more sensitive to demand characteristics (cues used by participants to work out what a study is about), and they are also more likely to comply with those demand characteristics. Marcus and Schutz (2005) found the personalities of volunteers were more agreeable and open to experience than those of non-volunteers, and they showed a tendency to be more extraverted.

Volunteer bias is especially likely when researchers are trying to recruit participants for a study on a sensitive topic. Strassberg and Lowe (1995) found several differences between volunteers and non-volunteers for several studies on human sexuality. The volunteers had had more sexual experience, had less sexual guilt, and reported a more positive attitude towards sexuality.

Sample size

An important issue relating to sampling is the total number of participants to be included in the sample. What is the ideal number of participants in each condition? That is a bit like asking how

KEY TERMS

Opportunity sampling: participants are selected because they are available, not because they are representative of a population.

Volunteer sampling: choosing research participants who have volunteered, e.g. by replying to an advertisement. Volunteer samples may not be representative of the general population, which means the research may not be generalisable.

Volunteer bias: any systematic differences between volunteers and non-volunteers.

Activities of the autonomic nervous system	
Sympathetic branch	**Parasympathetic branch**
Increased heart rate	Decreased heart rate
Reduced activity within the stomach	Increased activity within the stomach
Saliva production is inhibited (mouth feels dry)	Saliva production increased to aid digestion
Pupil dilation or expansion	Pupil contraction
Relaxation of the bronchi of the lungs	Constriction of the bronchi of the lungs
Glucose is released	Glucose is stored

Endocrine system

The ANS achieves its effects via the **endocrine system**, which consists of various ductless glands. Most importantly, the endocrine glands secrete or release **hormones** into the bloodstream—these hormones control ANS activity.

Hormones can have dramatic effects on our behaviour and emotions, especially stress, which can be regarded in part as an emotional reaction to stressors. Most hormones are slow acting because they are carried around the body relatively slowly by the bloodstream. The effects of hormones last for some time but typically gradually diminish as the situation becomes less stressful.

Nervous system	Endocrine system
• Consists of nerve cells	• Consists of ductless glands
• Acts by transmitting nerve impulses	• Acts by release of hormones
• Acts rapidly	• Acts slowly
• Direct control	• Indirect control
• Specific localised effects of neurotransmitters	• Hormones spread around the body
• Short-lived effects	• Hormones remain in the blood for some time

Homeostasis

The body's internal environment generally remains almost constant in spite of large changes in the external environment. This "steady state" or **homeostasis** is the result of ANS activity and is a fundamental part of the stress response. When an individual is placed under stress, the body strives to return to its normal steady state as soon as possible. The normal body state is controlled by the parasympathetic branch storing and conserving energy. The sympathetic branch produces arousal, which is necessary to deal with emergences.

The take-home message is as follows: we strive for a *balance* between parasympathetic and sympathetic activity. Stress is often experienced when this balance can't be achieved.

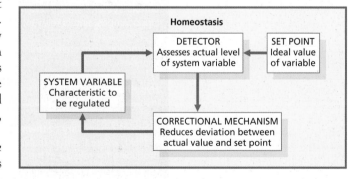

The Body's Response to Stress

It is now time to focus more directly on the ways in which the body responds to stressors, which are events imposing demands on us. What happens initially is that the individual engages in a process of appraisal in which they interpret the situation. Appraisal involves various thought processes and is influenced by stored memories of similar situations in the past. It occurs

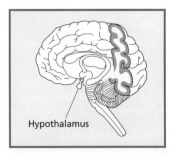

Hypothalamus

primarily in the cortex but also involves parts of the limbic system that are associated with emotional memories and processing. The **limbic system** consists of various cortical and subcortical structures that are associated with memory and emotional processing.

Of particular importance in emotional processing is the **amygdala**, which is an almond-shaped structure within the limbic system. It is very involved in emotional responses such as fear and anxiety but there is increasing evidence that it is of relevance to other emotions as well.

If appraisal processes involving the cortex and the amygdala indicate that the situation is stressful, this leads to activation of the hypothalamus. The **hypothalamus** is small (about the size of a fingernail), and it plays a major role in integrating activity within the autonomic nervous system. Of most relevance here, the hypothalamus is centrally involved in controlling the body's subsequent response when it is clear that the situation is stressful.

Stress (our reaction to a stressor) involves two rather separate systems within the body, both of which are under the control of the hypothalamus. First, there is the **sympathomedullary pathway**, which is often called the sympathetic adrenal medullary (SAM) system pathway or system. In what follows, we will use the two terms interchangeably.

Second, there is the **pituitary–adrenal system** or hypothalamic–pituitary–adrenocortical (HPA) axis. The body's response to stress depends very much on both of these systems. We will consider each system in turn (see figure opposite).

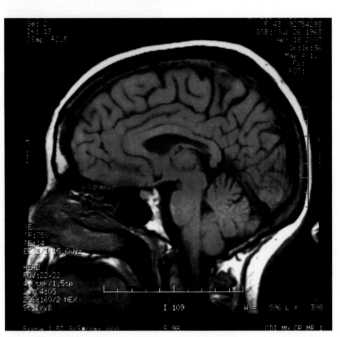

The hypothalamus triggers off the stress response. It is located at the base of the brain.

Sympathomedullary pathway: Sympathetic adrenal medullary (SAM) system

The bodily response to stress rapidly involves the sympathomedullary pathway or sympathetic adrenal medullary (SAM) system. There are several stages within the SAM system. First, activation within the hypothalamus leads to messages from the brainstem being sent to the adrenal medulla. The **adrenal medulla** is the inner part of the **adrenal glands,** which are located close to the kidneys.

KEY TERMS

Limbic system: a set of brain structures close to the brainstem; it includes the amygdala and hippocampus, and is relevant to hunger and memory as well as emotional processing.

Amygdala: a structure within the limbic system that is strongly associated with several emotions but especially fear or anxiety; it is buried deep within the temporal lobe.

Hypothalamus: the part of the brain that integrates the activity of the autonomic nervous system. It is involved with emotion, stress, motivation, and hunger.

Sympathomedullary pathway: the source of the immediate stress response, also known as fight or flight, where the hypothalamus activates the ANS, which in turn activates the adrenal medulla, producing the release of the stress hormones adrenaline and noradrenaline.

Pituitary–adrenal system: one of the two major systems involved in the stress response, where the hypothalamus activates the pituitary gland which in turn activates the adrenal cortex to release corticosteroid stress hormones.

Adrenal medulla: this is the inner part of the adrenal glands; it is involved in the stress response by releasing the hormones adrenaline and noradrenaline.

Adrenal glands: the endocrine glands that are located adjacent to, and covering, the upper part of the kidneys.

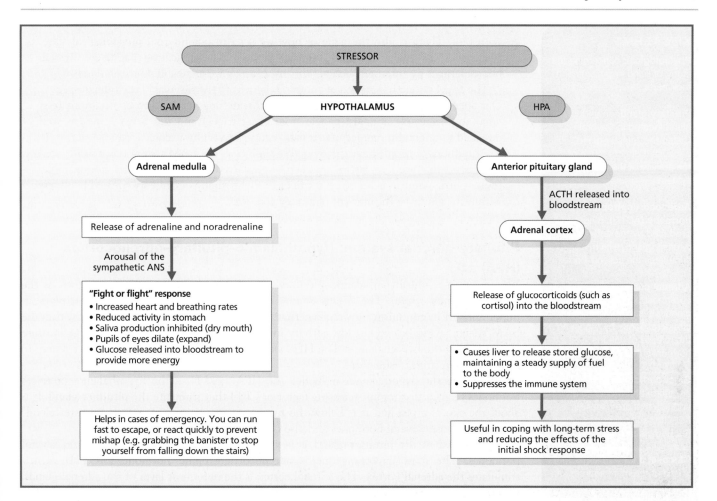

Second, the adrenal medulla secretes (releases) the hormones **adrenaline** and **noradrenaline** (Americans call these epinephrine and norepinephrine, respectively). Hormones are chemical substances that are produced by one tissue and then travel via the bloodstream to a second tissue.

Third, release of the hormones adrenaline (epinephrine) and noradrenaline (norepinephrine) leads to increased arousal of the sympathetic nervous system and reduced activity in the parasympathetic nervous system. These changes prepare us for "fight or flight".

More specifically, there are the following effects: an increase in energy; increased alertness; increased blood flow to the muscles; increased heart and respiration rate; reduced activity in the digestive system; and increased release of clotting factors into the bloodstream to reduce blood loss in the event of injury. Adrenaline and noradrenaline increase the output of the heart, which can cause an increase in blood pressure. These various changes involve the sympathetic nervous system. It typically operates fairly automatically—stressors cause our heart rate to increase, energy levels to increase, and blood pressure to increase without any conscious control on our part.

How can we explain **individual differences** in SAM system activity? There are undoubtedly several factors at work. Here we will simply consider genetic factors. Frigerio et al. (2009) studied the stress response in infants. Individual differences in SAM activity under stress were associated with specific genetic factors.

EVALUATION

Activity in the sympathomedullary pathway forms an important part of the stress response. It is an appropriate reaction of the body, because it prepares us for fight or flight. However, such SAM activity is not *only* associated with stress. For example, we have elevated levels of adrenaline and noradrenaline when we are concentrating hard

KEY TERMS

Adrenaline: one of the hormones (along with noradrenaline) produced by the adrenal glands, which increases arousal by activating the sympathetic nervous system and reducing activity in the parasympathetic system.

Noradrenaline: one of the hormones (along with adrenaline) produced by the adrenal glands that increases arousal by activating the sympathetic nervous system and reducing activity in the parasympathetic system.

Individual differences: the characteristics that vary from one individual to another, including several aspects of the stress response.

KEY TERMS

Physiological: concerning the study of living organisms and their parts.

Pituitary gland: an endocrine gland located in the brain. Called the "master gland" because it directs much of the activity of the endocrine system.

Adrenocorticotrophic hormone (ACTH): a hormone produced by the anterior pituitary gland, which stimulates the adrenal cortex.

Adrenal cortex: this is the outermost part of the adrenal glands; it is involved in the stress response by triggering the release of various hormones including cortisol.

Glucocorticoids: these are steroid hormones (e.g. cortisol) that are released from the adrenal cortex when the body is stressed.

Glucose: a form of sugar that is one of the main sources of energy for the brain.

Cortisol: a hormone produced by the adrenal gland that elevates blood sugar and is important in digestion, especially at times of stress.

on a task. There is also the issue of how we *perceive* our internal **physiological** state. Sometimes we perceive heightened activity in the SAM as indicating that we are stressed, but sometimes we interpret such activity as meaning we are excited or stimulated.

The SAM system has proved of enormous benefit to the survival of the human species. Our ancestors were faced by numerous very threatening and dangerous situations (e.g. large and aggressive animals; people from other tribes) and the SAM system is well designed to respond to immediate threats with vigorous physical activity.

As millions of people have discovered to their cost, the SAM system is not well suited to stressors that are long lasting and can't be resolved by physical action. For example, there is little point in being ready for fight or flight when you are very stressed by illness within the family or the amount of money you owe.

Pituitary–adrenal system: Hypothalamic–pituitary–adrenocortical (HPA) axis

We now turn to the hypothalamic–pituitary–adrenocortical (HPA) axis, also known as the pituitary–adrenal system. The details of its functioning are discussed below, but it plays an important part in minimising any damage that might be caused by excessive activity within the SAM system. As indicated already, activity in the HPA is initiated by (and in large measure controlled by) the hypothalamus. The HPA axis takes a little longer than the SAM system to be activated in stressful situations.

How does the hypothalamus influence the HPA axis? First, the hypothalamus produces hormones (e.g. corticotrophin-releasing factor or CRF) that stimulate the **pituitary gland**. It is about the size of a pea and it is below the hypothalamus. It is known as the "master gland" because it releases several hormones and also controls other bodily glands.

Second, when the pituitary gland is activated by the hypothalamus, it releases several hormones. The most important one is **adrenocorticotrophic hormone (ACTH)**, which stimulates the **adrenal cortex**. The adrenal cortex is the outermost layer of the adrenal glands, which, as mentioned earlier, are very close to the kidneys. As we are about to see, ACTH is strongly involved in the HPA axis stress response.

Third, ACTH in the adrenal cortex leads to the release of various **glucocorticoids**, which are hormones that influence **glucose** metabolism. The key glucocorticoid with respect to stress is **cortisol**, which is sometimes called the "stress hormone" because excess amounts are found in the urine of individuals experiencing stress.

The HPA axis

Hypothalamus

Anterior pituitary gland

Negative feedback

ACTH released

Adrenal glands

The measurement of stress

One way to measure stress is to use a lie detector. A lie detector, or more properly a "polygraph", is a machine used to tell if an individual is telling the truth. The machine measures a person's heart rate, blood pressure, breathing rate, and galvanic skin response (GSR). GSR tells us the extent to which your skin can conduct an electrical current because, when you sweat, the conductivity of your skin increases. These are all indicators of arousal of the sympathetic branch of the ANS. When a person is lying, their stress levels are elevated and so is their sympathetic arousal.

It would be nice if we could detect the difference between truth and lies so easily. However, people become sympathetically aroused for many reasons, such as fear of being falsely accused or being in a strange place. The polygraph is an excellent detector of nervousness but not of truthfulness. According to Forman and McCauley (1986) about half of all innocent people "fail" a lie detector test. In addition, many criminals are good liars and do not become aroused.

There are other physiological methods of measuring stress, including checking the size of the adrenal gland, which becomes enlarged under prolonged stress, and checking levels of cortisol in the urine.

How can we explain individual differences in HPA axis activity? First, genetic factors are important. Mormede et al. (2011) discussed twin studies in which identical twins were found to have much more similar HPA axis activity than fraternal twins.

Second, there are interesting gender differences. Males and females were exposed to achievement stressors (complex tasks) and to social rejection (being excluded from a conversation) (Stroud et al., 2002). Only males showed increased cortisol levels after exposure to achievement stressors and only females had increased cortisol after social rejection. These sex differences are consistent with stereotyped notions about men being more concerned than women about achievement and women being more concerned about social acceptance.

Effects of activity in the pituitary–adrenal system

- Good effect: Cortisol is important for coping with long-term stress, because it maintains a steady supply of fuel. More energy is available because of increased glucose levels.
- Good effects: The secretion of cortisol and other glucocorticoids has various useful functions:
  (i) The glucocorticoids help to conserve glucose for neural tissues.
  (ii) The glucocorticoids elevate or stabilise blood glucose concentrations.
  (iii) The glucocorticoids mobilise protein reserves.
  (iv) The glucocorticoids conserve salts and water.
- Good effect: Cortisol is important in reversing some of the body's initial responses to stress, thus putting bodily systems into a balanced state (Gevirtz, 2000).
- Bad effects: "The blood still has elevated levels of glucose (for energy) and some hormones (including adrenaline and the pituitary hormone ACTH), and the body continues to use its resources at an accelerating rate. Essentially, the organism remains on red alert" (Westen, 1996, p. 427).
- Bad effect: The anti-inflammatory action of glucocorticoids slows wound healing.
- Bad effect: Glucocorticoids suppress the immune system, which has the task of protecting the body against intruders such as viruses and bacteria. When immune responses are low, we are more likely to develop a disease (see Kiecolt-Glaser et al., 1984, 1995, discussed later in the chapter).

EXAM HINTS

If you are asked to outline two ways the body responds to stress, you can discuss the dual-stress response:

- The shock response: sympathomedullary pathway or sympathetic adrenal medullary system (SAM).
- The countershock response: pituitary–adrenal system (also known as the hypothalamic–pituitary–adrenocortical axis (HPA)).

Use examples of how the hormones released on each axis affect the body to ensure you write enough for 3 marks each, e.g.

- The sympathomedullary pathway produces adrenaline and noradrenaline, which increases the arousal of the sympathetic nervous system and so leads to increased heart beat, blood pressure, breathing rate, and inhibited digestion.
- The pituitary–adrenal system produces corticosteroids, which increase glucose release and suppress the immune system.

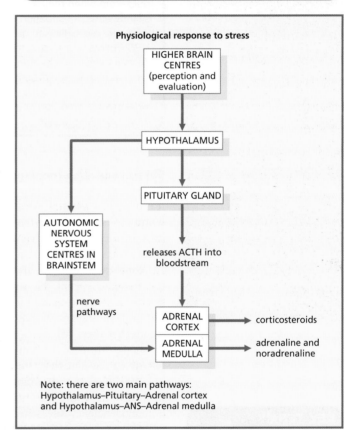

EVALUATION

The pituitary–adrenal system or HPA is of value in reducing some of the SAM system response to stress. We can see this by considering people without adrenal glands who can't produce the normal amounts of glucocorticoids. When exposed to a stressor, they must be given additional quantities of glucocorticoid to survive (Tyrell & Baxter, 1981). However, the beneficial effects of HPA activity are achieved at considerable cost, and it cannot continue indefinitely at an elevated level of activity. If the adrenal cortex stops producing glucocorticoids, this eliminates the ability to maintain blood glucose concentrations at the appropriate level.

I have discussed the sympathomedullary pathway, or SAM, and the pituitary–adrenal system, or HPA, as if they were different systems. This is no more than approximately

? It is normal to have a stress response reaction to a stressor—what change(s) have you noticed in your own body when faced with a stressful situation, such as a test or exam, or being told off? Could you feel your heart beating stronger, your breathing speeding up, or your muscles tensing?

correct. In fact, the two systems do *not* operate in complete independence of each other. As Evans (1998, p. 60) pointed out, "At the level of the central nervous system, the crucially important SAM and HPA systems can be considered as one complex: they are as it were the lower limbs of one body."

HOW SCIENCE WORKS: Stress as a bodily response

Heart rate is one measure that increases in the stress response, and this is easy to monitor by taking the pulse. This can be done manually or by using a pulse monitor, something psychology and biology departments often have in their equipment. This type of data is ratio data and does not depend on opinion, and so it is empirical. The equipment would enable you to measure accurately, and you could record your data methodically, for example by using a simple table.

You could do an experiment on willing participants aged 16 or over, measuring their pulse rate when they are sitting relaxed, and then doing this again when they are in a slightly stressful situation, such as doing a set of puzzles or a simple computer game with a time deadline to create mild stress. Of course, for obvious reasons as well as the BPS Ethical Guidelines, they must not be stressed more than they would be in any normal everyday situation. If you set up this experiment in a special room, a classroom for instance, it would be a laboratory experiment. But if you did it in the participant's own home it would be a field experiment. Each of these situations has strengths and weaknesses, and you could consider, on balance, which situation would give you the most scientific results.

Stress-Related Illness and the Immune System

It is often believed that stress can cause illness fairly directly by impairing the functioning of the **immune system**. This system is located in various parts of the body including the bone marrow, lymph nodes, tonsils, spleen, appendix, and small intestines. The immune system acts like an army, identifying and killing any intruders to the body.

Much remains to be discovered of the ways in which stress causes impaired functioning of the immune system. However, the high levels of adrenaline, noradrenaline, and cortisol associated with stress all play a part. Cells in the immune system have receptors for various chemical substances (hormones and neurotransmitters) involved in the stress response. That means that stress influences immune system functioning. Evans et al. (1997, p. 303) argued that we should "think of the immune system as striving to maintain a state of delicate balance". It is plausible to assume that stress can disrupt that "delicate balance".

We can see the importance of the immune system by considering **immunodeficiency diseases** in which its entire functioning suffers long-term or permanent damage. The best-known immunodeficiency disease is AIDS (acquired immune deficiency syndrome). AIDS increases the probability of premature death by making the individual less able to fight off infection.

As we will see, the effects of stress on the immune system and illness are complex. These effects depend very much on the type of stress, especially whether it is short-lasting (acute) or long-lasting (chronic). The immune system itself is complex and there is more than one type of immunity.

Types of immunity: Natural immunity and specific immunity

The first point that needs to be made is that there is an important distinction between natural immunity and specific immunity (Segerstrom & Miller, 2004). We will discuss the details of these two forms of immunity shortly. First, however, we will consider the key differences between these two types of immunity.

Natural immunity developed earlier in evolutionary history than specific immunity. This type of immunity involves very general processes—it responds in much the same way to most threats to the body. It is typically the body's first line of defence. Most other species rely very heavily on natural immunity. Their ability to protect themselves against foreign invaders indicates the effectiveness of this type of immunity.

KEY TERMS

Immune system: a system of cells (white blood cells) within the body that is concerned with fighting disease. The white blood cells, called leucocytes, include T and B cells and natural killer cells. They help prevent illness by fighting invading antigens such as viruses and bacteria.

Immunodeficiency diseases: diseases in which the functioning of the entire immune system is impaired either for a long period of time or permanently.

Specific immunity developed later in evolutionary history than natural immunity. As the name suggests, its response to threats to bodily functioning is much more *targeted* and specific. It takes longer than natural immunity to be effective.

Before proceeding, I should point out that the functioning of the immune system is complicated. Accordingly, I will focus on its most important aspects and functions.

Some cells of the immune system kill "invaders" by engulfing them. In this picture, lymphocytes are attacking an invading antigen.

Natural immunity

Natural immunity (often known as the innate immune system) is a vital part of the immune system. It is used successfully to attack a wide range of **pathogens** (infectious agents such as bacteria and viruses) that are capable of producing diseases. The initial task for the immune system is to distinguish between pathogens and healthy cells. This helps to ensure that its destructive powers are directed against pathogens.

The cells involved in natural immunity (e.g. **natural killer cells**) are all-purpose white blood cells that attack pathogens relatively rapidly. In addition to natural killer cells, other types of white blood cells involved in natural immunity are phagocytes and macrophages. All these cells play a key role in providing resistance to viral and bacterial infections.

The inflammatory response is of major importance to the functioning of natural immunity. This involves recruiting cells from the bloodstream into tissues to assist in the removal of pathogens and dead cells by increasing blood flow. The components of this part of the immune system are called natural or innate because they exist *before* the arrival of pathogens. As a result, they respond immediately when tissue damage or infection is detected. However, natural immunity is limited in that it typically provides relatively short-lasting immunity. It is also limited because it fails to recognise many viruses.

Specific immunity

As mentioned already, **specific immunity** (often known as adaptive immunity) developed later in evolutionary history than natural immunity. It is less primitive than the natural immunity system.

The cells involved in specific immunity are known as **lymphocytes** or white blood cells that develop in the lymph system; they include helper T cells and B cells. The cells involved in specific immunity are able to identify pathogens that are invading the body and to remember them in order to create immunity. They produce **antibodies**, which are proteins produced in blood used by the immune system to detect foreign molecules in the body (**antigens**) and then neutralise them. Antibodies are essential for our well-being—individuals who can't make antibodies are at risk of dying from overwhelming infection.

Let's consider how specific immunity works in a little more detail. There are numerous pathogens and each one has its own set of antigens. Specific immunity deals with this by responding to the presence of antigens by creating the appropriate antibodies. In contrast to natural immunity, this antibody response is acquired *after* the immune system has been exposed to an antigen.

In sum, specific or adaptive immunity has two key weapons at its disposal. First, there are lymphocytes that recognise antigens. Second, there are long-lived "memory" lymphocytes that remember specific antigens and so permit the immune system to respond rapidly when the same antigens re-appear.

Conclusions

From what has been said so far, it might be inferred that natural immunity and specific immunity operate entirely separately from each other. That is *not* the case. In fact, the chemicals released by lymphocytes within the specific immunity system can also influence the functioning of natural immunity. In addition, the processes involved in specific activity can be triggered by prior activity of the natural immunity system. In essence, natural and specific immunity act

KEY TERMS

Natural immunity: this is a part of the immune system that is relatively primitive but is of general value in attacking pathogens.

Pathogens: infectious agents such as viruses, parasites, and bacteria.

Natural killer cells: these are white blood cells that destroy pathogens.

Specific immunity: a part of the immune system that operates in a relatively specific and slow fashion.

Lymphocytes: white blood cells that are formed within the lymph system; important to the functioning of the immune system.

Antibodies: chemicals within the specific immunity system that are able to destroy antigens.

Antigens: foreign molecules in the body that trigger the production of antibodies by the immune system.

cooperatively based on their respective strengths—natural immunity provides a *rapid* response and specific immunity provides a *targeted* response.

The field of research in which the links between the immune system and stress and other psychological states are studied is called **psychoneuroimmunology (PNI)**. We will now discuss some of the important findings from PNI.

Findings: Effects of stress on the immune system

By the early 1980s, it was generally accepted that stress can make people more vulnerable to physical illness and psychological disorders. However, there wasn't much evidence concerning *how* stress had these effects. Kiecolt-Glaser et al. (1984) addressed this issue in a study using a naturally occurring stressful situation with which you will be familiar (perhaps too familiar!)—examinations.

KEY STUDY

Kiecolt-Glaser et al. (1984): Exam stress and the immune system

Blood samples were taken from medical students 1 month before their final examinations and again on the first day of those examinations. Natural killer cell activity (associated with natural immunity) *decreased* between the two samples, suggesting stress is associated with a *reduced* response of the immune system.

Kiecolt-Glaser et al. (1984) also obtained information about psychiatric symptoms, loneliness, and life events on both sampling occasions. They did this because some theories suggest all of these factors are associated with increased levels of stress. Immune responses were especially weak in those students who felt most lonely, as well as in those experiencing stressful life events or psychiatric symptoms such as depression or anxiety. This study suggested that stress could produce a lowered immune response. In addition, several other psychological factors (e.g. psychiatric symptoms; life events) were also associated with impaired functioning of the immune system.

Limitations

- First, although Kiecolt-Glaser et al. (1984) showed that stress can have a negative impact on the immune system, they didn't show that this effect on the immune system was sufficient to cause physical illness.
- Second, their study was restricted to medical students. As a result, we can't readily generalise the findings to other groups in society.
- Third, we have seen that the immune system is very complex. However, Kiecolt-Glaser et al. (1984) only considered one very small part of immune system functioning, namely, natural killer cell activity. It is possible that the negative effects of exam stress on natural killer cell activity were not present on most other aspects of immune system functioning. (e.g. specific immunity).

[?] This was a natural experiment. What are the advantages and disadvantages of such research?

Further evidence was reported by Kiecolt-Glaser et al. (1995). They tested the hypothesis that a psychological stressor (looking after a relative with Alzheimer's disease) can damage the immune system. It was decided to use slowing of wound healing as a measure of immune system damage. The experimental group consisted of women looking after a relative with Alzheimer's disease, and the control group consisted of women matched in age and family income with the caregivers. The caregivers (who had on average been looking after their relative for almost 8 years) scored much higher than the control women on a perceived stress scale.

The functioning of the immune system was studied by creating a small wound on the forearm close to the elbow. The time taken for the wound to heal was assessed by photographing the wound regularly and by observing the response to hydrogen peroxide (an absence of foaming indicated healing).

What did Kiecolt-Glaser et al. (1995) find? The healing time for the caregivers averaged 48.7 days compared to 39.3 days for the control women. In addition, the caregivers had a larger

KEY TERM

Psychoneuroimmunology (PNI): the study of the effects of both stress and other psychological factors on the immune system.

average wound size than the controls, especially during the first few days after the wound had been created. Analysis of the blood collected from the participants revealed that the caregivers produced significantly less interleukin-1β than controls under certain conditions. This may be important because interleukin-1β seems to play a role in speeding up wound healing.

A strength of the Kiecolt-Glaser et al. (1995) study is that they created the same wound in all the participants, so they could observe effects of stress on the immune system in a controlled way. An application of their findings is that it may assist in developing ways of speeding recovery from surgery. However, there are some weaknesses. Caregivers and controls may have differed in ways other than the level of psychological stress—for example, more caregivers were on medication, and this may have affected their immune system. The role of interleukin-1β in wound healing is somewhat speculative, and Kiecolt-Glaser et al. had no *direct* evidence that it was relevant.

There were only 13 participants in each group in the study by Kiecolt-Glaser et al. (1995). As a result, the findings needed to be repeated with a larger sample. In fact, very similar findings were reported by Marucha et al. (1998). A small wound was created on the hard palate of dental students both 3 days before a major examination and during the summer vacation. Wound healing took 40% longer on average when the students were stressed (i.e. shortly before an examination). Note that stress impaired wound healing even though the stress experienced by the students would have been much less than that experienced by the caregivers in the study by Kiecolt-Glaser et al. (1995).

Many studies have focused on immunosuppressive effects (something that suppresses the immune system). For example, Schliefer et al. (1983) studied husbands whose wives had breast cancer. The husbands' immune system functioned less well after their wives had died than before. Segerstrom and Miller (2004) analysed the findings from six studies in which the death of a spouse was the stressor. Overall, losing a spouse was associated with a highly significant reduction in the effectiveness of natural killer cells within the immune system.

How well do you feel these results [from Kiecolt Glaser] would generalise to all humans?

ACTIVITY: Stress and illness

Cohen, Tyrell and Smith (1991) showed that people are more likely to develop a cold if they are stressed. Stress would reduce the functioning of the immune system, making stressed individuals more vulnerable to infection. Cohen et al. conducted the study by giving participants nasal drops containing cold viruses. They measured stress by (1) recording recent life changes (see page 184) and (2) by asking the participants to what extent they felt 'out of control' (see locus of control on page 239).

You might try a similar study by designing two questionnaires: (1) ask about recent illnesses and use answers to give each participant an illness score, (2) ask about life changes and/or control and use answers to give each participant a stress score. You can then see if these two scores produce a positive correlation.

Findings: General overview

We have seen that long-term stressors can impair the functioning of the immune system. However, as Segerstrom and Miller (2004) pointed out, it wouldn't make any sense in evolutionary terms if humans were designed so that even short-term stressors impaired the immune system's functioning. An adaptive response would be for short-term stressors to be associated with enhanced functioning of at least some aspects of the immune system. As mentioned earlier, we need to distinguish between natural immunity and specific immunity. The cells involved in natural immunity have much more general effects than those involved in specific immunity. In addition, the former cells produce effects faster than the latter cells.

Segerstrom and Miller (2004) used meta-analysis (combining findings from many studies) to clarify the precise effects of stressors on the immune system. Their key findings were as follows:

- Short-lived stressors (e.g. public speaking) produce *increased* natural immunity (e.g. increased availability of natural killer cells) but don't alter specific immunity.
- Stressful event sequences involving loss of a spouse produce a reduction in natural immunity (e.g. reduced effectiveness of natural killer cells).

Segerstrom and Miller (2004) found that short-lived stressors, such as public speaking, increase the availability of natural killer cells.

- Stressful event sequences involving disasters produce small increases in natural and specific immunity.
- Life events are associated with significant reductions in natural and specific immunity in individuals over 55 years of age. However, life events aren't associated with changes in the immunity system in those under 55.

The take-home message from the very thorough review of Segerstrom and Miller (2004) is as follows: the precise effects of stressors on the immune system depend much more than is generally thought on the specific nature and duration of the stressor.

The focus of nearly all the research on chronic stress and the immune system has been on the notion that stress causes immune suppression. However, there is recent evidence suggesting that what actually happens is more complex than that. Robles et al. (2005) pointed out that the immune system is responsible for producing inflammatory responses that are of great usefulness in resolving infections and in repairing damaged tissue. If chronic stress simply causes immune suppression, we would predict that it would suppress these inflammatory responses. In fact, chronic stress typically leads to an *increase* in inflammatory responses (Robles et al., 2005).

Indirect effects of stress on the immune system

So far we have focused on *direct* effects of stress on the immune system. However, there are also *indirect* effects of stress. Stressed individuals smoke more, drink more alcohol, take less exercise, and sleep less than non-stressed individuals (Cohen & Williamson, 1991). Here we will consider the effects of alcohol consumption on the functioning of the immune system.

Molina et al. (2006) reviewed evidence showing that alcohol has numerous effects on the structural and cellular components of the immune system (natural immunity and specific immunity). Impaired functioning of the immune system due to alcohol makes individuals vulnerable to a wide range of pathogens. As a result, alcohol abuse is associated with a much increased risk of diseases such as HIV and hepatitis C.

Individual differences

Much research on the effects of stress on the immune system has paid little attention to individual differences. That limits our ability to apply the findings in the real world. We saw earlier in Segerstrom and Miller's (2004) review that the effects of stressful life events on immune system functioning are much greater in those over 55 years of age. Gouin et al. (2008) discussed more thoroughly the effects of chronic stress (looking after a family member with dementia) on older caregivers. Compared to non-caregivers of the same age, older caregivers showed premature ageing of the immune system and impaired control of viruses. Within the specific immunity system, the number of cells that recognise pathogens reduces in old age, and an increasing proportion of cells that "remember" previous pathogens is incompetent (Weng, 2006).

What needs to happen? Marshall (2011) argued that we need to devise better techniques for assessing individual risk of impaired immune system functioning. For example, biological markers (biomarkers) can be used to assess an individual's biological state. Those at most risk of impaired immune system functioning could then strive to minimise stress in their lives.

Stress can lead to an unhealthy lifestyle.

Why doesn't the immune system always function effectively?

In view of the great value of the immune system in preventing disease, it might seem to be ideal for it to be highly active all the time including during chronic stress. Why isn't that the case? There are two main reasons. First, consider **autoimmune diseases**, in which the immune system mistakenly regards healthy cells in the body as pathogens. Such immune system activity is very undesirable and is generally treated by using medication designed to reduce the immune response.

Second, considerable physiological resources are required to maintain an efficient immune response (Segerstrom, 2010). However, substantial resources are also needed to compensate for the loss of resources often associated with chronic stress (e.g. caused by bereavement or unemployment). If the total resources available are insufficient, it may be better to prioritise resource compensation than immune response maintenance.

EVALUATION

➕ Long-term stress produces changes in the immune system, most of which involve immune suppression.

➕ We now know that the precise effects of stress on the immune system depend on factors such as whether the stressor is short-term or long-term, the age of the person involved, and the type of immunity (specific immunity vs natural immunity).

➕ There are important practical applications of the research. Basic knowledge about the stressors that impair the immune system and the ways in which they impair it can be used by health professionals and others to anticipate possible problems (e.g. after surgery) and to provide appropriate interventions.

➖ We know that chronic stress can affect the immune system and can also increase the probability of certain illnesses. However, we still don't know the extent to which the effects of stress on susceptibility to disease depend on changes within the immune system. Bear in mind that stress could be associated with increased probability of various physical illnesses because stressed individuals may have unhealthy lifestyles (e.g. increased smoking and drinking).

➖ Related to the point above, the functioning of the immune system in many (or even most) stressed individuals is within the normal range (Bachen et al., 1997). When the effects on the immune system are limited, it seems unlikely that there would be much of an increase in an individual's chances of developing, say, coronary heart disease.

➖ The immune system is extremely complex, and so it is very hard to assess the quality of an individual's immune system. As a result, it is a gross oversimplification to say that stress impairs immune system functioning simply because there are effects of stress on certain small parts of the immune system. For example, Robles et al. (2005) reported that chronic stress *enhanced* some aspects of immune system functioning.

Section Summary

What is stress?

- Stress is an innate, defensive response to situations that threaten survival.
- The bodily response to stress can be explained by looking at:
  - the role of the autonomic nervous system;
  - the pituitary–adrenal system or hypothalamic–pituitary–adrenocortical axis.

> **KEY TERM**
>
> **Autoimmune diseases:** diseases that are caused by the immune system mistakenly attacking healthy body cells; examples include some forms of diabetes and inflammatory bowel disease.

- However, the beneficial effects of activity in this system (described below) are achieved at much cost, and it cannot continue indefinitely at an elevated level of activity.
- Continued stress can deplete our resources and lead to illness.

The autonomic nervous system (ANS)

- The ANS is concerned with involuntary movements and vital bodily functions and is automatic.
- It is divided into two branches:
  1. The sympathetic branch, which activates internal organs for flight or fight.
  2. The parasympathetic branch, which conserves energy and promotes metabolism.
- These two branches often operate in opposition to each other and maintain homeostasis.
- The ANS achieves its effects via the endocrine system, which produces hormones.
- In stress situations, the immediate response arouses the sympathetic branch (specifically, the sympathomedullary system or sympathetic adrenal medullary system), which prepares the individual for flight or fight.
- This is followed shortly by a second response, which is designed to minimise any damage caused by the shock response. It involves the pituitary–adrenal system or hypothalamic–pituitary–adrenocortical axis and seeks to return the body to its parasympathetic state.

Sympathomedullary pathway or sympathetic adrenal medullary system

- This pathway or system produces an increase in energy and increased alertness in response to a stressor.
- This system starts with activation of the hypothalamus that leads to activation of the adrenal medulla.
- Activation of the adrenal medulla leads to the release of the hormones adrenaline and noradrenaline. These hormones are associated with increased activity within the sympathetic nervous system.
- Activity in this pathway or system is sometimes interpreted as indicating stress and sometimes as indicating stimulation.

Pituitary–adrenal system or hypothalamic–pituitary–adrenocortical axis

- The pituitary–adrenal system or hypothalamic–pituitary–adrenocortical axis governs the stress response in that:
  1. The hypothalamus directs ANS activity via the corticotrophic releasing factor (CRF).
  2. CRF stimulates the anterior pituitary and this triggers the release of hormones in the endocrine system (a group of ductless glands).
  3. The pituitary hormone ACTH stimulates the adrenal cortex, which produces adrenaline and noradrenaline.
  4. The adrenal cortex also releases hormones such as cortisol (the "stress hormone") producing parasympathetic activity and sometimes suppression of the immune system.

Stress-related illness and the immune system

- Stress may cause illness by affecting the functioning of the immune system (the activity of lymphocytes, natural killer cells, and endorphins). The field that investigates this is called psychoneuroimmunology.
- It is important to distinguish between natural or innate immunity and specific or adaptive immunity.
- Natural immunity developed early in evolutionary history and involves a rapid, general response to infection. The inflammatory response is a key part of its functioning.
- Specific immunity developed relatively late in evolutionary history. It involves a slower but more targeted response than natural immunity. Cells involved in specific immunity

are able to recognise and destroy antigens; other cells "remember" antigens and so permit a rapid response when these antigens re-appear.

- There are two reasons why the immune system isn't always highly active: (1) if it is overactive, it can mistake healthy cells as pathogens; (2) there are considerable physiological costs associated with a very active immune system.

- The evidence indicates that stressful event sequences involving loss of a spouse reduce natural immunity, and that life events reduce natural and specific immunity in people over 55 years of age.

- Life events are not associated with changes in the immunity system in individuals under 55. In addition, short-lived stressors produce increased natural immunity but have no effect on specific immunity.

- Stress can impair the functioning of the immune system *indirectly* by leading the individual to engage in behaviours (e.g. excessive drinking of alcohol) that damage the immune system and increase the risk of disease.

- The immune system is very complex. It is generally oversimplified to claim stress has impaired the immune system when what has been found is that some small part has been adversely affected.

SECTION 11
STRESS IN EVERYDAY LIFE

A major way of considering stress is to examine the factors affecting how much stress we experience. In this section, I consider the most important stressors: life events or changes; daily hassles; workplace stress; and personality factors.

In addition to noting many sources of stress (i.e. stressors), we should also consider there are many different responses to stress. These include anxiety, depression, anger, and even happiness. The nature of the stress response depends on various other factors—what we might loosely term "the situation". As we will see, stress is associated with various physical illnesses. It is also associated with **psychosomatic health complaints**, which are problems with physical health thought to depend at least in part on psychological factors. Examples include migraine, high blood pressure, and some respiratory ailments.

Cox (1978) proposed a **transactional model** that described stress in terms of an *interaction* between the individual and his/her environment. Cox argued that stress is experienced when the perceived environmental demands are greater than the individual's ability to cope. The use of the term "transaction" refers to the *interaction* between the individual and the environment.

Here is an example showing the value of Cox's approach. Is driving a car in heavy traffic stressful? The answer is probably "Yes" for someone who has just started taking driving lessons. However, it is probably "No" for someone who is an experienced and confident driver.

After we have discussed various stressors in everyday life, we turn to ways of managing stress. These ways include various psychological and biological methods.

Cox's transactional model can explain why learners find driving stressful whereas experienced drivers don't. The learner has limited ability to meet the demands of handling a car in traffic, which means that the demands of the environment are greater than their perceived ability to cope. For experienced drivers the perceived demands of the environment are less than their perceived ability to cope.

Life Changes and Daily Hassles

Think of a situation that would make you very stressed. Most people imagine some major life event such as discovering you have a serious illness or that a close family member has died. There has been an enormous amount of research devoted to the stressful effects of numerous **life events**. Many life events (especially the most important or severe ones) produce high levels of stress and alterations in the individual's life patterns—these are known as **life changes**. After we have discussed life events and life changes, we will turn to hassles. **Daily hassles** are the minor challenges and interruptions (e.g. arguing with a friend; malfunctioning computer) of everyday life. On average, people experience at least one hassle on about 40% of the days in each week (Almeida, 2005).

Life changes or events

Two medical doctors, Holmes and Rahe (1967), were the first to record systematically the effects of life events. They observed that patients often experienced several life events or changes in the months before the onset of illness, and that these life events were associated with stress and poor health. In particular, these life events could be characterised as involving change from a steady state, such as getting divorced or moving house. Even positive events such as getting married or going on holiday seemed to be associated with stress. Holmes and Rahe suggested that the changes associated with major life events absorb "psychic [mental] energy", leaving less available for other matters such as physical defence against illness.

Holmes and Rahe (1967) needed some method for measuring life events to show associations or correlations among life events, stress, and illness. Accordingly, they developed the Social Readjustment Rating Scale (SRRS) by examining 5000 patient records and making a list of 43 life events that preceded illness (see Table). Nearly 400 participants rated each item in terms of the amount of stress it produced, and an arbitrary value of 50 was assigned to marriage as a reference point. The results were averaged and divided by 10 to get a measure of the individual

KEY TERMS

Life events: events that are common to many people, which involve change from a steady state.

Life changes: significant changes in the pattern of life, such as a divorce or a holiday, that require some kind of social readjustment. Each life change has a score and total scores over a year can predict psychological upset.

Daily hassles: the minor challenges and problems experienced in our everyday lives.

Life Events		
Rank	**Life event**	**Stress value**
1	Death of a spouse	100
2	Divorce	73
3	Marital separation	65
4	Jail term	63
5	Death of a close family member	63
6	Personal injury or illness	53
7	Marriage	50
8	Fired at work	47
9	Marital reconciliation	45
10	Retirement	45
13	Sex difficulties	39
23	Son or daughter leaving	29
38	Change in sleeping habits	16
40	Change in eating habits	15
41	Vacation	13
42	Christmas	12
43	Minor violations of the law	11

Adapted from Holmes, T., & Rahe, R. (1967). The social readjustment rating scale. *Journal of Psychosomatic Research*, *11*, 213–218.

events in terms of life change units (LCUs), representing the degree of stress caused by events. Total life event scores were worked out by adding up the LCUs for each event ticked on the scale.

Holmes and Rahe (1967) found that there was strong agreement on the ratings across different groups (e.g. male vs female; single vs married; black vs white; younger vs older). Thus, it seemed that the SRRS was a valid measure for all types of people. However, this research involved only American participants. McAndrew et al. (1998) asked Germans, Indians, South Africans, and Americans to rate the amount of stress associated with 32 life events or changes. All groups showed a high level of agreement on the relative stressfulness of these events, indicating that standard measures of life stress are valid cross-culturally.

Changes can be stressful, even the usually pleasant ones associated with going on holiday.

KEY STUDY

Rahe et al. (1970): Life events and illness

Rahe et al. (1970) carried out a study on 2500 male US naval personnel over a period of 6 months. The number of life events was assessed using a self-report questionnaire based on the Social Readjustment Rating Scale (SRRS). Each of the 43 life events had assigned to it a value (or life change unit, LCU) based on how much readjustment the event would require. Participants indicated how many of the life events they had experienced in the past 6 months. A total life change unit score (stress score) was calculated for each participant by adding up the LCUs of each life event. A health record was also kept of each participant during the 6-month tour of duty. A correlational analysis was carried out to test the association between total LCUs and incidence of illness.

Rahe et al. (1970) found a significant (but small) positive correlation of +0.118 between the total LCU (life change unit) score and illness. In other words, as total LCUs increased so did the incidence of illness. However, the strength of the association or relationship was weak even though it was significant because the sample size was large (2500). Implications include the importance of using stress management techniques when experiencing life events.

Why is the study by Rahe et al. (1970) important? First, it provided some of the first evidence that there is a genuine association between stressful life events and physical illness. Second, the study was an improvement on previous research, because careful records of physical illness were kept over a 6-month period. Third, the fact that physical health was assessed *after* the life events increases the chances that the life events were helping to cause problems with physical health rather than the other way around.

Limitations

There are various weaknesses with the study by Rahe et al. (1970). First, the correlational method was used, and so cause and effect can't be inferred—causation can only be inferred when an independent variable has been manipulated directly. Thus, we can't conclude that life events cause illness.

Second, it is likely that illness helped to cause certain life events rather than life events helping to cause illness. For example, two of the life-event items on the SRRS are change in eating habits and change in sleeping habits—it is perfectly possible that physical illness would produce such changes.

Third, the sample was biased because only American men were studied. Thus, the study was ethnocentric (as only one culture was sampled) and androcentric (as only males were sampled). As a result, the findings aren't representative of the wider population (e.g. other cultures; women).

ACTIVITY: The Social Readjustment Rating Scale

Find Holmes and Rahe's SRRS online and complete the scale to find your LCU. Consider why it is a limited measure of stress. Give reasons why we cannot infer cause and effect from the statistically significant correlation between life events and illness.

Findings

The evidence from numerous studies using the Social Readjustment Rating Scale (including the study by Holmes & Rahe, 1967) is that people who have experienced events totalling more than 300 LCUs over a period of 1 year are at greater risk than other people for numerous physical and mental illnesses. These illnesses include heart attacks, diabetes, TB, asthma, anxiety, and depression (Martin, 1989). However, the associations or correlations between LCUs and susceptibility to any particular illness tend to be rather low, indicating only a weak association between life events and illness.

The notion that the stressful life events we experience can have effects on our physical health is important, because it means we shouldn't only look for physical causes of physical illnesses. Several researchers carried out detailed studies to obtain stronger support for the above notion. Rahe et al. (1970) found a small but significant positive association between LCUs (life change units) and physical illness (see the box on the previous page).

Rahe and Arthur (1977) provided support for Rahe et al.'s (1970) findings. They found an increase of various psychological illnesses, athletic injuries, physical illness, and even traffic accidents, when LCUs were high. Pedersen et al. (2010) carried out a meta-analysis (combining the findings from many studies) on the effects of life events or changes on upper respiratory infection. Life events were associated with a significantly increased future risk of such infection.

The study by Pedersen et al. (2010) shows an association between life changes or events and a psychosomatic health complaint (i.e. upper respiratory infection). Hoes (1997) reviewed research on life events or changes and psychosomatic health complaints, finding that negative life changes were associated with numerous such complaints.

Negative life events or changes also increase the risk of very serious illness or early death. Degi et al. (2010) carried out a study on a representative sample of the Hungarian population. Individuals treated for cancer had experienced on average 29% more negative life events over the previous 5 years than those not treated for cancer.

Sbarra et al. (2011) carried out a meta-analysis based on 32 studies focusing on the effects of divorce on early death. Divorced individuals were 23% more likely than non-divorced ones to die early. Divorce may be associated with early death because it leads to reduced social support, reduced financial resources, and an unhealthy lifestyle (e.g. increased tobacco and alcohol use). Note that we can't be sure that early death was actually *caused* by divorce. People who get divorced are more likely than other people to have high hostility, depression, and substance use *before* divorce (Sbarra et al., 2011). Perhaps these aspects of divorced people's personalities and behaviour are responsible for their early death rather than the divorce itself.

Transactional model

Earlier we mentioned the transactional model (Cox, 1978), according to which an individual's stress level is determined by an *interaction* between environmental events and the individual. In other words, the impact of a life event (e.g. major financial problem; break-up of a romantic relationship) depends in part on characteristics of the individual experiencing the life event.

Kendler et al. (2004) tested the transactional model. Individuals who had experienced many severe life events during the preceding year were more likely than those experiencing fewer severe life events to have an onset of major depression. This finding suggests life events can cause stress-related psychological problems. However, Kendler et al. also found the effects of life events on the probability of developing major depression depended strongly on each individual's level of **neuroticism**, a personality dimension relating to the experience of anxiety, tension, and other negative emotions. The impact of severe life events in increasing the risk of major depression was substantially greater in those high in neuroticism. Thus, there was an interaction between life events and neuroticism.

Explanations

Why do life events/changes seem to have numerous negative effects? Remember some of the findings of the review by Segerstrom and Miller (2004) discussed earlier. They found the major life change of loss of one's spouse was associated with reduced natural immunity (a general form of immunity). In those aged over 55, life changes/events reduced both natural immunity and specific immunity. Thus, this is one mechanism by which life changes can impair physical health.

KEY TERM

Neuroticism: a personality dimension proposed by H.J. Eysenck; high scorers experience more intense negative emotional states than low scorers.

There is also evidence that life changes influence the level of cortisol (the "stress hormone"). Karlén et al. (2011) obtained cortisol levels from university students. Those who had experienced a serious life change in the previous three months had higher cortisol levels than the other students.

Causality?

It is generally assumed associations between life changes/events and stress responses occur because experiencing life changes *causes* increased stress. However, it is also possible that individuals who are generally highly stressed or are susceptible to stress have more life events/ changes. In other words, the causality may (at least in part) go in the *opposite* direction to that usually assumed.

Relevant evidence was reported by Van Os et al. (2001). They studied life events in individuals low and high in the personality dimension of neuroticism. Neuroticism assessed at the age of 16 predicted the number of stressful life events experienced 27 years later! Thus, individuals susceptible to stress have an increased likelihood of experiencing stressful life events. The take-home message is that some of the association between life changes and stress occurs because stress-prone individuals have more negative life changes.

> Some people who spend a lot of money on the National Lottery have received stress counselling because their failure to win is making them poor; others receive counselling because of the stress associated with winning large sums of money!

EVALUATION

➕ The Social Readjustment Rating Scale (and the research associated with it) represented a major breakthrough. It is now generally accepted that life events and changes of many kinds influence our well-being.

➕ The development of the SRRS by Holmes and Rahe in 1967 led to a huge increase in life-event research. One application of this research would be to develop techniques to minimise the amount of stress and ill health caused by life events. Another application would be to provide training in how to control those life events that can be controlled. These issues are discussed shortly.

➕ The negative effects of life changes or events seem to extend to numerous aspects of mental and physical health including psychosomatic health complaints.

➖ The research is correlational. As a result, it isn't clear whether life events have *caused* some stress-related illness or whether stress caused the life events. For example, divorce can cause stress, but someone who is already stressed may be more likely to behave in ways that lead to divorce. There is also the evidence of Van Os et al. (2001).

➖ The impact of most life events depends on the precise situation. For example, marital separation may be less stressful for someone who has already established an intimate relationship with another person. Some measures take account of the *context* in which people experience life events. This is the case with the Life Events and Difficulties Schedule (LEDS; see Harris, 1997). For example, consider the life event of losing your job. That is much more likely to cause stress if you have no money and very poor job prospects than if you have a million pounds in the bank and excellent job prospects. It is important to take subjective interpretations into account—it is not so much the events themselves but their meaning for us that matters. Cohen (1983) developed a "perceived stress scale" to assess this.

➖ The SRRS contains very diverse kinds of life events or changes. The assumption built into it that desirable life changes can cause stress-related illnesses has not attracted much support. The SRRS also muddles together events over which you have some control and those over which you have no control. The latter may be more stressful.

The data on life events are typically collected some time after they have occurred. This can cause unreliability—relatively minor life events can be forgotten within a period of a few months, and stressful events exaggerated once an illness diagnosis is made (Martin, 1989).

It is often assumed any serious life event can play a part in causing almost any type of illness. This has led to a relative ignoring of more *specific* effects. Finlay-Jones and Brown (1981) found anxious patients were more likely than depressed patients to have experienced danger events (involving future threats). On the other hand, depressed patients were more likely to have experienced loss events (involving past losses). It would be useful to have more such studies.

Daily hassles

Why might daily hassles be a better measure of stress than life events?

In our everyday lives, we often become stressed because of minor daily hassles. What are the main kinds of daily hassles? Almeida (2005) found 37% involved danger (e.g. potential for future loss), 30% involved loss (e.g. of money), and 27% were frustrations or events outside the individual's control. (In that last category, I must confess to "computer rage" when I can't make my computer do what I want!) People reported more psychological distress on days when they encountered hassles than on other days. However, college-educated adults had less psychological distress and fewer physical symptoms than less-educated ones, although experiencing more daily hassles, perhaps because they used more effective coping strategies.

DeLongis et al. (1982) pointed out that most people experience major life events very rarely whereas they frequently experience daily hassles. According to DeLongis et al., frequently occurring daily hassles are more important than rare life events in determining stress levels. They predicted the correlation between hassles and physical illness would be greater than that for life events.

DeLongis et al. (1982) used a life events scale and their own hassles scale to see which predicted later health problems better. They also considered how **uplifts**—events that make you feel good—affect health. Participants completed four **questionnaires** once a month for a year:

Almeida (2005) found that 27% of our daily hassles fall into the "outside of our control" category. Daily hassles such as traffic jams epitomise this kind of stressor.

- Hassles scale (117 hassles such as concerns about weight, rising prices, home maintenance, losing things, crime, and physical appearance).
- Uplifts scale (135 uplifts such as recreation, relations with friends, good weather, job promotion).
- Life events questionnaire (24 major events).
- A health status questionnaire covering overall health status, bodily symptoms, and energy levels.

DeLongis et al. (1982) found that both the frequency and intensity of hassles were significantly correlated with impaired overall health status and bodily symptoms. However, daily uplifts had little effect on health. There was no relationship between life events and health during the study, but there was one for the 2 years before the study.

A limitation with DeLongis et al.'s (1982) study is that the original sample consisted of people aged over 45. It may be inappropriate to generalise the findings to younger groups. Khan and Patel (1996) found that older people have less severe (and fewer) hassles than younger people.

Another limitation of DeLongis et al.'s (1982) study was that information about hassles and health was only obtained once a month. This approach placed much reliance on the participants' memory and may have been unreliable. Stone et al. (1987) adopted a preferable approach placing less reliance on memory. They considered the hassles and desirable events experienced

KEY TERMS

Uplifts: the positive events of everyday life that increase feelings of psychological well-being.

Questionnaire: a survey requiring written answers.

by participants developing a respiratory illness during the 10 days before its onset. These participants had experienced more hassles and fewer desirable events during that period than control participants who didn't develop a respiratory illness.

Massey et al. (2009) studied the frequency of headaches in adolescents. Adolescents experiencing many hassles tended to have more headaches than those who experienced few hassles.

Khan and Patel (1996) found that older people tended to have less severe (and fewer) hassles than younger people.

ACTIVITY: Daily hassles and illness

You could conduct your own research into the effects of stress and illness using your own daily hassles index. Some examples are given below from an index that was designed specifically for college students. Illness can be assessed by, for example, checking absenteeism or asking people to keep a diary for a short period.

Hassles Scale

Assess yourself by indicating how often each item irritates you, by entering a number between 1 and 10 in the box, where 10 = frequently, 5 = sometimes, and 0 = almost never.

Example items:

- ☐ Parking problems around campus
- ☐ Library too noisy
- ☐ Too little money
- ☐ Not enough close friends
- ☐ Conflicts with family
- ☐ Writing essays

- ☐ Careless bike riders
- ☐ Too little time
- ☐ Boring teacher
- ☐ Room temperatures
- ☐ Too little sleep
- ☐ Fixing hair in the morning

Adapted from Schafer, W. (1992), *Stress management for wellness (2nd Edn)*. New York: Harcourt Brace Jovanovich.

Explanations

Why do hassles have negative effects? Several factors have been identified. For example, daily hassles are associated with increased levels of cortisol (a stress-related hormone) (Sher, 2004), which may help to explain why they impair physical health.

Twisk et al. (1999) found people in their 20s experiencing increased numbers of daily hassles showed changes in their health-related behaviour. They became more likely to smoke but they had more physical activity. Another effect of hassles on health-related behaviour was reported by O'Connor et al. (2008). They found that individuals with the most daily hassles had increased consumption of high-fat, sugar-based snacks and reduced vegetable consumption. In other words, hassles led to the adoption of a less healthy diet.

Jain et al. (2007) studied the effects of hassles on the probability of the blood becoming abnormally thick, a condition that can increase the likelihood of blood clots. Hassles increased this probability whereas uplifts decreased it.

Finally, the effects of daily hassles depend on individuals' experience of major life events. The number of psychiatric symptoms reported by students experiencing major life events was greater if they also had substantial numbers of daily hassles (Johnson & Sherman, 1997). Thus, we should consider both daily hassles *and* life events.

Causality?

The major difficulty when interpreting findings on hassles and stress is the causality issue. Hassles could be associated with stress responses because hassles help to cause stress responses or because stress-prone individuals experience more hassles. This issue was examined by Barker (2011). Various personality measures were used at the start of the experiment and then life events and hassles were assessed 10 weeks later.

What did Barker (2011) find? Individuals high in neuroticism (personality dimension relating to negative emotions) at time 1 experienced more academic and interpersonal hassles than those low in neuroticism. Thus, at least some of the relationship between hassles and stress occurs because individuals who are stress-prone (i.e. high in neuroticism) experience more hassles in their everyday lives. This is the *opposite* direction of causality to the one that is usually assumed.

EVALUATION

➕ There is a moderate association between daily hassles and physical health.

➕ The fact that minor daily hassles are far more common than major life events suggests the importance of establishing the extent to which stress levels and physical health are affected by daily hassles.

➕ Some of the reasons why hassles might have negative effects on health have been identified. These include blood thickening, increased cortisol levels, and poorer health-related behaviour.

➕ It is useful to consider the combined effects of daily hassles and life events on physical and psychological health (e.g. Johnson and Sherman, 1997). Applications of this research include the provision of training in coping strategies to minimise the adverse effects of daily hassles on stress and health combined with providing individuals with an understanding that daily hassles can be more damaging than is often supposed.

➖ We are dealing with correlational data for the most part. That means it is hard to know whether hassles cause stress or whether stress-prone individuals experience more hassle.

➖ There are issues to do with individual differences in the meaning attached to occurrences. For example, a traffic jam may sometimes give you time to relax, whereas at other times it seems highly stressful. For this reason, DeLongis et al. (1988) produced a single "Hassles and Uplifts Scale" on which respondents could indicate the strength of a factor as a hassle or uplift.

➖ There has been much confusion about the distinction between daily hassles and chronic or long-lasting stressors (e.g. poor housing; strains of family life; unsatisfying work). Hahn and Smith (1999) presented participants with items from standard questionnaires designed to measure daily hassles or chronic stressors, and asked them to categorise each item. Many of the items allegedly measuring daily hassles were categorised as chronic stressors and vice versa. These findings suggest the distinction is unclear.

HOW SCIENCE WORKS: Stress in everyday life

Scientific research often uses a pilot study to check on the methodology—a small-scale trial run of the method and the data collection to see if they work. You could set up a pilot study for a study of daily hassles in your own age group. First you could print out a list of what you think are the 10 most frequent daily hassles, and ask participants to tick those with which they agree, and to add up to 3 that they feel you have missed out. You would then be able to analyse these data to find the 10 most frequent hassles for your sample. This would allow you, as a researcher, to evaluate your original list and modify it if necessary, before carrying out your main research project (using different participants from the pilot study). This is an illustration of good planning for an investigation into a psychological theory, in this instance the daily hassles theory.

the effects of majority influence, previously found in situations in which the stimulus was ambiguous, are so great that they are still present even when it is apparently obvious that the majority have responded incorrectly. (See the box below.)

 To what extent can we generalise about human behaviour from these studies?

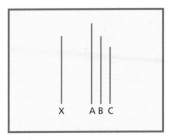

KEY STUDY

Asch's (1951) conformity study

Asch set up a situation in which (in some of his experiments) seven people all sat looking at a display. In turn, they said out loud which one of three lines A, B, or C was the same length as a given stimulus line X (see illustration on the right). All but one of the participants were confederates of the experimenter, that is, they were behaving as the experimenter told them to behave beforehand.

On "critical" trials, the confederates were instructed to give the same wrong answer unanimously. The one genuine participant was the last (or the last but one) to offer his/her opinion on each trial. The performance of participants exposed to such group pressure was compared to performance in a control condition in which there were no confederates.

Asch's participants weren't told the true nature of the study. Was this ethical?

Findings

What did Asch (1951) find? On the critical trials on which all the confederates gave the same wrong answer, the genuine participants showed majority influence by also giving the same wrong answer on 37% of trials. We need to compare this figure against the error rate in the control condition (with no group), which was only 0.7%. In other words, participants answered correctly over 99% of the time when there was no social pressure.

Many participants who gave wrong responses admitted they had yielded to majority influence because they didn't want to stand out. Individuals who gave only correct answers said they were confident in the accuracy of their own judgement or focused on performing the task as directed (i.e. striving to be accurate and correct).

The main conclusion of Asch's study is that a majority can influence a minority even in an unambiguous situation in which the correct answer is obvious (as shown by the almost perfect performance in the control condition). Asch showed convincingly that group pressure to conform in terms of majority influence is much stronger than had been thought previously. However, remember that the genuine participant actually gave the correct answer on about two-thirds of the crucial trials. Thus, many people can successfully resist majority influence.

Limitations

We will briefly discuss the main limitations with this study, some of which are discussed in more detail later. First, Asch's study was carried out in the United States in the late 1940s. This was a time at which conformity was high and "doing your own thing" was much less socially acceptable than in the 1960s and afterwards.

Second, Asch obtained some relevant evidence from questioning his participants. However, he didn't really explain *why* there was so much majority influence. He also failed to explain clearly *why* there were individual differences in the tendency to submit to majority influence (we consider this issue later).

Third, Asch's research raises important ethical issues. His participants didn't provide fully informed consent because they were misled about key aspects of the experimental procedures (e.g. the presence of confederates). In addition, they were placed in a difficult and embarrassing position—many of them became very anxious and distressed.

Fourth, even though this study by Asch (1951) is one of the most famous in the whole of social psychology, there was actually nothing very social about it because he used groups of strangers! Why this matters is discussed shortly.

EXAM HINT

Take note of the reasons why some people did NOT conform. In all, 25% of people never conformed in this study (that is, they always gave the correct line length). The reasons why they did this are mentioned in the study—make sure you know these, so you can use them when discussing independent behaviour, a topic that comes later in the chapter.

What does Asch's study tell us about non-conformity?

? Asch carried out his research in the United States. Why might the findings be different in other cultures?

Asch (1956) extended his original research. He manipulated various aspects of the situation to understand more fully the factors underlying conformity based on majority influence. He found majority influence increased as the number of confederates went up from one to three, but there was no increase between three and sixteen confederates. However, a small increase in conformity has sometimes been found as the number of confederates goes up above three. In addition, the precise effects of adding to the number of confederates depend on whether participants respond publicly or privately (Bond, 2005).

Asch (1956) found that another important factor was whether the genuine participant had a supporter (a confederate who gave the correct answer on all trials and answered before the genuine participant). Participants with a supporter showed majority influence on only 5% of crucial trials—this is a dramatic reduction from the 37% found by Asch (1951) when there was no supporter.

Temporal, Cultural, and Individual Difference Factors

The research discussed so far involved American participants who were tested in the Asch situation in the late 1940s and early 1950s. It would be unwise to assume such findings would necessarily be obtained at other times and in other cultures. Over the intervening decades, there have been considerable changes in views and behaviour in the United States and most other countries. There are also large differences across cultures. In addition, **individual differences** in personality and other factors (e.g. education) help to determine the extent of majority influence. In this section we will discuss temporal, cultural, and individual difference factors.

Temporal factors

? Why might engineering students be less likely to conform in these kinds of studies than other students?

Perrin and Spencer (1980) repeated Asch's study in England in the late 1970s. They found very little evidence of majority influence, and concluded that the Asch effect was "a child of its time". However, the low level of majority influence may have occurred because they used engineering students. These students had been given training in the importance of accurate measurement and so had more confidence in their own opinions about the length of the lines.

Smith and Bond (1993) reviewed studies that had used Asch's task in the United States. They concluded (1993, p. 124) that, "Levels of conformity in general had steadily declined since Asch's studies in the early 1950s." However, even the more recent studies still nearly all showed clear evidence of majority influence. How can we explain this trend? There is much evidence that the need for social approval went down in the United States between the 1950s and the early 1980s (Twenge & Im, 2007). Individuals with a low need for social approval are less likely to pay much attention to the views of others. In today's society, individuals "do their own thing".

Perrin and Spencer (1980) carried out two more studies. In one study, the participants were young men on probation. Mixed in with these genuine participants were confederates of the experimenter primed to give the same wrong answers. The level of conformity shown was about the same as in the Asch studies. In the other study, the participants and the confederates were both young unemployed men with Afro-Caribbean backgrounds. Once again, conformity levels were similar to those reported by Asch (1951).

Cultural factors

Bond and Smith (1996) reported a meta-analysis of cross-cultural studies of conformity using Asch's experimental design. The participants gave the wrong answer on average on 31.2% of trials across these studies, only slightly lower than the figure obtained by Asch. The highest figure was 58% wrong answers for Indian teachers in Fiji, and the lowest figure (apart from Perrin & Spencer, 1980) was 14% among Belgian students.

Social psychologists distinguish between individualistic and collectivistic cultures. Individualistic cultures (e.g. the United Kingdom and the United States) emphasise the desirability of individuals being responsible for their own well-being and having a sense of personal identity. In contrast, collectivistic cultures emphasise the priority of group needs over individual ones, and value the feeling of group identity and solidarity.

KEY TERM

Individual differences: the characteristics that vary from one individual to another; intelligence and personality are major ways in which individuals differ.

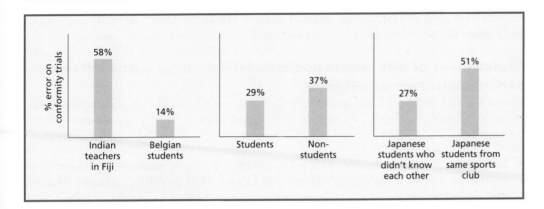

When Asch's study was replicated, cross-cultural differences emerged.

Kim and Markus (1999) found that a failure to show conformity is seen positively as *uniqueness* in individualistic cultures but negatively as *deviance* in collectivistic ones. Bond and Smith (1996) analysed numerous Asch-type studies in several countries. As expected, majority influence was greater in collectivistic cultures in Asia, Africa, and elsewhere (37.1% of trials) than in individualistic cultures in North America and Europe (25.3%). Thus, conformity is 50% greater in collectivistic cultures.

? What are some of the limitations of cross-cultural studies?

Individual differences

Some individuals conform more than others because of their biology or experience. Students made errors on 29% of crucial trials in the Asch task compared to 37% for non-students, perhaps because students are more independent than non-students in their thinking. Alternatively, their higher level of intelligence may make them more confident in their opinions.

? Why do you think students were less likely to conform (28%) than non-students (37%)

Some studies have found gender differences, with women being more affected by majority influence than men (Eagly & Carli, 1981). Eagly (1978) suggested that many of the studies are biased because they focus on "masculine" content, i.e. issues on which it is generally accepted that men are more knowledgeable than women. It would be expected that individuals who are very knowledgeable would be less open to influence than those who aren't. Maslach et al. (1987) used an equal number of feminine-relevant and masculine-relevant stories, and found no gender difference in conformity via majority influence.

Other research has also failed to find gender differences. For example, Kurosawa (1993) studied majority influence in the Asch situation with two or four confederates. There was no gender effect in either condition. However, those low in self-esteem showed more majority influence than those high in self-esteem when there were four confederates.

De Young et al. (2002) consider the impact of various personality dimensions on conformity. Individuals who were high in conscientiousness and/or agreeableness were more conformist than those low in those dimensions.

Conclusions

What conclusions should we draw from Asch's research? Asch (and many others) argued that his participants had a moral obligation to tell the truth. In other words, every participant had a responsibility to the truth, to "call it as he/she saw it". From that perspective, it is regrettable that 75% of the participants produced the wrong answer in response to group pressure at least once, and so exhibited mindless conformity. However, this argument is flawed, as is discussed below.

First, we mustn't overstate the amount of conformity. In fact, 25% of participants did *not* conform to the group's wrong answers at all, and nearly 70% defied the group on a majority of the trials.

Second, Asch and other researchers found many of their participants became aroused and somewhat distressed. Thus, they were aware of a strong conflict between producing the correct answer and their wish not to ignore the group.

Third, the participants were placed in a dilemma with no easy answer. Many of their "errors" can be seen as expressing their respect for group cohesion and their desire to avoid ridicule. Most participants gave a mixture of correct and incorrect answers because this was the best way for them to show group solidarity *and* perceptual accuracy (Hodges & Geyer, 2006). Perhaps Asch's participants should be praised rather than criticised!

Explanations of why people conform: informational social influence and normative social influence

One of the most influential attempts to identify the factors responsible for conformity based on majority influence was that of Deutsch and Gerard (1955). They proposed two possible explanations:

- **Informational social influence**: This is "an influence to accept information obtained from another as *evidence* about reality" (Deutsch & Gerard, 1955, p. 629). It generally involves majority influence due to the perceived superior knowledge or judgement of others, as in Sherif's (1935) study. For example, it might happen that several friends of yours all have the same view (but different from yours) about a topic in psychology about which they know more than you. It generally leads to a change in private as well as public opinion.

- **Normative social influence**: This is "an influence to conform with the positive expectations of another" (Deutsch & Gerard, 1955, p. 629). It involves majority influence due to wanting to be liked by the other members of the group (i.e. social approval) and to avoid being rejected. It undoubtedly played a major role in Asch's (1951, 1956) research. For example, when Asch (1956) had one confederate in a group of genuine participants give the wrong answer, the group laughed out loud at the confederate. When the confederate continued to give wrong answers, he/she was rejected by the group. Many people are motivated to avoid such embarrassment. Normative social influence affects public opinions but isn't likely to change private opinions.

It is easy to imagine that Deutsch and Gerard (1955) believed that one or other of the two forms of influence (but not both) would be operative at any given time. However, that was *not* what they thought. Deutsch and Gerard (1955, p. 629) argued that, "Commonly these two types of influence are found together." However, Deutsch and Gerard (1955) predicted that normative social influence would be especially important in the Asch-type situation in which the correct answer was unambiguous.

Before proceeding, we will briefly consider a factor that influences the extent of normative social influence. Suppose someone asked you to describe your best friend in detail. Your description would probably include some indication of the groups to which he/she belongs (e.g. student at college; hockey team member). According to social identity theory (Tajfel & Turner, 1979), we all have **social identities** based on the different groups to which we belong. Our sense of ourselves is strongly influenced by our social identities. Having a positive social identity makes us feel good about ourselves and enhances our self-esteem.

Why are social identities important in influencing conformity behaviour? We feel positively about the groups to which we belong (ingroups) but negatively about many other groups (outgroups). This produces **ingroup bias** (the tendency to favour one's ingroup over outgroups). As a result, we are more likely to be influenced by group members (and thus exhibit conformity) when they belong to our ingroup than when they do not.

Findings: Normative social influence

A useful starting point for understanding why participants often conform in the Asch situation is to ask them. That is what Asch (1951) did. Participants' self-reports focused on factors such as feeling self-conscious, fearing disapproval, and feeling anxious, suggesting that normative social influence was at work. Self-reports provide interesting data, but we can't be sure they accurately identify the reasons why people conform.

We could explain the level of conformity found in Asch's (1951) basic situation by assuming that the requirement to give their judgements out loud maximised normative social influence.

What is the difference between informational and normative social influence?

People might conform because of:

- Informational social influence
  - Why conform? Because you believe in the superior knwledge or judgement of others.
  - This leads people to change their private opinion.

- Normative social influence
  - Why conform? Because you want to be liked or respected by other members of the group.
  - This doesn't lead people to change their private opinion.

KEY TERMS

Informational social influence: when someone conforms because others are thought to possess more knowledge.

Normative social influence: when someone conforms in order to gain liking or respect from others.

Social identities: each of the groups with which we identify produces a social identity; our feelings about ourselves depend on how we feel about the groups with which we identify.

Ingroup bias: the tendency to view one's own group more favourably than other groups.

If so, conformity should be less if participants wrote down their judgements privately. Asch (1951) did precisely that, and conformity dropped to 12.5%. This happened because there is much less normative social influence when other group members are unaware of your judgements.

Bond (2005) carried out a meta-analysis of Asch-type studies in which the number of confederates varied. He compared studies in which participants responded publicly or privately. As expected, conformity increased in line with increasing number of confederates with public responding. However, the *opposite* was found with private responding—the more confederates there were, the *less* private conformity there was! These findings suggest increased public conformity with increasing numbers of confederates is mainly due to normative social influence.

Deutsch and Gerard (1955) assessed the role of normative social influence by extending Asch's research. They used several conditions varying in the likely importance of normative social influence but with the same information about the judgements of other group members available to them. Thus, any group differences should depend mainly on differences in normative social influence. The main conditions were as follows:

1. *Face-to-face situation*: this was very similar to Asch's situation with three confederates and the genuine participant announcing his/her judgements publicly.
2. *Anonymous situation*: the genuine participant gave his/her judgements anonymously in an isolated cubicle by pressing a button, believing that there were three other participants.
3. *Group situation*: this was like the anonymous situation except that the experimenter said a reward would be given to the groups making the most accurate decisions.

What would we expect to find? Normative social influence (and so conformity) should be greatest in the third condition (social pressure to conform) and least in the second condition. That was precisely what Deutsch and Gerard (1955) found. They also used a variation of the anonymous situation in which participants wrote down their judgements on a sheet of paper and then threw them away. In this situation (designed to minimise normative social influence) participants conformed on only 5% of trials.

Earlier we mentioned that Asch found that conformity decreased from 37% to 5% when a single confederate consistently gave the correct judgements. This could be due to reduced normative social influence (e.g. "Thank goodness I have some social support!") or to informational social influence (e.g. "Here is information suggesting there is no problem with my eyesight!"). However, Asch also found that a confederate of the experimenter giving judgements even more incorrect than the majority was as effective as an accurate confederate in reducing conformity. Presumably the inaccurate confederate reduced normative social influence more than informational social influence—the confederate didn't provide accurate information.

The effects of majority influence are much stronger when participants really care about the opinions of the other group members. Abrams et al. (1990) argued their first-year psychology participants would show more conformity if the other group members were perceived as belonging to an ingroup (first-year psychology students from a nearby university) than if they were perceived as belonging to an outgroup (students of ancient history).

The above manipulation had a dramatic effect—there was conformity on 58% of trials in the presence of an ingroup compared to only 8% with an outgroup. Asch failed to realise he could have obtained much stronger majority influence if he had replaced groups of strangers with ingroup members.

When might we expect normative social influence to be important? Suppose you were given an important, difficult task. In those circumstances, you might well rely on the information provided by other group members (i.e. informational social influence). That is what Baron et al. (1996) found. Participants were given easy and difficult versions of the same task and were told it was very important or unimportant. Substantial conformity effects were only found when the task was difficult and very important.

According to Baron et al. (1996), if a participant is told that a "counting the jelly beans" task is very important, he or she would be more likely to rely on, and be influenced by, the information provided by other group members.

Findings: Informational social influence

There is evidence from the Asch-type situation that informational social influence *can* be an important factor. Allen and Levine (1971) asked participants to make visual and other judgements in a group setting. There were three conditions: (1) participants had no support; (2) participants had a valid supporter with normal vision; and (3) participants had an invalid supporter with very poor vision who wore very thick glasses.

There was a very high level of conformity in the first condition (97% of critical trials) and a much lower level when there was a valid supporter (36%). The most interesting condition involved the invalid supporter, in which conformity was observed on 64% of critical trials. The lower conformity with a valid supporter than with an invalid one presumably occurred because the valid supporter reduced the group's informational social influence. However, the lower conformity with an invalid supporter than with no supporter is likely to reflect reduced normative social influence in the former condition.

So far we have focused mainly on the Asch situation. The processes involved are somewhat different in the Crutchfield situation (Crutchfield, 1955). This involves groups of five individuals sitting side by side in individual booths. They were shown slides containing multiple-choice questions and given the following instructions:

> *The slides call for various kinds of judgements—lengths of lines, areas of figures, logical completion of number series, vocabulary items, estimates of the opinions of others, expression of his own attitudes on issues, expression of his personal preferences for line drawings …*

There are two major differences between the Crutchfield situation and the Asch one. First, there is a less obvious group, in that participants in the Crutchfield situation can't see the other group members. Second, it is much harder to be confident of the correct answers in the Crutchfield situation, because many questions involve specialised knowledge or are based on opinions. Thus, participants are far more likely to be seeking information than in the Asch situation, and so informational social influence should be more important. Crutchfield (1955) found less intellectually effective participants showed more conformity, probably because they were more affected by informational social influence.

Lucas et al. (2006) also found evidence for informational social influence. Students answered easy and hard problems in mathematics. There was more conformity to the incorrect answers of others with hard problems than with easy ones, especially with students who doubted their mathematical ability. It is reasonable to assume that informational social influence would be greatest when individuals are given difficult problems and doubt their ability to solve them.

EVALUATION

➕ Conformity generally depends on some mixture of normative social influence (involving emotional processes) and informational social influence (involving cognitive processes). Thus, Deutsch and Gerard (1955) successfully identified two key processes underlying conformity behaviour.

➕ Some factors increasing or decreasing these types of social influence have been studied. Normative social influence is reduced when participants' judgements are anonymous and private, participants are permitted to throw away information about their judgements, or they have social support in the form of at least one supporter or dissenter from the majority. Informational social influence is greater when the situation is ambiguous, accuracy is crucial, a supporter possesses valid information, and the participants doubt their knowledge or ability.

➖ It is often not possible to decide whether the effects of any given factor on conformity behaviour are due to normative social influence, informational social influence, or some mixture of both. For example, conformity is markedly reduced if the genuine participant has one supporter. That supporter may provide social support (reducing the group's normative influence) and/or useful information (reducing the group's informational influence). We have no easy way of telling which type of social influence is more important.

- Deutsch and Gerard (1955) assumed that normative social influence would be extremely common, because it occurs whenever individuals seek social approval and acceptance. However, there is more to normative social influence than that. As discussed earlier, Abrams et al. (1990) found *seven* times as much conformity when the other group members belonged to one of the participants' ingroups rather than an outgroup. These findings suggest that group belongingness is much more powerful than simply the need for social approval.

- The extent of conformity behaviour depends on both the situation in which an individual finds himself/herself *and* his/her personal characteristics. For example, highly intelligent and knowledgeable individuals are less affected by informational social influence than those of lesser intelligence and knowledge. In addition, individuals with a great need to be positively regarded by others will be more affected by normative social influence than those with a lesser need. Most research has focused on situational determinants of social influence, and as yet we lack a clear idea of how situational and personal factors interact to determine conformity behaviour.

Types of Conformity Including Internalisation and Compliance

We have seen that there is much conformity through majority influence. Kelman (1958) argued it is important to distinguish between social influence in which individuals conform publicly but not privately and social influence in which their private beliefs change to agree with others. He used this distinction to outline three different kinds of social influence, discussed below. His approach was relatively broad, in that he considered social influence within society as well as within the laboratory.

1. **Internalisation** (genuine acceptance of group norms) occurs "when an individual accepts influence because the content of the induced behaviour—the ideas and actions of which it is composed—is intrinsically rewarding. He adopts the induced behaviour because it is congruent [consistent] with his value system" (Kelman, 1958, p. 53). Internalisation is involved when someone shows influence from other group members because he/she is really in agreement with their views. Since the *content* of the message matters with internalisation, it is likely to be thoroughly processed. Internalisation is most likely to be found when the person or group providing the influence is credible and communicates what appears to be valuable information. Of importance, internalisation always involves private conformity and often also involves public conformity.

2. **Compliance** (or group acceptance) occurs "when an individual accepts influence because he hopes to achieve a favourable reaction from another person or group. He adopts the induced behaviour because … he expects to gain specific rewards or approval and avoid specific punishments or disapproval by conforming" (Kelman, 1958, p. 53). As the influence is only *superficial*, compliance stops when there are no group pressures to conform. Compliance is most likely to be found when the person or group providing the influence is powerful and controlling. Of crucial importance, compliance involves conformity at a public but not at a private level—the individual's behaviour shows conformity but their private beliefs haven't changed.

3. **Identification** (or group membership) occurs "when an individual accepts influence because he wants to establish or maintain a satisfying self-defining relationship to another person or a group" (Kelman, 1958, p. 53). Identification is found when someone shows influence with respect to the demands of a given role in society, conforming to what is expected of them. It is seen in the behaviour of nurses, traffic wardens, and air hostesses regardless of how they may actually be feeling.

[?] Do some individuals and groups have more influence over you than others? If so, why do you think this might be the case?

[?] Which of these are examples of "true conformity"?

KEY TERMS

Internalisation: conformity behaviour where the individual has completely accepted the views of the majority.

Compliance: conforming to the majority view in order to be liked, or to avoid ridicule or social exclusion. Compliance occurs more readily with public behaviour than private behaviour, and is based on power.

Identification: conforming to the demands of a given role because of a desire to be like a particular person in that role.

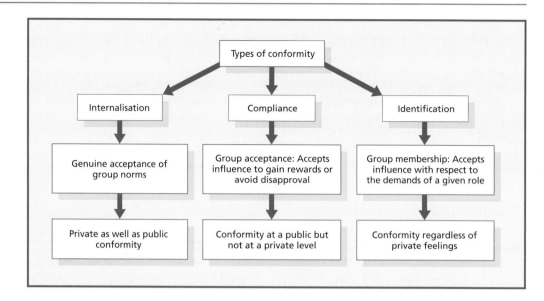

Kelman (1958) provided support for the distinction between compliance and internalisation. Black American students were presented with a message indicating it was important to maintain some private black colleges as all-black institutions to preserve black culture. This was a message initially opposed by most students.

In the compliance condition, the students were told the message came from a very powerful man who would withdraw funds from any college disagreeing with his position. In the internalisation condition, the same message was allegedly from a very credible source (a top expert on the problems of minority groups). After message presentation, participants completed a **questionnaire** concerning the relevant issues. Some students were told their answers would be shown to the person delivering the message (public responding), whereas others were told their answers were anonymous (private responding).

In the compliance condition, students were significantly more influenced by the message with public than with private responding. That suggests their private views hadn't really changed as a result of exposure to the message. In contrast, in the internalisation condition, the views expressed were very similar with public and private responding. Thus, these participants had been influenced by the message privately as well as publicly. Overall, the findings were consistent with Kelman's theoretical predictions.

We will consider identification later. For now we will consider internalisation and compliance in more detail.

Internalisation

As mentioned earlier, what is of central importance about internalisation is that there is private conformity and generally public conformity as well. In what circumstances would we expect to find conformity due to internalisation? According to Kelman (1958), this is most likely to happen when the majority appears knowledgeable. It is also likely to be important that members of the minority have little relevant knowledge to refute the majority position.

Earlier in the chapter we discussed research showing evidence of conformity due to internalisation. Sherif (1935) studied people's judgements on the apparent movement of a light that was actually stationary. Individuals rapidly adjusted their judgements to conform to those of the other group members: this shows public conformity. When the same individuals were tested on their own, their judgements typically remained similar to the ones they had given in the group situation. Since these judgements were given in the absence of any group, they indicate private conformity. Thus, the participants showed a mixture of public and private conformity suggestive of internalisation.

Why did internalisation occur in the Sherif (1935) research? The participants were in an ambiguous situation in which they had no relevant knowledge or experience to guide them. As a result, their internal and external judgements were both strongly influenced by the majority.

Internalisation occurs more often when there is majority informational social influence rather than normative social influence. Majority informational social influence is especially likely when the majority has (or appears to have) far more relevant expertise than the minority. For example, suppose you were at an A-level Psychology conference and you were in a small group discussing some issue. Suppose all the others were teachers of A-level Psychology and they all held the same view on some topic in psychology. Their majority influence on you would probably cause a change in your private and public views, and would thus involve internationalisation. The study by Lucas et al. (2006) discussed earlier is relevant at this point. They found that people who doubted their own mathematical ability were more likely than others to conform to the wrong answers to mathematical problems produced by the majority.

Moscovici (1980) argued in his conversion theory (discussed fully later) that majority influence rarely occurs through internalisation. According to him, people want to belong to the majority. This causes them to agree publicly with the majority position without taking the time to consider its arguments properly. As a result, majority influence does not lead to private attitude change and internalisation. Much research supports these predictions from conversion theory.

In fact, however, Moscovici's views are oversimplified. Martin et al. (2007) argued that minorities would engage in thorough processing of majority views provided the topic was of high personal relevance to them. Their findings supported this prediction. Of most relevance here, minorities showed more evidence of internalisation (private attitude change) when the majority message was of high rather than low personal relevance.

Finally, we consider the extreme majority influence that is found in many cults (especially destructive ones). Monroney (2008), who had herself previously belonged to a cult, carried out research on six former cult members. They all reported that there was enormous pressure to conform to group influence in several ways. First, they were told to shed their previous self and adopt a new cult self. Second, they were expected to have little or no contact with their family and friends. Third, they were rapidly enveloped in the culture of the cult: "All the participants, including myself, had instant friendships from other cult members. The cult became our family."

Monroney (2008) assessed the impact of the above pressures by asking her six participants to rate on a scale of 0–10 how controlling the cult environment had been. Four of them gave a rating of 10. The powerful majority influence causes internalisation, as can be seen in the extreme forms of behaviour that cult members are willing to engage in. For example, consider the Heaven's Gate cult in the United States. When its members were told to leave their physical bodies behind to find redemption in an extra-terrestrial Kingdom of Heaven, 39 of them committed suicide.

In sum, several aspects of the situation jointly determine whether majority influence involves internalisation:

- A knowledgeable majority.
- Minority members who lack relevant knowledge or experience.
- Situations in which there is majority informational social influence rather than normative social influence.
- Situations in which minority members engage in thorough processing of the majority views.
- Situations (e.g. cults) in which strong attempts are made to prevent minority members from being exposed to any views conflicting with those of the majority.

Compliance

Remember that compliance involves public conformity in the absence of private conformity. We have already discussed some of the strongest evidence for compliance—the famous studies by Asch. Asch (1951) found that participants tested on their own made the correct responses on over 99% of the trials. That means they had no difficulty whatsoever in identifying which of the three lines matched a given line. Thus, the fact that participants in the group situation conformed on about 35% of critical trials strongly suggests that their conformity was due to compliance.

We can obtain evidence about the extent of compliance by comparing the amount of conformity in the Asch situation when participants respond publicly and when they respond privately. Evidence of compliance would involve finding that conformity is much less with private than with public responding. We have already seen that public conformity is found on about 35% of trials. In contrast, Asch (1951) found private conformity occurred on only 12.5% of trials. When Deutsch and Gerrard (1955) used an anonymous situation in which participants wrote down their answers on a piece of paper and then threw them away, conformity dropped to only 5%.

One of the few studies directly comparing public and private responding in the Asch situation was reported by Insko et al. (1985). When the group size was small, conformity to the group was equal in the public and private conditions. When the group size was larger, however, there was more conformity in the public than the private condition. This difference indicates compliance.

The above findings suggest that much of the conformity found with public responding is superficial and is based on compliance. However, it is important to note that they do NOT indicate that all public responding in the Asch situation involves compliance. If that were the case, then we might expect to find no private conformity at all—that would mean producing wrong answers on only about 1% of the trials as Asch found when there was no group at all.

We saw earlier (Martin et al., 2007) that conformity often involves internalisation when minority members engage in thorough processing of the majority's message. What happens when minority members don't processing that message thoroughly? Martin et al. found that majority influence mostly involved compliance in those circumstances. This makes sense—your private beliefs are unlikely to be influenced by a message to which you pay little attention.

Why do participants in the Asch situation often respond to group pressure by pretending to agree with the group while privately disagreeing? The most obvious reason is because they want to avoid being ridiculed and then ignored by the other group members. Remember that Asch (1956) found that a single confederate who consistently produced the wrong answers was laughed at and then rejected by the rest of the group.

Another likely reason why individuals show compliance in the Asch situation is the more positive one of wanting to be fully accepted as belonging to the group. Such motivation should be much stronger if individuals perceive the other members as belonging to an ingroup rather than an outgroup. As predicted, public conformity was seven times more common with ingroups than with outgroups (Abrams et al., 1990).

In sum, several aspects of the situation determine whether conformity involves compliance:

- In the Asch situation, the number of people in the majority influences compliance-based conformity.
- Compliance is more likely when conformity depends on normative social influence.
- Situations in which the accuracy of group performance is important.
- Situations in which individuals fear ridicule produce compliance.
- Situations in which individuals regard the majority as their ingroup rather than outgroup.

CASE STUDY: Groupthink

Conformity to group opinion has many important applications, such as in juries and in the management committees of large organisations. The way individuals behave in these groups is likely to matter a lot. Janis (1972) coined the term "groupthink" to describe how the thinking of people in these situations is often disastrously affected by conformity.

Janis was describing the "Bay of Pigs" disaster to his teenage daughter and she challenged him, as a psychologist, to explain why such experts could make such poor decisions. (The Bay of Pigs invasion took place in 1961. President Kennedy and a group of government advisers made a series of bad decisions that resulted in this extremely unsuccessful invasion of the Bay of Pigs in Cuba—disastrous because 1000 men from the invasion force were only released after a ransom payment of $53,000,000 worth of food and medicine, and also because ultimately the invasion resulted in the Cuban missile crisis and a threat of nuclear war.) Janis suggested that there are a number of group factors that tend to increase conformity and result in bad decision-making:

- Group factors. People in groups do not want to be ostracised, they want to be liked and therefore tend to do things to be accepted as one of the group.
- Decisional stress. A group feels under pressure to reach a decision. To reduce this sense of pressure group members try to reach the decision quickly and with little argument.
- Isolation. Groups often work in isolation, which means there are no challenges to the way members are thinking.
- Institutional factors. Often people who are appointed to higher positions are those who tend to conform, following the principle that a good soldier makes a good commander.

Identification

As mentioned earlier, identification is found when individuals perform roles in ways expected of them. Consider the brutal attacks by prison guards on prisoners in American prisons during the 1960s. This behaviour may have been due mainly to prisons' social environment (e.g. rigid power structure). Thus, prison guards may have behaved as they felt was expected in their particular role—this is identification, and it is a **situational explanation**.

There is an alternative explanation. Perhaps those who put themselves in a position of power by becoming prison guards have aggressive or sadistic personalities. This is a **dispositional explanation**.

Wearing a uniform may lead individuals to conform to an expected role. This is known as "identification".

KEY STUDY

Zimbardo's Stanford prison experiment

Philip Zimbardo (1973) studied this important issue in the Stanford prison experiment, carried out in the basement of Stanford University's psychology department. Emotionally stable individuals acted as "guards" and "prisoners" in a mock prison. Zimbardo wanted to see whether hostility would be found in his mock prison. If hostility were found in spite of not using sadistic guards, this would suggest the power structure creates hostility.

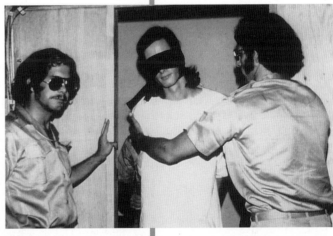

What happened was so unpleasant and dangerous that the entire experiment was stopped 8 days early! Violence and rebellion broke out within 2 days. The prisoners ripped off their clothing and shouted and cursed at the guards. In return, the guards violently put down this rebellion by using fire extinguishers. One prisoner showed such severe symptoms of emotional disturbance (disorganised thinking and screaming) that he was released after only 1 day. Over time, the prisoners became more subdued and submissive. At the same time, the use of force, harassment, and aggression by the guards increased steadily, and were clearly excessive reactions to the prisoners' submissive behaviour.

Some of the mock guards in Zimbardo's experiment became very aggressive during, and four of the mock prisoners had to be released early.

What conclusions can we draw? First, the study suggested that brutality and aggression in prisons are due mainly to the power structure. Thus, the study seems to show conformity by identification. However, real prison guards may be more sadistic than other people.

Second, the study showed how stereotypes about the kinds of behaviour expected of guards and prisoners influenced the participants' actions. According to Haney et al. (1973, p. 12), guard aggression "was emitted [shown] simply as a 'natural' consequence of being in the uniform of a 'guard' and asserting the power inherent in that role". More generally, identification was shown by the guards and prisoners, who both conformed closely to expected forms of behaviour. In addition, the guards all behaved in similar ways, and the same was true of the prisoners. This indicates a conformity effect, and may reflect the participants' need to be accepted by their fellow guards or prisoners.

Limitations

Various criticisms can be made of the Stanford prison experiment. First, the mock prison was very different from a real prison. For example, the participants knew they hadn't committed any crime and were free to leave.

continued over

KEY TERMS

Situational explanation: deciding that people's actions are caused by the situation in which they find themselves rather than by their personality.

Dispositional explanation: deciding that other people's actions are caused by their internal characteristics or dispositions.

KEY TERM

Participant reactivity:
the situation in which an
independent variable has an
effect on participants merely
because they know they are
being observed.

Second, the artificial set-up may have produced effects due to **participant reactivity**, with the guards and prisoners merely play-acting. However, the physical abuse and harassment shown by the prison guards went far beyond play-acting.

Third, some of the guards' hostility and aggression was due to following the experimenter's instructions rather than simply identifying with their role. When Zimbardo briefed the guards, he told them:

You can create in the prisoners … a sense of fear to some degree, you can create a notion of arbitrariness that their life is totally controlled by us, by the system, you, me—and they'll have no privacy … they can do nothing, say nothing that we don't permit. We're going to take away their individuality. (Zimbardo, 1989)

Fourth, the newspaper advertisement Zimbardo used to recruit participants indicated that it was a study of prison life. When Carnahan and McFarland (2007) used an almost identical advertisement, they found that those volunteering were high in aggressiveness. Thus, it is possible that the guards in the Stanford prison experiment behaved aggressively in part because of their aggressive personalities.

? How can the concept of "demand characteristics" be used to explain the behaviour of the participants in this study?

CASE STUDY: Zimbardo's defence

Zimbardo pointed out that all of his participants had signed a formal informed consent form, which indicated that there would be an invasion of privacy, loss of some civil rights, and harassment. He also noted that day-long debriefing sessions were held with the participants, so that they could understand the moral conflicts being studied. However, Zimbardo failed to protect his participants from physical and mental harm. It was entirely predictable that the mock guards would attack the mock prisoners, because that is exactly what had happened in a pilot study that Zimbardo carried out before the main study.

British study

Reicher and Haslam (2006) carried out a study for the BBC very similar to the Stanford prison experiment, using guards and prisoners selected to be well adjusted. However, the findings were very different. The guards didn't identify with their role, whereas the prisoners increasingly identified with theirs. As a result, the guards were overcome by the prisoners. As Reicher and Haslam (2006, p. 30) concluded, "People do not automatically assume roles that are given to them in the manner suggested by the role account that is typically used to explain events in the SPE [Stanford prison experiment] (Haney et al., 1973)." Thus, identification is *not* always found.

Why did the findings differ so much? Participants in the BBC prison study knew their actions would be seen by millions of television viewers. This might have encouraged the guards to behave gently. However, this doesn't explain why the guards failed to become more aggressive over time as their awareness of being filmed diminished. Perhaps people are now more aware of the dangers of conforming to stereotyped views, in part because of the publicity given to the Stanford prison experiment.

Differences between obedience and conformity	
OBEDIENCE	CONFORMITY
Occurs within a hierarchy. Actor feels the person above has the right to prescribe behaviour. Links one status to another. Emphasis is on power.	Regulate the behaviour among those of equal status. Emphasis is on acceptance
Behaviour adopted differs from behaviour of authority figure	Behaviour adopted is similar to that of peers
Prescription for action is explicit	Requirement of going along within the group is often implicit
Participants embrace obedience as an explanation for their behaviour	Participants deny conformity as an explanation for their behaviour

Obedience to Authority

This section is concerned with obedience to authority. What is obedience? According to Colman (2001 p. 501), it is "a form of social influence in which a person yields to explicit instructions or orders from an authority figure".

In nearly all societies, certain people are given power and authority over others. In our society, parents, teachers, and managers are invested with varying degrees of authority. Most of the time this doesn't cause any problems. If the doctor tells us to take some tablets three times a day, we accept he/she is the expert. If the school crossing attendant says "Cross now", it would be foolish not to obey—except if you could see a car approaching rapidly. However, the desirability of obeying authority is related to the reasonableness of their commands.

How does obedience differ from conformity?

Both obedience and conformity involve social pressure. In obedience the pressure comes from behaving as you are instructed to do, whereas in conformity the pressure comes from group norms. A further distinction can be made in terms of the effects on private opinion. Obedience is more likely to involve public behaviour only.

Research on obedience to authority differs in at least three ways from research on conformity. First, the participants are ordered to behave in certain ways rather than being fairly free to decide what to do. Second, the participant is of lower status than the person issuing the orders, whereas in studies of conformity the participant is usually of equal status to the group members trying to influence him or her. Third, participants' behaviour in obedience studies is determined by social power, whereas in conformity studies it is influenced mostly by the need for acceptance.

Obedience to unjust commands: Milgram

An issue that has interested psychologists for many years is to work out how far most people are willing to go in their obedience to authority. What happens if you are asked by a person in authority to do something you think is wrong? What we should do in those circumstances is refuse to obey. However, the lesson of history (e.g. Nazi Germany) seems to be that many ordinary people will do terrible things when ordered to do so.

Many people argue that only sadistic or psychopathic individuals would be so obedient to authority as to be prepared to do appalling things to another human being. Other people argue that most of us would probably be prepared to treat someone else very badly if ordered to do so by an authority figure. The famous (many would say infamous!) research of Stanley Milgram (see the box below) addressed this issue.

Unquestioning obedience to authority may have catastrophic consequences. The picture shows survivors of the Auschwitz concentration camp at the end of the war in 1945, following a decade of persecution, imprisonment, and genocide.

KEY STUDY

Milgram (1963): Obedience to authority

Milgram (1963) wanted to see whether people would risk someone else's life if ordered to do so. His first study was conducted at the prestigious Yale University. In this study, he aimed to see whether he could set up a situation in which participants were more obedient to authority than was generally believed to be the case.

Forty male volunteers (a self-selected sample) took part in a controlled observational study, which they were deceived into thinking was a test of learning. The naive participant was always assigned the role of "teacher" and a middle-aged confederate, "Mr Wallace", played the role of "learner". Mr Wallace was said to have a heart condition. A word association test was the learning task, and the naive participant was instructed to deliver an electric shock to the learner for each incorrect answer.

If the teacher was unwilling to administer the shocks, the experimenter told him/her to continue. The teacher and learner were in separate rooms with no voice contact. The measure of obedience was the strength of the electric shock administered

continued over

? Milgram's study is invariably described as an "experiment". Why might this be more correctly described as a "controlled observational study"?

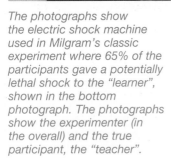

The photographs show the electric shock machine used in Milgram's classic experiment where 65% of the participants gave a potentially lethal shock to the "learner", shown in the bottom photograph. The photographs show the experimenter (in the overall) and the true participant, the "teacher".

Milgram's initial hypothesis was that German obedience during the Second World War was a facet of German culture. He was going to compare how Americans behaved with how Germans behaved but he found, to his astonishment, that Americans were extremely obedient—and therefore concluded that obedience was in human nature, not just German nature.

by the participants on a scale of 15 to 450 volts with 15-volt increments for each wrong answer. The participants understood that the highest levels of shock might be fatal, especially to a man with a heart condition. At 180 volts, the learner yelled, "I can't stand the pain", and by 270 volts the response had become an agonised scream. The participants didn't know until the end of the experiment that no shocks were actually administered. (The fact that no shocks were delivered shows psychologists are less sadistic than you may have started to believe!)

Would you have been willing to give the maximum (and potentially deadly) 450-volt shock? Milgram found that everyone he asked denied they personally would do any such thing. He also found that 110 experts on human behaviour (e.g. psychiatrists) predicted that no one would go to the 450-volt stage. In fact, all participants gave shocks up to the 300-volt level, and 65% of them (there was no gender difference) continued through to the highest level of 450 volts. As you can see, this was hugely different from expert predictions!

This study is important for various reasons. First, Milgram studied a phenomenon of great importance within most societies. Second, his findings were so strikingly different from prediction that they showed psychologists' ideas about obedience to authority needed rethinking. Third, they appeared to demonstrate that obedience to authority depends primarily on situational pressures (e.g. the experimental setting; the status of the experimenter; pressure exerted on the participant to continue) and is due surprisingly little to an individual's personality.

Limitations

There are several limitations with this study. First, the findings are limited in generalisability. The study was carried out in a laboratory of a prestigious university and the findings would probably have been much less impressive in less prestigious surroundings.

Second, there may have been **experimenter bias**. It is clear from Milgram's writings that he was keen to show that people are very obedient to authority.

Third, Orne and Holland (1968) argued that the research lacked mundane realism because the research set-up was in an artificial controlled environment unlike real life. However, experimental realism can compensate for a lack of mundane realism, and it can be argued that is the case with this study.

Fourth, Milgram (1963) didn't tell us what was different about the 35% of participants who refused to give the strongest electric shock. These individuals were less affected by the situational pressures involved than the other two-thirds of participants, but we don't know why.

Fifth, Milgram's research was very dubious ethically. Milgram totally failed to obtain informed consent from his participants, who simply didn't know what would happen. In addition, the participants weren't really free to leave the experiment if they wanted to—the experimenter urged them to continue when they indicated they wanted to stop.

Milgram (1974)

Milgram (1974) extended our knowledge about obedience to authority by carrying out several variations on his original experiment. He found there were two main ways obedience to authority could be reduced. The first way was to increase the obviousness of the learner's plight, which was done by comparing four situations (the percentage of totally obedient participants is in brackets):

- *Remote feedback*: The victim couldn't be heard or seen (66%).
- *Voice feedback*: The victim could be heard but not seen (62%).

- *Proximity*: The victim was only one metre away from the participant (40%).
- *Touch-proximity*: This was like the proximity condition except that the participant had to force the learner's hand onto the shock plate (30%).

The other main way obedience to authority could be lessened was by reducing the authority or influence of the experimenter in the following ways:

- Staging the experiment in a run-down office building rather than Yale University (48%).
- Giving the orders by telephone rather than having the experimenter sitting close to the participant (20.5%). (The effect of distance may help to explain why it is less stressful to kill people by dropping bombs from a plane than by shooting them at close range.)
- Making the experimenter an ordinary member of the public rather than a white-coated scientist (20%).
- Giving the participant two confederates (individuals working for the experimenter) who refused to give shocks (10%).

Milgram's (1974) variations on the original study give us greater insight into the conditions under which people obey unjust requests. They also show us something about independent behaviour, because in many situations a majority of participants behaved independently.

Major criticisms of Milgram's research approach concern the lack of **internal validity** and **external validity**, and the unethical nature of what he did. We will consider these criticisms now.

Validity of obedience research

The validity of any research refers to the extent to which it satisfies certain standards. There are several types of validity. One is internal validity, a measure of the extent to which the experimental design did the job it was supposed to do. If the experimental set-up wasn't believable then the participants probably wouldn't behave as they would generally do in such situations. It is called *internal* validity because it concerns what goes on inside the experiment.

Another form of validity is external validity, the extent to which the results of a study can be applied to other situations and other individuals. It is called *external* validity because it concerns issues outside the study's specific context. We will consider both forms of validity in relation to obedience research.

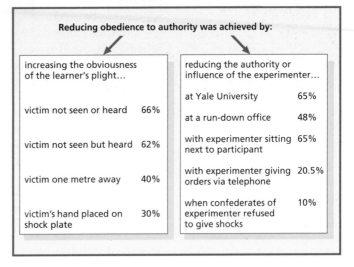

CASE STUDY: Stanley Milgram's other research

Milgram's name is synonymous with obedience research. However, he did conduct a number of other studies and was always seeking to test new ideas. Tavris (1974) called him "a man with a thousand ideas". He wrote songs, including a musical, and devised light-shows and machines.

In relation to conformity, Milgram tried the following with a group of students (Tavris, 1974). He asked them to go up to someone on an underground train and say "Can I have your seat?" The students all recoiled in horror at the idea. Why were they so frightened? Milgram tried the task himself, assuming that it would be easy, but when he tried to say the actual words to a stranger on the underground he froze. He found he was overwhelmed by paralysing inhibition, and suggested that this shows how social rules exert extremely strong pressure.

[?] What is the difference between internal and external validity?

Internal validity

Did Milgram's participants really believe they were giving the "learner" electric shocks? Orne and Holland (1968) claimed Milgram's experiment lacked experimental realism because the participants may have found it hard to believe in the set-up. For example, they might have questioned why the experimenter wasn't giving the shocks himself—why employ someone else if there wasn't some kind of trickery going on?

However, in a replication of Milgram's experiment by Rosenhan (1969), nearly 70% of participants reported that they believed the whole set-up. In a study by Turner and Solomon (1962), participants were willing to be *given* strong shocks, and so must have believed the experimental task. Coolican (1996) agrees with Milgram on the basis of film showing the participants in Milgram's (and Asch's) studies were taking the situation very seriously and appeared to be experiencing real distress.

Orne and Holland (1968) also considered the issue of demand characteristics in relation to internal validity. Demand characteristics are those cues in an experiment that "invite" participants to behave in certain predictable ways. One demand characteristic of any experiment is that participants should obey the experimenter's instructions. So, in Milgram's experiment, the reason the participants obeyed so completely was perhaps because this is how one should behave in an experiment.

Milgram's approach may also lack validity as a consequence of the fact that the participants behaved as they did because they had entered into a social contract with the experimenter. In exchange for payment ($4.50), participants might have felt they should obey the instructions they received—their behaviour didn't show obedience within the real world but only within a contractual relationship. They were told they could leave and still be paid but, at the same time, the instructions "You must continue" must have made it quite difficult to leave.

External validity

[?] Why do you think that the setting in which the experiments took place made such a difference?

External validity concerns the extent to which we can generalise the findings of a study. The main challenge to external validity in all of Milgram's research is that it was carried out in laboratory situations, and so the findings might not generalise to the real world. However, consider the point made earlier that experiments are like real-life social situations.

Another way to answer the external validity criticism is by reference to the distinction between experimental and mundane realism (Carlsmith et al., 1976). Any research set-up that is like real life can be said to have mundane realism in so far as it appears real rather than artificial to the participants. Some experiments lack mundane realism. However, experimental realism can compensate for this when the way the experiment is conducted is so involving the participants are fooled into thinking the set-up is real.

Milgram argued that his research had both mundane realism and experimental realism. It had mundane realism because the demands of an authority figure are the same regardless of whether the setting is artificial or occurring more naturally outside the laboratory. It also had experimental realism because the experiment must have been highly involving and engaging for the participants to have behaved as they did.

Probably the best-known replication of obedience research is a real-life study by Hofling et al. (1966). In this study, 22 nurses were phoned by someone claiming to be "Dr Smith". The nurses were asked to check that a drug called Astroten was available. When the nurses did this, they saw on the bottle that the maximum dosage was 10mg. When they reported back to Dr Smith, he told them to give 20mg of the drug to a patient.

There were two good reasons why the nurses should have refused to obey. First, the dose was double the maximum safe dose. Second, the nurses didn't know Dr Smith, and they were supposed to take instructions only from doctors they knew. However, the nurses' training had led them to obey instructions from doctors. There is a clear power structure in medical settings, with doctors in a more powerful position than nurses.

The nurses were more influenced by the power structure than by the hospital regulations: all but one did as Dr Smith instructed. However, when asked what other nurses would have done in the same circumstances, they all predicted that others would *not* have obeyed the instructions. Thus, the pressures to show obedience to authority are greater than most people imagine. This study raised important issues about hospital practices.

EXAM HINT

Notice how the terms experimental realism and mundane realism apply to an evaluation of Milgram's study. Make sure that you can link these issues appropriately to internal and external validity, i.e. you should be able to assess how experimental realism questions internal validity and how mundane realism questions external validity.

Similar findings to those of Hofling et al. (1966) were reported by Lesar et al. (1997) in a study on actual medication errors in American hospitals. Nurses typically carried out doctors' orders even when they had good reasons for doubting the wisdom of those orders. Krackow and Blass (1995) compared nurses who carried out (or refused to carry out) inappropriate doctors' orders in real life. Nurses who were compliant were more likely to attribute responsibility for potential harm to the doctor rather than to themselves.

Rank and Jacobsen (1997) found only 11% of nurses obeyed a doctor's instructions to give too high a dose to patients when they talked to other nurses beforehand. Thus, social support can reduce the tendency to obey authority. This resembles Milgram's (1974) finding that obedience was much less when the genuine participants were accompanied by two confederates refusing to give electric shocks.

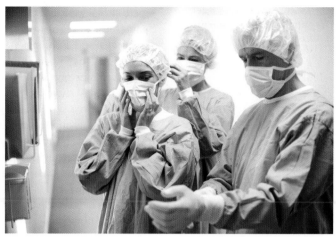

Hofling et al.'s (1966) study found that all but one of the nurses obeyed an unknown doctor's "dangerous" orders, even though they were only supposed to take instructions from doctors they knew. It is likely that the nurses were more influenced by the hierarchical power structure typical in their profession, than by the hospital regulations.

ACTIVITY: An observational study of obedience

Conduct an observational study of obedience in your school/college. Decide how you will issue an "order" and vary this across two conditions, e.g. presence and absence of an authority figure. Then measure the amount of obedience and disobedience to see if there is a difference between the two conditions. How will you measure this? What level of data will you obtain? How can you assess if there is a difference in the data? Consider the ethical and methodological issues raised by the study. Ensure that any request that is made is reasonable and one that would be made in everyday life.

Milgram's findings: Limited by time and place?

Milgram's studies were carried out in the United States during the 1960s and 1970s. Those limitations pose issues about the external validity of his research based on the time and culture in which it was carried out and the culture in which it was carried out.

In view of the ethical problems with Milgram's procedures, it has not been possible in recent times to try to replicate his findings directly. However, Dambrun and Vatiné (2010) managed to avoid the ethical problems. They put their French participants in an immersive video environment and told them the learner in the video was feigning discomfort and pain. In spite of the fact that this study took place about 40 years after most of Milgram's experiments, the percentage of participants prepared to administer the strongest electric shock was comparable in both cases.

Are Milgram's findings limited to the culture in which they were obtained? Relevant cross-cultural evidence was discussed by Smith and Bond (1993). Unfortunately, key aspects of the procedure varied from one culture to another, and so it is hard to interpret cross-cultural differences in obedience. However, the percentages of participants willing to give the most

---

HOW SCIENCE WORKS: Role play

One research method used by psychologists is 'role play' to avoid ethical problems such as psychological harm (see page 146). Many of the studies in this section of the book, such as Asch and Milgram, could not be replicated today because of the anxiety caused to participants. An alternative is to ask people to act *as if* they are a participant in the study and see how they behave and feel.

You could do this with either Asch's conformity study or Milgram's obedience study. Re-enact the whole study and afterwards interview the people who role-played confederates and the people who role-played participants. What did they feel? Did they feel pressured to conform or obey? Did they feel embarrassed?

EXAM HINT

The issue of ethics is important in all psychological studies but ethics are particularly relevant to studies of conformity and obedience. In an exam they can be useful in evaluating studies such as Asch, Milgram, Zimbardo's prison study, and Hofling. However, in order to make this an effective criticism, you need to make it clear in what way this is a limitation of the study—ethical issues do not challenge the results themselves, but they do challenge the kind of research that has been undertaken.

? To what extent can the same criticisms be applied to Meeus and Raaijmakers' study as were raised against Milgram's original experiment?

? In what way does Meeus and Raaijmakers' study have greater validity than Milgram's study?

? What are the main factors determining whether or not there is obedience to authority?

severe shock were very high in several countries: 80% or higher in studies carried out in Italy, Spain, Germany, Austria, and Holland, suggesting substantial obedience to authority.

Meeus and Raaijmakers (1995) carried out interesting research in Holland. They told participants they wanted to see how job applicants would handle stress in an interview. Each participant was given the role of being the interviewer, and the job applicants were actually confederates of the experimenter. The interviewer was told to create stress for the interviewee, and was given a set of negative statements to do this (e.g. "This job is too difficult for you"). Eventually the applicants pleaded with the interviewer to stop interrupting and then they refused to answer any more questions.

In spite of the obvious distress caused to the job applicant, 22 of 24 participants (interviewers) delivered all 15 "stress remarks". They clearly felt stressed themselves but tried to act as if nothing was wrong. The study by Meeus and Raaijmakers (1995) shows once again the willingness of individuals to obey an authority figure even when both their stress and that of the recipient is obvious.

Explanations of why people obey

People may obey because the situation they find themselves in somehow puts pressure on them to be obedient. Alternatively, it may be that people obey because obedience is a feature of human nature. Below, we consider situational and personality/dispositional explanations of obedience. As we see, there is merit in both kinds of explanation.

Situational factors

Burger (2011) identified five important situational factors, some of which have been largely overlooked. First, the participants found themselves in an entirely novel situation but assumed correctly that the experimenter had considerable experience with it. It is often hard to know how to behave in new situations, and so it was perhaps natural for most of the participants to do what the experienced experimenter told them to do.

Second, the participants in Milgram's research were given very little time to think about their actions. They had to find and read out the correct test item, note the learner's response, determine whether it was correct, and so on. If there was any delay on their part, they were told to move on to the next item by the experimenter. It seems likely that more participants would have refused to continue with the experiment with additional time to think about their actions.

Are we more likely to assume that this man is sleeping rough because of situational factors (he's been taken ill, forgotten his house keys) or dispositional factors (he can't keep a job, he's drunk and rowdy in accommodation, for example)?

Third, the experimenter repeatedly told concerned participants that he took full responsibility for what happened in the Milgram situation, which persuaded many of them to continue with the experiment. Tilker (1970) found there was much less obedience to authority when participants were told they (rather than the experimenter) were responsible for their actions.

Fourth, what was demanded of the participant increased slowly in 15-volt increments. This made it hard for participants to notice when researchers began to ask them to behave unreasonably. Think of the "foot-in-the-door" technique used by salespeople. They start with a minor request such as "Can I ask you a few questions?" (getting their foot metaphorically in the door) and then gradually make larger requests. Before you know it, you have bought some item you can't afford!

Fifth, it was only when participants delivered the tenth shock (at 150 volts) that the learner first protested and demanded to be released. This had a major impact on participants—more of the participants who refused to administer all the electric shocks stopped at this point than any other. More participants would probably have refused to obey the experimenter if the learner's anguish had been obvious earlier in the experiment.

Burger (2011) argued that these factors taken together undermine the notion that nearly everyone is willing to obey authority even when it is illegitimate. His central point is that

Milgram deliberately biased his situation to maximise the amount of obedience to authority. If the situation hadn't been a novel one, if participants had had more time to think, if the participants had been told they were personally responsible, if the increase in the shocks had been much greater, and if the learner had protested earlier, there would probably have been very little obedience to authority.

Why do you think situational explanations may be more common in some cultures than others?

Situational factors: Soft influences

Some researchers (e.g. Blass & Schmitt, 2001) draw a distinction between social power based on harsh *external* influences (e.g. hierarchy-based legitimate power) and social power based on soft influences *within* the authority figure (e.g. expertise; credibility). Milgram emphasised the importance of harsh influences, but soft influences are also important.

Blass and Schmitt presented participants with a 12-minute edited version of Milgram's documentary film, *Obedience*. Participants chose the best explanation for the strong obedience to authority shown in the film from the following choices based on various sources of power:

- *Legitimate*: experimenter's role as authority figure.
- *Expert*: experimenter's superior expertise and knowledge.
- *Coercive*: the power to punish the participant for non-compliance.
- *Informational*: the information conveyed to the participant was sufficient to produce obedience.
- *Reward*: the power to reward the participant for compliance.
- *Referent*: the power occurring because the participants would like to emulate the authority figure.

The sources of power most often chosen were in the order given above: legitimate power (a harsh influence) and expertise (a soft influence) were chosen most frequently, followed by coercive power (a harsh influence) and informational power (a soft influence). These findings are important in two ways. First, they show Milgram was only partially correct when explaining obedience to authority in terms of legitimate power. Second, they indicate that obedience to authority in the Milgram situation depends on at least two different sources of power.

Situational explanations

Milgram (1974) argued strongly that obedience to authority depends mostly on situational factors. More specifically, he identified three main features of the situation he used as being conducive to obedience:

1. Experience has taught us that authorities are generally trustworthy and legitimate, and so obedience to authority is often appropriate. For example, it would be disastrous if those involved in carrying out an emergency operation refused to obey the surgeon's orders!
2. The orders given by the experimenter moved gradually from the reasonable (small shocks) to the unreasonable (harmful shocks).
3. **Buffers**. These are aspects of the situation preventing the person from seeing the consequences of their actions. In Milgram's study, this occurred when the participants couldn't see the victim.

According to Milgram (1974), these various aspects of his situation led to the participants being put into an **agentic state**. In this state, they became the instruments of an authority figure and so ceased to act according to their conscience. Someone in the agentic state thinks, "I am not responsible, because I was ordered to do it."

In essence, Milgram was arguing that we have an unfortunate tendency to do as we're told provided the person doing the telling is an authority figure. This contrasts with our everyday lives, where we are generally in the **autonomous state**, in which we are aware of the consequences of our actions and feel in control of our own behaviour.

Milgram (1974) claimed that the tendency to adopt the agentic state "is the fatal flaw nature has designed into us". This led him to stress the links between his findings and the horrors of Nazi Germany (discussed in detail later in the chapter).

KEY TERMS

Buffers: aspects of situations that protect people from having to confront the results of their actions.

Agentic state: a state of feeling controlled by an authority figure, and therefore lacking a sense of personal responsibility.

Autonomous state: being aware of the consequences of our actions and therefore taking voluntary control of our behaviour.

EVALUATION

⊕ All the situational factors identified by Milgram do play a part in producing obedience to authority. As we saw earlier, Milgram (1974) found that obedience to authority was least when the authority of the experimenter was reduced and the obviousness of the learner's plight was maximised. Some of these situational factors have powerful effects. For example, full obedience to authority was reduced from 65% in the standard condition to only 10% when the participant had confederates who wouldn't give shocks.

⊕ In general terms, Milgram's original findings aren't limited by time or place. Similar findings to his have been obtained in numerous countries and in studies carried out many years after his.

⊕ There is some validity in the notion that a number of participants in the Milgram situation found themselves in an agentic state. Dambrun and Vatiné (2010) found that participants who gave the most electric shocks tended to hold the experimenter and the victim responsible for what happened rather than themselves. This refusal to accept personal responsibility is part of what is involved in the agentic state. In contrast, participants who gave the fewest shocks tended to accept personal responsibility and did not hold the experimenter or victim responsible.

⊖ Most participants in Milgram's studies did *not* find themselves in an agentic state. Most obedient participants experienced a strong conflict between the experimenter's demands and their own conscience. They seemed very tense and nervous, they perspired, they bit their lips, and they clenched and unclenched their fists. In addition, many of them argued strongly with the experimenter about what they were asked to do. Such behaviour indicates strongly they weren't in an agentic state.

⊖ As Burger (2011) argued, Milgram adopted a very biased approach to devising his experimental set-up. Factors such as the experimenter taking responsibility, denying the participants time to think, and only having the learner protest loudly some way into the experiment ensured that obedience levels were high.

⊖ Milgram (1974) didn't focus much on the role of individual differences in personality in determining the extent to which participants were obedient. The fact that 35% of participants weren't fully obedient in the standard Milgram situation indicates the situational pressures didn't influence all participants in the same way.

⊖ Milgram exaggerated the links between his findings and Nazi Germany. The values underlying Milgram's studies were the positive ones of increasing our understanding of human behaviour in contrast to the vile ideas prevalent in Nazi Germany. Most participants in Milgram's studies had to be watched closely to ensure their obedience, which wasn't necessary in Nazi Germany. Finally, most of Milgram's participants experienced great conflict and agitation, whereas those who carried out atrocities in Nazi Germany often seemed unconcerned about moral issues.

⊖ Milgram tried to justify his research ethically by claiming that the participants were fully debriefed afterwards about the purpose of the experiment and were pleased to have taken part. However, several of those participants reported that their experiences had been much more negative than claimed by Milgram. There is general agreement that exposing participants to considerable distress without having obtained their informed consent is ethically unacceptable. These ethical issues can be overcome by using virtual reality experiments or studies in which the participants know the learner isn't really receiving shocks (Dambrun & Vatiné, 2010).

Personality/dispositional explanations

Adorno et al. (1950) argued that obedience to authority could be mostly explained in terms of personality. According to them, some people have an **authoritarian personality**, making people obedient and prejudiced. Such individuals have the following characteristics:

- Rigid beliefs in conventional values.
- General hostility towards other groups.
- Intolerance of ambiguity.
- Submissive attitude towards authority figures.

Why are individuals with an authoritarian personality so obedient? Adorno et al. (1950) claimed such individuals were treated harshly as children, causing them to have much hostility towards their parents. This hostility remains unconscious, with the child seeming to idealise his/her parents. In later life, such children act submissively towards authority figures, and displace their hostility onto minority groups in the form of prejudice. These characteristics of the authoritarian personality make people especially likely to obey the orders of an authority figure.

Adorno et al. devised various questionnaires relating to their theory. The most important one was the **F (Fascism) Scale**, designed to measure the attitudes of the authoritarian personality (look at the box below). Adorno et al. gave the test to about 2000 people. Those who scored high on the F Scale also scored high on a scale measuring prejudice. This confirmed the validity of the scale.

Items from the F Scale devised by Adorno et al.

Indicate whether you hold slight, moderate, or strong support OR slight, moderate, or strong opposition to the following:

"Obedience and respect for authority are the most important virtues children should learn."

"Most of our social problems would be solved if we could somehow get rid of the immoral, crooked, and feeble-minded people."

"What the youth needs most is strict discipline, rugged determination, and the will to work for family and country."

"Familiarity breeds contempt."

"Sex crimes, such as rape and attacks on children, deserve more than mere imprisonment, such criminals ought to be publicly whipped."

Adorno et al. exaggerated the importance of a harsh environment in causing someone to develop the authoritarian personality. An alternative view is that genetic factors are important. This issue was addressed in a twin study by McCourt et al. (1999). Identical twins share 100% of their genes whereas fraternal twins share only 50%. If individual differences in the authoritarian personality depend in part on genetic factors, we would expect identical twins to be more similar to each other than fraternal twins. That is exactly what has been found (McCourt et al., 1999). However, these findings leave open the possibility that a harsh family environment may also play a role in the development of the authoritarian personality.

Altemeyer (1981) came up with the similar notion of **right-wing authoritarianism**. This consists of authoritarian submission to authority, authoritarian aggression towards wrongdoers, and conventionalism (a belief that there should be strict adherence to **social norms** and traditions).

Findings

Milgram (1974) found high scorers on the F Scale gave stronger shocks than low scorers when ordered to do so by an authority figure, thus indicating that personality plays a part in determining obedience to authority. However, the fact that about two-thirds of the participants in Milgram's experiments were fully obedient but far fewer people than that have an authoritarian personality means this approach only provides a partial explanation.

KEY TERMS

Authoritarian personality: identified by Adorno et al. as someone who is more likely to be obedient. These people tend to hold rigid beliefs, and to be hostile towards other groups and submissive to authority.

F (Fascism) Scale: a test of tendencies towards fascism. High scorers are prejudiced and racist.

Right-wing authoritarianism: a personality type consisting of submissiveness towards authority figures, authoritarian aggression, and strict adherence to social norms.

Social norms: the explicit and implicit rules that specify what forms of behaviour, beliefs, and attitudes are acceptable within a given society.

EXAM HINT

If you are asked to explain why people don't obey, don't describe Milgram's study. You might use some of this to support an explanation but the study itself is not an explanation.

Other studies have produced similar findings. Miller (1975) studied obedience to an order that the participants should grasp live electric wires for 5 minutes while working on some problems in arithmetic. Those scoring high on the F Scale were more likely to obey this order.

Altemeyer (1981) used his own scale to assess right-wing authoritarianism. High scorers gave more intense electric shocks than did low scorers on a verbal learning task. Dambrun and Vatiné (2010) also studied individual differences in right-wing authoritarianism in a study discussed already. They used an immersive video environment, and found that there was a moderate tendency for those high in right-wing authoritarianism to administer more shocks than low scorers.

Some of the strongest evidence of the importance of individual differences in personality in determining the extent of obedience to authority was reported by Haas (1966). Top management in a company ordered lower-level management staff to indicate which one of their superiors should be fired. They were told that their recommendation would serve as "the final basis for action". There was a fairly high correlation of +0.52 between hostility as a personality dimension and participants' degree of obedience.

Conclusions

Individual differences in personality help to explain why some participants show full obedience in the Milgram situation whereas others do not. A common theme running through the various personality dimensions is that individuals displaying much hostility towards other groups are most likely to be fully obedient. Milgram's experimental set-up provides a "strong" situation that is heavily biased towards making participants obedient. As a result, situational factors are very powerful and more important than personality. Later in the chapter we will be discussing personality again in the context of identifying individuals who are least likely to be obedient and to submit to social influence.

HOW SCIENCE WORKS: Obedience or conformity in everyday life

You could do a naturalistic observation of obedience or conformity in everyday life. This would comply with BPS Ethical Guidelines if you were careful to observe in a public place, and to respect your participants. How might you assess conformity to social norms? And how might you adjust your observation and data collection to reduce the chance of people feeling spied on, and in consequence becoming suspicious or agitated?

You could observe other customers in a fast food place, by sitting chatting with a friend and having a coffee so you look very ordinary. You could also have a magazine or newspaper on your table, and hidden in it a ready-drawn simple two-column grid on which you could tick the columns, one for conforming (people who clear away their own rubbish) and one for not conforming (people who leave their own rubbish). You would record no personal data at all, just ticks, and at the end of your observation you would total each column. Then you could see whether your prediction, your hypothesis, was supported by your data or not.

Section Summary

- Social influence involves an individual's attitudes and/or behaviour being affected by other people.

Conformity (majority influence)

- Conformity can be undesirable. However, it is important to adhere to certain social rules and group cohesion requires much conformity to group norms.
- Conformity occurs when individuals in groups adopt the behaviour, attitudes, or values of the majority.

- Asch found majority influence on about one-third of trials even when the correct response was obvious. Others have found that the effects of majority influence can be even greater when the majority is an ingroup.
- Conformity in the Asch situation has decreased over the years, probably due in part to a general reduction in the need for social approval.
- Conformity in the Asch situation is 50% higher in collectivistic cultures than in individualistic ones. This occurs because group cohesion is regarded as more important in collectivistic cultures.
- Most participants in the Asch situation give a mixture of correct and incorrect answers. By so doing, they show group solidarity *and* perceptual accuracy.

Informational social influence and normative social influence

- There are various reasons for majority influence, including normative social influence and informational social influence.
  - Normative social influence: people conform to be liked or to avoid ridicule.
  - Normative social influence is greater when the majority is larger rather than small.
  - Normative social influence is greater when individuals feel an involvement with the majority (e.g. they form an ingroup).
  - Normative social influence is greater when the task is difficult and important.
  - Informational social influence: people conform to gain information or because they are uncertain what to do.
  - There is increased informational social influence when individuals perceive the majority to have superior knowledge.
  - There is increased informational social influence when the situation is ambiguous.
  - Normative and informational social influence are generally present together.

Types of conformity including internalisation and compliance

- Kelman distinguished among compliance, internalisation, and identification. Compliance involves public conformity without internal agreement with other group members; internalisation involves public conformity plus internal agreement with others; and identification is conformity based on adhering to a given role in society.
- Conformity is most likely to take the form of internalisation when the majority is knowledgeable, when the minority members have no relevant knowledge, and when there is majority informational social influence.
- Situations that produce internalisation include those in which minority members process thoroughly the majority's views and those in which minority members lack experience.
- Compliance to the majority occurs when the majority is large, there is normative social influence, and the accuracy of the group's performance is important.
- Individuals show compliance when they fear ridicule or regard the majority as their ingroup.
- The Stanford prison experiment provides some evidence for identification with the roles of prison guards and prisoners. However, the key findings have proved hard to replicate.
- The Stanford prison experiment is flawed because of Zimbardo's excessive involvement in the actual conduct of the study.
- For reasons that aren't entirely clear, a British attempt to replicate the Stanford prison experiment was unsuccessful.

Obedience to authority

- Obedience to authority is behaving as instructed, usually in response to one individual.

Milgram's research

- Milgram's classic research showed that about two-thirds of people were prepared to administer potentially fatal electric shocks to another person. Similar findings have been obtained in several other cultures.
- Milgram discovered two ways in which obedience to authority could be reduced:
  1. Increasing the obviousness of the learner's plight;
  2. Reducing the authority or impact of the experimenter.
- There are issues of internal validity (believability of the set-up) and of external validity (generalising to real life). The fact that many participants were obviously distressed suggests reasonable internal validity. Replication of Milgram's findings when nurses were ordered to obey doctors suggests reasonable external validity.

Explanations of why people obey

- Milgram argued that his situation placed participants in an agentic state in which they surrendered responsibility for their actions to the experimenter, who was perceived as a legitimate source of power.
- The fact that many participants became distressed suggests they didn't surrender all responsibility.
- Milgram argued that the experimenter exerted harsh influence because he was regarded as a high-status power figure. However, there is evidence that much of the experimenter's power is via soft influence as a recognised expert.
- Milgram's findings owed much to the experimenter accepting full responsibility, to the gradual increase in the demands imposed on participants, and the fact that the learner only made his distress obvious following the tenth shock.
- It is important to consider factors within the individual as well as those within the situation. For example, individuals having an authoritarian personality are more likely than other people to be fully obedient in the Milgram situation. However, situational factors are more important than personality in determining obedience to authority.

SECTION 13
SOCIAL INFLUENCE IN EVERYDAY LIFE

In this section, we will be focusing on some of the most important ways social influence operates in our everyday lives. First, we consider why it is that some individuals manage to display independent behaviour in situations that cause most people to conform or to obey. Some of these factors are situational and others are to do with personality. Second, we consider the factors involved in social change within society. Research on social influence (including minority influence) assists us in understanding why and how social change occurs.

Explanations of Independent Behaviour, Including Locus of Control, How People Resist Pressures to Conform and Resist Pressures to Obey Authority

Social pressures to conform or to obey authority can exert powerful effects on people's behaviour. Indeed, in Milgram's (1963) initial research on obedience to authority, he found 65% (almost two-thirds) of participants were fully obedient. However, in virtually every experiment on majority influence and obedience to authority *some* people resisted the pressures to conform or obey and so exhibited **independent behaviour**. Even in Milgram's original research, 35% of participants behaved in an independent way. In experiments in the Asch situation, independent behaviour was exhibited on about two-thirds of the critical trials.

Locus of control

There are large individual differences between participants in their responses to situations such as those devised by Asch and by Milgram. It is, therefore, important to identify the characteristics of those individuals whose behaviour is independent. However, Milgram (1974, p. 205) was sceptical about the importance of individual differences: "The social psychology of this century reveals a major lesson: often, it is not so much the kind of person a man is as the kind of situation in which he finds himself that determines how he will act."

According to attribution theorists (e.g. Ross & Nisbett, 1991), people's behaviour can be caused *externally* (by situations) or *internally* (by dispositions, including personality). There is substantial obedience to authority in Milgram's situation because behaviour is under external or situational control rather than internal or dispositional control. Most participants' behaviour was determined by the experimenter's orders (an external or situational factor) rather than by their conscience (an internal or dispositional factor). Nearly everyone greatly underestimates the extent to which participants will be obedient because of the **fundamental attribution error**—the tendency to underestimate the degree to which behaviour is externally or situationally determined.

A similar account can be offered of conformity in the Asch situation. We could argue that participants in Asch's experiments were strongly influenced by an external factor (the opinions of other group members) but were sometimes not influenced by an internal factor (what they genuinely believed).

The attribution theory approach provides a way of predicting the kind of person most likely to resist majority influence and pressures to obey authority. We can distinguish between individuals who believe their behaviour is determined mainly by *external* factors (e.g. luck) and those who believe their behaviour is determined mainly by *internal* factors (e.g. their own ability and effort). We would expect those whose behaviour is most under the influence of internal factors to be more independent in their behaviour than those whose behaviour is strongly influenced by external factors. This could explain the behaviour of participants in both the Asch and Milgram situations.

Rotter (1966) devised a questionnaire assessing people's perceptions of control over personal outcomes, their generalised expectancies about the rewards they receive, and perceptions of control over entities such as governments. This questionnaire assessed **locus of control** (a personality dimension concerned with perceptions about the factors controlling what happens to us). This questionnaire indicates whether we perceive that what happens to us is under our own control (internal locus of control) or whether it is determined mainly by situational factors (external locus of control).

The prediction is that individuals with internal locus of control would be more likely than those with external locus of control to show independent behaviour in the Asch and Milgram situations. In addition, we might expect the difference in independent behaviour between internals and externals to be greater when the external pressures to conform (or to be obedient) are very strong than when they are weak—increasing external pressures should mostly affect externals who are very influenced by situational factors.

Many of Hitler's followers' levels of obedience may have been determined by situational factors (following orders) rather than dispositional factors (following internal moral resistance). This woman is unable to conceal her misery as she dutifully salutes the triumphant Hitler.

KEY TERMS

Independent behaviour: resisting the pressures to conform or to obey authority.

Fundamental attribution error: the tendency to explain the causes of another person's behaviour in terms of dispositional/personality rather than situational factors.

Locus of control: a personality dimension concerned with perceptions about the factors controlling what happens to us.

Can you think of a recent situation where you went against what you would have decided because of the "power of the situation"? This is an example of, in that instance, an external locus of control.

Findings: Conformity

The evidence generally supports the prediction that those with internal locus of control will be more independent in their behaviour than those with external locus of control. Shute (1975) studied the effects of peer pressure on attitudes to drugs. As predicted, participants with internal locus of control showed a smaller conformity effect than those with external locus of control.

London and Lim (1964) found internals were more independent than externals on a conformity task. The most convincing evidence was reported by Avtgis (1998), who carried out a meta-analysis of studies on the effects of locus of control on social influence and conformity. Those with internal locus of control showed a moderately strong tendency to show less social influence and majority influence than those with external locus of control.

In spite of several positive findings, there have been some failures to find any relationship between locus of control and majority influence. Williams and Warchal (1981) identified individuals having low and high scores for majority influence on Asch-type tasks. The two groups didn't differ significantly in locus of control, perhaps in part because there were only 10 participants in each group. However, those who showed little conformity were more assertive than those who conformed the most. These findings suggest that assertiveness may be more important than locus of control in producing independent behaviour.

Findings: Obedience

Locus of control predicts the extent to which individuals will conform in the Milgram situation (reviewed by Blass, 1991). For example, Holland (1967) carried out three versions of the Milgram experiment. Overall, 37% of the internals were disobedient in that they didn't administer the strongest electric shocks, compared to only 23% of externals.

Miller (1975) carried out a study in which the participants were told by the experimenter to give themselves electric shocks by grasping live electric wires (!) and to perform other tasks. The experimenter's apparent social status was manipulated—he seemed to have a low or a high bureaucratic authority. Participants with external locus of control were more obedient when told what to do by a high than a low bureaucratic authority. In contrast, those with internal locus of control weren't affected by the experimenter's social status. These findings make sense given that externals are generally more influenced by the situation and other people than are internals.

Other kinds of individual differences related to locus of control are also associated with independent behaviour. In conformity studies, participants exhibiting much independent behaviour have higher self-esteem than those displaying less independent behaviour. Kurosawa (1993) studied independent behaviour in an Asch-type situation with low conformity pressure (two confederates) or high conformity pressure (four confederates). Self-esteem didn't affect independent behaviour in the low pressure situation. However, those high in self-esteem showed more independent behaviour than those low in self-esteem in the high pressure situation.

Santee and Maslach (1982) found that students with high self-esteem were less likely than those with low self-esteem to agree with the solutions to a problem put forward by other students. Note that individuals high in self-esteem tend to have internal locus of control (Sterbin & Rakow, 1996). Thus, individuals high in self-esteem may show independent behaviour mainly because they have internal locus of control.

Real-world applications

We will briefly consider two ways in which internal locus of control is important in determining independent behaviour in the real world. First, consider eccentrics, 130 of whom were studied in depth by Weeks and James (1995). Most eccentrics clearly have an internal locus of control—they are non-conforming, they care little what others think of them, and they are opinionated and outspoken. These characteristics help eccentrics to challenge the established order and to make creative contributions in the artistic and scientific areas. Their achievements do not seem to be achieved at great personal cost, because most eccentrics are happy individuals.

Second, Oliner and Oliner (1988) studied 406 non-Jews who had (at considerable danger to themselves) rescued Jews from the Nazis during the Second World War, thus displaying a very high level of independent behaviour. These individuals tended to be high in social responsibility and in characteristics indicative of an internal locus of control.

In sum, both the real-world studies we have discussed show the value to society of an internal locus of control. Note, however, that other factors are also involved. For example, eccentrics tend to be intelligent, which helps them make a substantial contribution. Those non-Jews who rescued Jews in the War tended to have strong relationships with other people, which fostered their motivation to help the victims of the Nazis.

> **?** Why is it that people high in self-esteem are more likely to resist orders to obey?

EVALUATION

➕ As predicted by attribution theory, individuals with an internal locus of control show more independent behaviour (i.e. disobedience) than externals in the Milgram situation. It is assumed this occurs because internals focus more than externals on internal factors and less on the situation.

➕ The theory also correctly predicts that internals should display more independent behaviour (i.e. failure to conform) than externals in the Asch situation. This is explained on the basis that internals (more than externals) focus on internal factors rather than external, situational ones.

➕ There is some support (Miller, 1975) for the prediction that the difference in independent behaviour between internals and externals should be greater when situational pressures are greater than when they are weaker.

➕ Other personality factors (e.g. self-esteem) that predict independent behaviour are correlated in expected ways with measures of locus of control.

➕ Internal locus of control is associated with independent behaviour in eccentrics and those who rescued Jews victimised by the Nazis.

➖ Locus of control has typically been assessed by the Rotter scale, which provides a very *general* measure of whether a given individual has an external or internal locus of control. It is unlikely that such a general measure would allow us to predict accurately individuals' behaviour in the *specific* Asch and Milgram situations.

➖ The assumption that individuals whose behaviour is mainly controlled by internal factors will *always* show more independent behaviour is dubious. For example, psychopaths (who are very aggressive and uncaring) would not only administer the maximum shock in the Milgram situation, but would probably enjoy doing so. Psychopaths in the Milgram situation would be driven by internal factors (e.g. desire to hurt others) and so their total obedience is completely inconsistent with the attribution theory approach!

- *Several* internal and external factors are involved in the Asch and Milgram situations. As Sabini et al. (2001) pointed out, we could argue that independent behaviour involves a dominance of external factors over internal factors—precisely the opposite to the usual assumption. In the Milgram situation, independent individuals who show independent behaviour may be strongly influenced by an external or situational factor (the suffering of others) but relatively unaffected by an internal factor (the disposition to obey authority). In the Asch situation, independent individuals unaffected by majority influence may be more influenced by an external or situational factor (the experimenter's instructions to give correct answers) than by an internal factor (the need not to look like a fool). The desire to avoid embarrassment probably influences behaviour in the Asch situation.

- Attribution theory as applied to individual differences in locus of control focuses on situational factors leading to obedience/conformity and internal factors leading to disobedience/failure to conform. However, there are situational factors that could lead to disobedience/failure to conform and internal factors that could lead to obedience/conformity.

- The notion that internal and external factors are entirely separate is incorrect. For example, consider addicts. It is generally assumed they are driven by their internal cravings. However, their lives are very controlled by whatever it is that they crave. As Sabini et al. (2001, p. 8) pointed out, "The more internally controlled they [addicts] are, the more externally controlled they are." In similar fashion, psychopaths have very powerful internal desires to hurt others, and these desires cause them to seek situations in which these desires can be expressed (an external factor).

- Most research has focused on showing that internals display more independent behaviour than externals in a particular version of the Milgram or Asch situation. However, it follows from attribution theory that there should be larger differences between the groups in independent behaviour when the situational pressures are large than when they are small—in other words, the effects of locus of control on independent behaviour depend on the strength of the situational factors. However, this prediction has only rarely been tested.

How people resist pressures to conform

In the Asch situation, there is a severe conflict between the individual's desire to be accepted by the group and his/her desire to show competence by making judgements based on the evidence of his/her own eyes. It follows that resisting pressures to conform involves reducing the desire for group acceptance and/or increasing the desire to make the correct judgements.

There are various ways in which the desire for group acceptance can be reduced so as to increase the chances of resisting pressures to conform. First, if the individual participant has at least one supporter who agrees with his/her judgements, this reduces the need to be accepted by the group. In the real world (unlike the studies carried out by Asch), individuals often have the chance to seek out others who share their views rather than being required to provide immediate answers. In Asch's research, the presence of one supporting confederate drastically reduced conformity from 37% to 5%.

Second, and related to the first point, there are many famous examples of minorities who refused to conform and ultimately managed to achieve massive social changes. Later in the chapter, we consider the American civil rights movement that transformed the status of blacks within American society. Of crucial importance was the mutual support that the dissenting minority members provided for each other in their legitimate battles with the majority.

Third, the importance of what group members think about the individual can be reduced in the individual's mind if he/she regards the group as an outgroup and thus of little relevance to himself/herself. As we have seen, there was a huge reduction in conformity from 58% to only 8% when the other group members were perceived as an outgroup (Abrams et al., 1990).

There are also various ways in which the individual's desire to make correct judgements can be increased. First, what is most important is that individuals believe their behaviour is controlled or determined by internal factors rather than external ones. Such individuals (who are high in locus of control) have a high level of self-esteem and are thus better able to resist group pressure. In similar fashion, individuals who are assertive are more likely to attend to their inner thoughts rather than the views of the group.

Second, it is easier for individuals to emphasise their desire to be correct rather than to maintain group cohesion within individualistic cultures. As Kim and Markus (1999) found, failure to conform is regarded as a sign of uniqueness in individualistic cultures but as an indication of deviance in collectivistic ones.

Resisting pressures to obey

In the Milgram situation, there is a severe conflict between the individual's desire to be a "good" participant by following the experimenter's orders and their desire to treat the learner with respect. As a result, resisting pressures to obey authority involves reducing the perceived power of the experimenter or increasing the focus on the learner's suffering. This can be done in various ways, as we will see.

First, it is important that the individual participant accepts responsibility for his/her own actions and doesn't simply assume that the experimenter bears sole responsibility for what happens. There is much evidence that accepting personal responsibility is really important. As we saw earlier in a study by Dambrun and Vatiné (2010), participants who accepted personal responsibility administered fewer electric shocks than those who instead assigned blame to the experimenter and/or the victim.

Second, it is much easier for participants to resist the experimenter's order if they have some social support. This diminishes the impact of the experimenter on the participant's behaviour. Milgram showed the importance of social support by finding that total obedience was markedly reduced from about 65% to only 10% when there was a confederate who refused to administer electric shocks.

In the real world, individuals facing pressures to obey authority often have the opportunity to discuss what they should do with others, and this often makes it easier for them to resist such pressures. Remember the study by Rank and Jacobsen (1997) in which only 11% obeyed an unreasonable demand from a doctor when they had discussed the issue with other nurses.

Third, participants need to focus fully on the distress and pain suffered by the learner. People are much more likely to resist pressures to obey authority if they look at the situation from the learner's perspective. Individuals with an internal locus of control are more likely than those with an external locus of control to think in ways that maximise the chances they will resist pressure from the experimenter.

The importance of focusing on the learner's plight is shown by considering participants in Milgram's studies who eventually resisted the pressure to obey authority. The point at which most resisters stopped obeying the experimenter was when the learner started to protest loudly. Before that point, silence from the learner could be interpreted as indicating that he was coping well with the electric shocks.

Fourth, it is important to question the motives of authority figures when they issue unreasonable orders. Participants in the Milgram situation were impressed by the experimenter's legitimate and expert power (Blass & Schmitt, 2001). However, it can still be entirely appropriate to disobey authority figures possessing those two types of power.

Fifth, in the real world, the presence of highly respected role models who refuse to obey authority can greatly increase the probability that an individual will resist pressures to obey. Famous examples of such role models include Mahatma Gandhi and Martin Luther King (see later in the chapter).

> **?** Can you think of an example where conformity and/or obedience are very useful or essential, and an example of where they should be challenged?

KEY TERM

Social change: an alteration in the social structure of a society; minorities often try to produce social change to enhance the status of their group.

Sixth, it is easier for individuals to resist pressures to obey authority if they spend some time thinking about *all* of the relevant factors. Participants in the Milgram studies were pressured into responding rapidly by the experimenter (Burger, 2011), and this helped to prevent them from focusing clearly on the possible consequences of their actions.

HOW SCIENCE WORKS: Resisting pressure

Does personal experience fit in with psychological explanations? You could try to test psychological models about resisting pressure. It could be interesting to ask a few participants each to draw up a table, with clear headings. The left-hand column could be for real examples of resisting pressure from their individual personal experiences, e.g. choosing not to go to the cinema with friends as they'd already seen the film. The right-hand column could be for their explanation of how they resisted the pressure to conform or join in. When each person has given three or four examples you could look again at the theories and evaluate their usefulness in explaining these real-life behaviours. You could then work out which explanation or explanations seem to have more validity in the real world.

NB This exercise could raise some ethical issues if people have felt under pressure to conform in the past. Therefore all responses should be anonymous, and participants should have the right to withdraw and withhold their contribution at any time.

How Social Influence Research Helps us to Understand Social Change; the Role of Minority Influence in Social Change

This section is devoted to social change. **Social change** refers to large-scale alterations in the social order within a society. Well-known examples of social change (or attempted social change) include the suffragette movement that led to women getting the vote in the UK, the civil rights movement in the United States that led to blacks being given equal rights with whites, and the activities of numerous terrorist groups around the world.

Initially, I will consider the relevance of research on social influence to our understanding of social change. After that, we will focus more specifically on the ways in which minorities produce social change. The examples of social change I gave in the previous paragraph all involved minority influence. That is not coincidental—most of the greatest social changes over the past several centuries occurred because of the efforts and commitment of relatively small numbers of people.

An important real-life example of a minority influencing a majority was the suffragette movement in the early years of the 20th century. A relatively small group of suffragettes argued strongly for the initially unpopular view that women should be allowed to vote. The hard work of the suffragettes, combined with the justice of their case, finally led the majority to accept their point of view.

Social influence and social change

While reading this chapter, you may have found yourself worrying about the implications of the research for society. As a result of his research, Milgram (1974) became extremely pessimistic about the future: "The capacity for man to abandon his humanity, indeed the inevitability that he does so, as he merges his unique personality into the large institutional structures … is the fatal flaw nature has designed into us, and which in the long run gives our species only a modest chance for survival." In a similar vein, Milgram (1974) also referred to "the extreme willingness of adults to go to almost any lengths on the command of an authority".

The notion that evil behaviour (and an excessive willingness to obey authority) is not confined to a few psychopaths and other mentally ill individuals has been expressed by many other experts. For example, the philosopher Hannah Arendt argued that what was most horrifying about the Nazis was that they were "terrifyingly normal" rather than being extremely deviant.

It could be argued that Milgram's set-up was so artificial that his findings don't have any real relevance to everyday life. However, that argument doesn't stand up to scrutiny. We have seen that nurses in real-life situations will give patients too high doses of drugs if ordered to do so by a doctor (Hofling et al., 1966; Lesar et al., 1997). In addition, there is the Strip Search Prank Call Scam (Wolfson, 2005). Fast-food workers in the United States received phone calls from a prankster (not a researcher!) claiming to be a policeman. He persuaded many of the workers to strip and sexually abuse other workers.

For many people, the most compelling evidence that Milgram was right in assuming most people are willing to ignore their consciences in the face of authority comes from world history. The horrors of Nazi Germany perhaps provide the most obvious example. However, the genocide in Rwanda, the mass murders in Stalin's Russia, and the torture and abuse at Abu Ghraib prison in Iraq are other striking cases of immoral behaviour and obedience to authority.

Events such as the torture that was carried out on prisoners in Abu Ghraib support Milgram's findings that most people are prepared to ignore their own conscience in the face of authority.

Nazi Germany

Milgram (1974) believed his findings had direct relevance to the horrifying social changes that the Nazis imposed on Germany in the 1930s. We can use some of Milgram's findings to help to understand why the Nazis managed to change German society. First, as discussed earlier, two of the sources of social power at work in the Milgram situation are legitimate power (based on authority) and coercive power (based on the threat of punishment). Both of these power sources were important in Nazi Germany. The Nazis claimed legitimate power because they were more popular than any other party when they took over power. They also had coercive power because those who opposed them were treated harshly and were often killed.

Second, the Nazis imposed their appalling social changes on Germany through use of the foot-in-the-door technique—the demands imposed on German citizens gradually increased and so were harder to resist. Initially, there was only relatively modest discrimination against the Jews, but this increased systematically over time.

Third, the Nazi leaders generally accepted responsibility for the dreadful policies that they imposed on Germany. This meant that ordinary Germans could argue that they lacked personal responsibility for the changes occurring in Germany during the 1930s.

In spite of these similarities, Milgram minimised the differences between his situation and Nazi Germany. First, Milgram emphasised to his participants that the experiment was designed to achieve positive goals such as increasing our knowledge of human learning and memory. In contrast, the Nazis' goals were totally negative and abhorrent, including the systematic murder and eventual extermination of Jews, gypsies, and homosexuals.

Second, Milgram (1974) argued that people behaving in ethically unacceptable ways when obeying an authority figure do so because they have entered an agentic state in which they absolve themselves of all personal responsibility. That may well have been true of many Nazis working in concentration camps, but was certainly not true of the great majority of Milgram's participants. Their most common reaction was to show obvious signs of tension and unease and to be in emotional turmoil.

CASE STUDY: War criminals

After the Second World War, the Allies tried many of the high-ranking Nazi officers. At his trial in Jerusalem in 1961, Adolf Eichmann argued that he had only been obeying orders. He said he was not the "monster" that the newspapers described but simply an ordinary person caught up in an extraordinary situation. Eichmann was described as having no violent anti-Jewish feelings (Arendt, 1963). The argument was that he was an autonomous individual who became agentic when he joined the SS and subscribed to the military code of obedience to those in authority.

Third, most Nazis who committed atrocities against the Jews and others did so without minute-by-minute surveillance. In contrast, the participants in Milgram's experiments were much more obedient when the experimenter could see what they were doing than when he could not. Thus, Milgram's participants were less enthusiastic about obeying authority than were the Nazis.

In sum, the social change occurring in Nazi Germany depended in part on obedience to authority. This suggests that Milgram's research produced relevant findings. However, there is no comparison at all in moral terms. Milgram's participants were very concerned about what they were asked to do in spite of the alleged positive goals of the research. In contrast, most Nazis were unconcerned about the atrocities they carried out in spite of the appalling goals underlying Nazism.

Power structure

Obedience to authority is greater when the participant is of lesser status than the authority figure. In similar fashion, conformity is greater when the other group members are of higher status than the participant. An implication is that there will be more conformity and obedience to authority in hierarchical organisations or groups with large status differences than in non-hierarchical situations. It is no coincidence that many of the tragic situations that have occurred through undue obedience to authority (e.g. Nazi Germany; Abu Ghraib) have occurred in military groups, in which there is a very strong hierarchy.

CASE STUDY: The My Lai massacre

The My Lai massacre has become known as one of the most controversial incidents in the Vietnam War. On 14 December 1969 almost 400 Vietnamese villagers were killed in under 4 hours. The following transcript is from a CBS News interview with a soldier who took part in the massacre.

Q. How many people did you round up?

A. Well, there was about forty, fifty people that we gathered in the center of the village. And we placed them in there, and it was like a little island, right there in the centre of the village, I'd say … And …

Q. What kind of people—men, women, children?

A. Men, women, children.

Q. Babies?

A. Babies. And we huddled them up. We made them squat down and Lieutenant Calley came over and said, "You know what to do with them, don't you?" And I said yes. So I took it for granted that he just wanted us to watch them. And he left, and came back about ten or fifteen minutes later and said, "How come you ain't killed them yet?" And I told him that I didn't think you wanted us to kill them, that you just wanted us to guard them. He said, "No. I want them dead." So—

Q. He told this to all of you, or to you particularly?

A. Well, I was facing him. So, but the other three, four guys heard it and so he stepped back about ten, fifteen feet, and he started shooting them. And he told me to start shooting. So I started shooting, I poured about four clips into the group.

Q. You fired four clips from your …

A. M-16.

Q. And that's about how many clips—I mean, how many—

A. I carried seventeen rounds to each clip.

Q. So you fired something like sixty-seven shots?

A. Right.

Q. And you killed how many? At that time?

A. Well, I fired them automatic, so you can't—You just spray the area on them and so you can't know how many you killed 'cause they were going fast. So I might have killed ten or fifteen of them.

Q. Men, women and children?

A. Men, women and children.

Q. And babies?

A. And babies.

William Calley stood trial for his involvement in this massacre. His defence was that he was only obeying orders. Before the massacre Calley showed no criminal tendencies and afterwards he returned to a life of quiet respectability. His behaviour was that of a "normal" person. Kelman and Lawrence (1972) conducted a survey after the trial and found that half of the respondents said that it was "normal, even desirable" to obey legitimate authority.

Grounds for optimism

Many impressive examples of social change in society occurred due to the efforts of dissenters who stood up for their beliefs. A good example is Mahatma Gandhi (1869–1948), who always advocated non-violent resistance. He led numerous campaigns in India to reduce poverty, to increase women's rights, and to achieve independence from Britain for India. In 1930, he led the 250-mile Dandi Salt March to protest against the salt tax imposed by Britain. He was a charismatic figure who gradually gained massive support for most of his campaigns.

What kind of person is willing to resist unjust authority? On the basis of research on social influence, we might expect that individuals low in authoritarianism to be especially likely to stand up for their beliefs. Relevant evidence was reported by Mantell (1974), who found that young American men who were draft resisters during the Vietnam War mostly had very low scores on authoritarianism.

The importance of one or more dissenting voices can be seen in research on obedience to authority and in research on conformity. In Milgram's basic experiment, the participant decided whether to obey the authority figure on his/her own and about two-thirds of participants showed full obedience. There was markedly less full obedience to authority (10%) when participants were exposed to two dissenters who refused to give electric shocks.

In similar fashion, social support drastically reduces obedience to authority. For example, Rank and Jacobsen (1997) found only 11% of nurses obeyed a doctor's instructions to give too high a dose of medication to patients when they had the chance to talk to other nurses beforehand.

In sum, as Milgram (1974) pointed out, "When an individual wishes to stand in opposition to authority, he [sic!] does best to find support for his position from others in his group. The mutual support provided by men for each other is the strongest bulwark against the excesses of authority."

Role of minority influence in social change

Earlier in the chapter, we saw there are often powerful effects of majority influence on conformity behaviour. There are various reasons why we might expect **minority influence** (the beliefs and/ or behaviour of a minority being accepted by the majority) to be less than majority influence. Many majorities are powerful and controlling, and can administer rewards and punishments. In contrast, minorities typically don't command much power and can't administer rewards and punishments to the majority. However, minorities can have a strong influence provided they can produce credible and convincing messages.

Before discussing evidence that minorities can produce social change, I will discuss Moscovici's important theoretical contribution to our understanding of how minorities exert influence.

Conversion theory

Moscovici (1980, 1985) argued that conversion occurs when the majority is influenced by the views of the minority. **Conversion** typically affects private beliefs more than public behaviour. Individuals within the majority might still appear to go along with the majority (perhaps for their own safety), but privately their opinions have changed.

According to Moscovici, majority influence typically occurs after relatively brief and superficial processing of the majority's views, whereas minority influence generally occurs after detailed and thorough processing of the minority's views. Moscovici (1985) argued that conversion is most likely to occur under certain conditions:

1. *Consistency*: The minority must be consistent in their opinion.
2. *Flexibility*: The minority mustn't appear to be rigid and dogmatic.
3. *Commitment*: A committed minority will lead people to re-think their position and so produce conversion.
4. *Relevance*: The minority will be more successful if their views are in line with social trends.

Moscovici also suggested some behavioural styles minorities should have if they want to exert an influence. These include being consistent in order to demonstrate certainty, convey an

? Minority influence is probably of more importance than majority influence in terms of social change. Can you think of an example where a minority of one changed the course of human history?

? What is the difference between compliance and conversion?

KEY TERMS

Minority influence: a majority being influenced to accept the beliefs or behaviour of a minority.

Conversion: the influence of the minority on the majority. This is likely to affect private beliefs more than public behaviour.

alternative view, disrupt the norm, and draw attention to their views. In addition, they should act on *principles* rather than just talking about them, and should make *sacrifices* to maintain the view they hold. It also helps if they are similar in age, class, and gender to the people they are trying to persuade.

What successful minorities do is to force the majority to *think* in new ways about an issue. They cause one to "examine one's own responses, one's own judgements, in order to confirm and validate them" (Moscovici, 1980, p. 215).

There is a final factor. Moscovici argued that *distinctiveness* is an advantage for minorities. Thus, for example, a small minority of 18% is more distinctive than a large minority of 48% or a large minority. As predicted, distinctive minorities have more influence on the majority than non-distinctive minorities (Gardikiotis, 2011).

Findings

Moscovici et al. (1969) showed that a minority (especially if it is consistent) can influence a majority. There were four naive participants (the majority) and two confederates of the experimenter (the minority). All participants described the colours of blue slides. The minority described all slides as "green" (consistent condition) or two-thirds as "green" and one-third as "blue" (inconsistent condition). The participants showed minority influence (i.e. said "green") on 8.4% of trials with the consistent minority but only 1.25% of trials with the inconsistent minority.

Nemeth et al. (1974) confirmed that consistency is necessary for a minority to influence the majority. However, it isn't always sufficient. They essentially replicated Moscovici et al.'s study (1969) except their participants could respond with all the colours they saw in the slides rather than only a single colour. There were three main conditions:

1. The two confederates of the experimenter said "green" on 50% of the trials and "green-blue" on the other 50% in a random way.
2. As (1), except that the confederates said "green" to the brighter slides and "green-blue" to the duller ones, or vice versa.
3. The two confederates said "green" on every trial.

Nearly 21% of the majority's responses were influenced by the minority in condition 2, but the minority had no influence in conditions 1 and 3. The minority had no effect in condition 1 because it didn't respond consistently. The minority in condition 3 responded consistently, but its refusal to use more complex descriptions of the stimuli (e.g. "green-blue) made its behaviour seem rigid and unrealistic.

Martin et al. (2003) gave participants two messages, the second of which argued for the opposite position to the first one. According to Moscovici, resistance to changing participants' opinions when given the second message should have been greater when the first message was endorsed by a minority because it should have been processed more thoroughly. That is what they found.

Limitations

What are the main limitations of Moscovici's theory? First, Moscovici exaggerated the differences in how majorities and minorities exert influence.

Second, Moscovici did not attach sufficient importance to the *relationship* between the minority and the majority. David and Turner (1999) argued that minority influences will be found only when the minority is perceived as part of the ingroup. The participants were moderate feminists exposed to the minority views of extreme feminists. The views of the extreme feminists influenced the majority when the situation was set up as feminists vs non-feminists, because the extreme feminists were part of the ingroup. However, the views of the extreme feminists had little impact when there was a contrast between a moderate feminist majority and an outgroup of extreme feminists.

Social change produced by minorities

Research on minority influence is very relevant to understanding most of the major social changes in this country and around the world, and we will discuss its relevance very shortly. However, two points need to be made before doing so.

? How do the results of this study compare with the studies that looked at majority influence?

First, minorities have achieved social change in numerous ways, and so we must avoid oversimplifications. Second, it is often hard to identify the main factors responsible for social change in the real world. For example, historians continue to argue over the precise reasons that minorities such as the communists in Russia or the Nazis in Germany came to achieve power over the majority. This is perhaps inevitable given that we simply have to consider what happened and so can't make use of the experimental method. We will consider two examples of minority influence in the real world: (1) terrorists; and (2) the American civil rights movement.

Terrorism

Terrorism represents one way minority influence can be used to achieve social change. As Kruglanski and Fishman (2006) pointed out, terrorism is a tool or means to an end (e.g. overthrowing majority rule; putting an end to military occupation). According to the journalist Barbara Victor, terrorists are often motivated by a "fatal cocktail" involving religion, helpless deprivation, and nationalism.

Support for the notion of a fatal cocktail was reported by Kruglanski et al. (2009). They analysed video clips from farewell tapes of suicide terrorists, and interviews with captured terrorists and failed suicide terrorists. The terrorists' main motives for terrorism were nearly always based on an ideology or worldview involving religion and/or nationalism.

How much impact do terrorists have on majority opinion? Kruglanski et al. (2009) addressed this issue in a study carried out on the inhabitants of 12 Arab countries, Pakistan, and Indonesia. The participants indicated their support (or otherwise) for terrorist attacks on Americans. Those who endorsed individualistic goals (e.g. education; raising a family) were less supportive than those who endorsed collectivistic goals (e.g. defending one's nation or religion). Thus, majority members whose goals resembled those of the terrorists were more supportive of them.

Factors causing influence

What factors cause terrorists to have minority influence?

1. Most terrorist groups constantly put forward the same extreme views, and so they have the advantage of consistency.
2. Terrorists exhibit high levels of commitment and sacrifice, perhaps most obviously in the case of suicide terrorists.
3. Many terrorist groups are pursuing goals seen as relevant and appropriate by the majority. For example, consider the second intifada (uprising) in Palestine. About 80% of the Palestine population supported the use of terrorist tactics (including suicide bombings) against the Israelis.
4. Many terrorist groups are very successful at drawing attention to their views by committing atrocities that receive massive publicity.
5. Terrorist groups often portray themselves as an ingroup that represents the interests and goals of the majority. As we have seen, terrorists in several Arab countries attract more support from those members of the population who share their emphasis on defending one's religion and nation.
6. Terrorists try to present themselves as principled individuals seeking to maintain religious values they claim are under attack.
7. Terrorist groups are typically distinctive in the sense that they represent a tiny minority. As we have seen, distinctive groups tend to have more influence than less distinctive ones.

American civil rights movement

The civil rights movement in the United States in the 1950s and 1960s produced massive beneficial social change for blacks within American society. This movement involved very large numbers of people who were involved in thousands of different forms of civil disobedience. Here we will focus on only a few of the best-known events that occurred.

One key event occurred on 1 December 1955, when a black woman called Rosa Parks refused to give up her seat on a bus in Montgomery, Alabama to a white person. She was arrested, which led to the Montgomery Bus Boycott in which primarily black citizens refused to use the local bus network. This boycott caused major financial problems for the bus companies

EXAM HINT

Exam questions are likely to ask you to *use* your knowledge of social influence research, i.e. research on conformity, obedience and minority influence. For example, you will be given an example of how people's opinions have changed in the last decade about environmental issues and asked to use your knowledge of social influence research to explain how this has happened. Or you could be asked how you might set about changing people's views on an important environmental matter, based on your knowledge of social influence research.

Rosa Parks sits in the front of a bus in Montgomery, Alabama, after the Supreme Court ruled segregation illegal on the city bus system in 1956.

involved, and led one year later to a ruling that declared segregated buses were unconstitutional.

The Greensboro sit-ins formed another landmark. These sit-ins were triggered by four black students who sat down at the "whites only" counter at the Woolworth's store in Greensboro, North Carolina on 1 February 1960. The next day, more than 20 black students joined in the sit-in. There was widespread publicity for these sit-ins, which subsequently spread to many other cities in the South of the United States. The adverse publicity and loss of profit caused by the sit-ins led Woolworth's to stop their segregated policy in July 1960.

The final landmark event we will consider is the March on Washington for jobs and freedom on 28 August 1963. It was at a huge gathering connected to this March that Martin Luther King gave his famous "I have a dream" speech in which he emphasised the importance of racial harmony. This March played a significant role in the Civil Rights Act of 1964 that helped to eliminate racial discrimination in the United States.

Factors causing influence

Why was the minority (mostly black) involved in the civil rights movement so successful in achieving social change? Several factors were involved:

1. Those involved exhibited a very high level of commitment over a period of several years in terms of time and effort.
2. Those involved were willing to make sacrifices such as exposing themselves to abuse and to possible arrest. Their commitment and sacrifices convinced most Americans that they believed strongly in the rightness of their position.
3. The civil rights campaigners were entirely consistent in the views they endorsed and the changes to society that they wanted to achieve.
4. The civil rights movement attracted a huge amount of media attention. This led the white majority to think about the unequal position of blacks in American society.
5. It was very clear that those involved in civil rights were driven by principles (e.g. everyone is equal) that carried moral authority.
6. Martin Luther King was very successful at arguing that America should be a colour-blind society consisting of one large ingroup including blacks as well as whites.
7. There was a large increase in opportunities for tens of millions of Americans during the 1950s and early 1960s and much focus on individuals "doing their own thing". Thus, the civil rights movement was in some ways in tune with some of the major social trends of that era.

Conclusions

We have seen that minorities in many countries have been successful in producing major social change. Each example is idiosyncratic in some ways. However, there are several common themes. More specifically, most of the factors identified by Moscovici in his conversion theory seem to be important. Consider the very different examples of terrorism and the civil rights movement. In both cases, minority influence involves consistency of views and actions, commitment to the cause, sacrifices in order to achieve goals, considerable public attention, a principled position, trying to establish themselves as an ingroup, and identifying with current social trends.

The major limitation in trying to apply psychological research to social change is that it is impossible to establish cause and effect. The reason why this is the case is because all we have to rely on is the historical record. We can't know, for example, what would have happened in America if Martin Luther King had never existed. The Civil Rights Act was passed in the year after the Washington March at which he spoke, which suggests that the latter helped to cause the former. However, there were other important changes, notably, the assassination of President Kennedy on 22 November 1963 and his replacement by President Johnson. Since Johnson was more motivated than Kennedy to eliminate segregation, it is possible the change of President played an important role in producing social change.

Section Summary

Explanations of independent behaviour, including locus of control, how people resist pressures to conform and resist pressures to obey authority

Locus of control

- According to attribution theorists, individuals are most likely to display independent behaviour if they focus on internal or dispositional factors influencing their behaviour rather than situational ones.
- It follows from the above that individuals with an internal locus of control should show more independent behaviour than those with an external locus of control. There is support for this prediction in the Asch and Milgram situations.
- High self-esteem (associated with internal locus of control) is predictive of independent behaviour.
- Attribution theory is wrong in assuming that individuals whose behaviour is mainly controlled by internal factors will always show relatively independent behaviour. For example, psychopaths might focus on their internal desire to hurt other people, which would make them very inclined to be obedient in the Milgram situation.
- Attribution theory is also wrong in drawing a sharp distinction between internal and external factors.

How people resist pressures to conform

- There is more resistance in the Asch situation if individuals have a reduced desire for group acceptance (e.g. regarding the majority as an outgroup).
- In the real world, minorities (e.g. American civil rights campaigners) forming cohesive ingroups have often been very successful at resisting pressures to conformity and achieving social change.
- There is less conformity behaviour if the individual has at least some social support.
- There is more resistance in the Asch situation if individuals attend to their inner thoughts and have confidence in their own judgements (as shown by those with an internal locus of control).
- It is easier to resist conformity pressures in individualistic cultures than in collectivistic ones.

How people resist pressures to obey authority

- There is reduced obedience to authority if individuals accept full responsibility for their own actions rather than assigning blame to the experimenter and/or victim.
- The presence of social support greatly increases individuals' ability to resist pressures to obey authority.
- People who focus on the pain and suffering of others are more likely to resist unreasonable authority.
- Individuals who question the motives of authority figures are more likely to disobey authority figures.
- In the real world, the presence of a respected role model who resists authority can lead many other people to do the same.

How social influence research helps us to understand social change

- Nazi Germany resembled Milgram's situation in that legitimate and coercive power was used to produce obedience and the demands on individuals slowly became more unacceptable.

- Nazi Germany differed from Milgram's situation in that the Nazis' goals were abhorrent whereas those in Milgram's research were positive. In addition, there was much more denial of personal responsibility in Nazi Germany than in Milgram's situation.
- Beneficial social change typically involves dissenters (often low in authoritarianism) who receive social support from others.

The role of minority influence in social change

- According to Moscovici's conversion theory, minority influence requires the minority to be consistent, flexible, committed, and to have views in line with social trends.
- Minorities seeking to exert influence should have a behavioural style including conveying an alternative viewpoint, disrupting norms, drawing attention to their views, acting on principles, and making sacrifices.
- Social change produced by terrorists depends on most of the factors for minority influence identified by Moscovici. For example, they typically maintain a consistent position, and portray themselves as forming an ingroup fighting for principled ideas on behalf of the majority.
- Social change produced by civil rights campaigners in the United States also depended on most of the factors Moscovici claimed were required for minority influence. For example, they showed commitment by making many sacrifices and their actions were obviously based on moral principles that most people accepted.
- It is hard to establish cause and effect with social change because we have only the historical record available as evidence.

You have reached the end of the chapter on social psychology. Social psychology is an approach or perspective in psychology. The material in this chapter has exemplified the way that social psychologists explain behaviour. They look at behaviour in terms of the ways in which other people affect our behaviour. Nowhere is this clearer than in social influence research. Ancient astrologers believed that people's actions were affected by an airy fluid that flowed down from the heavenly bodies. This fluid force-field was called "*influentia*". The concept of influences comes from this—they are both invisible and very powerful, as we have seen.

Further Reading

- The whole topic of social influence is discussed in detail in M.W. Eysenck (2013) *Simply psychology (3rd Edn)* (Hove, UK: Psychology Press).

- Most of the topics discussed in this chapter are dealt with in various chapters in M. Hewstone, W. Stroebe, and K. Jonas (Eds) (2008) *Introduction to social psychology: A European perspective (4th Edn)* (Oxford: Blackwell).

- B.H. Hodges and A.L. Geyer (2006) A nonconformist account of the Asch experiments: Values, pragmatics, and moral dilemmas. *Personality and Social Psychology Review, 10,* 2–19. Hodges and Geyer show how Asch's conformity research has been misunderstood and misinterpreted.

- M.A. Hogg and G.M. Vaughan (2010) *Social psychology (6th Edn)* (Harlow, UK: Prentice Hall). Several chapters in this textbook contain comprehensive coverage of the topics discussed in this chapter.

Revision Questions

The examination questions aim to sample the material in this whole chapter. For advice on how to answer such questions refer to Chapter 1, Section 2.

1. The National Blood Service is always trying to recruit more people to become blood donors. They decide to consult a psychologist about how they might use psychological tactics to increase the number of donors.

   Using your knowledge of informational and normative social influence, suggest some possible strategies to encourage more people to become blood donors. (4 marks)

2. a. Identify **two** types of conformity and give examples of each. (2 marks + 2 marks)

   b. Outline and evaluate explanations of conformity. (12 marks)

3. a. Explain **one or more** reasons why people obey authority. (6 marks)

   b. Milgram conducted some well-known studies of obedience. Outline **one** other study of obedience. (4 marks)

   c. Milgram's studies on obedience have been criticised for lacking validity. Describe **one** way in which they lack validity. (2 marks)

4. a. Explain what is meant by *locus of control*. (3 marks)

   b. Locus of control can be used to explain independent behaviour. Outline **one** other explanation of independent behaviour. (3 marks)

   c. Outline **one** study that has shown how people resist pressures to conform. (4 marks)

5. Explain the role of minority influence in social change. (6 marks)

EXAM HINT

Some examination questions require you to apply your knowledge. They start with a "stem" describing a scenario (as in question 1 on this page). Whilst you probably have not seen the scenario before, if you have revised everything you will have the knowledge needed to answer the question. Just remember to apply your knowledge. You might briefly outline a theory or research study but then must use this to explain the scenario.

What you need to know

Section 14: Defining and explaining psychological abnormality p. 255

- Definitions of abnormality, including deviation from social norms, failure to function adequately and deviation from ideal mental health, and limitations of these definitions of psychological abnormality.
- The biological approach to psychopathology.
- Psychological approaches to psychopathology including the psychodynamic, behavioural, and cognitive approaches.

   This section explores the question "What is abnormality?" by looking at various possible definitions. What are the limitations of these definitions of abnormality? It may be possible to explain mental disorders in the same way that we explain physical illnesses—in terms of biological or physical causes. This is called the biological (or medical) approach. Alternatively, we could use psychological explanations, such as those based on learning theory (the behavioural approach) or on Freud's views (the psychodynamic approach), or we could use a cognitive approach. What are the implications of these approaches for treatment?

Section 15: Treating abnormality p. 284

- Biological therapies, including drugs and ECT (electroconvulsive therapy).
- Psychological therapies, including psychoanalysis, systematic de-sensitisation, and Cognitive Behavioural Therapy.

   Various forms of therapy for the treatment of mental disorders have been developed over the past hundred years. Most of these therapies are based on the biological and psychological approaches to abnormality discussed in Section 14. The effectiveness of the major biological and psychological therapies is discussed.

Psychopathology (Abnormality)

7

This chapter explores one major topic in the study of **individual differences**—abnormality. What is **abnormality**? If clinicians are to treat patients with mental disorders, they need to distinguish between normal and abnormal behaviour. However, first they must define abnormality. Mental disorder has been likened to physical illness—for example, having a cold is an abnormal and undesirable state. We will consider that definition a little later in the chapter.

Why do some people have mental disorders and others don't? Are mental disorders "caught" in the same way that you catch a cold, or do they depend on genetic factors and/or personality? We will explore mental abnormality and its potential undesirability in this chapter.

Most of our definitions of abnormality and our explanations for mental disorder are based on Western beliefs. In recent years, however, there has been a growing recognition that it is very important to take account of cultural and sub-cultural differences. This chapter takes account of these issues.

In the final section of the chapter, we consider the main therapeutic approaches used to treat individuals suffering from mental disorders. In general terms, we can place these therapies in two main categories: those that are mostly biological in emphasis and those that are primarily psychological.

SECTION 14
DEFINING AND EXPLAINING PSYCHOLOGICAL ABNORMALITY

Definitions of Abnormality

What is abnormality? The term "abnormal" is defined as "deviating from what is normal or usual". What, then, is meant by the term "normal"? Conforming to a standard of some sort is one answer to that question. But how do we establish the standard? Several approaches will be considered here—all of which have something in their favour:

1. The standard can be defined in social terms—what is considered socially acceptable or deviant.
2. We might use the notion of "adequate functioning"—being able to cope reasonably well with the demands of daily life.
3. There is the concept of **ideal mental health**—a state of contentment we all strive to achieve.

KEY TERMS

Individual differences: the characteristics that vary from one individual to another; intelligence and personality are major ways in which individuals differ.

Abnormality: an undesirable state producing severe impairment in a person's social and personal functioning, often causing anguish. Abnormal behaviour deviates from statistical or social norms, causes distress to the individual or others, and is seen as a failure to function adequately.

Ideal mental health: a state of contentment that we all strive to achieve.

Abnormal behaviour...?

...Not when rescuing a cat!

? In what ways are you abnormal?

Deviation from social norms

One important way of defining abnormality is based on the *impact* of an individual's behaviour on others. According to this approach, people behaving in a socially deviant and apparently incomprehensible way (especially if it upsets or distresses others) should be regarded as abnormal.

Social norms are the standards of behaviour that are regarded as acceptable within a given society. These standards of behaviour are expressed in the form of rules. Some rules are explicit (e.g. "You must not steal goods belonging to other people"), whereas other rules are implicit (e.g. "Don't talk negatively about your friends"; "Form an orderly queue at a bus stop"). As we might expect, explicit and implicit rules both vary from culture to culture and even from time to time within a culture.

The social norms approach allows us to account for desirability of a pattern of behaviour, both for the individual and for society as a whole. **Deviation from social norms** is regarded as abnormal and undesirable. Many people labelled as clinically abnormal do often behave in a socially deviant way. For example, anti-social personality disorder describes individuals who lack a conscience and behave aggressively towards others because they experience little or no guilt. Consider also the Case Studies described on the following pages.

Limitations of the social deviance approach

1. The concept of social deviancy is related to moral codes or standards, subjectively defined by a society, and these vary with prevailing social attitudes. For example, even until the latter part of the 20th century in Britain it was regarded as unacceptable for an unmarried woman to have a child. In the 19th century, single women who became pregnant were seen as social deviants and some were even locked up in psychiatric institutions as a result.

2. What is regarded as socially acceptable in many cultures is strongly influenced by political considerations. In Russia throughout much of the 20th century, individuals who disagreed with the communist government were called dissidents. Their attitudes were seen as symptoms of mental derangement and they were confined in mental hospitals. Using social deviancy to establish a standard allows serious abuses of human rights to occur. Szasz (1960) suggested that the concept of mental illness is a myth used by the state as a means of control. It is certainly open to such abuse.

3. Social deviance is defined by the *context* in which a certain behaviour occurs. Wearing very few clothes is acceptable on a beach but not in a business meeting. Slapping someone around the face is acceptable if you are an actor in a theatrical production but is unacceptable almost everywhere else.

4. Cultural context is also important. For example, the Kwakiutl Indians engage in a special ceremony in which they burn valuable blankets to cast shame on their rivals. If someone in our society deliberately set fire to his/her most valuable possessions, they would be regarded as very odd or mentally ill (Gleitman, 1986). Even within societies there are sub-cultural differences in relation to, for example, different religious groups that have different norms—the Mormons used to believe it is acceptable for a man to have several wives.

Moral codes

The subjective judgements we make when deciding whether or not a particular form of behaviour is normal are derived from the moral codes or standards that we have observed in the behaviour of significant others. We never become entirely independent in our moral thinking. Even as adults our thinking about morality often refers to a collective understanding of the right way to behave in a given situation. Someone who demonstrates a deviation from this may be perceived as either "mad" or "bad".

5. Social deviancy is not necessarily a bad thing. Some people are socially deviant because they have chosen a non-conformist lifestyle and others because their behaviour is motivated by high principles. Eccentrics deliberately fail to conform to many social norms. However, most eccentrics are happy and are on average less prone to mental illness than other people (Weeks & James, 1995). Consider also "deviants" in Nazi Germany who spoke out against the atrocities being committed or risked their lives to help the Jews.

6. The social deviance approach attaches too much importance to behaviour and de-emphasises what is going on inside individuals. For example, consider someone who is suffering from major depressive disorder. They may try very hard to ensure that their behaviour in public conforms to social norms in spite of the fact that they are suffering much internal distress and have a mental disorder. According to the social deviance approach, such individuals aren't abnormal.

7. Criminal behaviour obviously deviates from social norms. However, in most cases, criminals aren't regarded as abnormal. In crude terms, most criminals are seen as "bad" rather than "mad".

Camping in the middle of London may ordinarily be considered an abnormal behaviour in our society, but it is acceptable to those involved in a protest.

The fact that social deviance should be rejected as the only criterion of abnormality doesn't mean it is entirely irrelevant. After all, people derive much of their pleasure in life from their interactions with other people. As a result, most people find it important for a contented existence to avoid behaving in socially deviant ways that bemuse or upset others.

Failure to function adequately

The next possible way of defining abnormality is as a **failure to function adequately**. Most people who seek help from a clinical psychologist or psychiatrist are suffering from a sense of psychological distress or discomfort due to their inability to cope with their work and/or personal lives (Sue et al., 1994). We could say that this recognition of not functioning adequately could act as a standard of abnormality.

In most societies there are *expectations* about how people should live their lives and how they should contribute to the social groups around them. When an individual can't meet these obligations, then both we (and usually they) feel they aren't functioning adequately. Rosenhan and Seligman (1989) suggested that the concept of distress and failure to function adequately can be extended to include a number of behaviours.

According to Rosenhan and Seligman (1989), the most suitable approach to defining mental abnormality may be to identify a set of seven abnormal characteristics. Each on its own may not be sufficient to cause a problem. However, when several are present, they are symptomatic of abnormality. The fewer features that are displayed, the more an individual can be regarded as normal. This approach enables us to think in terms of *degrees* of normality and abnormality rather than whether or not a behaviour or person is abnormal. Here are the seven features identified by Rosenhan and Seligman:

- *Suffering.* Most abnormal individuals report that they are suffering, and so this is a key feature of abnormality. However, nearly all normal individuals grieve when a loved one dies, and some abnormal individuals (e.g. psychopaths or those with anti-social personality disorder) treat other people very badly but don't suffer themselves.
- *Maladaptiveness.* Maladaptive behaviour prevents an individual from achieving major life goals such as enjoying good relationships with other people or working effectively. Most abnormal behaviour is maladaptive in this sense. However, maladaptive behaviour can also be due to a lack of relevant knowledge or skills.

KEY TERM

Failure to function adequately: a model of abnormality based on an inability to cope with day-to-day life caused by psychological distress or discomfort.

CASE STUDY: Sarah, a case of agoraphobia with panic disorder

Sarah, a woman in her mid-thirties, was shopping for bargains in a crowded department store during the January sales. Without warning and without knowing why, she suddenly felt anxious and dizzy. She worried that she was about to faint or have a heart attack. She dropped her shopping and rushed straight home. As she neared home, she noticed that her feelings of panic lessened.

A few days later she decided to go shopping again. On entering the store, she felt herself becoming increasingly anxious. After a few minutes she had become so anxious that a shopkeeper asked her if she was alright and took her to a first aid room. Once there her feelings of panic became worse and she grew particularly embarrassed at all the attention she was attracting.

After this she avoided going to the large store again. She even started to worry when going into smaller shops because she thought she might have another panic attack, and this worry turned into intense anxiety.

Eventually she stopped shopping altogether, asking her husband to do it for her.

Over the next few months, Sarah found that she had panic attacks in more and more places. The typical pattern was that she became progressively more anxious the further away from her house she got. She tried to avoid the places where she might have a panic attack but, as the months passed, she found that this restricted her activities. Some days she found it impossible to leave the house at all. She felt that her marriage was becoming strained and that her husband resented her dependence on him.

Clearly Sarah's behaviour was abnormal, in many of the ways described in the text. It was socially deviant and it interfered with her ability to function adequately, both from her own point of view and from that of her husband. She did not have many of the signs of mental healthiness, and suffered from the mental disorder of agoraphobia with panic disorder.

(Adapted from Stirling & Hellewell (1999).)

- *Vividness and unconventionality of behaviour*. The ways in which abnormal individuals behave in various situations differ substantially from how most people behave. However, the same is true of non-conformists and eccentrics.
- *Unpredictability and loss of control*. Abnormal individuals' behaviour is often very variable and uncontrolled, and is also inappropriate. However, most people sometimes behave like this (e.g. after binge drinking).
- *Irrationality and incomprehensibility*. A common feature of abnormal behaviour is that it isn't clear why anyone would choose to behave in that way. However, we might simply not know the reasons for it.
- *Observer discomfort*. Those who see the unspoken rules of social behaviour being broken by others often experience some discomfort. However, observer discomfort may reflect cultural differences in behaviour and style rather than abnormality.
- *Violation of moral and ideal standards*. Behaviour may be judged to be abnormal when it violates established moral standards. However, the majority of people may fail to maintain those standards, which may be out of date or imposed by minority religious or political leaders. For example, various common sexual practices are illegal in parts of the United States.

One serious problem with Rosenhan and Seligman's features is that most involve making subjective judgements. For example, behaviour causing severe discomfort to one observer may have no effect on another. Behaviour that violates one person's moral standards may be consistent with another person's moral standards. Another problem with some features is that they also apply to people who are non-conformists or who simply have their own idiosyncratic style. However, there are no clear objective measures of abnormality that we can use.

Limitations of the "failure to function" approach

The first limitation of this approach is that it is very *imprecise*. Abnormality is defined as a failure to function adequately and yet it isn't possible to define the key terms clearly. Inadequate functioning is a matter of degree, and it is entirely arbitrary to draw a dividing line between adequate and inadequate functioning. It is very unlikely that different people would agree where the dividing line should be drawn.

> **ACTIVITY: The seven features of abnormality**
>
> Imagine a continuum from extremely abnormal behaviour at one end to normality at the other. At what point does our behaviour become unacceptable? Bearing in mind Rosenhan and Seligman's definitions, consider the experiences described below. For each one describe what would be acceptable behaviour and what would be regarded as abnormal. For example, what kind of expression of grief would go beyond the bounds of normality?
>
> *Suffering*: Grief at the loss of a loved one.
> *Maladaptiveness*: Disregard for one's own safety, e.g. taking part in extreme sports.
> *Vividness and unconventionality*: Tattooing or body piercing.
> *Unpredictability and loss of control*: Losing one's temper.
> *Irrationality and incomprehensibility*: Remaining friendly towards someone who is hostile.
> *Observer discomfort*: Laughing at inappropriate times, e.g. when someone is describing a sad event.
> *Violation of moral and ideal standards*: Removing one's clothes to sunbathe on the beach.
>
> - Are the criteria we use influenced by our cultural and personal backgrounds?
> - Try to think of other examples for each standard.

The "failure to function" approach assumes individuals who aren't functioning adequately are behaving abnormally. It also assumes that individuals who are functioning aren't abnormal. There is some merit in both of these assumptions, but they are often incorrect.

We will start with the assumption that inadequate functioning indicates abnormal behaviour. A major problem with this assumption is that it doesn't take sufficient account of *situational context*. Consider the following examples. In most contexts, the behaviour of a man with a machine gun who kills 20 people would be regarded as abnormal; in a war situation, he might be a hero. It is usually regarded as abnormal for someone to spend several weeks or months in a state of deep depression. However, that is a normal reaction if someone very close to you has just died.

Second, the assumption doesn't take fully into account the fact that notions of abnormality vary within any given culture at different periods in history. For example, how homosexuality is regarded within American culture has altered over successive editions of DSM (*Diagnostic and Statistical Manual of Mental Disorders*). This is the system used to classify mental illness in America. It is used by clinicians to diagnose mental disorders.

In DSM-II, published in 1968, homosexuality was classified as a sexual deviation. In DSM-III, published in 1980, homosexuality was no longer categorised as a mental disorder. However, there was a new category of "ego-dystonic homosexuality" that was used only for homosexuals wishing to become heterosexual. In DSM-III-R, this last category had disappeared. However, a category of "sexual disorder not otherwise specified" with "persistent and marked distress about one's sexual orientation" was added. This remained the case in DSM-IV, which was published in 1994. However, even today many people continue to view homosexuality as an aberrant mental state.

Another problem with this way of defining abnormality is that not all people who experience mental disorder are aware of their failure to function. For example, individuals suffering from schizophrenia often deny they have a problem (see the Case Study overleaf). It is distressing to others, who may be able to judge that the individual isn't functioning adequately and seek help on his/her behalf.

On the positive side, it is relatively easy to assess the consequences of dysfunctional behaviour (e.g. absenteeism from work; inadequate work performance) to measure the level of functioning. However, value judgements are still required. That means that the "failure to function adequately" model is tied to the social deviancy one.

The model doesn't recognise the individual's subjective experience. Inevitably, however, such judgements are made by others, and those judgements are influenced by social and cultural beliefs and biases.

CASE STUDY: Simon, a boy with acute schizophrenia

Simon lived at home with his parents. Over some months his parents had become increasingly concerned about his behaviour. He had grown reclusive, spending a lot of time in his room, and he had lost contact with his friends. His parents feared he might be taking drugs. They decided to call the doctor when they found that he had scratched the words "good" and "evil" on his arms, along with other unusual symbols. The GP was also concerned and contacted a psychiatrist who visited Simon at home. Simon at first pretended to be out. After some negotiation, he agreed to let the psychiatrist in. Initially, Simon was very suspicious and denied that there was a problem. Eventually, he told the psychiatrist that he was very worried about all the evil in the world, and had discovered that he could tell whether people were good or evil just by looking at them. He described receiving messages from the radio and TV.

The psychiatrist was concerned when Simon said that he left the house at night to look for evil people, believing it was his duty to fight them. The psychiatrist found that Simon's bedroom was painted black and the curtains were taped shut. The walls were covered with crucifixes and mystical symbols, and Simon slept with a large knife near his bed in case he was confronted by evil people at night.

Simon was asked if he was willing to be admitted to a local hospital. He refused, saying he did not need help. The psychiatrist was sufficiently concerned about the possible risks to Simon or others that he arranged for Simon to be admitted under the Mental Health Act. For the first few weeks in hospital, Simon continued to claim that he was not ill and did not need treatment. Drug therapy resulted in significant improvements and he eventually returned home, continuing with his medication.

(Adapted from J.D. Stirling & J.S.E. Hellewell, 1999, *Psychopathology*. London: Routledge.)

What about the assumption that individuals who are functioning adequately aren't abnormal? There are several reasons for doubting the correctness of this assumption. A prime example is the English doctor Harold Shipman. He was a serial killer who was responsible for the deaths of at least 218 of his patients. In spite of his appalling crimes, Shipman managed to function adequately enough to escape detection for many, many years. Even when his crimes were discovered, the police were surprised how quiet and dull Shipman appeared to be.

We also need to consider psychopaths. Psychopathy is a mental disorder characterised by superficial charm, frequent lying, and a lack of concern about other people. Many psychopaths commit violent crimes and are imprisoned. However, other psychopaths lead successful lives and even become business leaders. How can some psychopaths apparently function adequately in spite of having a mental disorder? Gao and Raine (2010) argued that such psychopaths are highly intelligent and so can achieve their goals by non-violent methods.

Deviation from ideal mental health

If we take the view that abnormality is related to the lack of a "contented existence", then we might seek a definition in terms of deviation from ideal mental health. This is the view taken by **humanistic psychologists** such as Carl Rogers and Abraham Maslow. They both felt **self-actualisation** (fulfilment of one's potential) was a key standard and goal for human endeavour. Very few people are fully self-actualised, so don't worry if you are only partially fulfilling your potential!

Rogers (1959) was the founder of **client-centred therapy**. This has been extremely influential and has played a major role in the development of counselling. Rogers believed that maladjustment or abnormal development occurred when a child received only conditional love from his/her parents. What this means is that the child only receives love from his/her parents if the child behaves in certain ways. The resulting conflict between the self-concept and the ideal self means that the individual will try to be someone else to receive the love he/she wants.

Healthy psychological development occurs through receiving *unconditional* positive regard from significant others (i.e. love is given regardless of the child's behaviour). This leads to high **self-esteem** and self-acceptance. It frees the individual from seeking social approval and enables him/her to seek self-actualisation.

Maslow (1954) was interested in the factors driving or motivating individuals. He claimed we seek first to have our basic needs satisfied (e.g. hunger; safety). After that, people are driven by "higher" motives such as love, belonging, and knowledge. The highest motive of all is to seek self-actualisation (see diagram).

Humanists wanted to define the ultimate goals of human behaviour. Normal people would strive for these goals, and abnormality results from a failure to achieve them.

KEY TERMS

Humanistic psychology: an approach to psychology that focuses on higher motivation, self-development, and on each individual as unique.

Self-actualisation: fulfilling one's potential in the broadest sense.

Client-centred therapy: a form of humanistic therapy introduced by Rogers and designed to increase the client's self-esteem and reduce incongruence between self and ideal self.

Self-esteem: the feelings that an individual has about himself or herself.

Jahoda (1958) argued that the concepts of abnormality and normality were useless because their definition varies as a function of the group or culture we are considering. She suggested it was preferable to identify the criteria for positive mental health and then look at the frequency of their distribution in any population. Jahoda tried to identify common concepts used when describing mental health. She proposed that there were six categories that **clinicians** typically related to mental health:

KEY TERM

Clinician (or clinical psychologist): a person who works in clinical psychology, concerned with the diagnosis and treatment of abnormal behaviour.

1. *Self-attitudes.* High self-esteem and a strong sense of identity are related to mental health.
2. *Personal growth.* The extent of an individual's actual growth, development, or self-actualisation is important.
3. *Integration.* This is a "synthesising psychological function" that integrates or combines the above two concepts. It can be assessed in terms of the individual's ability to cope with stressful situations.
4. *Autonomy.* This is the degree to which an individual is independent of social influences. We must be careful here, because ignoring social influences can be a sign of mental illness!
5. *Perception of reality.* This is a prime factor in mental health. Individuals with good mental health don't need to distort their perception of reality, and they exhibit empathy and social sensitivity.
6. *Environmental mastery.* The extent to which an individual is successful and well-adapted, including the ability to love, adequacy at work and at play, good interpersonal relations, efficiency in meeting situational requirements, capacity for adaptation and adjustment, and efficient problem solving. Most of us probably don't succeed in all these areas!

Jahoda's approach has the advantage of being positive. It seeks to identify the characteristics that people need in order to be mentally or psychologically healthy rather than identifying the problems. As a result, the six categories she identified could be translated into useful therapeutic aims (treatment goals).

Maslow characterised Einstein as an individual who demonstrated "self-actualisation"—including characteristics such as self-acceptance, resistance to cultural influences, empathy, and creativeness.

Limitations of the ideal mental health approach

The ideal mental health approach has the advantage of focusing on positive characteristics—on health rather than illness. However, this approach has several limitations:

1. Any set of values is inevitably linked to a given culture and historical period. Many psychologists (e.g. Oyserman et al., 2002) distinguish between individualistic cultures and collectivistic ones. Individualistic cultures (e.g. the United Kingdom; the United States) emphasise independence and personal control. In contrast, collectivistic cultures (e.g. China; Japan) focus on interdependence and considering oneself as a member of a group.

   Jahoda's list of mentally healthy behaviours such as self-attitudes, autonomy, and personal growth makes much more sense in individualistic cultures than in collectivistic ones. For example, Heine et al. (1999) discussed research in which

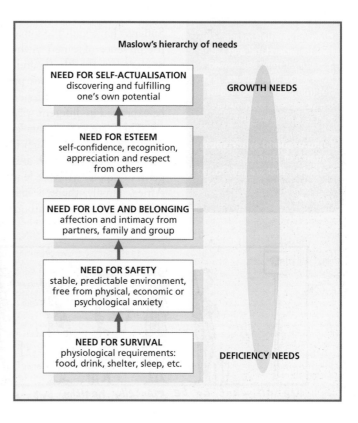

Maslow's hierarchy of needs

NEED FOR SELF-ACTUALISATION
discovering and fulfilling one's own potential

GROWTH NEEDS

NEED FOR ESTEEM
self-confidence, recognition, appreciation and respect from others

NEED FOR LOVE AND BELONGING
affection and intimacy from partners, family and group

NEED FOR SAFETY
stable, predictable environment, free from physical, economic or psychological anxiety

NEED FOR SURVIVAL
physiological requirements: food, drink, shelter, sleep, etc.

DEFICIENCY NEEDS

EXAM HINT

You need to be able to describe each definition of abnormality that is on the specification in sufficient detail to gain full marks:
- *Deviation from social norms*: Remember these are culturally relevant and era dependent.
- *Failure to function adequately*: Be able to include some (not necessarily all) of Rosenhan and Seligman's criteria for failure to function, e.g. personal distress, observer discomfort, and maladaptiveness.
- *Deviation from ideal mental health*: Consider Jahoda's criteria for ideal mental health, e.g. positive self-attitudes, autonomy, perception of reality.

European Canadian and Japanese students ranked 20 traits in terms of how much they ideally would like to possess them. European Canadians rated self-confidence as the trait they would *most* like to possess, whereas the Japanese rated it as the trait they would *least* like to possess.

2. The vague criteria for ideal mental health are hard to measure. For example, how can we rate positive interpersonal relations or self-acceptance?

3. The "healthy behaviours" identified by Jahoda are ideals. Very few people ever achieve them, so many (or even most) of us could be classified as abnormal. However, it could be argued that abnormality involves a substantial falling short on most or all of the criteria for ideal mental health. That raises the tricky issue of how much of a falling short is required for behaviour to be regarded as abnormal.

4. Humans are social animals and so having close personal relationships with other people is of central importance to ideal mental health. Jahoda refers to this under environmental mastery, but still de-emphasises its importance.

5. There seems to be an implicit assumption that any given individual's mental health remains fairly constant over time. However, that is probably the exception rather than the rule. Most people have a period of reduced mental health after someone close to them dies, and an important failure is generally followed by reduced self-esteem.

6. Eccentrics often focus obsessively on their work and/or hobbies, and many of them aren't very interested in the opinions or the company of other people. Thus, they would seem to fall short of ideal mental health. In spite of that, as we saw earlier, eccentrics tend to be happier than other people. This suggests most of them have good mental health.

7. However, Jahoda's approach may not provide useful criteria for identifying what constitutes abnormality. A psychological scale that measures psychological concepts (e.g. a person's level of self-esteem) can't provide an objective measurement.

Cultural relativism

A fundamental limitation with all the definitions of abnormality we have examined is that they are culturally specific. The notion of **cultural relativism** means that value judgements are *relative* to individual cultural contexts. As a result, we can't make absolute statements about what is normal and abnormal in human behaviour. This is very clear if we consider **culture-bound syndromes** (patterns of abnormal behaviour typically found only in a single culture).

Dhat syndrome is a culture-bound syndrome found among males of the Indian subcontinent. Sufferers have multiple somatic complaints, and blame their physical and mental exhaustion on the presence of semen in their urine. The origins of this lie in the Hindu belief that semen is produced in the blood, and that the loss of semen will result in illness. Chadda and Ahuja (1990) examined various patients with *dhat* and concluded they were suffering from either neurotic depression or anxiety neurosis. Thus, a single underlying disorder (e.g. depression) may be expressed in different ways from one culture to another.

There are many other culture-bound syndromes, and we will briefly mention three more here. *Ghost sickness*, which is common in Native American tribes, has as its main symptom an excessive focus on death and on those who have died. *Koro* involves extreme anxiety that the penis or nipples will recede into the body and possibly cause death. It is found in south and east Africa. Finally, there is *amok* (originally identified in Malaysia), which involves brooding followed by a violent outburst.

We all want to be mentally healthy, but should we all want to be totally "normal"?

The importance of the cultural context can be seen if we go back to the seven features of abnormality proposed by Rosenhan and Seligman (1989; see page 258). Many of those features refer to behaviour defined by the social norms or expectations of the culture. That is certainly true of vividness and unconventionality of behaviour; irrationality and incomprehensibility; and observer discomfort. In other words, abnormality has a somewhat different meaning across cultures. For example, hallucinations are considered normal in certain situations in some societies, but in the West they are seen as a manifestation of a mental disorder.

Finally, it is important to strike the right balance. Some features identified by Rosenhan and Seligman can be thought of as universal indicators of undesirable behaviour for the individual concerned and those around them. Examples include a refusal to eat, chronic depression, a fear of going outdoors, and anti-social behaviour. Thus, there are some universal indicators of abnormality, even though most behavioural signs of abnormality are culture-specific.

DSM-IV-TR

How do psychiatrists and clinical psychologists go about the task of diagnosing mental disorders (abnormal conditions)? They often use the *Diagnostic and Statistical Manual of Mental Disorders* (DSM), which contains over 200 disorders. The current version of DSM is DSM-IV-TR (text revision), published in 2000. According to this version, a mental disorder (abnormal condition) is "a clinically significant behavioural or psychological syndrome or pattern that occurs in an individual [which] is associated with present distress ... or disability ... or with a significant increased risk of suffering." In general terms, an individual is likely to have a mental disorder if their condition interferes with their ability to cope with work and/or their personal lives.

How is DSM-IV-TR used to decide whether someone has a mental disorder and, if so, which disorder? The emphasis is on the signs and symptoms of mental disorders rather than on the underlying causes. A major reason is that there is little agreement on the underlying causes of most mental disorders. Some signs and symptoms tend to be found together and so form a syndrome. Schizophrenia can be regarded as a syndrome involving symptoms such as disorganised speech, lack of emotion, hallucinations, and delusions.

Of most relevance here, DSM-IV-TR makes use of a scale of global assessment of functioning, although this is not of central importance in diagnosis. This is designed to assess the patient's social, occupational, and psychological functioning. As such, its main emphasis closely resembles the approach based on failure to function adequately that was discussed earlier. This scale also resembles the approach based on deviation from social norms, but to a lesser extent. It is of least relevance to the approach based on deviation from ideal mental health.

Conclusions

Concepts differ very much in their precision. "Abnormality" is an imprecise concept. Abnormal behaviour can take different forms and can involve different features. Moreover, there is no single feature that can always be relied on to distinguish between normal and abnormal behaviour. What is needed is to identify the main features that are *much more likely* to be found in abnormal than in normal individuals. The seven features proposed by Rosenhan and Seligman

EXAM HINT
- You are most likely to be asked to give ONE limitation of any of the definitions of abnormality. However, you may also be asked to answer an essay question so you need to know some other criticisms (limitations and/or strengths). You must be able to ELABORATE the limitation sufficiently for 3 marks.
- Culture bias works well for all three definitions. Use examples of social norms changing across cultures and examples of how the criteria for failure to function and ideal mental health can be viewed differently across cultures to make sure your answer is DETAILED and FOCUSED on the definition specified in the question.

Labels and symptoms

Imagine that you are in a situation where you have been wrongly diagnosed as suffering from a mental disorder such as schizophrenia. How would you react to such a situation? Would you be incredulous? Furious? Tearful? Shocked and withdrawn? How could all those emotions be interpreted by those people whose job it is to assess your mental condition?

(1989) may offer a combined and realistic approach. The more of these features possessed by an individual, the greater the likelihood that he or she will be categorised as abnormal.

Alternatively, we could adopt a multi-criterion approach to defining abnormality. In essence, that could involve combining the three approaches we have been discussing in this section. Suppose we were trying to decide whether a given individual was abnormal. If they failed to function adequately, their behaviour deviated in several ways from social norms, and their mental health deviated considerably from the ideal, we would probably be very confident that they were abnormal.

On the other hand, suppose their behaviour didn't deviate from social norms but their mental health deviated very much from the ideal. That would suggest that they were experiencing inner distress but were somehow managing to behave normally. In contrast, an approximation to ideal mental health combined with behaviour deviating from social norms might indicate that the individual is an eccentric who is perfectly content but doesn't care about the impact of their behaviour on other people.

In sum, there are degrees of abnormality. Abnormality can manifest in terms of behaviour and/or in terms of inner distress. If we use all three approaches to defining abnormality, we can obtain a clearer idea of the ways in which someone is and is not abnormal.

Biological and Psychological (Including Psychodynamic, Behavioural, and Cognitive) Approaches to Psychopathology

A different way to consider abnormality is to focus on explanations of *why* it happens. Several approaches to abnormality have been put forward over the years. These approaches have been very influential, because the form of treatment for any given mental disorder is based in part on our understanding of the causes of that disorder. In what follows, we will be using the term **psychopathology** often. Psychopathology means the study of mental illness.

The dominant approach at one time was the **biological (medical) approach**, in which mental disorders are regarded as illnesses. Most **psychiatrists** accept this approach, whereas most clinical psychologists reject it in favour of psychological approaches. There are also numerous psychologically-based approaches to abnormality, focusing on different factors and/or attitudes to life.

We can distinguish between one-dimensional and multi-dimensional causal approaches (Durand & Barlow, 2006). According to one-dimensional approaches, the origins of a mental disorder can be traced to a *single* underlying cause. For example, severe depression might be caused by a major loss (e.g. death of a loved one) or schizophrenia by genetic factors. In practice, one-dimensional approaches have been replaced by multi-dimensional approaches assuming that any given mental disorder is typically caused by *several* factors in interaction.

One way of expressing the multi-dimensional perspective is in terms of the **diathesis–stress approach**. According to this approach, the occurrence of psychological disorder depends on two factors:

1. Diathesis: a genetic vulnerability or predisposition to disease or disorder.
2. Stress: some severe or disturbing environmental event.

If the multi-dimensional approach is correct, it follows that we may need to combine the insights of the biological and psychological approaches. That is the position we adopt here. We assume that each approach is partially correct, and that a full understanding of the origins of

KEY TERMS

Psychopathology: the study of mental illness or mental disorders; abnormal psychology.

Biological (medical) model: an approach to abnormality that regards mental disorders as illnesses with a physical cause.

Psychiatrist: a medically trained person who specialises in the diagnosis and treatment of mental disorders.

Diathesis–stress approach: the notion that psychological disorders occur when there is a genetically determined vulnerability (diathesis) and relevant stressful conditions.

mental disorders requires us to combine information from all of them. Here we will focus on the four most important ones: biological, psychodynamic, behavioural, and cognitive approaches.

The biological approach

The essence of the biological (medical) approach is that "abnormal behaviours result from physical problems and should be treated medically". Thus, mental disorders are illnesses with a physical cause, so we should approach mental disorders from the perspective of medicine.

Four kinds of medical explanation can be used to explain the cause of abnormality. Below we discuss all four.

Infection

Germs or micro-organisms such as bacteria or viruses produce disease states. Many common physical illnesses (e.g. measles, influenza) are caused in this way. Some mental illnesses have also been linked to micro-organisms. This approach is of limited value because most mental disorders don't have a single cause.

Micro-organisms have been suggested as a cause of schizophrenia. Barr et al. (1990) found there was an increased incidence of schizophrenia in children whose mothers had flu when they were pregnant, suggesting the disorder might be a disease. However, this approach to schizophrenia is very limited and ignores several important factors. For example, people with schizophrenia tend to have experienced a high number of stressful life events in the few weeks before its onset (Day et al., 1987), a finding that can't be explained in terms of infection.

Favaro et al. (2011) considered the incidence of anorexia nervosa (a serious eating disorder in which the patient is severely underweight) in women. Those exposed to chickenpox or rubella when they were foetuses were about 50% more likely to have anorexia nervosa than those who hadn't been exposed to those virus infections. However, anorexia nervosa depends much more on genetic factors and on having perfectionist parents than on being exposed to such virus infections.

Genetic factors

Individuals may inherit predispositions to certain illnesses. These predispositions are carried by genes. One way to show the inheritance of mental disorder is by looking at patterns of such disorders within families or twin pairs. If a disorder is caused genetically, we would expect individuals who are closely related (and so share many genes) to be more likely to have it. However, closely related individuals within a family are likely to experience more similar environments (e.g. living in the same home) than those who aren't closely related. That can make it hard to decide whether the presence of a given mental disorder in two closely related individuals is due to the similarity of their genes or to the similarity in their environment.

The most useful way of deciding whether genetic factors are important is to carry out twin studies. **Monozygotic twins** (identical twins) share 100% of their genes whereas fraternal or **dizygotic twins** share only 50% of their genes. For any given disorder, the key measure is the **concordance rate**: this is the likelihood that, if one twin has the disorder, the other twin also has it.

If genetic factors are important, the concordance rate should be higher in identical than fraternal twins. That has been found for several disorders. Gottesman (1991) summarised the findings from about 40 twin studies on schizophrenia, finding the concordance rate was 48% for identical twins but only 17% for fraternal twins. McGuffin et al. (1996) found that the concordance rate for major depression was 46% for identical twins and 20% for fraternal twins. Craddock and Jones (1999) found with bipolar disorder (also known as manic-depressive disorder) that the concordance rate was 40% for identical twins compared to between 5% and 10% for fraternal twins, siblings, and other close relatives.

Identical twins offer the opportunity of conducting a natural experiment. They are the same genetically so any differences in their behaviour should be due to the environment. However, they usually experience rather similar environments as well.

KEY TERMS

Monozygotic twins: identical twins who share 100% of their genes with each other.

Dizygotic twins: fraternal twins who share 50% of their genes with each other.

Concordance rate: in twin studies, the probability that if one twin has a given disorder the other twin also has the same disorder.

The biological approach to abnormality: Genes

How much of our behaviour is determined by our personal mix of genes is uncertain, but it is a fact that they do affect behaviour. A unique example of this is in the Batista family in the Dominican Republic. For example, out of ten children in this family there were four boys born with normal *female* genitalia, but at puberty, about age 12, the vaginas of these four closed and healed over, two testicles descended, and normal penises grew. Similar physical changes have occurred in related families in the village and these have been found to be the result of a recessive pair of genes. The question is whether this clearly unusual physical development could be classed as psychological abnormality—what do you think, and why?

? How might research on gene-mapping be of use when counselling prospective parents?

Another way to study **genetic** influences is to show that particular genes are more likely to be present in individuals with a disorder than in those without the disorder. **Gene-mapping** studies have found several genes that may be involved in particular disorders. Wang et al. (2010) carried out a meta-analysis of studies concerned with the specific genes associated with schizophrenia and bipolar disorder (a disorder in which there are depressive and manic episodes). Several specific genes were identified, including many that were related to both disorders.

In sum, genetic factors are important for several disorders. However, several other factors are also involved. There would be a concordance rate of 100% for identical twins if any disorder depended only on genetic factors. In fact, in the studies we have discussed, the concordance rate was always below 50%.

Biochemistry

A third possible cause of abnormality lies in the patient's **biochemistry**. For example, several theorists have argued that one factor involved in schizophrenia is an excessive amount of dopamine, a chemical substance in the brain. However, most research has only identified *correlations* between the disorder and the raised biochemical levels. What this means is that we can't be certain whether the excessive amount of dopamine is *cause* or *effect*. Schizophrenia may cause dopamine levels to rise rather than excessive dopamine levels playing a role in the onset of schizophrenia.

However, recent research by Howes et al. (2011) is more informative. They studied patients at ultra-high risk of psychosis. Those with the highest levels of dopamine in a part of the brain known as the striatum were most likely to develop schizophrenia. Thus, dopamine overactivity *predicted* subsequent schizophrenia, which suggests it may have played a causal role.

Some evidence that biochemical changes can have significant effects on the symptoms of abnormality comes from drug studies using patients. For example, depression is often associated with low levels of the neurotransmitter serotonin, although the findings are somewhat inconsistent (Nordquist & Oreland, 2010). Prozac, a well-known drug that increases serotonin activity, reduces the symptoms of depression (Hirschfeld, 1999). This is consistent with the hypothesis that abnormal levels of serotonin play a role in producing depression.

KEY TERMS

Genetic: information from genes, the units of inheritance.

Gene-mapping: determining the effect of a particular gene on physical or psychological characteristics.

Biochemistry: the study of the chemical processes of living organisms.

Neuroanatomy: the anatomy of the nervous system, i.e. the study of its structure and function.

PET scans of a normal (left) and schizophrenic human brain.

Neuroanatomy

A fourth possible cause lies in **neuroanatomy**—the structure of the nervous system. For example, many brain-imaging studies indicate that the brains of people with schizophrenia differ from those of healthy individuals. Lawrie and Abukmeil (1998) reviewed 40 brain-imaging studies. On average, people with schizophrenia have smaller brain volume than healthy controls, but the lateral ventricles (fluid-filled open spaces in the brain) were about 40% larger in people with schizophrenia. Once again, we can't be sure whether the brain differences partly caused the schizophrenia or whether schizophrenia caused the neuroanatomical changes.

EVALUATION OF THE BIOLOGICAL APPROACH

➕ The biological (medical) approach has had an enormous influence on the terms used to refer to mental disorder and their treatment. As Maher (1966, p. 22) pointed out, deviant behaviour

is termed pathological and is classified on the basis of symptoms, classification being called diagnosis. Processes designed to change behaviour are called therapies, and are [sometimes] applied to patients in mental hospitals. If the deviant behaviour ceases, the patient is described as cured.

➕ The biological approach is clearly successful with some psychological conditions. For example, phenylketonuria (PKU), which is a cause of mental retardation, can be treated simply and effectively by physical means. In this condition, an individual is born with an inability to metabolise (process) the amino acid phenylalanine. As a result, the concentration of phenylalanine increases, and there is permanent brain damage. PKU is preventable if infants are given a special diet low in phenylalanine.

➕ The biological approach has the merit of being based on well-established sciences such as medicine and biochemistry.

➕ Some forms of mental disorder (especially schizophrenia) can be understood from the perspective of the biological approach, and numerous mental disorders are caused *in part* by genetic factors. Drug therapies based on the biological approach have often proved effective in at least reducing symptoms.

➖ There is generally only a loose analogy between physical and mental illness. It is easier to establish the causes of most physical illnesses than mental ones, and symptoms of mental disorders are often more subjective.

➖ The biological approach applies much better to some mental disorders (e.g. schizophrenia) than others (e.g. phobias). Genetic factors are especially important in schizophrenia, but even here environmental factors play a major role.

➖ When biological differences (e.g. in biochemistry, in brain structure) are found between individuals with and without a given mental disorder, it is tempting to conclude that the biological differences caused the mental disorder. In fact, since we only have correlational evidence, we don't know whether the biological differences caused the mental disorder or whether the biological differences are a by-product of having the disorder.

➖ The biological model is too narrow in its focus. It focuses on biological causes of mental disorder but ignores cultural factors, social factors (e.g. severe life events; inadequate social support), and psychological factors (e.g. distorted beliefs about oneself and the world).

➖ Thomas Szasz (pronounced "sas") claimed mental illnesses are more appropriately described as "problems in living" than as disease:

It is customary to define psychiatry as a medical speciality concerned with the study, diagnosis, and treatment of mental illness. This is a worthless and misleading definition. Mental illness is a myth. Psychiatrists are not concerned with mental illnesses and their treatment ... In actual practice they deal with personal, social and ethical problems in living ... the notion of a person "having a mental illness" is scientifically crippling. It provides professional assent to a popular rationalisation, namely that problems of living ... expressed in terms of so called psychiatric symptoms are basically similar to bodily disease (1960, p. 269).

Szasz's objections to the medical or biological approach are not made very clear in the above quotation (as you will probably agree!), so I will try to clarify matters. First, he pointed out that we generally don't hold someone responsible if they have a physical illness and we tend to do the same if they have a so-called mental illness. He felt this was very undesirable ethically, because it stops people accepting responsibility for themselves and for their own lives.

Second, putting a label on someone (e.g. "You're a schizophrenic!") can create problems for the individual concerned. People identified as suffering from a mental illness are often rejected by others in the same way as someone identified as a prostitute or criminal.

We could turn Szasz's argument on its head. The notion that individuals with mental disorders are suffering from an illness could be regarded as ethically desirable—it suggests they aren't responsible for their condition and so shouldn't feel guilty. However, it may be undesirable to encourage individuals with mental disorders to hand over complete responsibility for their recovery to experts in treating "mental illness".

Assumptions of the biological approach

- All mental disorders have a physical cause (micro-organisms, genetics, biochemistry, or neuroanatomy).
- Mental illnesses can be described in terms of clusters of symptoms.
- Symptoms can be identified, leading to the diagnosis of an illness.
- Diagnosis leads to appropriate physical treatments.

The psychodynamic approach

The **psychodynamic approach to psychopathology** is based on the assumption that mental disorders have their origins in psychological factors rather than physical or biological ones. More specifically, unresolved unconscious conflicts are of central importance in triggering metal disorders.

The term "psychodynamic" refers to a group of explanations designed to account for the *dynamics* of behaviour, or the forces that motivate it. Sigmund Freud's theory is the best-known example. He put forward the first psychodynamic approach, which he called psychoanalysis. Sigmund Freud (1856–1939) practised as a psychiatrist in Vienna and collected a lot of information from his patients about their feelings and experiences, especially those relating to early childhood.

Psychodynamic theory explains human development in terms of an interaction between innate drives (e.g. the desire for pleasure) and early experience (the extent to which early desires were gratified). The idea is that individual personality differences can be traced back to early conflicts between desire and experience. For example, a child may want to behave badly (e.g. steal sweets) but be in conflict because of the guilt experienced afterwards. Some of these conflicts remain with the adult, influencing his or her behaviour, and can cause mental disorders. Accordingly, we turn to Freud's description of development.

Structure of personality

You probably imagine most of the mind exists at the conscious level. The fact that you are generally consciously aware of why you have the emotions you do, and why you behave as you do, suggests our conscious mind has full access to all relevant information about ourselves. However, Freud's views were very different. He argued the conscious mind is like the tip of an iceberg, with most of the mind (as with an iceberg) out of sight.

Freud assumed there were *three* levels of the mind:

- The conscious—those thoughts that are currently the focus of attention; in other words, what we are thinking about at any moment.

Sigmund Freud, 1856–1939.

KEY TERM

Psychodynamic approach to psychopathology: an approach that regards the origin of mental disorders as psychological rather than physical, and suggests that mental illness arises out of unresolved unconscious conflicts.

- The preconscious—information and ideas that can be retrieved easily from memory and brought into consciousness.
- The unconscious—this is the largest part of the mind, containing information almost impossible to bring into conscious awareness. Much of the information in the unconscious mind relates to very emotional experiences from our past (e.g. being bullied at school; being rejected by someone very important to us).

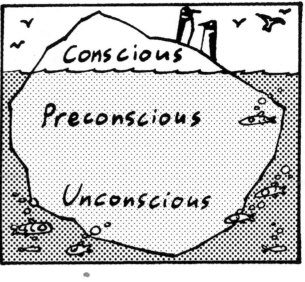

We have just seen that Freud assumed the mind exists at three different levels. He also assumed the mind is divided into *three* parts. In broad terms, Freud argued that the mind contains basic motivational forces (the id), the cognitive system used to perceive the world and for thinking and problem solving (the ego), and a conscience based on the values of family and of society generally (the superego). Let's now consider each part in more detail.

1. **Id.** This contains basic motivational forces, especially innate sexual and aggressive instincts. The id follows the pleasure principle, with the emphasis being on *immediate* satisfaction. It is located in the unconscious mind. The sexual instinct is known as **libido.**
2. **Ego.** This is the conscious, rational mind, and it develops during the first two years of life. It works on the **reality principle**, taking account of what is going on in the environment.
3. **Superego.** This develops at about the age of 5. It embodies the child's conscience and sense of right and wrong. It is formed when the child adopts the values of the same-sex parent (the process of identification).

Defence mechanisms

According to Freud, there are frequent *conflicts* among the id, ego, and superego, causing the individual to experience anxiety. What generally happens is that there are conflicts between the id (which wants immediate satisfaction) and the superego (which wants the person to behave in line with society's rules). These conflicts force the ego to devote much time to trying to resolve them. The ego protects itself by using various defence mechanisms (strategies designed to reduce anxiety).

Defence mechanisms are used to reduce the anxiety caused by unresolved conflicts. However, they act more as sticking plaster than as a way of sorting out an individual's problems. Some of the main defence mechanisms are as follows:

1. **Repression.** Keeping threatening thoughts out of consciousness, e.g. not remembering a potentially painful dental appointment.

KEY TERMS

Id: in Freudian theory, that part of the mind motivated by the pleasure principle and sexual instincts.

Libido: sexual desire; a major motivational force located within the id.

Ego: the conscious, rational part of the mind, which is guided by the reality principle.

Reality principle: the drive on the part of the ego to accommodate to the demands of the environment.

Superego: in Freud's theory, the part of the mind that embodies one's conscience. It is formed through identification with the same-sex parent.

Repression: a main ego defence mechanism suggested by Freud, where anxiety-causing memories are kept out of conscious memory to protect the individual. This is a type of motivated forgetting, and the repressed memories can sometimes be recalled during psychoanalysis.

Defence mechanisms

Another example of a defence mechanism is reaction formation, e.g. in an adult who has developed a fear of close, intimate relationships due to a disappointment or hurt experienced during childhood. As a consequence, when this adult meets someone to whom they feel a strong attraction, they may subconsciously experience the opposite emotion of dislike, or even hatred.

KEY TERMS

Displacement: one of the defence mechanisms identified by Freud in which impulses are unconsciously moved away from a very threatening object towards a non-threatening one.

Projection: attributing one's undesirable characteristics to others, as a means of coping with emotionally threatening information and protecting the ego.

Denial: failure to accept consciously threatening thoughts and events.

Intellectualisation: excessive thinking about emotionally threatening events in order to minimise their emotional impact.

Oedipus complex: Freud's explanation of how a boy resolves his love for his mother and feelings of rivalry towards his father by identifying with his father.

Fixation: in Freudian terms, spending a long time at a given stage of development because of over- or under-gratification.

Regression: in Freudian terms, returning to an earlier stage of development as a means of coping with anxiety.

2. **Displacement**. Unconsciously moving impulses away from a threatening object and towards a less threatening object, e.g. someone who has been made angry by their teacher may shout at their brother.
3. **Projection**. An individual may attribute their undesirable characteristics to others, e.g. someone who is unfriendly may accuse other people of being unfriendly.
4. **Denial**. Refusing to accept the existence or reality of a threatening event, e.g. patients suffering from life-threatening diseases often deny their lives are affected.
5. **Intellectualisation**. Thinking about threatening events in ways that remove the emotion from them (e.g. responding to a car ferry disaster by thinking about ways of improving ferry design).

Psychosexual development

One of Freud's key assumptions was that adult personality depends very much on childhood experiences. In his theory of psychosexual development, Freud assumed all children go through *five* stages:

1. *Oral stage* (occurs during the first 18 months of life). During this stage, the infant obtains satisfaction from eating, sucking, and other activities using the mouth.
2. *Anal stage* (between about 18 and 36 months of age). Toilet training takes place during this stage, which helps to explain why the anal region becomes so important.
3. *Phallic stage* (between 3 and 6 years of age). The genitals become a key source of satisfaction during this stage. At about the age of 5, boys acquire the **Oedipus complex**, in which they have sexual desires for their mother and therefore want to get rid of their father, who is a rival. They then also fear their father, who might realise what they are thinking. This complex is resolved by identification with their father, involving adopting many of their father's attitudes and developing a superego.

   So far as girls are concerned, Freud argued that girls come to recognise they don't have a penis and blame their mother for this. The girl's father now becomes her love-object and she substitutes her "penis envy" with a wish to have a child. This leads to ultimate identification with her same-sex parent. If you think Freud's ideas of what goes on in the phallic stage are very fanciful (and also remarkably male-centred), you're absolutely right!
4. *Latency stage* (from 6 years of age until the onset of puberty). During this stage, boys and girls spend very little time together.
5. *Genital stage* (from the onset of puberty and throughout adult life). During this stage, the main source of sexual pleasure is in the genitals and experiencing such pleasure with a partner.

Development of adult personality and mental disorders

Freud coupled the theory of psychosexual development with a theory of personality. If a child experiences severe problems or excessive pleasure at any stage of development, this leads to **fixation**, in which basic energy or libido becomes attached to that stage for many years. Later in life, adults who experience very stressful conditions are likely to show **regression**, in which their behaviour becomes less mature, and more like that displayed during a psychosexual stage at which they fixated as children. According to Freud, these processes of fixation and regression play important roles in determining adult personality. Some personality types are shown in the figure opposite, along with descriptions and a link to the stage of psychosexual development at which fixation may have occurred.

How did Freud explain the development of mental disorders? As just discussed, adults who experience great difficulties show regression typically occurs back to a stage at which they had previously fixated. More serious mental disorders are associated with regression further back into childhood. Thus, for example, individuals suffering from schizophrenia (which involves a loss of contact with reality) regress to an earlier age of their lives than individuals suffering from neuroses or anxiety disorders.

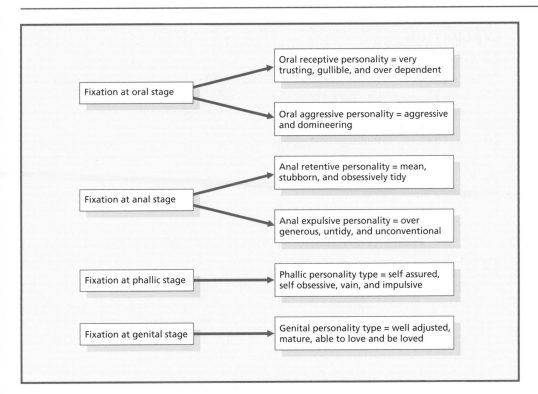

Freud suggested that adult personality types could be linked with fixations during each stage of development.

Positive aspects of the Freudian approach

Freud's work is often criticised, and it is true that it is difficult to verify the workings of the subconscious mind through scientific investigations. However, post-Freudian study of the importance of subjective feelings and experience has been a major undertaking in both psychology and other different fields such as creative writing, literary theory, and art history. Freud's ideas about the importance of the subconscious mind were one of the most profound influences on human thought of the 20th century, leading to in-depth questioning of human motives and intentions. It is hard for us to think about the world without employing Freudian concepts.

Findings

There has been much research on repression. The most relevant studies are those on clinical patients with recovered previously repressed memories of child abuse. Some of these recovered memories aren't genuine but rather were due to direct suggestions from the therapist. However, there is convincing evidence that many recovered memories are entirely genuine (Geraerts et al., 2007).

There has also been much research on displacement. Marcus-Newhall et al. (2000) carried out a meta-analysis of 82 studies concerned with displaced aggression (aggressive behaviour directed towards someone not responsible for making the individual angry). Displaced aggression was a moderately strong and replicable finding. The main limitation was that the time interval between the individual becoming angry and the opportunity to show displaced aggression was typically only a few minutes. Freud argued that displaced aggression can be found at much longer time intervals, but we don't have the necessary evidence for this.

As we have seen, Freud assumed most adult mental disorders have their roots in childhood experiences or personality development in childhood. The evidence is mixed, but there is some support. Kendler et al. (1996) considered the role of childhood experiences. They studied adult female twins who had experienced parental loss through separation in childhood. These twins showed an above-average tendency to suffer from depression and alcoholism in adult life.

Caspi et al. (1996) considered the role of childhood personality in subsequent problems. They studied 3-year-olds, and then carried out a follow-up 18 years later. Children with an introverted personality at the age of 3 tended to be depressed at the age of 21. Children under-controlled at the age of 3 were more likely to have developed anti-social personality disorder by the time they reached 21.

EXAM HINT

Exam questions will ask you, for example, to describe the psychodynamic approach to psychopathology. They will not ask you to describe the psychodynamic approach. This means you will receive few if any marks for simply describing Freud's personality theory. You must use this theory to explain why some people develop mental disorders.

The same advice applies to all the psychological explanations in this section—your answers must focus on psychopathology.

EVALUATION

⊕ Freud put forward the first systematic approach to abnormality focusing specifically on *psychological* factors as the cause of mental disorder and on psychological forms of treatment. Before Freud, nearly all explanations of mental illness were in terms of physical causes or ideas such as possession by evil spirits.

⊕ Freud and his psychodynamic theory have had an enormous impact on psychology. Indeed, he is the most influential psychologist of all time.

⊕ Psychoanalysis paved the way for later psychological approaches and forms of therapy. In essence, Freud focused very much on the individual and his/her personal conflicts dating back to childhood. In contrast, later psychodynamic therapists put more emphasis on the patient's current social and relationship problems.

⊕ The psychodynamic approach identified traumatic childhood experiences as a factor in the development of adult disorders. There is reasonable evidence for this (Comer, 2001), but Freud exaggerated the role played by such experiences. More generally, the notion that childhood experiences and childhood personality development play a role in adult mental disorder has received some support (Caspi et al., 1996; Kendler et al., 1996).

⊕ A strength of the psychodynamic approach concerns the notion of defence mechanisms. Some of the evidence is controversial, but there is clear support for defence mechanisms such as repression and displacement.

⊕ Freud was right to emphasise the importance of the unconscious mind. However, the unconscious mind is less complex than Freud assumed.

⊖ Freud was relatively uninterested in the *current* problems his clients were facing. Even if childhood experiences stored in the unconscious influence the development of mental disorders, that doesn't mean adult experiences can be ignored.

⊖ Freud focused too much on sexual factors as the cause of mental disorders. Freud over-emphasised sex because he developed his theory at a time of great sexual repression, which caused sex to be repressed in many minds (Banyard & Hayes, 1994). Most modern psychodynamic therapists believe sexual problems are a *result* of poor relationships with others rather than a direct cause of disorder (as assumed by Freud).

⊖ The psychodynamic approach isn't based on a solid foundation of scientific research. Freud's theoretical views emerged from his interactions with clients in the therapeutic situation. This provided a weak form of evidence because what Freud's patients said in therapy was often influenced by his biases and preconceptions. Freud's observations were largely based on a rather narrow sample of people: white, middle-class, Victorian Viennese women. That limits the extent to which we can generalise his ideas to other types of patient.

⊖ The psychodynamic approach is limited because it ignores genetic factors involved in the development of mental disorder.

⊖ The psychodynamic approach has a strong emphasis on neuroses (the anxiety disorders) and on depression. As a result, it has been applied mainly to clients suffering from anxiety disorders or depression rather than more severe disorders (e.g. schizophrenia).

- Many of Freud's key concepts (e.g. id, ego, superego, fixation) are imprecise, making it hard to assess their usefulness.

- Finding an association between having had a troubled childhood and adult mental disorder doesn't prove the troubled childhood helped to *cause* the adult mental disorder.

- Freud's stage-based theory suggests that personality development occurs in a neater and tidier way than is actually the case.

Ethical implications of the psychodynamic approach

One implication of the psychodynamic approach is that individuals aren't really responsible for their own mental disorders because those disorders depend on unconscious processes. However, the notion that adult mental disorders have their basis in childhood experiences suggests that parents or other caregivers are partly to blame. This can easily cause them distress if they believe they are responsible for their child's disorder.

Very serious issues are raised by numerous recent cases of **false memory syndrome**. In these cases, clients undergoing psychotherapy have made allegations about childhood physical or sexual abuse that have sometimes turned out to be untrue (e.g. Lief & Fetkewicz, 1995). Note, however, that many memories of abuse are genuine.

Freud argued that males and females have their own biologically determined sexual natures, and anxiety disorders or depression can develop when their natural sexual development is thwarted. This approach is dubious because it ignores the importance of cultural differences in sexual attitudes and behaviour. It is also very sexist in its emphasis on the notion that behavioural differences between men and women stem from biology rather than social and cultural factors.

> **Assumptions of the psychodynamic approach**
>
> - Much of our behaviour is driven by unconscious motives.
> - Childhood is a critical period in development.
> - Mental disorders arise from unresolved, unconscious conflicts originating in childhood.
> - Resolution occurs through accessing and coming to terms with repressed ideas and conflicts.

? Considering that Freud was working in a strict Victorian society, why was sexual behaviour so strongly emphasised in his theory of development?

The behavioural approach

The **behavioural approach to psychopathology** developed out of the behaviourist approach to psychology put forward mainly by John Watson and Fred Skinner. According to this approach, individuals with mental disorders possess maladaptive forms of behaviour, which they have learned. Most of this learning takes the form of classical conditioning or operant conditioning. Subsequent neo-behaviourists such as Bandura (1965) identified another basic form of learning known as observational learning. This occurs when an individual learns certain responses simply by observing someone else and then imitating their behaviour.

The behavioural approach is defined in part by what it doesn't emphasise as well as by what it does. The approach differs from most others in that there is very little consideration of the client's internal thoughts and feelings, and the underlying cause of the client's disorder isn't explored. Instead, the focus is mainly on the client's behavioural symptoms.

Classical conditioning

The origins of behaviourism lie in Ivan Pavlov's (1849–1936) work as a physiologist. He was conducting research into the digestive system and accidentally discovered a new form of learning by association. This is how it happened. When his experimental dogs were offered food, saliva production increased. But he also noticed something particularly interesting—salivation started to increase as soon as a researcher opened the door to bring them the food. The dogs had learned that "opening door" signalled "food coming soon". It was in their nature to salivate when they smelled food—a reflex response—but the dogs had now *learned* a link between "door" and their reflex response (salivation). What Pavlov had demonstrated is **classical conditioning**, which is learning by association.

KEY TERMS

False memory syndrome: a condition where an adult "recovers" apparently repressed memories. In fact the memories are for events that did not happen, thus "false memory".

Behavioural approach to psychopathology: an approach to abnormality which considers that individuals who suffer from mental disorders possess maladaptive forms of behaviour, which have been learned.

Classical conditioning: learning through association; a neutral stimulus becomes associated with a known stimulus–reflex response.

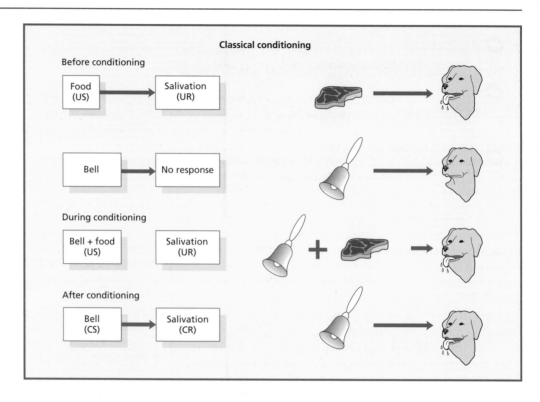

Just to make the basic idea clear, here is another example of classical conditioning. Imagine you go to the dentist. As you lie down on the reclining chair, you may feel frightened. *Why* are you frightened *before* the dentist has caused you any pain? The sights and sounds of the dentist's surgery lead you to expect or predict that you are shortly going to be in pain. Thus, you have formed an *association* between the neutral stimuli of the surgery and the painful stimuli involved in drilling.

Drilling is an unconditioned stimulus (US) and fear is an unconditioned response (UR). No learning is required for this stimulus–response (S–R) link, which is why both stimulus and response are described as "unconditioned". The sights and sounds of the dentist's surgery form a neutral stimulus (NS). There is no inborn reflex response to being in the surgery.

If an NS and a US occur together repeatedly they become associated, until eventually the NS also causes the UR. Now the NS is called a conditioned stimulus (CS) and the UR becomes a conditioned response (CR) to this—the CS will produce the CR. A new stimulus–response

CASE STUDY: John Watson

At the time the "Little Albert" study was conducted, Watson was a major figure in behaviourism and psychology. In 1913 he published a key paper arguing that psychology had to throw out introspection as a research method, and dismiss vague concepts such as "the mind" in order to become a respectable science. Psychologists, he suggested, should instead focus on observable, directly measurable behaviours. In short, he was largely responsible for founding the behaviourist movement, drawing on the ideas of Pavlov.

At the time, he was the Professor of Psychology at Johns Hopkins University, Baltimore, USA, where he conducted research into animal behaviour until 1918, when he turned his attention to conditioning infants. However in 1920 he was involved in a rather sensational divorce as a result of his affair with his research assistant Rosalie Rayner, whom he subsequently married. This led him to resign from his job and he went into the advertising business. He continued to have an interest in psychology, publishing a book on infant and child care, but for the most part devoted himself entirely to business where he applied the principles of behaviourism to the world of advertising. In fact he probably was the first applied psychologist and had an extremely successful second career.

KEY STUDY

Watson and Rayner (1920): Classical conditioning

John B. Watson and Rosalie Rayner (1920) showed in a classic study that emotions could be classically conditioned in the same way as any other response is conditioned. Their participant was an 11-month-old boy called "Little Albert", who was reared almost from birth in a hospital. At the start of the experiment, Watson and Rayner found out that items such as a white rat, a rabbit, and white cotton wool didn't trigger any fear response. In other words, they could all be regarded as neutral stimuli.

Watson and Rayner (1920) then induced a fear response (unconditioned response) by striking a steel bar with a hammer (unconditioned stimulus). This startled Albert and made him cry. After that, they gave him a white rat to play with. As he reached to touch it, they struck the bar to make him frightened. They repeated this three times, and did the same 1 week later. After that, when they showed the rat to Albert he began to cry, rolled over, and started to crawl away quickly. Classical conditioning had occurred, because the previously neutral or conditioned stimulus (i.e. the rat) produced a conditioned fear response.

Watson and Rayner found that now the sight of any object that was white and furry (e.g. a white fur coat; a Father Christmas beard) provoked a fear response. This is called **generalisation** — Albert had learned to generalise his fear of the white rat to other similar objects. They intended to "re-condition" Albert to eliminate these fearful reactions. However, he was taken away from the hospital before this could happen.

The research of Watson and Rayner (1920) is very relevant to the behavioural approach to abnormality. It showed how high levels of fear and anxiety could occur through a learning process.

Limitations

There are several limitations with this study. First, it was a case study based on only one participant. We don't know whether the findings that Watson and Rayner (1920) obtained with Little Albert would also have been obtained with other young children. Second, the researchers assessed Little Albert's fear responses in a limited way. For example, they didn't make any use of physiological measures. Third, there are obvious ethical issues about reducing a young child to tears and leaving him frightened of many innocuous objects. Fourth, it proved hard to repeat the findings on Little Albert when attempts were made to condition people to fear neutral stimuli by pairing them with unpleasant ones (Davison et al., 2004).

Watson and Rayner taught a boy ("Little Albert") to fear white fluffy objects by striking a metal bar (unconditioned stimulus) every time he touched the previously unfeared object (neutral stimulus). Thus, they demonstrated that fears could be learned through classical conditioning.

link has been learned, and you start to experience fear before the dentist has set to work on you.

It is possible that Little Albert developed a *phobia*, which is an extreme fear causing the individual concerned to avoid the feared stimulus. Mowrer (1947) developed a two-process theory to explain the origins of phobias. The first stage involves classical conditioning (e.g. linking the white rat and the loud noise). The second stage involves operant conditioning (discussed shortly). What happens here is that avoidance of the phobic stimulus reduces fear and this reduction in fear is reinforcing or rewarding.

Specific phobia, in which there is an extreme fear reaction to a specific type of stimulus (e.g. snakes; spiders), is recognised as a mental disorder even though it is nothing like as serious as most other mental disorders. The evidence provides only modest support for the notion that specific phobias develop as a result of conditioning experiences with the phobic stimulus. Many phobic individuals have not had prior traumatic experiences with the objects (e.g. snakes) of which they are frightened. DiNardo et al. (1988) found about 50% of dog-phobic individuals had become very anxious during an encounter with a dog, which seems to support conditioning theory. However, about 50% of healthy controls without dog phobia had also had an anxious encounter with a dog!

? Try to use classical conditioning to explain an abnormal behaviour.

KEY TERMS

Generalisation: in classical conditioning, the tendency to transfer a response from one stimulus to another that is quite similar.

Specific phobia: extreme fear and avoidance of specific kinds of stimuli (e.g. snakes, spiders).

Reinforcement increases the likelihood that the behaviour will be repeated...

Operant conditioning

Classical conditioning is important but it doesn't explain *all* learning. B. F. Skinner (1904–1990) developed **operant conditioning**, a form of learning that is controlled by its consequences. More specifically, responses followed by reward (known technically as **positive reinforcement**) are produced more and more often whereas those followed by punishment are produced less and less.

The essence of operant conditioning can be seen in Skinner's (1938) experiments with rats. A rat was placed in a cage with a lever sticking out on one side. When the lever was pressed, a pellet of food was delivered. At first, the rat accidentally pressed the lever but soon learned that there was a link between lever pressing and food appearing. Skinner argued that the rat *operated* on the environment. When there was a reward or reinforcement (food), this increased the chances of the response occurring again.

The simplest procedure is continuous reinforcement, in which each response is followed by reward. However, that is rare in everyday life. That led Skinner to study the effects of other schedules of reinforcement. One of the main schedules is variable ratio reinforcement in which every nth response on average is rewarded but the actual gap between two rewarded responses may be very small or fairly large. The variable ratio schedule led to the fastest rate of responding because it creates high levels of motivation. This schedule applies to gambling, which helps to explain why gamblers find it so hard to stop their addiction.

What is the relevance of operant conditioning to mental disorder? We will briefly consider two examples. First, individuals suffering from addictions obtain much positive reinforcement from their addiction, and this prevents them from stopping it. Second, one of the problems that individuals with depression have is that they find most pleasurable activities less rewarding or reinforcing than do non-depressed individuals. This helps to create the apathy characteristic of depression.

KEY TERMS

Operant conditioning: learning through reinforcement; a behaviour becomes more likely because the outcome is reinforced. It involves learning contingent on the response.

Positive reinforcement: a reward (e.g. food; money) that serves to increase the probability of any response produced shortly before it is presented.

Observational learning: learning through imitating or copying the behaviour of others (especially when that behaviour is rewarded or reinforced).

Vicarious learning: learning and imitating certain patterns of behaviour by observing someone else (especially when their behaviour is rewarded).

Classical conditioning

- Unconditioned stimulus (US) e.g. food → causes → reflex response e.g. salivation.
- Neutral stimulus (NS) e.g. bell → causes → no response.
- NS and US are paired in time (they occur at the same time).
- NS (e.g. bell) is now a conditioned stimulus (CS) → which produces → a conditioned response (CR) (a new stimulus–response link is learned, the bell causes salivation).

Operant conditioning

- A behaviour that has a positive effect is more likely to be repeated.
- Positive and negative reinforcement (escape from aversive stimulus) are agreeable.
- Punishment is disagreeable.

Social learning theory

Operant conditioning involves learning a new response because that response has previously resulted in a reward or reinforcement. Bandura (1986) further developed conditioning theory. He argued that **observational learning** or **vicarious learning** is important—learning by imitating someone else's behaviour. Observational learning is especially likely to influence behaviour when the other person's behaviour is rewarded or reinforced (vicarious reinforcement).

One of Bandura's key insights was that the early behaviourists (e.g. Skinner, 1938) were wrong to attach so much importance to the need to produce *responses* that are then rewarded if learning is to occur. In our everyday lives we learn much by watching and observing others rather than responding.

Observational learning may be relevant to several mental disorders. For example, Mineka et al. (1984) found monkeys developed snake phobia simply by watching another monkey experience fear in the presence of a snake. The same principle applies to humans. In a study by Bandura and Rosenthal (1966), participants observed someone responding to a buzzer by pretending to be in pain (e.g. twitching; shouting). After the participants had observed this reaction several times, they experienced fear whenever they heard the buzzer. Askew and Field (2008) reviewed research in this area, and concluded there is considerable evidence that clinical fears in humans can be acquired through vicarious learning.

EVALUATION OF THE BEHAVIOURAL APPROACH

➕ The basic concepts in the behavioural approach (stimulus; response; reinforcement; modelling) are easier to observe and to measure than those emphasised in other models.

➕ Conditioning experiences play a role in the development of some mental disorders (e.g. phobias).

➕ There is compelling evidence that much human learning is based on operant conditioning and observational learning, and this probably accounts for some of the maladaptive learning shown by individuals with mental disorders.

➕ The experiences people have in life (including the forms of conditioning to which they have been exposed) do play a part in the development of mental disorders. The behavioural approach has the advantage over the psychodynamic approach in that it focuses on the symptoms that concern the client (i.e. maladaptive patterns of behaviour) rather than what happened to the client many years earlier.

➖ It is hard to apply the findings of laboratory studies to explain the origins of mental disorders. As Comer (2001, p. 63) pointed out, "There is still no indisputable evidence that most people with psychological disorders are victims of improper conditioning." We rarely know for sure the details of the learning experiences of anyone suffering from a mental disorder, which makes it hard to test the behavioural model thoroughly. To show that a patient's reinforcement history was responsible for his or her disorder, we would need to have detailed information about rewards or reinforcements received over many years.

➖ The behavioural approach *exaggerates* the importance of environmental factors in causing disorders and *minimises* the role of genetic factors. As a result, it is of little value in explaining disorders such as schizophrenia in which genetic factors are important.

➖ The behavioural approach minimises the role played by internal processes (e.g. thinking, feeling). This makes it more relevant to disorders with observable behavioural symptoms (e.g. specific phobia involving avoidance of certain stimuli) rather than to disorders with few clear behavioural symptoms (e.g. generalised anxiety disorder in which the central symptom is excessive worrying).

➖ Most conditioning research has involved non-human species. The findings obtained can be misleading, because conditioning is less important in humans than other

Behavioural approaches to the treatment of mental disorders have been successful but they assume that the patient and therapist share the same goals for behaviour. In what way might such treatments be seen as "social manipulation"?

species. This is because language and complex cognitive processes (e.g. problem solving; decision making) are much more important in humans than in any other species.

⊖ The behavioural approach is oversimplified and rather narrow in scope. It is likely that only a few mental disorders depend to any great extent on the individual's conditioning history.

⊖ There are ethical problems with some of the forms of treatment based on the behavioural model. Aversion therapy involves giving very unpleasant stimuli (e.g. electric shocks or nausea-inducing drugs) to clients in order to stop some undesirable form of behaviour, such as drinking in alcoholics. There has been much controversy about the morality of causing high levels of pain and discomfort.

Assumptions of the behavioural approach

• All behaviour is learned, and maladaptive behaviour is no different.
• This learning can be understood in terms of the principles of conditioning and modelling.
• What was learned can be unlearned, using the same principles.
• The same laws apply to human and non-human animal behaviour.

The cognitive approach

The **cognitive approach to psychopathology** grew out of dissatisfaction with the behavioural approach's focus on *external* factors (stimuli and responses). According to the cognitive approach, we need to consider *internal*, mental influences, and the power of the individual to shape his or her own thinking.

The central notion in the cognitive approach is that individuals suffering from mental disorders have distorted and irrational thinking—they suffer from maladaptive thinking rather than maladaptive behaviour as in the behavioural model. Many of these thoughts have a "must" quality about them (Warren & Zgourides, 1991). For example, "I *must* perform well and/or win the approval of others, or else it's awful", "You *must* treat me fairly and considerately and not unduly frustrate me, or it's awful", "My life conditions *must* give me the things I want easily and with little frustration ... or else life is unbearable." These distorted thoughts can play an important role in the development of mental disorders.

The cognitive approach has been applied most often to individuals suffering from anxiety and depression. Such individuals do have irrational thoughts. For example, Newmark et al. (1973) found that 65% of anxious clients (but only 2% of healthy individuals) agreed with the statement, "It is essential that one be loved or approved by virtually everyone in his [sic!] community." The statement, "One must be perfectly competent, adequate, and achieving to consider oneself worthwhile", was agreed to by 80% of anxious patients compared with 25% of healthy individuals.

Anxious and depressed patients have distorted views and attitudes about themselves and the world around them. For example, those with panic disorder often have catastrophic beliefs (e.g. that when they perceive their heart racing, this indicates they are about to have a heart attack) (Clark, 1986). Those with social phobia (involving excessive fear about social situations) often believe that they are in imminent danger of social disgrace and humiliation.

Albert Ellis: Rational-emotive therapy

Albert Ellis (1962) was one of the first therapists to adopt the cognitive approach with his rational-emotive therapy. He argued that anxiety and depression occur as the final stage in a three-point sequence (see the figure opposite). According to his A-B-C model, anxiety and depression do *not* occur as a direct result of unpleasant events but rather are produced by the irrational thoughts triggered by unpleasant events.

More specifically, an unpleasant event occurs at point A (adversity). At point B (beliefs), the individual puts his or her own interpretation on this unpleasant event. If the interpretation is negative or self-defeating, the individual experiences anxiety and/or depression at point C (consequences). However, if the individual interprets the unpleasant event in a positive or realistic way, this greatly reduces the amount of anxiety or depression experienced. Ellis (1962) argued that individuals who are anxious or depressed should create a point D. This is a dispute belief system allowing them to interpret life's events in ways avoiding emotional distress.

Critics of rational-emotive therapy argue that Ellis attached too much importance to cognitive factors such as beliefs and not enough to emotional ones. A more telling criticism is that people often find it very difficult to act on their beliefs. Someone may firmly believe that cigarette smoking or overeating is damaging their health but may still find it hard to stop smoking or to go on a diet.

Beck's approach

Beck (1976) used the term **cognitive triad** to refer to the unrealistic negative thoughts of depressed patients in the three areas of themselves, the world, and the future. Depressed individuals regard themselves as helpless, worthless, and inadequate. They interpret events in the world in an unrealistically negative and defeatist way, and they see the world as posing obstacles that can't be handled. Finally, they see the future as totally hopeless because their worthlessness will prevent their situation improving.

These negative thoughts depend on cognitive schemas. A **cognitive schema** is "a well-organised cognitive structure of stored information and memories that forms the basis of core beliefs about self and others" (Beck & Dozois, 2011).

Two maladaptive forms of thinking in depressed patients are negative automatic thoughts and over-generalisation. Negative automatic thoughts (e.g. "I always make a mess of things") are triggered effortlessly when depressed individuals experience failure. Over-generalisation involves drawing very general negative conclusions from specific evidence (e.g. failing to obtain one job is taken to mean the depressed person will never find a job again).

Causality

The crucial issue is whether the distorted and unrealistic thoughts of clients with various mental disorders actually played a part in the development of the mental disorder. Perhaps clients only

> **?** Think of an occasion when you felt helpless or worthless. Could you try to re-interpret the occasion in a more positive way?

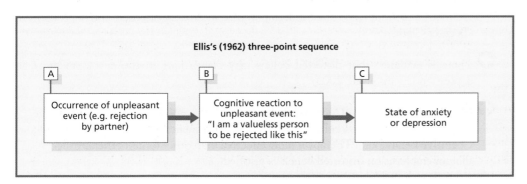

Ellis's (1962) three-point sequence

A	B	C
Occurrence of unpleasant event (e.g. rejection by partner)	Cognitive reaction to unpleasant event: "I am a valueless person to be rejected like this"	State of anxiety or depression

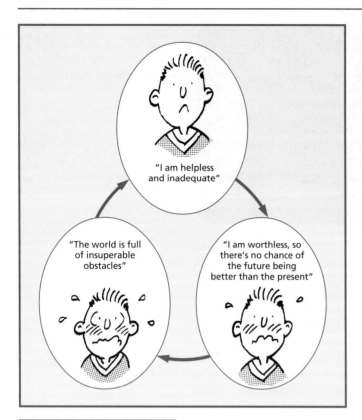

"I am helpless and inadequate"

"The world is full of insuperable obstacles"

"I am worthless, so there's no chance of the future being better than the present"

Assumptions of the cognitive approach

- Maladaptive behaviour is caused by faulty and irrational cognitions.
- It is the way you think about a problem, rather than the problem itself, that causes mental disorder.
- Individuals can overcome mental disorders by learning to use more appropriate cognitions.
- Aim to be positive and rational.

KEY TERM

Safety-seeking behaviours: actions taken by individuals with anxiety disorders to reduce their anxiety level and prevent feared consequences.

start having these unrealistic thoughts *after* having developed an anxiety disorder or depression. If so, this is a real problem—it would mean distorted thoughts have nothing to do with causing mental disorders!

Evidence that unrealistic thoughts may occur *before* a disorder develops and may play a part in its occurrence was reported by Evans et al. (2005), who assessed negative or dysfunctional self-beliefs in women in the 18th week of pregnancy. Women with the highest scores for negative self-beliefs were 60% more likely to become depressed subsequently than those with the lowest scores. Negative self-beliefs predicted the onset of depression 3 years later, which is strong evidence that negative or dysfunctional beliefs can play a role in causing depression.

What maintains irrational thoughts?

A key question raised by the cognitive approach is the following: *Why* do individuals with anxiety disorders or depression maintain distorted and irrational thoughts and beliefs year after year in the face of contrary evidence from the world around them?

I will answer the above question with respect to social phobia and panic disorder. Social-phobics fear they will experience catastrophe (e.g. public humiliation) in social situations even though they haven't actually experienced any such catastrophes. According to Clark and Wells (1995), they do so because they use **safety-seeking behaviours** designed to reduce the anxiety experienced in social situations. These safety-seeking behaviours include avoiding eye contact, talking very little, and avoiding talking about themselves. People with social phobia mistakenly believe these safety-seeking behaviours are all that stands between them and social catastrophe. In fact, these safety-seeking behaviours prevent them from discovering that their extreme social fears are irrational.

Patients with panic disorder have catastrophic cognitions about fainting, having a heart attack, or being paralysed with fear. According to such patients, these catastrophes haven't happened because they use safety-seeking behaviours such as holding on to people, distracting themselves, or trying to exercise during a panic attack (Salkovskis et al., 1996).

EVALUATION OF THE COGNITIVE APPROACH

➕ The cognitive approach to psychopathology has become very influential in recent years; this is reflected in the increase in cognitive therapy and Cognitive Behavioural Therapy (discussed later).

➕ Distorted and irrational beliefs are very common among patients with mental disorders, and seem to be of central importance in anxiety disorders and depression (Beck & Clark, 1988).

➕ There is evidence that distorted beliefs may play a part in the development of depression (Evans et al., 2005).

➕ Of major importance in Cognitive Behavioural Therapy is the attempt to eliminate the biased and distorted beliefs of individuals with mental disorders. The fact that Cognitive Behavioural Therapy is more effective than other forms of therapy suggests that an emphasis on distorted beliefs is justified.

We know that individuals suffering from anxiety or depression have numerous distorted beliefs. However, we need more research to determine whether distorted beliefs help to cause the disorder (as predicted by the cognitive approach) or whether they are merely a *consequence* of having a mental disorder.

Related to the above point, the cognitive approach isn't very explanatory. As Davison and Neale (1996, p. 46) pointed out, "That a depressed person has a negative schema [organised knowledge] tells us that the person thinks gloomy thoughts. But everyone knows that such a pattern of thinking is actually part of the diagnosis of depression."

Little attention is paid to the role of social and interpersonal factors or of individuals' life experiences in producing mental disorders.

The cognitive approach is limited in that genetic factors are ignored. Indeed, all the factors emphasised within the biological model approach are ignored.

The cognitive approach has mainly been applied to anxiety and depression. Its potential relevance to disorders having an important biological basis (e.g. schizophrenia) is limited.

HOW SCIENCE WORKS: Defining and explaining psychological abnormality

The various approaches' explanations of psychological abnormality really are different. You can demonstrate this by producing a set of four posters, one for each approach (biological; psychodynamic; behavioural; cognitive). Each one should identify the key assumptions of the approach, the actual explanation the approach offers, and a summary of the main strengths and limitations of that explanation. Make your posters as lively as possible. Finally you could use your analysis of the models, i.e. your posters, to evaluate the different models' explanations of abnormality. The posters will be useful revision tools too!

Section Summary

Deviation from social norms

- This is one way of defining abnormality. Social groups have norms of what is considered to be socially acceptable behaviour. Deviation from them is abnormal and undesirable.
- This approach has been criticised as follows:
  - Deviation from social norms depends on subjective moral standards and can be influenced by political considerations.
  - The same behaviour may deviate from the social norms of some cultures but not others.
  - Eccentrics deviate from social norms but are typically happy and well-adjusted.
  - The definition ignores the role of social context. In some cases (e.g. Nazi Germany) it may be desirable to be socially deviant.
  - This approach focuses too much on people's behaviour and not enough on their internal states.

Failure to function adequately

- This approach suggests that abnormality can be defined in terms of an inability to function adequately in day-to-day life and social interactions.

- An absence of distress and the ability to function are standards of normal behaviour.
- This approach has the benefit of taking the individual's experience into account. However, it has been criticised as follows:
  - How do we determine whether a person is functioning adequately?
  - Not all those with mental disorders are aware of their own distress or dysfunction.
  - The definition raises concerns about cultural bias and subjectivity as judgements by others on their behalf may be biased.
  - Rosenhan and Seligman have extended the "failure to function" model to cover seven features associated with abnormality, but these also rely on making subjective judgements.
  - Inadequate functioning may reflect the situational context rather than mental disorder.
  - Some individuals (e.g. Harold Shipman; psychopaths) may appear to function adequately in spite of being abnormal in important ways.

Deviation from ideal mental health

- Another approach suggests abnormality can be defined in terms of deviation from ideal mental health.
- Humanistic psychologists consider the factors that may be important for normal development such as unconditional positive regard. They also see self-actualisation as an ultimate goal.
- This approach has been criticised as follows:
  - It is based on abstract and culturally relative ideals (e.g. personal growth) not shared by collectivistic societies. There are cultural variations in how to identify psychological health.
  - There have been changes in what is regarded as ideal mental health throughout history.
  - Unlike physical health, it is difficult to measure psychological health.
  - Nearly everyone's mental health deviates from the ideal, but we can't identify the point at which this is indicative of abnormality.

Limitations with all these approaches

- Cultural relativism is a problem in all three of the approaches described. The definitions inevitably refer to some subjective, culturally determined set of values.
- However, there are also cultural universals—behaviours such as anti-social behaviour or chronic depression are universally viewed as abnormal and undesirable.
- The resolution may lie in using a combined approach that focuses on which features are more likely to be associated with abnormality.

Approaches to psychopathology

- There are five major approaches to psychopathology, each of which provides explanations for the treatment of mental disorders. They are:
  - Biological (medical) approach
  - Psychodynamic approach
  - Behavioural approach
  - Cognitive, and now cognitive behavioural, approach
  - Diathesis–stress approach
- These approaches are not mutually exclusive, and all have contributed to our understanding of the causes of mental disorders.

Biological approach to abnormality

- This approach suggests the causes of mental disorders resemble those of physical illness.
- Clusters of symptoms can be identified and a diagnosis made, followed by suitable treatment.

- There is some evidence that the following may account for mental disorders:
  - genetics
  - biochemistry
  - neuroanatomy
  - infections
- While this approach has received some scientific support and has contributed to treatments, it has been criticised in that:
  - It focuses on symptoms rather than the person's thoughts and feelings.
  - It is less appropriate for disorders with psychological symptoms such as the anxiety disorders.
  - There is some debate as to whether mental disorders are basically similar to physical illnesses.
  - The treatments based on the medical approach (e.g. drugs, ECT, psychosurgery) may have unpleasant side effects and their effectiveness has been challenged.

Psychodynamic approach to psychopathology

- This approach suggests the causes of mental disorders arise from unresolved unconscious conflicts and traumas of early childhood and in problems with personality development.
- According to Freud, defence mechanisms (e.g. repression) reduce the anxiety caused by unresolved conflicts but do not resolve an individual's problems.
- There are five stages of personality development, and mental disorders involve the individual regressing to an earlier stage of development.
- Although this approach has offered insights into anxiety disorders and has changed the perception of mental illness, it has been criticised in that:
  - It is hard to disprove and thus is rather unscientific.
  - It focuses too much on sexual problems rather than interpersonal and social issues.
  - Insufficient attention is paid to the role of genetic factors in the development of mental disorders.
  - It raises ethical concerns about the problems of false memory syndrome, sexism, and parental blame.

Behavioural approach

- This approach suggests that mental disorders are caused by learning maladaptive behaviour via conditioning or observational learning.
- This approach offers people with mental disorders hope, in that it implies that their behaviour can be changed—anything that is learned can be unlearned using the same techniques.
- The approach is most suited to explaining and treating those disorders in which the emphasis is on external behaviour (e.g. phobias).
- Ethically, there are advantages such as the lack of blame attached to a person with a mental disorder. However, the approach has been criticised in that:
  - It is somewhat oversimplified and ignores individual differences.
  - It is based on animal research.
  - It de-emphasises the importance of cognitive processes (e.g. thoughts and beliefs).
  - Its emphasis on changing behaviour means it is less suitable for treating mental disorders lacking clear behavioural symptoms.
  - The treatments developed from this approach can be painful and manipulative (e.g. aversion therapy).

Cognitive approach

- This approach suggests mental disorders stem from distorted and irrational beliefs, and there is no doubt that patients with anxiety disorders and depression have distorted beliefs.

- According to Ellis's ABC model, an unpleasant event occurring at point A (adversity) can lead the individual to interpret the event in a threatening way at point B (beliefs). This causes anxiety and/or depression at point C (consequences), which can be combated by using the dispute belief system (point D).
- The distorted beliefs of those with mental disorders are maintained in part because safety-seeking behaviours prevent patients from discovering what is really happening.
- This approach has been criticised in that:
  - It is generally not clear whether the distorted thinking is an effect of the disorder or the cause.
  - Another issue is that the cognitive approach has been applied mainly to anxiety and depression, and its relevance to other mental disorders is largely unknown.
  - It de-emphasises the role of social factors and life experiences in causing mental disorders.
  - It implies that individuals are somehow to blame for their problems.
- Over the past 30 years or so, a cognitive behavioural approach has been suggested that combines the cognitive and behavioural approaches.

The diathesis–stress approach
- This model is a multi-dimensional approach.
- It suggests individuals may have a genetic vulnerability (diathesis) that can be triggered by environmental factors (stress).

SECTION 15
TREATING ABNORMALITY

Individuals with mental disorders exhibit a wide range of symptoms. There may be problems associated with thinking (e.g. the distorted beliefs of anxious and depressed individuals), with behaviour (e.g. the avoidance behaviour of the phobic person), or with physiological and bodily processes (e.g. the highly activated physiological system of someone with post-traumatic stress disorder). Note, however, that thinking, behaviour, and physiological processes are all highly *interdependent*.

Therapeutic approaches to mental disorder could focus on producing changes in thinking, in behaviour, or in physiological functioning. At the risk of over-simplification, this is precisely what has happened. The psychodynamic approach is designed to change thinking, and the same is true of cognitive therapy. Behaviour therapy, as its name implies, emphasises the importance of changing behaviour. Cognitive Behavioural Therapy, which represents a combination of cognitive and behaviour therapy, aims to change clients' thinking *and* their behaviour. Biological therapies (e.g. drug therapy; electroconvulsive therapy) focus on physiological and biochemical changes.

When considering various forms of therapy, we must avoid the treatment aetiology fallacy (MacLeod, 1998). This is the mistaken notion that the success of a given form of treatment reveals the cause of the disorder. For example, aspirin is an effective cure for headache. However, that doesn't mean that a lack of aspirin causes headaches!

Biological Therapies

Biological therapies are forms of treatment involving manipulations of the body. Biological therapies mostly involve the administration of drugs and they are associated with the biological approach. According to the biological approach, mental disorders develop because of abnormalities in bodily functioning (especially within the brain), and drugs can reduce or eliminate those abnormalities.

KEY TERM

Biological therapies: forms of treatment that involve manipulations of the body, e.g. drugs or ECT.

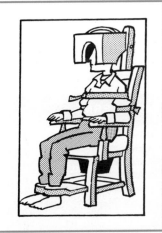

KEY TERM

Placebo effect: positive responses to a drug or form of therapy based on the patient's beliefs that the drug or therapy will be effective, rather than on the actual make-up of the drug or therapy.

Apart from drug therapy, two other main forms of biologically based therapy are electroconvulsive therapy (ECT) and psychosurgery. I will discuss drug therapy and ECT in detail shortly, but will first briefly refer to psychosurgery. Psychosurgery involves carrying out brain surgery to treat mental disorders. Pioneering work was carried out by Antonio Egas Moniz. He carried out prefrontal lobotomies, in which fibres running from the frontal lobes to other parts of the brain were cut.

Early somatic therapy

There have been many bizarre treatments for mental illness over the course of history, from blood-letting and purging (use of laxatives), to ice baths. In 1810, Dr Benjamin Rush invented the restraining chair. Herman and Green (1991) quote his description of its effectiveness:

> *I have contrived a chair and introduced it to our Hospital to assist in curing madness. It binds and confines every part of the body. By keeping the trunk erect, it lessens the impetus of blood toward the brain … It acts as a sedative to the tongue and temper as well as to the blood vessels.*

Rush coined the word *Tranquiliser* as a name for his apparatus and patients were confined in it for up to 24 hours at a time. No one today would be surprised that this would subdue anyone, regardless of their mental state.

In the film *One Flew Over the Cuckoo's Nest*, a lobotomy operation ends Randle Patrick McMurphy's rebellion against the hospital authorities. Moniz claimed such operations made schizophrenic and other patients less violent and agitated. However, lobotomies have very serious side effects, including apathy, diminished intellectual powers, and even coma and death. In addition, psychosurgery poses immense ethical issues. As a result, lobotomies stopped being performed many years ago in most countries.

Drug therapy

How can we show a given drug is effective in treating a particular disorder? It might seem as if all we need to do is to assign patients to two groups, one receiving the drug and the other receiving nothing. In fact, that is *not* an adequate approach because of the placebo effect. The **placebo effect** occurs when patients given an inactive substance or placebo (e.g. a salt tablet) show reduced symptoms. In other words, if you *think* something is going to make you better, it may do so simply through "the power of the mind".

In the film One Flew Over the Cuckoo's Nest, Jack Nicholson played Randle Patrick McMurphy, who inspired and awakened his fellow patients, while falling out with the authorities. Eventually, the character is lobotomised, and becomes calmer and easier to handle, but loses all his intellectual spark and energy.

? Why do you think that many people won't take drugs for mental problems?

The ideal is a double-blind study in which neither the patient nor the therapist knows whether the patient is receiving an active drug or a placebo. In such a study, the expectations of the patient and therapist can't influence the outcome. In what follows, we will consider drug therapy for depression, anxiety, and schizophrenia in turn.

Depression

There are two main forms of depression. First, there is **major depressive disorder**, characterised by sadness, depressed mood, tiredness, and loss of interest in various activities. Second, there is **bipolar disorder,** a mood disorder characterised by depressive and manic (elated) episodes. Bipolar disorder is the more serious condition and is harder to treat.

Individuals with major depressive disorder often have low levels of the neurotransmitters serotonin and noradrenaline. Accordingly, drugs are designed to rectify these low levels. The most common ones are the serotonin re-uptake inhibitors (SSRIs) (e.g. Prozac). SSRIs prevent the re-uptake of serotonin by the presynaptic neuron, so allowing it to have an enhanced effect on the postsynaptic neuron. As a result, such drugs increase serotonin activity without influencing other neurotransmitters such as noradrenaline.

DeRubeis et al. (2005) compared drug therapy using one of the SSRIs against cognitive therapy in the treatment of patients with major depressive disorder. About 58% of the patients in each group showed much improvement due to treatment.

Hollon et al. (2005) studied relapse (recurrence of symptoms) of depressed patients successfully treated in the study by DeRubeis et al. (2005). Of those who had received drug therapy, 76% suffered a relapse. That was much higher than the relapse rate of 31% for patients who had received cognitive therapy.

Depressed patients taking SSRIs are less likely to suffer from dry mouth and constipation than those taking other drugs for depression, and overdosing is rare. However, SSRIs conflict with some other forms of medication and some side effects have been reported (e.g. nausea; insomnia).

Bipolar disorder

The most commonly used drug for bipolar disorder is lithium. Lithium has beneficial effects in 80% of patients. Geddes et al. (2004) carried out a meta-analysis of studies on lithium therapy for bipolar disorder. Lithium was effective in preventing relapses after most symptoms had been eliminated. However, its effectiveness was significantly greater in preventing relapses of manic than depressive symptoms. Another advantage of lithium is that it often improves patients' moods within 5–14 days.

There are some problems with the use of lithium. First, it produces various side effects (e.g. impaired coordination, tremors, and digestive problems). Second, Baldessarini et al. (1999) reported that bipolar patients who stopped taking lithium were 20 times more likely to commit suicide than those who continued to take it.

? It has sometimes been suggested that bipolar disorder is higher among very creative people, and that the manic phase of the disorder can particularly heighten creativity. How might this affect some sufferers' decisions about whether or not to take drug treatment such as lithium?

KEY TERMS

Major depressive disorder: a disorder characterised by symptoms such as sad depressed mood, tiredness, and loss of interest in various activities.

Bipolar disorder: a mood disorder in which there are depressive and manic (elated) episodes.

CASE STUDY: Virginia Woolf

The author Virginia Woolf, who committed suicide in 1941 at the age of 59, was plagued by an intermittent form of depression. This affliction appears to have been bipolar depression, but was accompanied by extreme physical symptoms and psychotic delusions. In her biography of Woolf, Hermione Lee (1997) unravels the series of treatments administered to Woolf between 1895, when she experienced her first breakdown, and the 1930s. Later, Woolf's husband Leonard made detailed notes on her breakdowns (Lee, 1997, pp. 78–179):

In the manic stage she was extremely excited; the mind raced; she talked volubly and, at the height of the attack, incoherently; she had delusions and heard voices ... During the depressive stage all her thoughts and emotions were the exact opposite ...

she was in the depths of melancholia and despair; she scarcely spoke; refused to eat; refused to believe that she was ill and insisted that her condition was due to her own guilt.

During the period from 1890 to 1930, Woolf consulted more than 12 different doctors, but the treatments barely altered during this time. They tended to consist of milk and meat diets to redress her weight loss; rest to alleviate her agitation; sleep and fresh air to help her regain her energy. Lithium had not yet been discovered as a treatment for manic depression. Instead, bromide, veronal, and chloral, most of which are sedatives, were prescribed. Lee points out that there is great uncertainty about the neuropsychiatric effects of some of these drugs, and Woolf's manic episodes may well have been the result of taking these chemicals.

Anxiety disorders

Patients with anxiety disorders (especially generalised anxiety disorder in which excessive worrying is the central symptom) are often given drugs. The most popular anti-anxiety drugs are the benzodiazepines (e.g. Librium and diazepam) (see Chapter 5). These drugs bind to receptor sites in the brain that generally receive the neurotransmitter GABA. The benzodiazepines increase the ability of GABA to bind to these sites, which enhances the ability of GABA to inhibit bodily arousal and anxiety.

The benzodiazepines are reasonably effective in the treatment of generalised anxiety disorder (Rickels et al., 2000), and have also been used to treat social phobia (a condition involving excessive anxiety about social events). Mitte (2005) found in a meta-analysis of 65 studies that drug therapies in the treatment of generalised anxiety disorder are mostly effective. Indeed, they are comparably effective to Cognitive Behavioural Therapy.

Liebowitz et al. (1999) studied patients who had been treated successfully by Cognitive Behavioural Therapy or drug therapy. There was a relapse in 33% of patients who had received drug therapy vs 0% for those who had received Cognitive Behavioural Therapy.

Benzodiazepines can produce several unwanted effects. First, anxious symptoms often return when patients stop taking the drugs. Second, there are various side effects (e.g. lack of coordination; poor concentration; memory loss; sedative effects). Third, Stewart (2005) found in a meta-analysis that long-term use of benzodiazepines was associated with various cognitive impairments. However, there was some improvement after the drugs were withdrawn. Fourth, there is the danger of drug escalation, with patients taking progressively larger doses of the drug to achieve the same effect. Fifth, there can be physical dependence, with patients finding it difficult to manage without drugs.

 In what instances might a GP feel justified in prescribing drugs such as diazepam or Librium? What other forms of treatment would benefit an anxious patient, together with or instead of drugs?

Disorder	Drug/group of drugs	How they work	Drawbacks
Depression (major)	SSRIs (e.g. Prozac)	Increase serotonin activity by preventing its re-uptake by the presynaptic neuron	Preoccupation with suicide and violence
Depression (bipolar)	Lithium	Anti-mania, but mechanism is imperfectly understood	Side effects on CNS, cardiovascular, and digestive systems. Overdose can be fatal
Anxiety disorders	Benzodiazepines (e.g. diazepam, Librium)	Have a sedative effect on the CNS	Drowsiness, lethargy, impairments of long-term memory. Withdrawal symptoms and possible addiction
Schizophrenia	Neuroleptic drugs (e.g. Thorazine, Prolixin, Haldol)	Reduce delusions, hallucinations	Little effect on lack of motivation and emotion, social withdrawal. Some patients report grogginess, sedation, difficulty concentrating, dry mouth, blurred vision
	Atypical anti-psychotic drugs (e.g. clozapine)	As neuroleptics, but with fewer side effects	Expensive. May produce fatal blood disease in 1–2% of patients

Schizophrenia

When discussing drug effects on **schizophrenia**, we must distinguish between the positive and negative symptoms of schizophrenia. The positive symptoms include the presence of delusions and hallucinations, whereas the negative symptoms include lack of motivation, lack of emotion, and social withdrawal. There are two main categories of drugs: (1) conventional or neuroleptic drugs; and (2) the newer atypical drugs.

KEY TERM

Schizophrenia: a very severe disorder characterised by hallucinations, delusions, lack of emotion, and very impaired social functioning.

CASE STUDY: Chemotherapy saves lives

Novelist blames depression in son's apparent overdose
Danielle Steel says he was manic-depressive

When Nicholas Traina was found dead of an apparent overdose during the weekend, his mother, novelist Danielle Steel, was heartbroken but not entirely surprised. Though her 19-year-old son had a history of drug use, the problem was much deeper: for his entire short life, Traina was tormented by mental illness. "The only time he messed around with drugs was when his medications failed him and he was desperate," Steel told *The Chronicle* in the first interview she has given since her son's death on Saturday. "This was not some wild kid, this was a very sick kid. The awful thing is I knew for years. He was manic-depressive, and wrestled with mental illness all his life. The biggest agony of my life is that for years, no one would listen to me that he was sick until we found a doctor in LA about 4 years ago who gave him amazing medication. He understood because he was manic-depressive, too."

(Adapted from an article in the *San Francisco Chronicle*, 17 September 1997.)

To Dad, girl was Satan and thought he was Messiah when he killed daughter, 6, court told

Paranoid schizophrenic Ron England believed he was the Messiah ridding the world of evil when he murdered his mother and 6-year-old daughter, a psychiatrist says.

Dr Ian Jacques told a coroner's inquest yesterday England still does not believe his daughter, Jenny, and her grandma, Marian Johnston, are dead.

Jacques said England—who'd sworn off medication treating his severe mental illness—was "almost functioning on auto-pilot and getting his instructions (to kill) from television." England called 911 on April 2, 1996, to report he'd killed his mother and daughter at their home in Bowmanville. Marian Johnston, 79, was found slumped on her bed in pyjamas, housecoat and black boots. The former public health nurse, who'd helped England win supervised custody of Jenny over her biological parents, had been stabbed 34 times. On the floor lay Jenny with a knife embedded in her heart. She'd been stabbed 89 times.

(Adapted from an article in the *Toronto Sun*.)

Neuroleptic drugs are conventional drugs often used in the treatment of schizophrenia. Common neuroleptic drugs include Thorazine, Prolixin, and Haldol. They block the activity of the neurotransmitter dopamine within 48 hours, and their effects on dopamine are believed to be important in therapy. The major neuroleptic drugs are more effective at reducing positive symptoms than negative ones.

Neuroleptic drugs produce side effects. Windgassen (1992) found that 50% of schizophrenic patients taking neuroleptics reported grogginess or sedation, 18% reported concentration problems, and 16% had blurred vision. Other side effects include muscle rigidity, tremors, and foot shuffling. More than 20% of patients who take neuroleptic drugs for over a year develop **tardive dyskinesia**. The symptoms include involuntary sucking and chewing, jerky movements of the limbs, and writhing movements of the mouth or face.

Schizophrenia is increasingly treated with atypical anti-psychotic drugs (e.g. Clozaril; Risperdal; Zyprexa). These drugs have fewer side effects than the neuroleptic drugs and benefit more patients (85% vs 65%, respectively: Awad & Voruganti, 1999). The atypical drugs are of much more use in helping schizophrenic patients suffering mainly from negative symptoms. Finally, many side effects of the conventional drugs (especially tardive dyskinesia) are absent with the atypical drugs.

The atypical drugs can produce serious side effects. Schizophrenic patients taking clozapine have a 1–2% risk of developing agranulocytosis. This involves a substantial reduction in white blood cells, and the condition can be life threatening.

KEY TERM

Tardive dyskinesia: some of the long-term effects of taking neuroleptic drugs, including involuntary sucking and chewing, jerky movements, and writhing movements of the mouth or face.

OVERALL EVALUATION

➕ Drug therapy often produces clear-cut beneficial effects when used to treat depression, anxiety, and schizophrenia.

➕ Drug therapy often works rapidly, which is of vital importance if, for example, a severely depressed individual is in danger of committing suicide. The fact that it works rapidly can provide patients with reassurance that their symptoms can be controlled.

? To what extent should practical concerns take precedence over ethical issues?

⊕ Drug therapy is as effective as cognitive behavioural therapy in the treatment of generalised anxiety disorder (Mitte, 2005) and major depressive disorder.

⊕ Drug therapy has shown progress in that newer drugs are generally more effective than previous ones. In the treatment of schizophrenia, for example, the atypical drugs are not only more effective than the neuroleptic drugs, but are also at least as effective as any other form of treatment. This is impressive given that schizophrenia is notoriously hard to treat.

⊖ Drug therapy for most mental disorders is palliative (it reduces the symptoms) but it isn't curative (it doesn't eliminate the underlying processes responsible for the disorder). For example, depressed patients are typically concerned about past losses and their personal relationships, but these are not the focus of therapy. This raises serious questions about the appropriateness of drug therapy given that patients want to be cured rather than having to take drugs over long periods of time.

⊖ Drug therapy ignores the factors that are of central importance in other forms of therapy: childhood experiences; biased interpretations of events; maladaptive behaviour; and so on.

⊖ Since it is only palliative, relapse is more common after drug therapy than after other types of therapy. This restricts its value as a form of therapy.

⊖ It is often difficult to know precisely *why* any given drug is effective in the treatment of a particular disorder because of our limited understanding of the underlying biochemical factors. This raises ethical issues about the desirability of giving patients drugs whose effects on the body are poorly understood.

⊖ Typically, about 30% of patients fail to respond to any given drug or show only very modest beneficial effects. However, patients who don't respond to one drug often respond to a different one.

⊖ There can be problems of drug dependence, with patients finding it very hard to cope without drugs.

⊖ The drop-out rate is often rather high when drug therapy is used.

⊖ Nearly all drugs have unwanted side effects. Some of these side effects (e.g. tardive dyskinesia; agranulocytosis) can be very serious and even life threatening.

Electroconvulsive therapy (ECT)

Electroconvulsive therapy (ECT) is used mainly in the treatment of major depressive disorder. What happens in ECT is that an electric current is passed through the head to produce a convulsion. In the past, ECT produced broken bones, patient terror, and memory loss. However, various changes in treatment have been introduced to reduce or eliminate these problems:

1. Strong muscle relaxants are given to patients to prevent or minimise convulsions.
2. The current is generally only passed through the non-dominant brain hemisphere rather than through both hemispheres. This reduces the danger of memory loss, but on average reduces treatment effectiveness.
3. Anaesthetics are used to put patients to sleep during ECT, minimising the chances of experiencing terror.

Many studies designed to assess the effectiveness of ECT have compared it against simulated ECT, in which patients are exposed to the equipment and believe falsely they have received

> **KEY TERM**
>
> **Electroconvulsive therapy (ECT):** a form of therapy used to treat depressed patients, in which brain seizures are created by passing an electric current through the head.

ECT. This is done to ensure that the beneficial effects of ECT are genuine and not simply a placebo effect—seeing the equipment and believing you are receiving shocks might be enough to reduce symptoms in the absence of any actual shocks.

ECT and psychosurgery

Some forms of treatment based on the biological model include fairly drastic methods such as electroconvulsive therapy (ECT) and brain surgery. However, ECT is not the barbaric treatment it once was. Patients are given sedatives before treatment and then brief shocks are applied to the non-dominant hemisphere of the brain. The treatment has been found to be successful for patients suffering from chronic depression, and long-term side effects are unusual (Stirling & Hellewell, 1999).

Brain surgery (psychosurgery) is used in extremely rare conditions where no other treatment seems appropriate. As mentioned earlier, the techniques involved were first pioneered by Antonio Egas Moniz (1937). These techniques were used on large numbers of patients, especially those who were prone to aggression and violence. When it was discovered that psychosurgery often caused very severe problems (e.g. loss of personality; coma), the number of operations dropped dramatically. In view of the dangers of Moniz's techniques, it is ironic that he was shot by one of the patients on whom he had operated!

Depression

When is ECT used rather than anti-depressant drugs to treat major depressive disorder? The great majority of patients are initially treated by anti-depressant drugs rather than ECT. However, some patients have poor tolerance of anti-depressant drugs or don't respond when given them, and such patients are sometimes given ECT. ECT is also often the treatment of choice in the case of patients with very severe depression when *rapid reduction* in symptoms is especially important. This can be essential in cases of severe depression in which suicide attempts are possible.

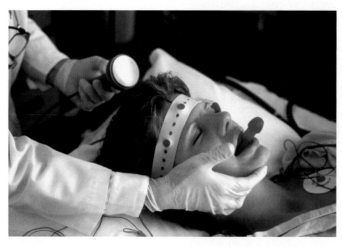

Electroconvulsive therapy has been found to be quite effective in cases of severe depression, though the reasons why it might be effective are uncertain.

How effective is ECT in the treatment of depression? The findings are encouraging. For example, Petrides et al. (2001) reported that between 65% and 85% of depressed patients had a favourable response to ECT. Pagnin et al. (2004) carried out a meta-analysis in which the effectiveness of ECT was compared against various types of anti-depressant drugs and simulated ECT. ECT was more effective in the treatment of depression than anti-depressant drugs or simulated ECT. Grunhaus et al. (2002) compared the effectiveness of ECT in patients with major depressive disorder and with bipolar disorder. They found that 57% of the patients responded positively to ECT and both groups of patients benefited equally.

What kinds of patients benefit most from ECT? This issue was addressed by de Vreede et al. (2005) in a study on patients with major depression. They identified four patient factors predicting good response to ECT: age above 65 years; the absence of a psychotic depression (involving more severe symptoms); the absence of a personality disorder; and responding well to anti-depressants.

Schizophrenia

ECT is also used in the treatment of schizophrenia, but much less frequently than for depression. Tharyan and Adams (2005) carried out a meta-analysis (combining many findings) on the effects of ECT in treating schizophrenia. It had beneficial short-term effects, but smaller than those obtained with drugs.

In a study by Chanpattana (2007), schizophrenics who had previously proved resistant to treatment received ECT on its own or in combination with neuroleptic drugs. ECT produced a marked reduction in positive symptoms (e.g. delusions; hallucinations; bizarre behaviour), especially when used in combination with drug therapy. ECT plus drug therapy also led to significant improvements in quality of life. However, ECT failed to reduce negative symptoms (e.g. absence of motivation and emotion; language deficits).

In sum, ECT can be useful when used in combination with drugs. This is especially the case when it is important to produce rapid reductions in symptoms. It is less clear that ECT produces long-term benefits to patients with schizophrenia.

Given that the full implications of ECT are poorly understood, do you think it is ever right to administer such treatments to vulnerable patients?

EVALUATION

⊕ ECT has proved moderately effective in the treatment of major depression.

⊕ ECT has proved of value in treating schizophrenia, especially when combined with drug therapy.

⊖ There is still no detailed understanding of precisely why ECT is effective. It has numerous effects on the brain, including affecting neurotransmission and probably producing structural changes in neuronal networks. However, it is hard to establish *which* effects are the important ones in reducing the symptoms of depression.

⊖ ECT is associated with various side effects including memory loss and other cognitive impairments, although most of these problems are short term rather than long term.

⊖ ECT is generally most effective at reducing symptoms when given to both hemispheres at a high dose. However, those are the conditions in which side effects are most common.

⊖ ECT is less effective in the treatment of depression among patients who are below 65 years of age, who respond poorly to anti-depressants, and who have a psychotic depression and a personality disorder (de Vreede et al., 2005).

⊖ While ECT has been shown to benefit people with schizophrenia in the short term, it is less clear that it conveys long-term benefits to them.

⊖ The use of ECT raises ethical issues because of its potential dangers. Most patients dislike receiving ECT, and some may be pressured into accepting this form of therapy.

⊖ The fact that we don't know precisely why ECT works makes it hard to improve its effectiveness. It also means that psychiatrists can't tell patients the precise risks involved.

Psychological Therapies

Psychological therapies involve the use of psychological techniques to produce beneficial changes in individuals suffering from mental disorders. There are many psychological therapies, but we will be focusing on only a few of the main ones. First, we consider psychoanalysis, which was developed by Sigmund Freud about 100 years ago. Psychoanalysis influenced the development of many other psychodynamic therapies subsequently. Second, we consider behaviour therapy, which was developed mainly in the United States and the United Kingdom in the middle of the 20th century. More specifically, we will discuss in detail one technique used in behaviour therapy—systematic de-sensitisation. Third, we consider Cognitive Behavioural Therapy. That form of therapy developed out of behaviour therapy, and started becoming influential from the 1970s onwards.

KEY TERM

Psychological therapies: forms of treatment that involve the use of various psychological techniques, e.g. psychoanalysis.

Psychoanalysis

Psychoanalysis was the first fully developed psychological therapy for the treatment of mental disorders. It was proposed by Sigmund Freud in the early years of the 20th century. Psychoanalysis has been used to treat individuals with many mental disorders. However, it is mostly used to treat those suffering from neuroses (the anxiety disorders) or from depression. In general terms, psychoanalysis has been very successful—the whole notion of "talking cures", which is very widely accepted nowadays, owes its origins to Freud.

Therapeutic method

Freud argued that the best way to cure neuroses was to allow the client to gain access to his or her repressed ideas and conflicts and to face up to whatever emerged from the unconscious. These repressed thoughts mostly refer to childhood and to the conflicts between the instinctive (e.g. sexual) motives of the child and the restraints imposed by his or her parents. These repressed thoughts represent "unfinished business" and it is crucial in psychoanalysis for patients to come to terms with the conflicts involved and to resolve them.

The client should focus on the feelings associated with the previously repressed ideas, and shouldn't simply regard them unemotionally. *Emotional involvement* is necessary for the client to appreciate the full significance of the events and ideas recovered from the unconscious and thus to gain insight. **Insight** "involves a conscious awareness of some of the wishes, defences, and compromises … that have interacted to produce emotional conflict or deficits in psychological development" (Kivlighan et al., 2000, p. 50).

How can we uncover repressed memories and permit the client to gain insight into the causes of his or her mental disorder? Freud used three main methods. The first method, and one

CASE STUDY: Anna O

Freud's theory was largely based on the observations he made during consultations with patients. He suggested that his work was similar to that of an archaeologist, who digs away layers of earth before uncovering what he or she was seeking. In a similar way, the psychiatrist seeks to dig down to the unconscious and discover the key to the individual's personality dynamic.

"Anna O. was a girl of twenty-one, of a high degree of intelligence. Her illness first appeared while she was caring for her father, whom she tenderly loved, during the severe illness which led to his death. The patient had a severe paralysis of both right extremities, disturbance of eye-movements, an intense nausea when she attempted to take nourishment, and at one time for several weeks a loss of the power to drink, in spite of tormenting thirst. She occasionally became confused or delirious and mumbled several words to herself. If these same words were later repeated to her, when she was in a hypnotic state, she engaged in deeply sad, often poetically beautiful, day dreams, we might call them, which commonly took as their starting point the situation of a girl beside the sick-bed of her father. The patient jokingly called this treatment 'chimney sweeping'.

Dr. Breuer [Freud's colleague] soon hit upon the fact that through such cleansing of the soul more could be accomplished than a temporary removal of the constantly recurring mental 'clouds'.

During one session, the patient recalled an occasion when she was with her governess, and how that lady's little dog, that she abhorred, had drunk out of a glass. Out of respect for the conventions the patient had remained silent, but now under hypnosis she gave energetic expression to

her restrained anger, and then drank a large quantity of water without trouble, and woke from hypnosis with the glass at her lips. The symptom thereupon vanished permanently.

Permit me to dwell for a moment on this experience. No one had ever cured an hysterical symptom by such means before, or had come so near understanding its cause. This would be a pregnant discovery if the expectation could be confirmed that still other, perhaps the majority of symptoms, originated in this way and could be removed by the same method.

Such was indeed the case, almost all the symptoms originated in exactly this way, as we were to discover. The patient's illness originated at the time when she was caring for her sick father, and her symptoms could only be regarded as memory symbols of his sickness and death. While she was seated by her father's sick bed, she was careful to betray nothing of her anxiety and her painful depression to the patient. When, later, she reproduced the same scene before the physician, the emotion which she had suppressed on the occurrence of the scene burst out with especial strength, as though it had been pent up all along.

In her normal state she was entirely ignorant of the pathogenic scenes and of their connection with her symptoms. She had forgotten those scenes. When the patient was hypnotized, it was possible, after considerable difficulty, to recall those scenes to her memory, and by this means of recall the symptoms were removed."

(Adapted from Sigmund Freud, 1910, The origin and development of psychoanalysis. *American Journal of Psychology*, 21, 181–218.)

that he initially used extensively, was hypnosis. Freud and Breuer (1895) treated a young woman called Anna O, who suffered from several neurotic symptoms (e.g. paralysis; nervous coughs). Hypnosis uncovered a repressed memory of Anna hearing the sound of dance music coming from a nearby house while she was nursing her dying father, and feeling guiltily that she would rather be dancing. Her nervous coughing stopped after that repressed memory came to light.

Freud gradually lost interest in hypnosis, partly because many clients were hard or impossible to hypnotise. Another problem is that individuals under hypnosis become very suggestible. As a result, little reliance can be placed on the accuracy of what they claim to remember when hypnotised.

The second method was **free association**. In this method, the client responds with the first thing coming into his or her mind when presented with certain words or ideas. Free association is ineffective if the client shows *resistance* and is reluctant to say what he or she is thinking. Nevertheless, the presence of resistance (revealed by long pauses) suggests the client is getting close to an important repressed idea, and that further probing by the therapist is needed.

The client is reluctant to say what he or she is really thinking.

The third method used by Freud was dream analysis, which he described as "the via regia [royal road] to the unconscious". Freud argued that the mind has a censor that keeps repressed material out of conscious awareness. This censor is less vigilant (it nods off?) during sleep, and so repressed ideas from the unconscious are more likely to appear in dreams than in waking thought. These repressed ideas emerge in disguised form because of their unacceptable nature. As a result, the therapist works with the client to work out the true meaning of each dream.

Dream analysis

There are various schools of thought on the significance of dreams and their possible biological function. Freud and Jung believed that dreams signified the thoughts and feelings of the unconscious mind and are therefore necessary to allow the mind to explore them. Others have suggested that dreams perform no concrete function, but this view has been contested by referring to examples of sleep deprivation. Sleep-deprived participants tend to experience an increase in dreaming sleep when they are finally permitted to sleep.

What is your view on the role of dreams? How might psychologists test your views scientifically?

Progress in therapy depends partly on **transference**. This involves the client transferring onto the therapist the powerful emotional reactions previously directed at his or her own parents or other highly significant others. These intense feelings can be negative or positive and the client is usually unaware of what is happening. Transference often provides a direct link back to the client's childhood by providing a re-creation of dramatic conflicts experienced at that time. Transference can facilitate the uncovering of repressed memories.

Findings

We will consider two main issues. First, the effectiveness of psychoanalytic therapy is discussed. Second, we consider whether its effectiveness involves the processes emphasised by Freud.

Effectiveness

How effective is psychoanalysis? It is hard to answer that question, because psychoanalysis as originally practised has increasingly been replaced by various psychodynamic therapies based in part on Freud's ideas. These psychodynamic therapies owe much to Freud's influence in that the emphasis is on making sense of emotionally loaded information in the unconscious. However,

? How can you account
for the appeal of
psychoanalysis?

they represent a development of classical psychoanalysis in two main ways. First, there is more consideration of the client's current worries and concerns in psychodynamic therapy. Second, psychodynamic therapies typically focus more on the client's social relationships, whereas psychoanalysis emphasises the patient as an individual.

Psychodynamic therapy is moderately effective. Matt and Navarro (1997) considered 63 meta-analyses in which different types of therapy had been compared. On average, 75% of clients receiving treatment improved more than the average untreated control person. Behaviour therapy and cognitive therapy (discussed shortly) tended to be more effective than psychodynamic therapy. However, Matt and Navarro argued those differences were more apparent than real. Clients treated by behaviour or cognitive therapy often had less serious symptoms than those treated by psychodynamic therapy.

Other research supports Matt and Navarro (1997). Leichsenring (2001) carried out a meta-analysis to compare the effectiveness of psychodynamic therapy and Cognitive Behavioural Therapy. There were no differences between the two forms of therapy in 97% of the comparisons, which included comparing the number of depressive symptoms, general psychiatric symptomatology, and social functioning.

However, psychoanalysis and psychodynamic therapy have limited effectiveness in various ways. First, psychodynamic therapy has rarely been shown to be significantly more effective than alternative forms of therapy (Fonagy et al., 2005). Second, psychoanalysis and psychodynamic therapy tend to be most effective with clients who are well-educated. For psychoanalysis to be effective, clients must express their innermost thoughts and feelings coherently, which is easier for well-educated individuals to do.

Third, psychoanalysis and psychodynamic therapy are relatively ineffective in the treatment of schizophrenia. An important reason is that schizophrenia is in some ways a biological disorder and as such is not likely to be easily treated by a "talking cure".

Assumptions and processes

A central assumption underlying psychoanalysis (and a controversial one!) is that many adult mental disorders have their origins in childhood. This assumption may well be true in some cases. Kendler et al. (1996) in a study mentioned earlier studied the effects on female twins of parental loss in childhood. These twins showed an above-average tendency to suffer from alcoholism and depression in adulthood. Caspi et al. (1996) found children inhibited at the age of 3 were more likely than other children to suffer from major depression at the age of 21. They were also more likely to have attempted suicide. However, these effects were not large.

We mustn't exaggerate the importance of early childhood in causing adult mental disorder. The onset of mental disorder is often triggered by *recent* events. Kendler et al. (1998) studied the probability of female adults developing major depression as a function of the number of stressful life events in the preceding month. The percentages were as follows: 0.9% (0 events); 3.4% (1 event); 6.8% (2 events); and 23.8% (3 events).

It is hard to test Freud's notion that insight is of crucial importance for recovery because the concept is rather vague. Høglend et al. (1994) found psychiatrists showed poor agreement among themselves concerning the insight levels shown by anxious and depressed patients in therapy. However, Høglend et al. (2000) used a scale to assess insight in clients with a range of problems (mostly anxiety or depression) who received psychotherapy. They found 46% of the clients showed increased insight during therapy. However, that doesn't necessarily mean the recovery shown by the clients was *caused* by increased insight.

The findings of Kivlighan et al.'s (2000) study supported Freud's prediction that the levels of insight demonstrated by clients would increase as the psychoanalytic sessions progress.

Impressive findings on the value of insight in therapy using the Insight Rating Scale (in which experts evaluate clients' reports of the counselling session just finished) were reported by Kivlighan et al. (2000). They studied 12 clients who received 20 sessions in psychoanalytic counselling. There were steady decreases in symptoms across sessions and progressive increases in insight. Of key importance, clients showing an increase in insight had reduced symptoms over the following week. This suggests (as predicted by Freud) that insight helped to cause symptom reduction.

According to Freud, transference is very important in psychoanalysis because it provides a major way for the client to recover repressed memories and so achieve insight. Most evidence doesn't support this view. Høglend et al. (2006) carried out an experimental study. Clients, mostly suffering from anxiety or depression, received psychotherapy. They were assigned at random to two groups, one involving much more focus on transference than the other. The two groups didn't differ in therapy outcome, suggesting that transference isn't important in producing recovery from mental disorder.

EVALUATION

➕ Psychoanalysis has a very important place in the history of therapy. It was the first systematic form of psychological treatment for mental disorders, and has strongly influenced several subsequent forms of therapy.

➕ Developments of psychoanalysis such as psychodynamic therapy have proved moderately effective (Matt & Navarro, 1997). Some critics (e.g. H.J. Eysenck, 1985) emphasise that this therapeutic approach is less effective than later forms of therapy. However, it is remarkable that a form of therapy originally put forward 100 years ago is almost as effective as much more recent forms of therapy.

➕ Another strength of psychoanalysis is that it appears that insight plays an important role in promoting recovery from mental illness.

➖ Most clients treated by psychoanalysis have reported repressed memories of childhood, as predicted by Freud. However, there is a real danger that much of what the client says is influenced by suggestions implanted previously by the therapist and so may not reflect his or her genuine views. Evidence that the therapist can distort what patients remember was reported by Lief and Fetkewicz (1995). They found that 80% of adult patients who admitted reporting false recovered memories had therapists who made direct suggestions they had been the victims of childhood sexual abuse.

➖ On average, psychoanalysis and psychodynamic therapy are somewhat less effective than other forms of therapy. This is especially the case with schizophrenia, which can be regarded in some ways as a biological disorder.

➖ Some concepts of central importance to Freud's therapeutic approach are very vague. For example, it has proved hard to find valid ways of measuring concepts such as "insight" and "transference".

➖ Psychoanalysis had too narrow a focus. Insufficient attention was paid to the individual's *current* problems and the difficulties he or she has at the social and interpersonal level.

➖ It is assumed that insight produces recovery. It seems about as likely that recovery leads to insight.

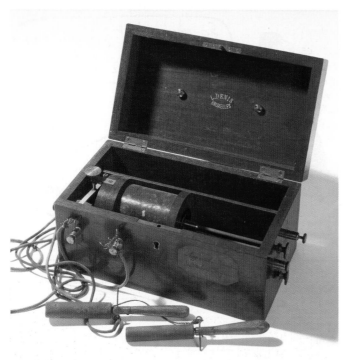

A very early example of an induction coil device used in 18th-century electric-shock therapy. Today, aversion therapy utilises much more sophisticated methods and equipment.

Psychoanalysis and psychodynamic therapy have generally been most successful with less severe mental disorders. With such disorders, there is much evidence that successful treatment depends to a large extent on factors such as the warmth and empathy (emotional understanding) of the therapist (Stevens et al., 2000). Thus, uncovering repressed childhood experiences may not contribute much to the beneficial effects of psychoanalysis or psychodynamic therapy.

Behaviour therapy

We discussed the behavioural approach earlier in the chapter. According to that approach, most mental disorders are caused by maladaptive ways of behaving. This approach led to the development of behaviour therapy. Behaviour therapy was developed during the 1950s and 1960s, but its origins go back several decades before that. Behaviour therapists argue that since maladaptive learning causes mental disorders, the best treatment consists of appropriate new learning.

Behaviour therapists believe that abnormal behaviour develops through conditioning (discussed earlier in the chapter). There are two main forms of conditioning: (1) classical conditioning involving learning by association; and (2) operant conditioning involving learning by reinforcement or reward. Behaviour therapists argue that classical and operant conditioning can change unwanted behaviour into more desirable patterns of behaviour.

Consider how behaviour therapists might treat someone suffering from alcoholism. According to behaviour therapists, what is needed is to replace the undesirable response of drinking alcohol when it is presented, with the response of avoiding it. This can be done by aversion therapy. For example, an alcoholic is given a drug (e.g. Antabuse) causing him or her to vomit or have great difficulty in breathing if he or she starts to drink alcohol. This often causes the alcoholic to change his or her behaviour and cease drinking in the short term. However, aversion therapy tends to be less effective in the long term (Roth & Fonagy, 2005).

Aversion therapy

- (US) Electric shock → (UR) fear
- (NS) Pornographic pictures → pleasure

Conditioning: Pornographic pictures associated with electric shock

- (CS) Pornographic pictures → (CR) fear

- (US) Vomiting → (UR) displeasure
- (NS) Alcohol → pleasure

Conditioning: Alcohol associated with vomiting

- (CS) Alcohol → (CR) displeasure

Systematic de-sensitisation

Systematic de-sensitisation (often written without a hyphen) is one of the main techniques within **behaviour therapy**. It is historically important because it was one of the first such techniques to be developed. It was introduced by Joseph Wolpe (1958, 1969) to treat individuals suffering from **phobias** involving excessive fear of certain stimuli (e.g. snakes; spiders).

According to behaviour therapists, phobias develop through classical conditioning, with the phobic object being associated with some aversive or unpleasant event (discussed earlier in

KEY TERMS

Systematic de-sensitisation: a form of behaviour therapy designed to treat phobias, in which relaxation training and a fear hierarchy are used.

Behaviour therapy: therapy based on the assumption that the best way to treat mental disorders is through techniques that allow the individual to learn new forms of behaviour more appropriate than their current behaviour. More specifically, classical and operant conditioning are used to replace unwanted patterns of behaviour.

Phobias: severe and irrational fear of objects such as snakes or spiders leading to a strong tendency to avoid the feared objects.

What is unwanted behaviour?

The term "unwanted behaviour" leads to questions about who decides which behaviour is disliked, unwanted, or abnormal. Usually the client himself or herself will decide that symptoms (e.g. phobic reactions) need treatment. Some behaviour is so anti-social that everyone agrees it is undesirable. However, it is possible for behaviour that those in authority decide is unacceptable to be labelled as "mental illness". Could the behaviour of rebellious young people, trade union activists, or lonely old people be construed as "undesirable" and in need of modification? Has this ever happened as far as you know?

this chapter). According to this account, phobic individuals would be much more likely than other people to have had a frightening experience with the phobic object. In fact, however, dog-phobic people were no more likely than anyone else to report frightening experiences with a dog (DiNardo et al., 1988). Only 2% of water-phobic children claimed to have had a direct conditioning experience involving water (Menzies & Clarke, 1993).

What is involved in systematic de-sensitisation? The first stage is to provide clients with relaxation training in which they learn how to engage in deep muscle relaxation.

Second, clients construct a fear hierarchy with the assistance of their therapist. A **fear hierarchy** consists of a list of situations or objects producing fear in the client, starting with those causing only a small amount of fear and moving on to those causing increasingly great levels of fear. For example, the first item on the list of a snake-phobic person might be a small, harmless snake 50 feet away, with subsequent items featuring larger and more dangerous snakes closer to the client.

Third, clients learn how to use their relaxation techniques while imagining the objects or situations they fear, starting with those at the bottom of the fear hierarchy. The therapist describes the object or situation, and the client tries to form a clear image of it. The client often engages in covert de-sensitisation during therapy sessions and places himself/ herself in progressively more frightening real-life situations between sessions. An alternative approach is to present the actual object or situation itself (in vivo de-sensitisation).

When the client can imagine the less feared items in the fear hierarchy without experiencing fear, he or she moves on to the next items. Eventually, the client can confront the most feared object or situation in the fear hierarchy without fear, at which point he or she is regarded as cured.

Systematic de-sensitisation puts demands on the expertise of the therapist. For example, it is essential to the success of systematic de-sensitisation that the therapist identifies the reasons for the client's anxiety. Consider someone who is very fearful of social situations. This fear may be totally irrational or it may occur because the individual concerned lacks social skills. If the latter is the case, then training in social skills is required in addition to systematic de-sensitisation.

Fear of dogs

If an individual has a fear of dogs, systematic de-sensitisation could be used to overcome this. The client might have learned their fear in the following way:

* Child is bitten by dog. Unpleasant bite (US) → fear (UR).
* Dog (NS) paired with US, becomes CS → fear (now CR).

This can be overcome by associating the dog with a new response—relaxation.

* Dog (CS) → fear (CR).
* Dog paired with new UCS (relaxation) → pleasant feelings (CR).

KEY TERM

Fear hierarchy: a list of feared situations or objects, starting with those creating only small amounts of fear and moving on to those creating large amounts of fear; used in the treatment of phobias.

What are the two main explanations for how systematic desensitisation works in treating phobias?

Why does systematic de-sensitisation work?

As we will see shortly, systematic de-sensitisation has proved to be a moderately effective form of treatment for phobia. How does it work? Several answers have been proposed. Wolpe (1958) argued that individuals learn through a process of conditioning to associate certain specific stimuli (e.g. snakes) with anxiety. The individual learns to produce a response *incompatible* with anxiety (e.g. deep muscle relaxation) in the presence of the anxiety-evoking stimulus.

Wolpe used the term **reciprocal inhibition** to refer to the process of inhibiting anxiety by substituting a competing response. If relaxation is going to be successful in inhibiting the client's anxiety, the amount of anxiety triggered by imagining the phobic stimulus must not be too great. That explains why systematic de-sensitisation starts with stimuli creating only a small amount of anxiety.

A different explanation was proposed by Wilson and Davison (1971). According to them, the crucial process is **extinction**, which occurs when a response repeatedly produced in a given situation in the absence of reinforcement loses its strength. More specifically, imagining the phobic stimulus produces the anxiety response but there are no adverse consequences (e.g. being bitten by a snake). This lack of consequences eventually reduces the strength of the anxiety response. According to this explanation, *all* that matters is repeated non-reinforced exposure to the phobic stimulus.

There is a crucial difference in prediction between the reciprocal inhibition and extinction accounts—according to the former, deep muscle relaxation is essential, whereas it is almost irrelevant according to the latter.

Findings

Choy et al. (2007) reviewed the literature on the effectiveness of systematic de-sensitisation in the treatment of phobias. Systematic de-sensitisation was generally moderately effective in reducing anxiety levels. However, its effects on avoidance of the feared object or situation were less consistent. For example, Rosen et al. (1976) found in a study on animal phobia that clients treated with systematic de-sensitisation were as likely as controls to continue to avoid the feared animals.

Four studies have assessed the long-term effects of systematic de-sensitisation by carrying out a follow-up several months after the end of treatment. According to Choy et al. (2007), the treatment gains (decreased anxiety and avoidance) present at the end of treatment were maintained at follow-up. For example, Denholtz et al. (1978) found 60% of clients treated for flying phobia continued to fly during the 3½-year follow-up period.

Does systematic de-sensitisation work because of reciprocal inhibition (with muscle relaxation inhibiting the anxiety response) or because of extinction (non-reinforced exposure to the feared stimulus)? The most direct approach to answering this question is to compare systematic de-sensitisation with and without relaxation. Levin and Gross (1985) reviewed the relevant literature. The picture was confused. In 10 studies, systematic de-sensitisation without relaxation was as effective as de-sensitisation with relaxation. However, there were 15 studies in which relaxation contributed to the success of systematic de-sensitisation!

McGlynn et al. (1981) shed some light on the apparently inconsistent findings. They pointed out that extinction occurs only slowly over time. Thus, there would be very little extinction of anxiety if clients spent only a short period of time imagining each item in the fear hierarchy and if there were only a few treatment sessions. In such circumstances, any beneficial effects of systematic de-sensitisation would depend on relaxation and reciprocal inhibition. As they predicted, relaxation was generally important in treatment when there was little opportunity for extinction to occur.

We can pursue this issue by considering exposure therapy. In **exposure therapy**, phobic individuals are exposed to the object or situation they fear for lengthy periods of time until their anxiety level is substantially reduced. In recent years, this form of therapy has been developed into virtual reality exposure therapy, in which a computer program produces a virtual environment simulating the phobic situation.

Exposure therapy provides maximal scope for extinction to occur but doesn't involve muscle relaxation. If extinction is the crucial process in curing phobias,

KEY TERMS

Reciprocal inhibition: the process of inhibiting anxiety by substituting a competing response.

Extinction: elimination of a conditioned response when the conditioned stimulus is not followed by the unconditioned stimulus or a response is not followed by a reward.

Exposure therapy: a form of therapy in which patients are exposed to the object or situation they fear for lengthy periods of time until their anxiety level is substantially reduced.

exposure therapy should be very effective. However, if muscle relaxation is essential, then exposure therapy shouldn't be effective.

In fact, exposure therapy is consistently effective, with traditional exposure therapy and virtual reality exposure therapy producing similar success rates. Both forms of exposure therapy are often more effective than systematic de-sensitisation (Choy et al., 2007). However, there is one problem with exposure therapy—prolonged exposure to feared stimuli can create intense levels of anxiety, and so the drop-out rate is sometimes rather high.

In exposure therapy, individuals are exposed to the source of their anxiety for a prolonged period until their fear subsides.

EVALUATION

✚ Systematic de-sensitisation was one of the first techniques to be developed within behaviour therapy. It played a role in the subsequent development of related techniques such as exposure therapy and virtual reality exposure therapy.

✚ It is based on solid theoretical grounds, namely, the notion that through conditioning individuals can learn to replace the anxiety response to feared stimuli with a relaxation response.

✚ The basic ingredients of systematic de-sensitisation (muscle relaxation; fear hierarchy; association of phobic stimuli with relaxation responses) can easily be manipulated to see whether each one is important in successful treatment.

✚ Systematic de-sensitisation is of proven effectiveness. In the great majority of studies, individuals treated with systematic de-sensitisation improved more than those receiving no treatment (Choy et al., 2007).

✚ Systematic de-sensitisation poses few ethical issues. The use of a fear hierarchy and deep muscle relaxation are designed to ensure that clients don't experience very unpleasant levels of anxiety.

➖ It is a form of therapy specifically designed to reduce anxiety, and so is only relevant to the anxiety disorders. Even within the anxiety disorders, it can only be used when the stimuli producing a client's anxious state can be identified. It wouldn't be appropriate to use systematic de-sensitisation with someone suffering from generalised anxiety disorder, because that condition involves excessive worrying about numerous, ill-defined situations.

➖ Many phobias (e.g. snake phobia; spider phobia) treated by systematic de-sensitisation are relatively trivial in that they don't have the crippling effects on everyday life of other mental disorders such as depression or schizophrenia. However, systematic de-sensitisation has been used successfully to treat social phobia (excessive fear of social situations), and social phobia can severely disrupt people's lives.

➖ Most evidence (e.g. Choy et al., 2007) indicates that exposure therapy is more effective than systematic de-sensitisation in the treatment of phobias. This helps to explain why there has been a pronounced reduction in the use of systematic de-sensitisation over the years (McGlynn et al., 2004).

There is a lack of clarity about precisely *why* systematic de-sensitisation is effective. However, Wolpe probably exaggerated the importance of muscle relaxation. Muscle relaxation often adds nothing to the effectiveness of systematic de-sensitisation, and exposure therapy is effective without making any use of muscle relaxation.

Cognitive Behavioural Therapy

What is **Cognitive Behavioural Therapy**? As the name implies, Cognitive Behavioural Therapy involves elements of cognitive therapy and behaviour therapy. The basic notion is that the client needs to change his or her inappropriate behaviour *and* his or her dysfunctional thoughts. It is claimed that changing behaviour and thoughts produces more effective therapy than focusing primarily on behaviour (behaviour therapy) or on beliefs (cognitive therapy).

Four basic assumptions underlie Cognitive Behavioural Therapy (Kendall & Hammen, 1998):

1. Clients typically respond on the basis of their *interpretations* of themselves and the world around them rather than on the basis of what is *actually* the case. Of central importance is the notion of **interpretive bias**—the tendency shown by most anxious and depressed patients to interpret ambiguous stimuli and situations in a negative or threatening way. Interpretive biases are especially common with respect to interpretations concerning the individual himself/herself.
2. Thoughts, behaviours, and feelings are inter-related, and all influence each other. Thus, no single factor is more important than the others.
3. In order for therapeutic interventions to be successful, therapists must clarify and change how people think about themselves and about the world around them. A major part of this involves reducing or eliminating their interpretive biases about themselves and the world around them.
4. It is important to change both the client's cognitive processes and his or her behaviour. The reason is that the benefits of therapy are likely to be greater than when only cognitive processes or behaviour change.

Beck (1976) proposed a form of Cognitive Behavioural Therapy. As discussed earlier, he argued that the negative and maladaptive thoughts of depressed and anxious patients depend on cognitive schemas (organised cognitive structures about the self and others). According to him, therapy should involve more than simply changing such thoughts and replacing them with more appropriate and positive ones. He also emphasised the use of homework assignments requiring clients to behave in certain ways they found hard. For example, a client suffering from social phobia (with excessive fear of social situations) might be told to initiate a conversation with everyone in his or her office over the following few days.

ACTIVITY: Dysfunctional thoughts

Devise a situation like the following example and describe how the thoughts, emotions, and behaviour that result from it could be changed.

It is your birthday and you are given a surprise invitation to meet your friends at lunchtime to celebrate. You are disappointed to find that your best friend does not join you and gives no reason or apology.

	Irrational/negative	Rational/positive
Thoughts	He/she is annoyed with you but won't say why	Maybe he/she was under pressure with work, etc.
Emotions	Hurt and upset. Perhaps you aren't friends after all	Disappointed, but sure you'll get together soon to celebrate
Behaviour	Treat him/her with cool detachment next time you meet	Ring him/her to arrange to meet

---

In what ways might a person's thoughts about themselves influence the way they react in a particular situation?

KEY TERMS

Cognitive Behavioural Therapy: a development of cognitive therapy in which attempts to change behaviour directly are added to thought and belief restructuring.

Interpretive bias: the tendency shown by most anxious and depressed patients to interpret ambiguous stimuli and situations in a negative or threatening way.

CASE STUDY: Cognitive Behavioural Therapy

Here is a concrete example of Cognitive Behavioural Therapy (Clark, 1996) involving a 40-year-old man with panic disorder (a disorder involving frequent panic attacks). The client tried to protect himself against having a heart attack during panic attacks by taking paracetamol and by breathing deeply. The hypothesis that this was what prevented him from having a heart attack was tested by the therapist and the client alternately sprinting and jogging around a football pitch. In addition, the client was given the homework of taking strenuous daily exercise without trying to control his breathing. The client rapidly accepted that his problem centred on his own mistaken beliefs.

Hypothesis testing

A crucial ingredient in homework assignments is *hypothesis testing*. Clients typically predict that carrying out their homework assignments will make them feel anxious or depressed, and so they are told to test their predictions. The clients' hypotheses are generally shown to be too pessimistic. Discovering that many of their fears are groundless speeds recovery.

Safety-seeking behaviours

Earlier in the chapter we considered the issue of how anxious individuals maintain their mistaken beliefs and interpretations of the world over long periods of time. Part of the answer is safety-seeking behaviours, which are used to reduce the level of anxiety. For example, patients with panic disorder often have the mistaken belief that they are in danger of having a heart attack and dying when they have a panic attack. They may maintain this belief by adopting the safety-seeking behaviour of keeping very still when they experience a panic attack, imagining this behaviour protects them against having a heart attack. It follows from this analysis that preventing patients from using safety-seeking behaviours should assist in eliminating their mistaken beliefs.

Findings

How effective is Cognitive Behavioural Therapy? A very thorough attempt to answer that question was made by Butler et al. (2006). They considered the findings from 16 meta-analyses concerned with the therapeutic value of Cognitive Behavioural Therapy based on almost 10,000 patients. This form of therapy was notably successful in treating major depressive disorder, generalised anxiety disorder, panic disorder with or without agoraphobia, social phobia, and post-traumatic stress disorder.

In addition, Cognitive Behavioural Therapy was more effective than anti-depressants in the treatment of major depressive disorder especially in terms of the long-term persistence of its beneficial effects. Finally, it is useful in the treatment of schizophrenia, and would be valuable if used in conjunction with atypical anti-psychotic drugs.

According to advocates of Cognitive Behavioural Therapy, it is important to identify and to eliminate the interpretive biases (unduly negative interpretations) possessed by clients. For example, individuals with social anxiety or social phobia typically interpret their own social behaviour as being less skilled and more inept than is actually the case. One effective way of reducing this interpretive bias involves the use of video feedback. Harvey et al. (2000) asked socially anxious individuals to give a speech while being videoed. They then predicted what they would see when the video was shown to them.

Nearly all of socially anxious individuals showed interpretive bias—they discovered when viewing the video that their social performance was much better than they had predicted. The reduction in this interpretive bias has been found to assist in treatment (see Eysenck, 1997, for a review).

It is assumed within Cognitive Behavioural Therapy that safety-seeking behaviours may help to maintain anxious patients' mistaken beliefs and so reduce the value of therapy. For example, exposure therapy (putting patients in feared situations) is assumed to be effective with social-phobics because it allows them to disconfirm their unrealistically negative views about the dangers of social situations. Safety-seeking behaviours (e.g. avoiding eye contact; keeping quiet) may prevent effective disconfirmation of those negative views.

? Why has cognitive behavioural therapy become such a popular therapeutic treatment for many mental disorders?

Evidence supporting the above assumptions was reported by Morgan and Raffle (1999). They instructed social-phobics receiving exposure therapy (e.g. giving talks in public) to avoid safety-seeking behaviours, whereas others weren't given those instructions. As predicted, those patients instructed to avoid safety-seeking behaviours showed more improvement from therapy.

Which component of Cognitive Behavioural Therapy is more effective? Dobson et al. (2008) considered this issue in a study on patients with major depression. Some of them received only cognitive therapy (designed to eliminate maladaptive thoughts) whereas others received only behaviour therapy (engagement with rewarding activities). Both forms of therapy were about equally effective in preventing subsequent relapse or recurrence of depression, and both were more effective than drug therapy.

EVALUATION

⊕ Cognitive Behavioural Therapy has established itself over the past 30 years as one of the most important and most commonly used forms of treatment for several mental disorders.

⊕ Cognitive Behavioural Therapy combines features of cognitive therapy and of behaviour therapy. As such, it is broader and more effective than either of the forms of therapy from which it arose.

⊕ Cognitive Behavioural Therapy is based on research carried out by behaviourists and by cognitive psychologists (see earlier in this chapter). As a result, it is based on a solid scientific foundation.

⊕ Cognitive Behavioural Therapy has shown itself to be clearly effective (and generally more effective than other forms of therapy) in the treatment of major depression, generalised anxiety disorder, panic disorder with agoraphobia, and post-traumatic stress disorder (Roth & Fonagy, 2005). That is a considerable achievement.

⊕ The beneficial effects of Cognitive Behavioural Therapy when used with patients having panic disorder, schizophrenia or depression are more long lasting than those of drug therapy (Butler et al., 2006; Dobson et al., 2008). This is the case because Cognitive Behavioural Therapy is designed to cure the causes of these disorders whereas drug therapy focuses only on reducing the symptoms.

⊕ The effectiveness of exposure therapy (used in behaviour therapy) is increased when patients avoid safety-seeking behaviours as predicted by cognitive-behaviour therapists (e.g. Salkovskis et al., 1999).

⊖ There are many mental disorders for which it may have less to offer than other forms of therapy. For example, it is less effective in treating schizophrenia than are family intervention programmes involving the families of schizophrenic patients, or drug therapy. However, Cognitive Behavioural Therapy is of some value in treating schizophrenia (Butler et al., 2006).

⊖ Those who advocate Cognitive Behavioural Therapy may exaggerate the importance of cognitive processes. Many clients develop more rational and less distorted ways of thinking about important issues with no beneficial changes in their maladaptive behaviour. In addition, many of the beliefs of anxious and depressed patients simply reflect the reality of their difficult everyday lives, rather than being distortions of that reality!

⊖ Cognitive Behavioural Therapy de-emphasises factors regarded as important in other forms of therapy. For example, little attention is paid to physiological or biological processes, and the emphasis is on current problems rather than traumatic childhood experiences.

⊖ Patients with anxiety disorders or depression are very concerned about their emotional state. Cognitive Behavioural Therapy with its emphasis on hypothesis testing can seem too "cold" and "rational" to emotionally disturbed patients (James Walsh, pers. comm.).

⊖ Cognitive Behavioural Therapy often involves a complex mixture of cognitive and behavioural ingredients. As a result, it can be hard to determine precisely *which* ingredients are more and less responsible for the success of treatment.

⊖ Some aspects of Cognitive Behavioural Therapy raise ethical issues. This is certainly the case with exposure therapy, which can involve very high or intolerance levels of anxiety. As a result, many patients drop out of exposure therapy. There can also be ethical issues about the desirability of telling patients that the problem lies within them rather than reality.

You have reached the end of the chapter on individual differences. Individual differences is an approach or perspective in psychology. The material in this chapter has exemplified this approach in so far as abnormal behaviour is one of the ways that individuals vary. Individual differences can be explained in terms of biological (physiological), behaviourist (learning theory), psychoanalytic, and cognitive explanations. All of these explanations have also appeared elsewhere in this book and are important "tools" for explaining behaviour.

Section Summary

Biological therapies
- Biological therapies involve manipulation of the body.
- Major depressive disorder is treated with various drugs, of which the serotonin re-uptake inhibitors (SSRIs) are the ones most commonly used.
- Lithium is the drug most commonly used to treat bipolar disorder. It is effective but can produce tremors and digestive problems.
- Anxiety disorders are often treated with the benzodiazepines. These drugs are moderately effective but can produce poor concentration, sedative effects, and physical dependence.
- Schizophrenia is treated by neuroleptic and atypical anti-psychotic drugs. The latter drugs have fewer side effects and are generally more effective.
- Problems with drug therapy include the following:
  - Fairly frequent relapse because drugs don't address the causes of the disorder
  - Limited understanding of *why* drugs are effective
  - Drug dependence
  - High drop-out rates
  - Unwanted side effects
- ECT is mostly used to treat major depressive disorder but is also used to treat schizophrenia.

- ECT is generally effective and can produce rapid symptom reduction in depression. However, it is less effective in patients under the age of 65.
- ECT can produce memory loss and other cognitive impairments.

Psychoanalysis

- A central goal in psychoanalysis is for the client to gain insight into the emotional significance of his or her traumatic and distressing childhood experiences.
- Insight can be produced by hypnosis, free association, dream analysis, and transference.
- Psychoanalysis has proved moderately effective and is of huge historical significance.
- Problems with psychoanalysis include the following:
  - Many traumatic childhood memories may be distorted by the therapist's influence.
  - Concepts such as "insight" and "transference" are very vague.
  - Transference doesn't seem to promote recovery as Freud claimed.
  - Freud assumed that insight helped to cause recovery, but it may well be that recovery causes insight.
  - This form of therapy is too narrow—it focuses on childhood experiences while de-emphasising the client's current social and interpersonal difficulties.
  - Psychoanalysis may work because of the warmth and responsiveness of the therapist rather than its specific content.

Systematic de-sensitisation

- Systematic de-sensitisation is used in the treatment of phobias. It involves muscle relaxation, the construction of a fear hierarchy, and the replacement of an anxious response to phobic stimuli with relaxation.
- Systematic de-sensitisation was one of the first techniques developed within behaviour therapy. It is based on solid theoretical grounds and is moderately effective.
- Problems with systematic de-sensitisation include the following:
  - It is only of much relevance to the anxiety disorders.
  - Even within the anxiety disorders, it is hard to use with generalised anxiety disorder, because that disorder involves numerous general worries and concerns rather than fears of specific stimuli.
  - Exposure therapy is generally more effective than systematic de-sensitisation. This suggests that muscle relaxation is not needed to treat phobias successfully.

Cognitive Behavioural Therapy

- Cognitive Behavioural Therapy evolved out of behaviour therapy and cognitive therapy.
- It involves changing the client's cognitive processes and behaviour in order to eliminate his or her interpretive biases and mistaken beliefs.
- It is assumed that mistaken interpretations and beliefs are maintained by safety-seeking behaviours.
- Cognitive Behavioural Therapy is very effective in treating anxiety disorders and depression.
- Cognitive Behavioural Therapy leads to less relapse and recurrence of mental disorders than does drug therapy.
- Problems with this form of therapy include:
  - It is less effective than other therapies in treating schizophrenia.
  - It exaggerates the importance of cognitive processes in changing people's behaviour.
  - Cognitive Behavioural Therapy tends to ignore biological factors and the events of childhood.
  - The complexity of therapy means that it is hard to know precisely which ingredients are most effective.

Further Reading

- There are several excellent and thorough textbooks on abnormal psychology. The main issues within abnormal psychology are discussed in an accessible and reader-friendly way in R.J. Comer (2009) *Abnormal psychology (7th Edn)* (New York: Worth).

- A second textbook that can be recommended because of its focus on the main issues in abnormal psychology is V.M. Durand and D.H. Barlow (2013) *Essentials of abnormal psychology (6th Edn)* (Belmont, CA: Thomson/Cengage).

- There is detailed coverage of major forms of therapy and an assessment of their effectiveness in A. Roth and P. Fonagy (2005) *What works for whom?: A critical review of psychotherapy research (2nd Edn)* (New York: Guilford Press).

> **EXAM HINT**
>
> Some examination questions require you to apply your knowledge. They start with a "stem" describing a scenario (as in question 4 on this page). Whilst you probably have not seen the scenario before, if you have revised everything you will have the knowledge needed to answer the question. Just remember to apply your knowledge. You might briefly outline a theory or research study but then must use this to explain the scenario.

Revision Questions

The examination questions aim to sample the material in this whole chapter. For advice on how to answer such questions refer to Chapter 1, Section 2.

1. a. Outline **two** definitions of abnormality. (3 +3 marks)

    b. Explain **one** limitation of each of the definitions answered in (a.). (2+2 marks)

2. a. Evaluate the behavioural approach to psychopathology. (6 marks)

    b. Outline the cognitive approach to psychopathology. (6 marks)

3. a. Describe and evaluate **one or more** biological therapy used to treat abnormality. (12 marks)

    b. Explain what is involved in Cognitive Behavioural Therapy. (3 marks)

4. A research study is conducted to compare the effectiveness of drug therapy vs Cognitive Behavioural Therapy to treat a person with depression. Each participant in the study is assessed before treatment starts and again assessed 8 weeks later.

    Outline **two** ethical issues that might arise in this study. (2 marks + 2 marks)

References

Abrahamsson, K.H., Berggren, U., Hallberg, L.R-M., & Carlsson, S.G. (2002). Ambivalence in coping with dental fear and avoidance: A qualitative study. *Journal of Health Psychology, 7*, 653–664.

Abrams, D., Wetherell, M., Cochrane, S., Hogg, M.A., & Turner, J.C. (1990). Knowing what to think by knowing who you are: Self-categorisation and the nature of norm formation, conformity and group polarisation. *British Journal of Social Psychology, 29*, 97–119.

Adorno, T.W., Frenkel-Brunswik, E., Levinson, D., & Sanford, R. (1950). *The authoritarian personality.* New York: Harper.

Ainsworth, M.D.S., & Bell, S.M. (1970). Attachment, exploration and separation: Illustrated by the behaviour of one-year-olds in a strange situation. *Child Development, 41*, 49–67.

Ainsworth, M.D.S., Blehar, M.C., Waters, E., & Wall, S. (1978). *Patterns of attachment: A psychological study of the strange situation.* Hillsdale, NJ: Lawrence Erlbaum Associates Inc.

Allen, B.P., & Lindsay, D.S. (1998). Amalgamations of memories: Intrusion of information from one event into reports of another. *Applied Cognitive Psychology, 12*, 277–285.

Allen, V.L., & Levine, J.M. (1971). Social support and conformity: The role of independent assessment of reality. *Journal of Experimental Social Psychology, 7*, 48–58.

Almeida, D.M. (2005). Resilience and vulnerability to daily stressors assessed via diary methods. *Current Directions in Psychological Science, 14*, 64–68.

Altemeyer, B. (1981). *Right-wing authoritarianism.* Winnipeg: University of Manitoba Press.

Amelang, M., & Schmidt-Rathjens, C. (2003). Personality, cancer and coronary heart disease: Fictions and facts in the aetiological research. *Psychologische Rundschau, 54*, 12–23.

Anderson, J. (1972). Attachment out of doors. In N. Blurton-Jones (Ed.), *Ethological studies of child behaviour.* Cambridge, UK: Cambridge University Press.

Antoni, M.H., Cruess, D.G., Cruess, S., Lutgendorf, S., Kumar, M., et al. (2000). Cognitive-behavioural stress management interaction effects on anxiety, 24-hr urinary norepinephrine output, and T-cytotoxic/suppressor cells over time among symptomatic HIV infected gay men. *Journal of Consulting and Clinical Psychology, 68*, 31–45.

Arendt, H. (1963). *Eichmann in Jerusalem: A report on the banality of evil.* New York: Viking Press.

Arnett, J. (2008). The neglected 95%: Why American psychology needs to become less American. *American Psychologist, 63*, 602–614.

Aronson, E. (1988). *The social animal (5th Edn).* New York: Freeman.

Asch, S.E. (1951). Effects of group pressure on the modification and distortion of judgements. In H. Guetzkow (Ed.), *Groups, leadership and men.* Pittsburgh, PA: Carnegie.

Asch, S.E. (1956). Studies of independence and conformity: A minority of one against a unanimous majority. *Psychological Monographs, 70* (Whole no. 416).

Ashton, H. (1997). Benzodiazepine dependency. In A. Baum, S. Newman, J. Weinman, R. West, & C. McManus (Eds), *Cambridge handbook of psychology, health and medicine.* Cambridge, UK: Cambridge University Press.

Askew, C., & Field, A.P. (2008). The vicarious learning pathway to fear 40 years on. *Clinical Psychology Review, 28*, 1249–1265.

Atkinson, R.C., & Shiffrin, R.M. (1968). Human memory: A proposed system and its control processes. In K.W. Spence & J.T. Spence (Eds), *The psychology of learning and motivation, Vol. 2.* London: Academic Press.

Avtgis, T.A. (1998). Locus of control and persuasion, social influence, and conformity: A meta-analytic review. *Psychological Reports, 83*, 899–903.

Awad, A.G., & Voruganti, L.N. (1999). Quality of life and new antipsychotics in schizophrenia: Are patients better off? *International Journal of Social Psychiatry, 45*, 268–275.

Bachen, E., Cohen, S., & Marsland, A.L. (1997). Psychoimmunology. In A. Baum, S. Newman, J. Weinman, R. West, & C. McManus (Eds), *Cambridge handbook of psychology, health, and medicine.* Cambridge, UK: Cambridge University Press.

Baddeley, A.D. (1966). The influence of acoustic and semantic similarity on long-term memory for word sequences. *Quarterly Journal of Experimental Psychology, 18*, 302–309.

Baddeley, A.D. (2001). Is working memory still working? *American Psychologist, 56*, 851–864.

Baddeley, A.D., & Hitch, G.J. (1974). Working memory. In G.H. Bower (Ed.), *The psychology of learning and motivation, Vol. 8.* London: Academic Press.

Baddeley, A.D., Thomson, N., & Buchanan, M. (1975). Word length and the structure of short-term memory. *Journal of Verbal Learning and Verbal Behavior, 14*, 575–589.

Bahrick, H.P., Bahrick, P.O., & Wittinger, R.P. (1975). Fifty years of memory for names and faces: A cross-sectional approach. *Journal of Experimental Psychology: General, 104*, 54–75.

Bahrick, H.P., Hall, L.K., & Da Costa, L.A. (2008). Fifty years of memory of college grades: Accuracy and distortions. *Emotion, 8* (no. 1), 13–22.

Bakermans-Kranenburg, M.J., van IJzendoorn, M.H., & Juffer, F. (2003). Less is more: Meta-analyses of sensitivity and attachment interventions in early childhood. *Psychological Bulletin, 129*, 195–215.

Baldessarini, R.J., Tondo, L., & Hennen, J. (1999). Effects of lithium treatment on suicidal behaviour in bipolar manic-depressive disorders. *Journal of Clinical Psychiatry, 60*, 77–84.

Bales, R.F. (1950). *Interaction process analysis: A method for the study of small groups.* Reading, MA: Addison-Wesley.

Bandura, A. (1965). Influences of models' reinforcement contingencies on the acquisition of initiative responses. *Journal of Personality and Social Psychology, 1*, 589–593.

Bandura, A. (1986). *Social foundations of thought and action: A social cognitive theory*. Englewood Cliffs, NJ: Prentice Hall.

Bandura, A., & Rosenthal, T.L. (1966). Vicarious classical conditioning as a function of arousal level. *Journal of Personality and Social Psychology, 3*, 54–62.

Banyard, P., & Hayes, N. (1994). *Psychology: Theory and application*. London: Chapman & Hall.

Barker, D.B. (2011). Self-selection for stressful experiences. *Stress and Health, 27*, 194–205.

Baron, R.S., VanDello, J., & Brunsman, B. (1996). The forgotten variable in conformity research: The impact of task importance on social influence. *Journal of Personality and Social Psychology, 71*, 915–927.

Barr, C.E., Mednick, S.A., & Munk-Jorgenson, P. (1990). Exposure to influenza epidemics during gestation and adult schizophrenia: A forty-year study. *Archives of General Psychiatry, 47*, 869–874.

Barrett, H. (1997). How young children cope with separation: Toward a new conceptualization. *British Journal of Medical Psychology, 70*, 339–358.

Bartlett, F.C. (1932). *Remembering: A study in experimental and social psychology*. Cambridge, UK: Cambridge University Press.

Bates, J.E., Marvinney, D., Kelly, T., Dodge, K.A., Bennett, D.S., & Pettit, G.S. (1994). Child-care history and kindergarten adjustment. *Developmental Psychology, 30*, 690–700.

Beck, A.T. (1976). *Cognitive therapy of the emotional disorders*. New York: New American Library.

Beck, A.T., & Clark, D.A. (1988). Anxiety and depression: An information processing perspective. *Anxiety Research, 1*, 23–36.

Beck, A.T., & Dozois, D.J.A. (2011). Cognitive therapy: Current status and future directions. *Annual Review of Medicine, 62*, 397–409.

Beckett, C., Castle, J., Rutter, M., & Sonuga-Barke, E.J. (2010). VI. Institutional deprivation, specific cognitive functions, and scholastic achievement: English and Romanian adoptee (ERA) study findings. *Monographs of the Society for Research in Child Development, 75*, 125–142.

Bellezza, F.S. (1982). Updating memory using mnemonic devices. *Cognitive Psychology, 14*, 301–327.

Belsky, J., & Fearon, R.M.P. (2002). Early attachment security, subsequent maternal sensitivity, and later child development: Does continuity in development depend upon continuity of caregiving? *Attachment and Human Development, 4*, 361–387.

Belsky, J., & Rovine, M. (1987). Temperament and attachment security in the Strange Situation: A rapprochement. *Child Development, 58*, 787–795.

Belsky, J., & Rovine, M.J. (1988). Nonmaternal care in the first year of life and the security of parent–infant attachment. *Child Development, 59*, 157–167.

Belsky, J., Vandell, D.L., Burchinal, M., Clarke-Stewart, K.A., McCartney, K., & Tresch Owen, M. (2007). Are there long-term effects of early child care? *Child Development, 78*, 681–701.

Berens, P.L., & Ostrosky, J.D. (1988). Use of beta-blocking agents in musical performance induced anxiety. *Drug Intelligence and Clinical Pharmacy, 22*, 148–149.

Bjork, R.A., & Bjork, E. L. (1992). A new theory of disuse and an old theory of stimulus fluctuation. In A. Healy, S. Kosslyn, & R. Shiffrin (Eds), *From learning processes to cognitive processes: Essays in honor of William K. Estes, Vol. 2*, pp. 35–67. Hillsdale, NJ: Erlbaum.

Blass, T. (1991). Understanding behaviour in the Milgram obedience experiment: The role of personality, situations, and their interactions. *Journal of Personality and Social Psychology, 60*, 398–413.

Blass, T., & Schmitt, C. (2001). The nature of perceived authority in the Milgram paradigm: Two replications. *Current Psychology, 20*, 115–121.

Bokhorst, C.L., Bakermans-Kranenburg, M.J., Fearon, R.M.P., van IJzendoorn, M.H., & Schuengel, C. (2003). The importance of shared environment in mother–infant attachment security: A behavioural genetic study. *Child Development, 74*, 1769–1782.

Bond, R. (2005). Group size and conformity. *Group Processes and Intergroup Roles, 6*, 331–354.

Bond, R., & Smith, P.B. (1996). Culture and conformity: A meta-analysis of studies using Asch's line judgement task. *Psychological Bulletin, 119*, 111–137.

Borge, A.I.H., Rutter, M., Côté, S., & Tremblay, R.E. (2004). Early childcare and physical aggression: Differentiating social selection and social causation. *Journal of Child Psychology and Psychiatry, 45*, 367–376.

Bothwell, R.K., Brigham, J.C., & Pigott, M.A. (1987). An exploratory study of personality differences in eyewitness memory. *Journal of Social Behavior and Personality, 2*, 335–343.

Bower, G.H. (1973). How to ... uh ... remember. *Psychology Today, 7*, 63–70.

Bower, G.H., & Clark, M.C. (1969). Narrative stories as mediators for serial learning. *Psychonomic Science, 14*, 181–182.

Bower, G.H., Clark, M.C., Lesgold, A.M., & Winzenz, D. (1969). Hierarchical retrieval schemes in recall of categorised word lists. *Journal of Verbal Learning and Verbal Behavior, 8*, 323–343.

Bowlby, J. (1944). Forty-four juvenile thieves: Their characters and home life. *International Journal of Psycho-Analysis, 25*, 19–52 and 107–127.

Bowlby, J. (1951). *Maternal care and mental health*. Geneva, Switzerland: World Health Organisation.

Bowlby, J. (1953). *Child care and the growth of love*. Harmondsworth, UK: Penguin.

Bowlby, J. (1969). *Attachment and love, Vol. 1: Attachment*. London: Hogarth.

Brantigan, C.O., Brantigan, T.A., & Joseph, N. (1982). Effect of beta blockade and beta stimulation on stage fright. *American Journal of Medicine, 72*, 88–94.

Brewer, N., Weber, N., & Semmler, C. (2005). Eyewitness identification. In N. Brewer & K.D. Williams (Eds), *Psychology and law: An empirical perspective*. New York: Guilford Press.

British Psychological Society (2009). http://www.bps.org.uk/sites/default/files/documents/code_of_ethics_and_conduct.pdf

Bronfenbrenner, U. (1988). Interacting systems in human development. In N. Bolger, A. Caspi, G. Downey, & M. Moorehouse (Eds), *Persons in context: Developmental processes* (pp. 25–49). New York: Cambridge University Press.

Brown, G.W., & Harris, T. (1978). *Social origins of depression*. London: Tavistock.

Brown, R. (1986). *Social psychology: The second edition*. New York: The Free Press.

Bruce, T.J., & Saeed, S.A. (1999). Social anxiety disorder: A common, under-recognised mental disorder. *American Family Physician, 60*, 2311–2322.

Bruck, M., & Melnyk, L. (2004). Individual differences in children's suggestibility: A review and synthesis. *Applied Cognitive Psychology, 18*, 947–996.

Bruner, E.M., & Kelso, J.M. (1980). Gender differences in graffiti: A semiotic perspective. *Women's Studies International Quarterly, 3*, 239–252.

Bryant, B., Harris, M., & Newton, D. (1980). *Children and minders*. London: Grant McIntyre.

Budd, J.W. (2004). Mind maps as classroom exercises. *Journal of Economic Education, 35*, 35–46.

Buehler, R., Griffin, D., & Ross, M. (1994). Exploring the "planning fallacy": Why people underestimate their task completion times. *Journal of Personality and Social Psychology, 67*, 366–381.

Burger, J.M. (2011). Alive and well after all these years. *Psychologist*, *24*, 654–657.

Bus, A.G., & van IJzendoorn, M.H. (1988). Attachment and early reading: A longitudinal study. *Journal of Genetic Psychology*, *149*(2), 199–210.

Butler, A.C., Chapman, J.E., Forman, E.M., & Beck, A.T. (2006). The empirical status of cognitive-behavioural therapy: A review of meta-analyses. *Clinical Psychology Review*, *26*, 17–31.

Buzan, T., & Buzan, B. (1993). *The mind map book*. London: BBC Books.

Bystrova, K., Ivanova, V., Edhborg, M., Matthiesen, A.-S., Ransjö-Arvidson, A.B., Mukhamedrakhimov, R.M., et al. (2009). Early contact versus separation: Effects on mother-infant interaction one year later. *Birth*, *36*, 97–109.

Campbell, D.T., & Stanley, J.C. (1966). *Experimental and quasi-experimental designs for research*. Chicago: Rand McNally.

Campbell, J.J., Lamb, M.E., & Hwang, C.P. (2000). Early child-care experiences and children's social competence between 1 ½ and 15 years of age. *Applied Developmental Science*, *4*, 166–175.

Carlsmith, H., Ellsworth, P., & Aronson, E. (1976). *Methods of research in social psychology*. Reading, MA: Addison-Wesley.

Carnaham, T., & McFarland, S. (2007). Revisiting the Stanford Prison Experiment: Could participant self-selection have led to the cruelty? *Personality and Social Psychology Bulletin*, *33*, 603–614.

Cartwright, S., & Cooper, C. (1997). *Managing workplace stress*. London: Sage.

Caspi, A., Mofitt, T.E., Newman, D.L., & Silva, P.A. (1996). Behavioral observations at age 3 years predict adult psychiatric disorders: Longitudinal evidence from a birth cohort. *Archives of General Psychiatry*, *53*, 1033–1039.

Centofanti, A.T., & Reece, J. (2006). The cognitive interview and its effect on misleading postevent information. *Psychology, Crime & Law*, *12*, 669–683.

Chadda, R.K., & Ahuja, N. (1990). Dhat syndrome. A sex neurosis of the Indian subcontinent. *British Journal of Psychiatry*, *156*, 577–579.

Chamberlain, S.R., Muller, U., Deakin, J.B., Cortlett, P.R., Dowson, J., Cardinal, R.N., et al. (2007). Lack of deleterious effects of buspirone on cognition in healthy male volunteers. *Journal of Psychopharmacology*, *21*, 210–215.

Chanpattana, W. (2007). A questionnaire survey of ECT practice in Australia. *Journal of ECT*, *23*, 89–92.

Charlton, A. (1998). TV violence has little impact on children, study finds. *The Times*, 12 January, p. 5.

Chida, Y., & Steptoe, A. (2009). The association of anger and hostility with future coronary heart disease: A meta-analytic review of prospective evidence. *Journal of the American College of Cardiology*, *53*, 936–946.

Chincotta, D., Underwood, G., Abd Ghani, K., Papadopoulou, E., & Wreskinksi, M. (1999). Memory span for Arabic numerals and digit words: Evidence for a limited-capacity visuo-spatial storage system. *Quarterly Journal of Experimental Psychology*, *52*, 325–351.

Choy, Y., Fyer, A.J., & Lipsitz, J.D. (2007). Treatment of specific phobia in adults. *Clinical Psychology Review*, *27*, 266–286.

Clark, D.M. (1986). A cognitive approach to panic. *Behaviour Research and Therapy*, *24*, 461–470.

Clark, D.M. (1996). Panic disorder: From theory to therapy. In P. Salkovskis (Ed.), *Frontiers of cognitive therapy*. New York: Guilford Press.

Clark, D.M., & Wells, A. (1995). A cognitive model of social phobia. In R.R.G. Heimberg, M. Liebowitz, D.A. Hope, & S. Scheier (Eds), *Social phobia: Diagnosis, assessment and treatment*. New York: Guilford Press.

Clarke-Stewart, A. (1989). Infant day care: Maligned or malignant? *American Psychologist*, *44*, 266–273.

Clarke-Stewart, K.A., Gruber, C.P., & Fitzgerald, L.M. (1994). *Children at home and in day care*. Hillsdale, NJ: Lawrence Erlbaum Associates Inc.

Claxton, G. (1980). Cognitive psychology: A suitable case for what sort of treatment? In G. Claxton (Ed.), *Cognitive psychology: New directions*. London: Routledge & Kegan Paul.

Cohen, G. (1983). *The psychology of cognition (2nd Edn)*. London: Academic Press.

Cohen, N. J., & Squire, L. R. (1980). Preserved learning and retention of pattern analyzing skill in amnesia: Dissociation of knowing how and knowing that. *Science*, *210*, 207–210.

Cohen, S., Tyrrell, D.A.J., & Smith, A.P. (1991). Psychological stress and susceptibility to the common cold. *New England Journal of Medicine*, *325*, 606–612.

Cohen, S., & Williamson, G.M. (1991). Stress and infectious disease in humans. *Psychological Bulletin*, *109*, 5–24.

Colman, A.M. (2001). *A dictionary of psychology*. Oxford: Oxford University Press.

Comer, R.J. (2009). *Abnormal psychology (7th Edn)*. New York: Worth.

Conrad, R. (1964). Acoustic confusions in immediate memory. *British Journal of Psychology*, *55*, 75–84.

Conway, A.R.A., Kane, M.J., & Engle, R.W. (2003). Working memory capacity and its relation to general intelligence. *Trends in Cognitive Sciences*, *7*, 547–552.

Coolican, H. (1994). *Research methods and statistics in psychology (2nd Edn)*. London: Hodder & Stoughton.

Coolican, H. (1996). *Introduction to research methods and statistics in psychology*. London: Hodder & Stoughton.

Coolican, H. (2004). *Research methods and statistics in psychology (4th Edn)*. London: Hodder & Stoughton.

Cooper, L.A., & Shepard, R.N. (1973). Chronometric studies of the rotation of mental images. In W.G. Chase (Ed.), *Visual information processing*. New York: Academic Press.

Cowan, N., Elliott, E.M., Saults, J.S., Morey, C.C., Mattox, S., Hismjatullina, A., & Conway, A.R.A. (2005). On the capacity of attention: Its estimation and its role in working memory and cognitive aptitudes. *Cognitive Psychology*, *51*, 42–100.

Cox, T. (1978). *Stress*. London: Macmillan Press.

Craddock, N., & Jones, I. (1999). Genetics of bipolar disorder. *Journal of Medical Genetics*, *36*, 585–594.

Crowley, B.J., Hayslip, B., & Hobdy, J. (2003). Psychological hardiness and adjustment to life events in adulthood. *Journal of Adult Development*, *10*, 237–248.

Crutchfield, R.S. (1955). Conformity and character. *American Psychologist*, *10*, 191–198.

Cumberbatch, G. (1990). *Television advertising and sex role stereotyping: A content analysis* [Working paper IV for the Broadcasting Standards Council]. Communications Research Group, Aston University, Birmingham, UK.

Curtiss, S. (1989). The independence and task-specificity of language. In M.H. Bornstein & J.S. Bruner (Eds), *Interaction in human development*. Hillsdale, NJ: Lawrence Erlbaum Associates Inc.

Dahiya, A., & Girdhar, Y. (2011). Impact of stress on work-life balance: An overview. *Strategies and Innovations for Sustainable Organizations*, 286–301.

Dalton, A.L., & Daneman, M. (2006). Social suggestibility to central and peripheral misinformation. *Memory*, *14*, 486–501.

Dambrun, M., & Vatiné, E. (2010). Reopening the study of extreme social behaviour: Obedience to authority within an immersive video environment. *European Journal of Social Psychology*, *40*, 760–773.

Daneman, M., & Carpenter, P.A. (1980). Individual differences in working memory and reading. *Journal of Verbal Learning and Verbal Behavior, 19,* 450–466.

David, B., & Turner, J.C. (1999). Studies in self-categorisation and minority conversion: The in-group minority in intragroup and intergroup contexts. *British Journal of Social Psychology, 38,* 115–134.

Davidson, J.R.T. (2004). Use of benzodiazepines in social anxiety disorder, generalized anxiety disorder, and posttraumatic stress disorder. *Journal of Clinical Psychiatry, 65*(Suppl. 5), 29–33.

Davidson, J.R.T., DuPont, R.L., Hedges, D., & Haskins, J.T. (1999). Efficacy, safety, and tolerability of venlafaxine extended release and buspirone in outpatients with generalised anxiety disorder. *Journal of Clinical Psychiatry, 60,* 528–535.

Davison, G.C., & Neale, J.M. (1996). *Abnormal psychology (rev. 6th Edn).* New York: Wiley.

Davison, G., Neale, J.M., & Kring, A.M. (2004). *Abnormal psychology with cases.* Hoboken, NJ: John Wiley & Sons.

Day, A.L., Therrien, D.L., & Carroll, S.A. (2005). Predicting psychological health: Assessing the incremental validity of emotional intelligence beyond personality, Type A behaviour, and daily hassles. *European Journal of Personality, 19,* 519–536.

Day, R., Nielsen, J.A., Korten, A., Ernberg, G., et al. (1987). Stressful life events preceding the acute onset of schizophrenia: A cross-national study from the World Health Organization. *Culture, Medicine and Psychiatry, 11,* 123–205.

De Beni, R., Moè, A., & Cornoldi, C. (1997). Learning from texts or lectures: Loci mnemonics can interfere with reading but not with listening. *European Journal of Cognitive Psychology, 9,* 401–415.

Deffenbacher, K.A., Bornstein, B.H., Penrod, S.D., & McGorty, K. (2004). A meta-analytic review of the effects of high stress on eyewitness memory. *Law and Human Behavior, 28,* 687–706.

Degi, C.L., Balg, P., Kopp, M., Kallay, E., Thayer, J.F., & Csikai, E.L. (2010). Depressive symptoms, negative life events and incidence of lifetime treatment of cancer in the Hungarian population. *Journal of Cognitive and Behavioral Psychotherapies, 10,* 39–57.

de Jonge, J., van Vegchel, N., Shimazu, A., Schaufell, W., & Dormann, C. (2010). A longitudinal test of the demand-control model using specific job demands and specific job control. *International Journal of Behavioral Medicine, 17,* 125–133.

De Leon, C.F.M., Powell, L.H., & Kaplan, B.H. (1991). Change in coronary-prone behaviours in the recurrent coronary prevention project. *Psychosomatic Medicine, 33,* 407–419.

DeLongis, A., Coyne, J.C., Dakof, G., Folkman, S., & Lazarus, R.S. (1982). The impact of daily hassles, uplifts and major life events to health status. *Health Psychology, 1,* 119–136.

DeLongis, A., Folkman, S., & Lazarus, R.S. (1988). The impact of daily stress on health and mood: Psychological and social resources as mediators. *Journal of Personality and Social Psychology, 54,* 486–495.

De Man, A., Morrison, M., & Drumheller, A. (1993). Correlates of socially restrictive and authoritarian attitudes toward mental patients in university students. *Social Behavior and Personality: An International Journal, 21,* 333–338.

Denholtz, M.S., Hall, L.A., & Mann, E. (1978). Automated treatment for flight phobia: A 3½-year follow-up. *American Journal of Psychiatry, 135,* 1340–1343.

Denollet, J. (2005). DS14: Standard assessment of negative affectivity, social inhibition, and Type D personality. *Psychosomatic Medicine, 67,* 89–97.

Denollet, J., Schiffer, A.A., & Spek, V. (2010). A general propensity to psychological distress affects cardiovascular outcomes: Evidence from research on the Type D (distressed) personality profile. *Circulation: Cardiovascular Quality and Outcomes, 3,* 546–57.

DeRubeis, R.J., Hollon, S.D., Amsterdam, J.D., Shelton, R.C., Young, P.R., Salomon, R.M., et al. (2005). Cognitive therapy vs. medications in the treatment of moderate to severe depression. *Archives of General Psychiatry, 62,* 409–416.

Deutsch, M., & Gerard, H.B. (1955). A study of normative and informational influence upon individual judgement. *Journal of Abnormal and Social Psychology, 51,* 629–636.

De Vreede, I.M., Burger, H., & van Vliet, I.M. (2005). Prediction of response to ECT with routinely collected data in major depression. *Journal of Affective Disorders, 86,* 323–327.

De Wolff, M.S., & van Ijzendoorn, M.H. (1997). Sensitivity and attachment: A meta-analysis on parental antecedents of infant attachment. *Child Development, 68,* 571–591.

De Young, C.G., Peterson, J.B., & Higgins, D.M. (2002). Higher-order factors of the Big Five predict conformity: Are there neuroses of health? *Personality and Individual Differences, 33,* 533–552.

Diener, E., & Crandall, R. (1978). *Ethics in social and behavioural research.* Chicago: The University of Chicago Press.

DiNardo, P.A., Guzy, L.T., Jenkins, J.A., Bak, R.M., Tomasi, S.F., & Copland, M. (1988). Aetiology and maintenance of dog fears. *Behaviour Research and Therapy, 26,* 241–244.

Dobson, K.S., Hollon, S.D., Dimidjian, S., Schmaling, K.B., Kohlenberg, R.J., Gallop, R.J., et al. (2008). Randomised trial of behavioural activation, cognitive therapy, and antidepressant medication in the prevention of relapse and recurrence in major depression. *Journal of Consulting and Clinical Psychology, 76,* 468–477.

Dodson, C.S., & Krueger, L.E. (2006). I misremember it well: Why older adults are unreliable eyewitnesses. *Psychological Bulletin & Review, 13,* 770–775.

Dollard, J., & Miller, N.E. (1950). *Personality and psychotherapy.* New York: McGraw-Hill.

Dunst, C.J., & Kassow, D.Z. (2008). Caregiver sensitivity, contingent social responsiveness, and secure infant attachment. *Journal of Early and Intensive Behavior Intervention, 5,* 40–56.

Durand, V.M., & Barlow, D.H. (2013). *Essentials of abnormal psychology (6th Edn).* Belmont, CA: Wadsworth.

Durkin, K. (1995). *Developmental social psychology: From infancy to old age.* Oxford, UK: Blackwell.

Durrett, M.E., Otaki, M., & Richards, P. (1984). Attachment and the mother's perception of support from the father. *International Journal of Behavioral Development, 7,* 167–176.

Dyer, C. (1995). *Beginning research in psychology.* Oxford, UK: Blackwell.

Eagly, A.H. (1978). Sex differences in influenceability. *Psychological Bulletin, 85,* 86–116.

Eagly, A.H., & Carli, L. (1981). Sex of researchers and sex-typed communications as determinants of sex differences in influenceability: A meta-analysis of social influence studies. *Psychological Bulletin, 90,* 1–20.

Eakin, D.K., Schreiber, T.A., & Sergent-Marshall, S. (2003). Misinformation effects in eyewitness memory: The presence and absence of memory impairment as a function of warning and misinformation accessibility. *Journal of Experimental Psychology: Learning, Memory, and Cognition, 29,* 813–825.

Ein-Dor, T., Mikuliner, M., Doron, G., & Shaver, P.R. (2010). The attachment paradox: How can so many of us (the insecure ones) have no adaptive advantages? *Perspectives on Psychological Science, 5,* 123–141.

Ellis, A. (1962). *Reason and emotion in psychotherapy.* Secaucus, NJ: Prentice-Hall.

Erel, O., Oberman, Y., & Yirmiya, N. (2000). Maternal versus nonmaternal care and seven domains of children's development. *Psychological Bulletin, 126*, 727–747.

Ericsson, K.A. (1988). Analysis of memory performance in terms of memory skill. In R.J. Sternberg (Ed.), *Advances in the psychology of human intelligence, Vol. 4*. Hillsdale, NJ: Lawrence Erlbaum Associates Inc.

Ericsson, K.A., & Chase, W.G. (1982). Exceptional memory. *American Scientist, 70*, 607-615.

Evans, J., Heron, J., Lewis, G., Araya, R, & Wolke, D. (2005). Negative self-schemas and the onset of depression: Longitudinal study. *British Journal of Psychiatry, 186*, 302–307.

Evans, P. (1995). Cognitive-behavioral treatment of Type A behaviour pattern: a critical review. *Psicologia Conductual, 3*, 183–194.

Evans, P. (1998). Stress and coping. In M. Pitts & K. Phillips (Eds), *The psychology of health (2nd Edn)*. London: Routledge.

Evans, P., Clow, A., & Hucklebridge, F. (1997). Stress and the immune system. *The Psychologist, 10*(7), 303–307.

Eysenck, H.J. (1985). *Decline and fall of the Freudian empire*. London: Viking.

Eysenck, M.W. (1990). *Happiness: Facts and myths*. Hove, UK: Psychology Press.

Eysenck, M.W. (1997). *Anxiety and cognition: A unified theory*. Hove, UK: Psychology Press.

Eysenck, M.W. (2011). How to improve your memory. *Psychology Review, 17*, 11–13.

Farrand, P., Hussain, F., & Hennessy, E. (2002). The efficacy of the 'mind map' study technique. *Medical Education, 36*, 426–431.

Favaro, A., Tenconi, E., Ceschin, L., Zanetti, T., Bosello, R., & Santonastaso, P. (2011). In utero exposure to virus infections and the risk of developing anorexia nervosa. *Psychological Medicine, 41*, 2193–2199.

Fearon, R.P., Bakermans-Kraenburg, M., van IJzendoorn, M.H., Lapsley, A.-M., & Roisman, G.I. (2010). The significance of insecure attachment and disorganisation in the development of children's externalising behaviour: A meta-analytic study. *Child Development, 81*, 435–456.

Festinger, L., Riecken, H.W., & Schachter, S. (1956). *When prophecy fails*. Minneapolis: University of Minnesota Press.

Finlay-Jones, R.A., & Brown, G.W. (1981). Types of stressful life events and the onset of anxiety and depressive disorders. *Psychological Medicine, 11*, 803–815.

Fisher, R.P., Geiselman, R.E., & Amador, M. (1990). A field test of the cognitive interview: Enhancing the recollections of actual victims and witnesses of crime. *Journal of Applied Psychology, 74*, 722–727.

Fisher, R.P., Geiselman, R.E., Raymond, D.S., Jurkevich, L.M., & Warhaftig, M.L. (1987). Enhancing enhanced eyewitness memory: Refining the cognitive interview. *Journal of Police Science and Administration, 15*, 291–297.

Flaxman, P.E., & Bond, F.W. (2010). A randomised worksite comparison of acceptance and commitment therapy and stress inoculation training. *Behaviour Research and Therapy, 48*, 816–820.

Foa, E.B., Dancu, C.V., Hembree, E.A., Jaycox, L.H., Meadows, E.A., & Street, G.P. (1999). A comparison of exposure therapy, stress inoculation training, and their combination for reducing posttraumatic stress disorder in female assault victims. *Journal of Consulting and Clinical Psychology, 67*, 194–200.

Fonagy, P., Matthews, R., & Pilling, S. (2005). *The Mental Health Outcome Measurement Initiative: Best practice guidance for local implementation adapted from the Report from the Chair of the Outcomes Reference Group*. National Institute for Mental Health in England.

Forman, R.F., & McCauley, C. (1986). Validity of the positive control polygraph test using the field practice model. *Journal of Applied Psychology, 71*, 691–698.

Fraley, R.C., & Spieker, S.J. (2003). What are the differences between dimensional and categorical models of individual differences in attachment? Reply to Cassidy (2003), Cummings (2003), Sroufe (2003), and Waters and Beauchaine (2003). *Developmental Psychology, 39*, 423–429.

Franzoi, S.L. (1996). *Social psychology*. Madison, WI: Brown & Benchmark.

Freud, A., & Dann, S. (1951). An experiment in group upbringing. *Psychoanalytic Study of the Child, 6*, 127–168.

Freud, S., & Breuer, J. (1895). Studies on hysteria. In J. Strachey (Ed.), *The complete psychological works, Vol. 2*. New York: Norton.

Friedman, M., & Rosenman, R.H. (1959). Association of specific overt behaviour pattern with blood and cardiovascular findings. *Journal of the American Medical Association, 96*, 1286–1296.

Friedman, M., & Rosenman, R.H. (1974). *Type A behaviour and your heart*. New York: Knopf.

Frigerio, A., Ceppi, E., Rusconi, M., Giorda, R., Raggi, M.E., & Fearon, P. (2009). The role played by the interaction between genetic factors and attachment in the stress response. *Journal of Child Psychology and Psychiatry, 50*(12), 1513–1522.

Gaab, J., Blättler, N., Menzi, T., Stoyer, S., & Ehlert, U. (2003). Randomised controlled evaluation of the effects of cognitive-behavioural stress management on cortisol responses to acute stress in healthy subjects. *Psychoneuroendocrinology, 28*, 767–779.

Galbally, M., Lewis, A.J., van IJzendoorn, M., & Permezel, M. (2011). The role of oxytocin in mother–infant relations: A systematic review of human studies. *Harvard Review of Psychiatry, 19*, 1–14.

Ganster, D.C., Fox, M.L., & Dwyer, D.J. (2001). Explaining employees' health care costs: A prospective examination of stressful job demands, personal control, and physiological reactivity. *Journal of Applied Psychology, 86*, 954–964.

Ganster, D.C., Schaubroeck, J., Sime, W.E., & Mayes, B.T. (1991). The nomological validity of the Type A personality among employed adults. *Journal of Applied Psychology, 76*, 143–168.

Gao, Y., & Raine, A. (2010). Successful and unsuccessful psychopaths: A neurobiological model. *Behavioral Science and Law, 28*, 194–210.

Gardikiotis, A. (2011). Minority influence. *Social and Personality Psychology Compass, 5/9*, 679–693.

Gates, G.A., Saegert, J., Wilson, N., Johnson, L., Shepherd, A., & Hearne, E. (1985). Effect of beta blockade on singing performance. *Annals of Otolaryngology, Rhinology and Laryngology, 94*, 570–574.

Gathercole, S., & Baddeley, A.D. (1990). Phonological memory deficits in language-disordered children: Is there a causal connection? *Journal of Memory and Language, 29*, 336–360.

Geddes, J.R., Burgess, S., Hawton, K., Jamison, K., & Goodwin, G.M. (2004). Long-term lithium therapy for bipolar disorder: Systematic review and meta-analysis of randomised controlled trials. *American Journal of Psychiatry, 161*, 217–222.

Geiselman, R.E., & Fisher, R.P. (1997). Ten years of cognitive interviewing. In D.G. Payne & F.G. Conrad (Eds), *Intersections in basic and applied memory research*. Mahwah, NJ: Lawrence Erlbaum Associates Inc.

Geiselman, R.E., Fisher, R.P., MacKinnon, D.P., & Holland, H.L. (1985). Eyewitness memory enhancement in police interview: Cognitive retrieval mnemonics versus hypnosis. *Journal of Applied Psychology, 70*, 401–412.

Geraerts, E., Schooler, J.W., Merckelbach, H., Jelicic, M., Hunter, B.J.A., & Ambadar, Z. (2007). Corroborating continuous and discontinuous memories of childhood sexual abuse. *Psychological Science, 18,* 564–568.

Gevirtz, R. (2000). Physiology of stress. In D. Kenney, J. Carlson, J. Sheppard, & F.J. McGuigan (Eds), *Stress and health: Research and clinical applications.* Sydney: Harwood Academic Publishers.

Gewirtz, J.L. (1991). Identification, attachment, and their developmental sequencing in a conditioning frame. In J.L. Gewirtz (Ed.), *Attachment and dependency* (pp. 213–229). Oxford: Winston.

Gilbert, G.N., & Mulkay, M. (1984). *Opening Pandora's box: A sociological analysis of scientists' discourse.* Cambridge, UK: Cambridge University Press.

Glanzer, M., & Cunitz, A.R. (1966). Two storage mechanisms in free recall. *Journal of Verbal Learning and Verbal Behavior, 5,* 351–360.

Gleitman, H. (1986). *Psychology (2nd Edn).* London: Norton.

Goa, K.L., & Ward, A. (1986). Buspirone: A preliminary review of its pharmacological properties and therapeutic efficacy as an anxiolytic. *Drugs, 32,* 114–129.

Goldfarb, W. (1947). Variations in adolescent adjustment of institutionally reared children. *American Journal of Orthopsychiatry, 17,* 499–557.

Goleman, D. (1991, November 26). Doctors find comfort is a potent medicine. *The New York Times.*

Gottesman, I.L. (1991). *Schizophrenia genesis: The origins of madness.* New York: W.H. Freeman.

Gouin, J.P., Hantsoo, L., & Kiecolt-Glaser, J.K. (2008). Immune dysregulation and chronic stress among older adults: A review. *Neuroimmunomodulation, 15,* 251–259.

Griffiths, M.D. (1993). Fruit machine addiction in adolescence: A case study. *Journal of Gambling Studies, 9*(4), 387–399.

Gross, J., & Hayne, H. (1999). Drawing facilitates children's verbal reports after long delays. *Journal of Experimental Psychology: Applied, 5,* 265–283.

Grossman, K., Grossman, K.E., Spangler, S., Suess, G., & Uzner, L. (1985). Maternal sensitivity and newborn responses as related to quality of attachment in Northern Germany. In J. Bretherton & E. Waters (Eds), Growing points of attachment theory. *Monographs of the Society for Research in Child Development, 50,* No. 209.

Grunhaus, L., Schreiber, S., Dolberg, O.T., Hirshman, S., & Dannon, P.N. (2002). Response to ECT in major depression: Are there differences between unipolar and bipolar depression? *Bipolar Disorders, 4*(Suppl. 1), 91–93.

Guiton, P. (1966). Early experience and sexual object choice in the brown leghorn. *Animal Behaviour, 14,* 534–538.

Haas, K. (1966). Obedience: Submission to destructive orders as related to hostility. *Psychological Reports, 19,* 32–34.

Hahn, S.E., & Smith, C.S. (1999). Daily hassles and chronic stressors: Conceptual and measurement issues. *Stress Medicine, 15,* 89–101.

Haney, C., Banks, W.C., & Zimbardo, P.G. (1973). Interpersonal dynamics in a simulated prison. *International Journal of Criminology and Penology, 1,* 69–97.

Harlow, H.F. (1959). Love in infant monkeys. *Scientific American, 200,* 68–74.

Harlow, H.F., & Harlow, M.K. (1962). Social deprivation in monkeys. *Scientific American, 207*(5), 136–146.

Harris, T. (1997). Life events and health. In A. Baum, S. Newman, J. Weinman, R. West, & C. McManus (Eds), *Cambridge handbook of psychology, health, and medicine.* Cambridge, UK: Cambridge University Press.

Harrison, L.J., & Ungerer, J.A. (2002). Maternal employment and infant–mother attachment security at 12 months postpartum. *Developmental Psychology, 38,* 758–773.

Harrison, V., & Hole, G.J. (2009). Evidence for a contact-based explanation of own-age bias in face recognition. *Psychonomic Bulletin & Review, 16,* 264–269.

Harvey, A.G., Clark, D.M., Ehlers, A., & Rapee, R.M. (2000). Social anxiety and self-impression: Cognitive preparation enhances the beneficial effects of video feedback following a stressful social task. *Behaviour Research and Therapy, 38,* 1183–1192.

Hay, D.F., & Vespo, J.E. (1988). Social learning perspectives on the development of the mother–child relationship. In B. Birns & D.F. Hay (Eds), *The different faces of motherhood.* New York: Plenum Press.

Haynes, S.G., Feinleib, M., & Kannel, W.B. (1980). The relationship of psychosocial factors to coronary heart disease in the Framingham Study: III. Eight-year incidence of coronary heart disease. *American Journal of Epidemiology, 111,* 37–58.

Hazan, C., & Shaver, P.R. (1987). Romantic love conceptualised as an attachment process. *Journal of Personality and Social Psychology, 52,* 511–524.

Heather, N. (1976). *Radical perspectives in psychology.* London: Methuen.

Heine, S.J., Lehman, D.R., Markus, H.R., & Kitayama, S. (1999). Is there a universal need for positive self-regard? *Psychological Review, 106,* 766–794.

Henrich, J., Heine, S.J., & Norenzayan, A. (2010). The weirdest people in the world. *Behavioral and Brain Sciences, 33,* 61–83.

Herman, D., & Green, J. (1991). *Madness: A study guide.* London: BBC Education.

Hirschfeld, R.M. (1999). Efficacy of SSRIs and newer antidepressants in severe depression: Comparison with TCAs. *Journal of Clinical Psychiatry, 60,* 326–335.

Hitch, G., & Baddeley, A.D. (1976). Verbal reasoning and working memory. *Quarterly Journal of Experimental Psychology, 28,* 603–621.

Hodges, B.H., & Geyer, A.L. (2006). A nonconformist account of the Asch experiments: Values, pragmatics, and moral dilemmas. *Personality and Social Psychology Review, 10,* 2–19.

Hodges, J., & Tizard, B. (1989). Social and family relationships of ex-institutional adolescents. *Journal of Child Psychology and Psychiatry, 30,* 77–97.

Hoes, M.J.A.J.M. (1997). Adverse life events and psychosomatic disease. *Current Opinion in Psychiatry, 10,* 462–465.

Hofling, K.C., Brotzman, E., Dalrymple, S., Graves, N., & Pierce, C.M. (1966). An experimental study in the nurse–physician relationship. *Journal of Nervous and Mental Disorders, 143,* 171–180.

Hogg, M., & Vaughan, G. (2005). *Social Psychology (4th Edn).* London: Prentice-Hall.

Høglend, P., Amlo, S., Marble, A., Bøgwald, K.P., Sørbye, O., Sjaastad, M.C., et al. (2006). Analysis of the patient–therapist relationship in dynamic psychotherapy: An experimental study of transference interpretations. *American Journal of Psychiatry, 163,* 1739–1746.

Høglend, P., Bøgwald, K-P., Amlo, S., Heyerdahl, O., Sørbye, O., Marble, A., et al. (2000). Assessment of change in dynamic psychotherapy. *Journal of Psychotherapy Practice and Research, 9,* 190–199.

Høglend, P., Engelstad, V., Sørbye, O., et al. (1994). The role of insight in exploratory psychodynamic psychotherapy. *British Journal of Medical Psychology, 67,* 305–317.

Holland, C.D. (1967). Sources of variance in the experimental investigation of behavioural disturbance. *Dissertation Abstracts International, 29,* 2802A (University Microfilm No. 69–2146).

Hollon, S.D., DeRubeis, R.J., Shelton, R.C., Amsterdam, J.D., Salomon, R.M., O'Reardon, J.P., et al. (2005). Prevention of relapse following cognitive therapy vs. medications in moderate to severe depression. *Archives of General Psychiatry, 62,* 417–422.

Holmes, T.H., & Rahe, R.H. (1967). The social readjustment rating scale. *Journal of Psychosomatic Research, 11,* 213–218.

Howes, C., Matheson, C.C., & Hamilton, C.E. (1994). Maternal, teacher, and child care correlates of children's relationships with peers. *Child Development, 65*(1), 264–273.

Howes, O.D., Bose, S.K., Turkheimer, F., Valli, I., Egerton, A., Valmaggia, L.R., et al. (2011). Dopamine synthesis capacity before onset of psychosis: A prospective [18F]-DOPA PET imaging study. *American Journal of Psychiatry, 168,* 1311–1317.

Hsu, L., & Hsieh, S-I. (2005). Concept maps as an assessment tool in a nursing course. *Journal of Professional Nursing, 21,* 141–149.

Ihlebaek, C., Løve, T., Eilertsen, D.E., & Magnussen, S. (2003). Memory for a staged criminal event witnessed live and on video. *Memory, 11,* 319–327.

Immelmann, K. (1972). Sexual and other long-term aspects of imprinting in birds and other species. In D.S. Lehrmann, R.A. Hinde, & E. Shaw (Eds), *Advances in the study of behaviour, Vol. 4.* New York: Academic Press.

Insko, C.A., Smith, R.H., Alicke, M.D., Wade, J., & Taylor, S. (1985). Conformity and group size: The concern with being right and the concern with being liked. *Personality and Social Psychology Bulletin, 11,* 41–50.

Ismail, M.N., Ngah, N.A., & Umar, I.N. (2010). The effects of mind mapping with cooperative learning on programming performance, problem solving skill and metacognitive knowledge among computer science students. *Journal of Educational Computing Research, 42,* 35–61.

Jackson, S., & Goldschmied, E. (2004). *People under three: Young children in day care (2nd Edn).* London: Taylor & Francis.

Jacobs, J. (1887). Experiments on 'prehension'. *Mind, 12,* 75–79.

Jacobs, S.R., & Dodd, D.K. (2003). Student burnout as a function of personality, social support, and workload. *Journal of College Student Development, 44,* 291–303.

Jacobson, J.L., & Wille, D.E. (1986). The influence of attachment pattern on developmental changes in peer interaction from the toddler to the preschool period. *Child Development, 57,* 338–347.

Jacoby, L.L., Bishara, A.J., Hessels, S., & Toth, J.P. (2005). Aging, subjective experience, and cognitive control: Dramatic false remembering by older adults. *Journal of Experimental Psychology: General, 134,* 131–148.

Jahoda, M. (1958). *Current concepts of positive mental health.* New York: Basic Books.

Jain, S., Mills, P.J., Von Kanel, R., Hong, S.Z., & Dimsdale, J.E. (2007). Effects of perceived stress and uplifts on inflammation and coagulability. *Psychophysiology, 44,* 154–160.

Jamal, M. (1990). Relationship of job stress and Type-A behaviour to employees' job satisfaction, organisational commitment, psychosomatic health problems, and turnover motivation. *Human Relations, 43,* 727–738.

James, O. (1997). Serotonin: A chemical feel-good factor. *Psychology Review, 4,* 34.

Janis, I. (1972). *Victims of groupthink: A psychological study of foreign-policy decisions and fiascos.* Boston: Houghton-Mifflin.

Johansson, G., Aronson, G., & Lindstroem, B.O. (1978). Social psychological and neuroendocrine stress reactions in highly mechanised work. *Ergonomics, 21,* 583–599.

Johnson, J.G., & Sherman, M.F. (1997). Daily hassles mediate the relationship between major life events and psychiatric symptomatology: Longitudinal findings from an adolescent sample. *Journal of Social and Clinical Psychology, 16,* 389–404.

Johnson, M.K., Hastroudi, S., & Lindsay, D.S. (1993). Source monitoring. *Psychological Bulletin, 114,* 3–28.

Kagan, J. (1984). *The nature of the child.* New York: Basic Books.

Kagan, J., Kearsley, R.B., & Zelazo, P.R. (1980). *Infancy: Its place in human development.* Cambridge, MA: Harvard University Press.

Kahneman, D., & Tversky, A. (1979). Intuitive prediction: Biases and corrective procedures. *TIMS Studies in Management Science, 12,* 313–327.

Kalakoski, V., & Saariluoma, P. (2001). Taxi drivers' exceptional memory of street names. *Memory & Cognition, 29,* 634–638.

Karasek, R.A. (1979). Job demands, job decision latitude and mental strain: Implications for job design. *Administrative Science Quarterly, 24,* 285–308.

Karlén, J., Ludvigsson, J., Frostell, A., Theodorsson, E., & Faresjö, T. (2011). Cortisol in hair measured in young adults – A biomarker of major life stressors? *BMC Clinical Pathology, 11*/1.

Keast, A., Brewer, N., & Wells, G.L. (2007). Children's metacognitive judgments in an eyewitness identification task. *Journal of Experimental Child Psychology, 97*(4), 286–314.

Kelman, H.C. (1958). Compliance, identification and internalisation: Three processes of attitude change. *Journal of Conflict Resolution, 2,* 51–60.

Kelman, H.C. (1972). The rights of the subject in social research: An analysis in terms of relative power and legitimacy. *American Psychologist, 27,* 989–1016.

Kelman, H., & Lawrence, L. (1972). Assignment of responsibility in the case of Lt. Calley: Preliminary report on a national survey. *Journal of Social Issues, 28,* 177–212.

Kendall, P.X., & Hammen, C. (1998). *Abnormal psychology (2nd Edn).* Boston, MA: Houghton Mifflin.

Kendler, K.S., Karkowski, L., & Prescott, C.A. (1998). Stressful life events and major depression: Risk period, long-term contextual threat and diagnostic specificity. *Journal of Nervous and Mental Disease, 186,* 661–669.

Kendler, K.S., Kuhn, J., & Prescott, C.A. (2004). The interrelationship of neuroticism, sex, and stressful life events in the prediction of episodes of major depression. *American Journal of Psychiatry, 161,* 631–636.

Kendler, K.S., Neale, M.C., Prescott, C.A., Kessler, R.C., Heath, A.C., Corey, L.A., et al. (1996). Childhood parental loss and alcoholism in women: A causal analysis using a twin-family design. *Psychological Medicine, 26,* 79–95.

Kenny, D.T. (2006). Music performance anxiety: Origins, phenomenology, assessment and treatment. context: *Journal of Music Research, 5,* 1–10.

Keogh, E., Bond, F.W., & Flaxman, P.E. (2006). Improving academic performance and mental health through a stress management intervention: Outcomes and mediators of change. *Behaviour Research and Therapy, 44,* 339–357.

Keppel, G., & Underwood, B.J. (1962). Proactive inhibition in short-term retention of single items. *Journal of Verbal Learning and Verbal Behavior, 1,* 153–161.

Khan, F., & Patel, P. (1996). A study of the impact of hassles versus life events on health outcome measures in students and the general population. *Proceedings of the British Psychological Society, 4*(1), 32.

Khoshaba, D.M., & Maddi, S.R. (2001). *HardiTraining.* Newport Beach, CA: Hardiness Institute.

Kiecolt-Glaser, J.K., Garner, W., Speicher, C.E., Penn, G.M., Holliday, J., & Glaser, R. (1984). Psychosocial modifiers of immunocompetence in medical students. *Psychosomatic Medicine, 46,* 7–14.

Kiecolt-Glaser, J.K., Marucha, P.T., Malarkey, W.B., Mercado, A.M., & Glaser, R. (1995). Slowing of wound healing by psychological stress. *Lancet, 346,* 1194–1196.

Kim, H., & Markus, H.R. (1999). Uniqueness or deviance, harmony or conformity: A cultural analysis. *Journal of Personality and Social Psychology, 77*, 785–800.

Kivlighan, D.M., Multon, K.D., & Patton, M.J. (2000). Insight and symptom reduction in time-limited psychoanalytic counselling. *Journal of Counselling Psychology, 47*, 50–58.

Klag, S., & Bradley, G. (2004). The role of hardiness in stress and illness: An exploration of the effect of negative affectivity and gender. *British Journal of Health Psychology, 9*, 137–161.

Klauer, K.C., & Zhao, Z. (2004). Double dissociations in visual and spatial short-term memory. *Journal of Experimental Psychology: General, 133*, 355–381.

Klaus, M.H., & Kennell, J.H. (1976). *Parent–infant bonding.* St Louis: Mosby.

Kobasa, S.C. (1979). Stressful events, personality, and health: An inquiry into hardiness. *Journal of Personality and Social Psychology, 37*, 1–11.

Kobasa, S.C., Maddi, S.R., Puccetti, M.C., & Zola, M.A. (1985). Effectiveness of hardiness, exercise and social support as resources against illness. *Journal of Psychosomatic Research, 29*, 525–533.

Köhnken, G., Milne, R., Memon, A., & Bull, R. (1999). The cognitive interview: A meta-analysis. *Psychology of Crime Law, 5*, 3–27.

Koluchová, J. (1976). The further development of twins after severe and prolonged deprivation: A second report. *Journal of Child Psychology and Psychiatry, 17*, 181–188.

Koluchová, J. (1991). Severely deprived twins after twenty-two years' observation. *Studia Psychologica, 33*, 23–28.

Konkle, T., Brady, T.F., Alvarez, G.A., & Oliva, A. (2010). Scene memory is more detailed than you think: The role of categories in visual long-term memory. *Psychological Science, 21*, 1551–1556.

Korotkov, D., Perunovic, M., Claybourn, M., Fraser, I., Houihan, M., Macdonald, M., et al. (2011). The Type B behaviour pattern as a moderating variable of the relationship between stressor chronicity and health behaviour. *Journal of Health Psychology, 16*, 397–409.

Krackow, A., & Blass, T. (1995). When nurses obey or defy inappropriate physician orders: Attributional differences. *Journal of Social Behavior and Personality, 10*, 585–594.

Kruglanski, A.W., Chen, X., Dechesne, M., Fishman, S., & Orehek, C. (2009). Fully committed: Suicide bombers' motivation and the quest for personal significance. *Political Psychology, 30*, 331–357.

Kruglanski, A.W., & Fishman, S. (2006). Terrorism between "syndrome" and "tool". *Current Directions in Psychological Science, 15*, 45–48.

Kumsta, R., Kreppner, J., Rutter, M., Beckett, C., Castle, J., Stevens, S., et al. (2010). Deprivation-specific psychological patterns. *Monographs of the Society for Research in Child Development, 75*, 48–78.

Kurosawa, K. (1993). The effects of self-consciousness and self-esteem on conformity to a majority. *Japanese Journal of Psychology, 63*, 379–387.

Kutakoff, L., Levin, J., & Arluke, A. (1987). Are the times changing? An analysis of gender differences in sexual graffiti. *Sex Roles, 16*, 1–7.

Larsen, J.D., Baddeley, A.D., & Andrade, J. (2000). Phonological similarity and the irrelevant speech effect: Implications for models of short-term memory. *Memory, 8*, 145–157.

Lau, J., Antman, E.M., Jimenez-Silva, J., Kuperlnik, B., Mostpeller, F., & Chalmers, T.C. (1992). Cumulative meta-analysis of therapeutic trials for myocardial infarction. *New England Journal of Medicine, 327*, 248–254.

Lau, R., & Russell, D. (1980). Attributions in the sports pages. *Journal of Personality and Social Psychology, 39*, 29–38.

Lawrie, S.M., & Abukmeil, S.S. (1998). Brain abnormality in schizophrenia. A systematic and quantitative review of volumetric magnetic resonance imaging studies. *British Journal of Psychiatry, 172*, 110–120.

Leach, P., Barnes, J., Malmberg, L.E., Sylva, K., Stein, A., and the FCCC team. (2008). The quality of different types of child care at 10 and 18 months: A comparison between types and factors related to quality. *Early Child Development and Care, 2*, 177–209.

Lee, C., Gavriel, H., Drummon, P., Richards, J., & Greenwald, R. (2002). Treatment of PTSD: Stress inoculation training with prolonged exposure compared to EMDR. *Journal of Clinical Psychology, 58*, 1071–1089.

Lee, H. (1997). *Virginia Woolf.* London: Vintage.

Leichsenring, F. (2001). Comparative effects of short-term psychodynamic psychotherapy and cognitive-behavioural therapy in depression: A meta-analytic approach. *Clinical Psychology Review, 21*, 40–419.

Lesar, T.S., Briceland, L., & Stein, D.S. (1997). Factors related to errors in medication prescribing. *Journal of the American Medical Association, 277*, 312–317.

Levin, R.B., & Gross, A.M. (1985). The role of relaxation in systematic desensitization. *Behavior Research and Therapies, 23*(2), 187–196.

Liebowitz, M.R., Heimberg, R.G., Schneier, F.R., Hope, D.A., Davis, S., Holt, C.S. et al. (1999). Cognitive-behavioural group therapy versus phenelzine in social phobia: Long-term outcomes. *Depression and Anxiety, 10*, 89–98.

Lief, H., & Fetkewicz, J. (1995). Retractors of false memories: The evolution of pseudo-memories. *The Journal of Psychiatry & Law, 23*, 411–436.

Lindsay, D.S., Allen, B.P., Chan, J.C.K., & Dahl, L.C. (2004). Eyewitness suggestibility and source similarity: Intrusions of details from one event into memory reports of another event. *Journal of Memory and Language, 50*, 96–111.

Lippa, R.A., Collaer, M.L., & Peters, M. (2010). Sex differences in mental rotation and line angle judgments are positively associated with gender equality and economic development across 53 nations. *Archives of Sexual Behavior, 39*, 990–997.

Littman, A.B., Fava, M., McKool, K., Lamon-Fava, S., & Pegg, E. (1993). Buspirone therapy for Type A behavior, hostility, and perceived stress in cardiac patients. *Psychotherapy and Psychosomatics, 59*(2), 107–110.

Locke, E.A. (1968). Toward a theory of task motivation and incentives. *Organizational Behavior and Human Performance, 3*, 157–189.

Lockwood, A.H. (1989). Medical problems of musicians. *New England Journal of Medicine, 320*, 221–227.

Loftus, E. (1979). *Eyewitness testimony.* Cambridge, MA: Harvard University Press.

Loftus, E.F. (1992). When a lie becomes memory's truth: Memory distortion after exposure misinformation. *Current Directions in Psychological Science, 1*, 121–123.

Loftus, E.F. (2004). Memories of things unseen. *Current Directions in Psychological Science, 13*, 145–147.

Loftus, E.F., Loftus, G.R., & Messo, J. (1987). Some facts about "weapons focus". *Law and Human Behavior, 11*, 55–62.

Loftus, E.F., & Palmer, J.C. (1974). Reconstruction of automobile destruction: An example of the interaction between language and memory. *Journal of Verbal Learning and Verbal Behavior, 13*, 585–589.

Logie, R.H., Baddeley, A.D., Mane, A., Donchin, E., & Sheptak, R. (1989). Working memory and the analysis of a complex skill by secondary task methodology. *Acta Psychologica, 71*, 53–87.

London, P., & Lim, H. (1964). Yielding reason to social pressure: Task complexity and expectation in conformity. *Journal of Personality, 33*, 75–98.

Love, J.M., Harrison, L., Sagi-Schwartz, A., van IJzendoorn, M.H., Ungerer, J.A., Raikes, H., et al. (2003). Child care quality matters: How conclusions may vary with context. *Child Development, 74*, 1021–1033.

Lozoff, B. (1983). Birth and "bonding" in non-industrial societies. *Developmental Medicine and Child Neurology, 25*, 595–600.

Lucas, T., Alexander, S., Firestone, I.J., & Baltes, B.B. (2006). Self-efficacy and independence from social influence: Discovery of an efficacy–difficulty effect. *Social Influence, 1*, 58–80.

Lucassen, N., Tharner, A., van IJzendoorn, M.H., Bakermans-Kranenburg, M.J., Volling, B.L., Verhulst, F.C., et al. (2011). The association between paternal sensitivity and infant–father attachment security: A meta-analysis of three decades of research. *Journal of Family Psychology, 25*, 986–992.

Maccoby, E.E. (1980). *Social development: Psychological growth and the parent–child relationship.* San Diego, CA: Harcourt Brace Jovanovich.

MacLeod, A. (1998). Therapeutic interventions. In M.W. Eysenck (Ed.), *Psychology: An integrated approach.* Harlow, UK: Addison Wesley Longman.

Maddi, S.R. (2007). Relevance of hardiness assessment and training to the military context. *Military Psychology, 19*, 61–70.

Maher, B.A. (1966). *Principles of psychopathology: An experimental approach.* New York: McGraw-Hill.

Main, M., & Solomon, J. (1986). Discovery of a disorganised disoriented attachment pattern. In T.B. Brazelton & M.W. Yogman (Eds), *Affective development in infancy.* Norwood, NJ: Ablex.

Main, M., & Weston, D.R. (1981). The quality of the toddler's relationship to mother and father: Related to conflict behaviour and the readiness to establish new relationships. *Child Development, 52*, 932–940.

Mandler, G. (1967). Organisation and memory. In K.W. Spence & J.T. Spence (Eds), *The psychology of learning and motivation: Advances in research and theory, Vol. 1.* London: Academic Press.

Mantell, D.M. (1974). *True Americanism: Green Berets and war resisters.* New York: Teachers College Press.

Marcus, B., & Schutz, A. (2005). Who are the people reluctant to participate in research? Personality correlates of four different types of non-response as inferred from self- and observer ratings. *Journal of Personality, 73*, 959–984.

Marcus-Newhall, A., Pedersen, W.C., Carlson, M., & Miller, N. (2000). Displaced aggression is alive and well: A meta-analytic review. *Journal of Personality and Social Psychology, 78*, 670–689.

Marmot, M.G., Bosma, H., Hemingway, H., Brunner, E., & Stansfeld, S. (1997). Contribution of job control and other risk factors to social variations in coronary heart disease incidence. *Lancet, 350*, 235–239.

Marsh, P., Fox, K., Carnibella, G., McCann, J., & Marsh, J. (1996). *Football violence in Europe.* The Amsterdam Group.

Marshall, G.D. (2011). The adverse effects of psychological stress on immunoregulatory balance: Applications to human inflammatory diseases. *Immunology and Allergy Clinics of North America, 31*, 133–137.

Marshall, N.L. (2004). The quality of early child care and children's development. *Current Directions in Psychological Science, 13*, 165–168.

Martin, R.A. (1989). Techniques for data acquisition and analysis in field investigations of stress. In R.W.J. Neufeld (Ed.), *Advances in the investigation of psychological stress.* New York: Wiley.

Martin, R., Hewstone, M., & Martin, P.Y. (2003). Resistance to persuasive messages as a function of majority and minority status. *Journal of Experimental Social Psychology, 39*, 585–593.

Martin, R., Martin, P.Y., Smith, J.R., & Hewstone, M. (2007). Majority versus minority influence and prediction of behavioural intentions and behaviour. *Journal of Experimental Social Psychology, 43*, 763–771.

Marucha, P.T., Kiecolt-Glaser, J.K., & Favagehi, M. (1998). Mucosal wound healing is impaired by examination stress. *Psychosomatic Medicine, 60*, 362–365.

Maslach, C., Santee, R.T., & Wade, C. (1987). Individuation, gender role, and dissent: Personality mediators of situational forces. *Journal of Personality and Social Psychology, 53*, 1088–1093.

Maslow, A.H. (1954). *Motivation and personality.* New York: Harper.

Massey, E.K., Garnefski, N., Gebhardt, W.A., & van der Leeden, R. (2009). Daily frustration, cognitive coping and coping efficacy in adolescent headache: A daily diary study. *Headache, 49*, 1198–1205.

Matt, G.E., & Navarro, A.M. (1997). What meta-analyses have and have not taught us about psychotherapy effects: A review and future directions. *Clinical Psychology Review, 17*, 1–32.

Matthews, K.A. (1988). Coronary heart disease and Type A behaviour: Update on an alternative to the Booth-Kewley and Friedman (1987). Quantitative review. *Psychological Bulletin, 104*, 373–380.

Matthews, K.A., Glass, D.C., Rosenman, R.H., & Bortner, R.W. (1977). Competitive drive, Pattern A, and coronary heart disease: A further analysis of some data from the Western Collaborative Group. *Journal of Chronic Diseases, 30*, 489–498.

Mayall, B., & Petrie, P. (1983). *Childminding and day nurseries: What kind of care?* London: Heinemann Educational Books.

McAndrew, F.T., Akande, A., Turner, S., & Sharma, Y. (1998). A cross-cultural ranking of stressful life events in Germany, India, South Africa, and the United States. *Journal of Cross-Cultural Psychology, 29*, 717–727.

McCourt, K., Bouchard, T.J., Lykken, D.T., Tellegen, A., & Keyes, M. (1999). Authoritarianism revisited: Genetic and environmental influences examined in twins reared apart and together. *Personality and Individual Differences, 27*, 985–1014.

McGlynn, F.D., Mealiea, W.L., & Landau, D.L (1981). The current status of systematic desensitisation. *Clinical Psychology Review, 1*, 149–179.

McGlynn, F.D., Smitherman, T.A., & Gothard, K.D. (2004). Comment on the status of systematic desensitisation. *Behavior Modification, 28*, 194–205.

McGuffin, P., Katz, R., Watkins, S., & Rutherford, J. (1996). A hospital-based twin register of the heritability of DSM-IV unipolar depression. *Archives of General Psychiatry, 53*, 129–136.

McNamara, P., Belsky, J., & Fearon, P. (2003). Infant sleep disorders and attachment: Sleep problems in infants with insecure-resistant versus insecure-avoidant attachments to mother. *Sleep and Hypnosis, 5*, 7–16.

Meeus, W.H.J., & Raaijmakers, Q.A.W. (1995). Obedience in modern society: The Utrecht studies. *Journal of Social Issues, 51*(3), 155–175.

Meichenbaum, D. (1977). *Cognitive-behaviour modification: An integrative approach.* New York: Plenum Press.

Meichenbaum, D. (1985). *Stress inoculation training.* New York: Pergamon.

Meichenbaum, D.H., & Deffenbacher, J.L. (1985). Stress inoculation training. *The Counseling Psychologist, 16*, 69–90.

Menges, R.J. (1973). Openness and honesty versus coercion and deception in psychological research. *American Psychologist, 28*, 1030–1034.

Menzies, R.G., & Clarke, J.C. (1993). The aetiology of childhood water phobia. *Behaviour Research and Therapy, 31*, 499–501.

Metra, M., Nodari, S., D'Aloia, A., Bontempi, L., Boldi, E., & Cas, L.D. (2000). A rationale for the use of [beta]-blockers as standard treatment for heart failure. *American Heart Journal, 139,* 511–521.

Milgram, S. (1963). Behavioural study of obedience. *Journal of Abnormal and Social Psychology, 67,* 371–378.

Milgram, S. (1974). *Obedience to authority: An experimental view.* New York: Harper & Row.

Miller, F.D. (1975). *An experimental study of obedience to authority of varying legitimacy.* Unpublished doctoral dissertation, Harvard University.

Miller, G.A. (1956). The magical number seven, plus or minus two: Some limits on our capacity for processing information. *Psychological Review, 63,* 81–97.

Miller, T.Q., Turner, C.W., Tindale, R.S., Posavac, E.J., & Dugoni, B.L. (1991). Reasons for the trend toward null findings in research on Type A behaviour. *Psychological Bulletin, 110,* 469–485.

Milne, R., & Bull, R. (2002). Back to basics: A componential analysis of the original cognitive interview mnemonics with three age groups. *Applied Cognitive Psychology, 16,* 743–753.

Mineka, S., Davidson, M., Cook, M., & Kuir, R. (1984). Observational conditioning of snake fear in rhesus monkeys. *Journal of Abnormal Psychology, 93,* 355–372.

Mitte, K. (2005). A meta-analysis of the efficacy of psycho- and pharmacotherapy in panic disorder with and without agoraphobia. *Journal of Affective Disorders, 88,* 27–45.

Miyake, A., Friedman, N.P., Emerson, M.J., Witzki, A.H., Howerter, A., & Wager, T. (2000). The unity and diversity of executive functions and their contributions to complex "frontal lobe" tasks: A latent variable analysis. *Cognitive Psychology, 41,* 49–100.

Molina, P.E., Happel, K.I., Zhang, P., Kolls, J.K., & Nelson, S. (2006). Focus on: Alcohol and the immune system. *Alcohol Research & Health, 33,* 97–108.

Mols, F., & Denollet, J. (2010). Type D personality in the general population: A systematic review of health status, mechanisms of disease, and work-related problems. *Health and Quality of Life Outcomes, 8,* Article no. 9.

Moniz, E. (1937). Prefrontal leucotomy in the treatment of mental disorders. *American Journal of Psychiatry, 93,* 1379–1385.

Monroney, L. (2008). Translating from a cult back into society. brahmakumaris.info/forum/viewtopic.php?f=11&t=2737.

Morgan, H., & Raffle, C. (1999). Does reducing safety behaviours improve treatment response in patients with social phobia? *Australian and New Zealand Journal of Psychiatry, 33,* 503–510.

Mormede, P., Foury, A., Barat, P., Corcuff, J.-B., Terenina, E., Marissal-Arvy, N., et al. (2011). Molecular genetics of hypothalamic-pituitary-adrenal axis activity and function. *Annals of the New York Academy of Sciences, 1220,* 127–136.

Morris, P.E. (1979). Strategies for learning and recall. In M.M. Gruneberg & P.E. Morris (Eds), *Applied problems in memory.* London: Academic Press.

Morris, P.E., & Reid, R.L. (1970). The repeated use of mnemonic imagery. *Psychonomic Science, 20,* 337–338.

Moscovici, S. (1980). Toward a theory of conversion behaviour. In L. Berkowitz (Ed.), *Advances in experimental social psychology, Vol. 13.* New York: Academic Press.

Moscovici, S. (1985). Social influence and conformity. In G. Lindzey & E. Aronson (Eds), *Handbook of social psychology (3rd Edn).* New York: Random House.

Moscovici, S., Lage, E., & Naffrenchoux, M. (1969). Influence of a consistent minority on the responses of a majority in a colour perception task. *Sociometry, 32,* 365–380.

Moskovitz, S. (1983). *Love despite hate: Child survivors of the Holocaust and their adult lives.* New York: Schocken.

Moss, P., & Melhuish, E.C. (1991). *Future Directions for daycare policy and research.* In P. Moss & E.C. Melhuish (Eds), *Current issues in day care for young children* (pp. 131–136). London: HMSO.

Mowrer, O.H. (1947). On the dual nature of learning: A reinterpretation of "conditioning" and "problem-solving". *Harvard Educational Review, 17,* 102–148.

Mueller, S.T., Seymour, T.L., Kieras, D.E., & Meyer, D.E. (2003). Theoretical implications of articulatory duration, phonological similarity, and phonological complexity in verbal working memory. *Journal of Experimental Psychology: Learning, Memory & Cognition, 29,* 1353–1380.

Mueller-Johnson, K., & Ceci, S.J. (2004). Memory and suggestibility in older adults: Live event participation and repeated interview. *Applied Cognitive Psychology, 18,* 1109–1127.

Myrtek, M. (2001). Meta-analyses of prospective studies on coronary heart disease, Type A personality, and hostility. *International Journal of Cardiology, 79,* 245–251.

Nemeth, C., Swedlund, M., & Kanki, G. (1974). Patterning of the minority's responses and their influence on the majority. *European Journal of Social Psychology, 4,* 53–64.

Nesbit, J.C., & Adescope, O.O. (2006). Learning with concept and knowledge maps: A meta-analysis. *Review of Educational Research, 76,* 413–448.

Newmark, C.S., Frerking, R.A., Cook, L., & Newmark, L. (1973). Endorsement of Ellis' irrational beliefs as a function of psychopathology. *Journal of Clinical Psychology, 29,* 300–302.

NICHD Early Child Care Research Network (1997). The effects of infant child care on infant–mother attachment security: Results of the NICHD study of early child care. *Child Development, 68*(5), 860–879.

NICHD Early Child Care Research Network (2002). Child-care structure → process → outcome: Direct and indirect effects of child-care quality on young children's development. *Psychological Science, 13,* 199–206.

NICHD Early Child Care Research Network (2003a). Does quality of child care affect child outcomes at age 4? *Developmental Psychology, 39,* 451–469.

NICHD Early Child Care Research Network (2003b). Does amount of time spent in child care predict socioemotional adjustment during the transition to kindergarten? *Child Development, 74,* 976–1005.

NICHD Early Child Care Research Network (2006). Infant–mother attachment: Risk and protection in relation to changing maternal caregiving quality over time. *Developmental Psychology, 42,* 38–58.

Nisbett, R.E., & Wilson, T.D. (1977). Telling more than we can know: Verbal reports on mental processes. *Psychological Review, 84,* 231–259.

Nordquist, N., & Oreland, L. (2010). Serotonin, genetic variability, behaviour and psychiatric disorders—A review. *Upsala Journal of Medical Sciences, 115,* 2–10.

O'Connor, D.B., Jones, F., Conner, M., McMillan, B., & Ferguson, E. (2008). Effects of daily hassles and eating style on eating behaviour. *Health Psychology, 27,* S20–S31.

O'Connor, T.G., Caspi, A., De Fries, J.C., & Plomin, R. (2000). Are associations between parental divorce and children's adjustment genetically mediated? An adoption study. *Developmental Psychology, 36,* 429–437.

O'Connor, T.G., & Croft, C.M. (2001). A twin study of attachment in preschool children. *Child Development, 72,* 1501–1511.

Oliner, S.P., & Oliner, P.M. (1988). *The altruistic personality.* New York: Free Press.

Orne, M.T. (1962). On the social psychology of the psychological experiment: With particular reference to demand characteristics and their implications. *American Psychologist, 17*, 776–783.

Orne, M.T., & Holland, C.C. (1968). On the ecological validity of laboratory deceptions. *International Journal of Psychiatry, 6*(4), 282–293.

Oyserman, D., Coon, H.M., & Kemmelmeier, M. (2002). Rethinking individualism and collectivism: Evaluation of theoretical assumptions and meta-analyses. *Psychological Bulletin, 128*, 3–72.

Papagno, C., Valentine, T., & Baddeley, A.D. (1991). Phonological short-term memory and foreign-language learning. *Journal of Memory & Language, 30*, 331–347.

Pagnin, D., de Queiroz, V., Pini, S., & Cassano, G.B. (2004). Efficacy of ECT in depression: A meta-analytic review. *Journal of ECT, 20*, 13–20.

Parke, R.D. (1981). *Fathers.* Cambridge, MA: Harvard University Press.

Pedersen, A., Zachariae, R., & Bovbjerg, D.H. (2010). Influence of psychological stress on upper respiratory infection—A meta-analysis of prospective studies. *Psychosomatic Medicine, 72*, 823–832.

Pennebaker, J.W., Hendler, C.S., Durrett, M.E., & Richards, P. (1981). Social factors influencing absenteeism due to illness in nursery school children. *Child Development, 52*, 692–700.

Pepler, D.J., & Craig, W.M. (1995). A peek behind the fence: Naturalistic observations of aggressive children with remote audiovisual recording. *Developmental Psychology, 31*, 548–553.

Perfect, T.J., Wagstaff, G.F., Morre, D., Andrews, B., Cleveland, V., Newcombe, S., et al. (2008). How can we help witnesses to remember more? It's an (eyes) open and shut case. *Law and Human Behavior, 32*, 314–324.

Perrin, S., & Spencer, C. (1980). The Asch effect: A child of its time. *Bulletin of the British Psychological Society, 33*, 405–406.

Peterson, C., Seligman, M.E., & Valliant, G.E. (1988). Pessimistic explanatory style is a risk factor for physical illness: A thirty-five year longitudinal study. *Journal of Personality and Social Psychology, 55*, 23–27.

Peterson, L.R., & Peterson, M.J. (1959). Short-term retention of individual verbal items. *Journal of Experimental Psychology, 58*, 193–198.

Petrides, G., Fink, M., Husain, M.M., et al. (2001). ECT remission rates in psychotic versus nonpsychotic depressed patients: A report from CORE. *Journal of ECT, 17*, 244–253.

Pickel, K.L. (1999). The influence of context on the "weapon focus" effect. *Law and Human Behavior, 23*, 299–311.

Posada, G., Gao, Y., Fang, W., Posada, R., Tascon, M., Scholmerich, A., et al. (1995). The secure-based phenomenon across cultures: Children's behaviour, mothers' preferences, and experts' concepts. *Monographs of the Society for Research in Child Development, 60*, 27–48.

Posner, M.I. (1969). Abstraction and the process of recognition. In J.T. Spence & G.H. Bower (Eds), *The psychology of learning and motivation: Advances in learning and motivation, Vol. 3.* New York: Academic Press.

Pozzulo, J.D., & Lindsay, R.C.L. (1998). Identification accuracy of children versus adults: A meta-analysis. *Law and Human Behavior, 22*, 549–570.

Rahe, R.H., & Arthur, R.J. (1977). Life change patterns surrounding illness experience. In A. Monat & R.S. Lazarus (Eds), *Stress and coping.* New York: Columbia University Press.

Rahe, R.H., Mahan, J., & Arthur, R. (1970). Prediction of near-future health-change from subjects' preceding life changes. *Journal of Psychosomatic Research, 14*, 401–406.

Rank, S.G., & Jacobsen, C.K. (1977). Hospital nurses' compliance with medication overdose orders: A failure to replicate. *Journal of Health and Social Behaviour, 18*, 188–193.

Reicher, S., & Haslam, S.A. (2006). Rethinking the psychology of tyranny: The BBC prison study. *British Journal of Social Psychology, 45*, 1–40.

Rickels, K., DeMartinis, N., & Aufdrembrinke, B. (2000). A double-blind, placebo-controlled trial of abecarnil and diazepam in the treatment of patients with generalised anxiety disorder. *Journal of Clinical Psychopharmacology, 20*, 12–18.

Ridley, S.M., McWilliam, R.A., & Oates, C.S. (2000). Observed engagement as an indicator of child care programme quality. *Early Education and Development, 11*, 133–146.

Robbins, T.W., Anderson, E.J., Barker, D.R., Bradley, A.C., Fearnyhough, C., Henson, R., et al. (1996). Working memory in chess. *Memory & Cognition, 24*, 83–93.

Robertson, J., & Bowlby, J. (1952). Responses of young children to separation from their mothers. *Courier Centre International de l'Enfance, 2*, 131–142.

Robertson, J., & Robertson, J. (1971). Young children in brief separation. *Psychoanalytic Study of the Child, 26*, 264–315.

Robles, T.F., Glaser, R., & Kiecolt-Glaser, J.K. (2005). Out of balance: A new look at chronic stress, depression, and immunity. *Current Directions in Psychological Science, 14*, 111–115.

Roediger, H.L. III, & Karpicke, J.D. (2006). Test-enhanced learning: Taking memory tests improves long-term retention. *Psychological Science, 17*, 249–255.

Rogers, C.R. (1959). A theory of therapy, personality, and interpersonal relationships as developed in the client-centred framework. In S. Koch (Ed.), *Psychology: A study of a science.* New York: McGraw-Hill.

Roggman, L.A., Langlois, J.H., Hubbs-Tait, L., & Rieser-Danner, L.A. (1994). Infant daycare, attachment and the "file-drawer" problem. *Child Development, 65*, 1429–1443.

Rönnlund, M., Nyberg, L., Backman, L., & Nilsson, L.G. (2005). Stability, growth, and decline in adult life span development of declarative memory: Cross-sectional and longitudinal data from a population-based study. *Psychology and Aging, 20*, 3–18.

Rosen, G.M., Glasgow, R.E., & Barrera, M., Jr. (1976). A controlled study to assess the clinical efficacy of totally self-administered systematic desensitization. *Journal of Consulting and Clinical Psychology, 44*, 208–217.

Rosenberg, M.J. (1965). When dissonance fails: On eliminating evaluation apprehension from attitude measurement. *Journal of Personality and Social Psychology, 1*, 28–42.

Rosenhan, D. (1969). Some origins of concern for others. In P. Mussen, J. Langer, & M. Covington (Eds), *Trends and issues in developmental psychology.* New York: Holt, Rinehart & Winston.

Rosenhan, D.L., & Seligman, M.E.P. (1989). *Abnormal psychology (2nd Edn).* New York: Norton.

Rosenthal, R. (1966). *Experimenter effects in behavioural research.* New York: Appleton-Century-Crofts.

Rosenthal, R. (2003). Covert communication in laboratories, classrooms, and the truly real world. *Current Directions in Psychological Science, 12*, 151–154.

Rosenthal, R., & Jacobson, L. (1968). *Pygmalion in the classroom.* New York: Holt, Rinehart & Winston.

Ross, L., & Nisbett, R.E. (1991). *The person and the situation: Perspectives of social psychology.* Philadelphia: Temple University Press.

Roth, A., & Fonagy, P. (2005). *What works for whom?: A critical review of psychotherapy research (2nd Edn).* New York: Guilford Press.

Rothbaum, F., Kakinuma, M., Nagaoka, R., & Azuma, H. (2007). Attachment and amae: Parent–child closeness in the United

States and Japan. *Journal of Cross-Cultural Psychology, 38,* 465–486.

Rothbaum, F., Pott, M., Azuma, H., & Weisz, J. (2000). The development of close relationships in Japan and the United States: Paths of symbiotic harmony and generative tension. *Child Development, 71,* 1121–1142.

Rotter, J.B. (1966). Generalised expectancies for internal versus external control of reinforcement. *Psychological Monographs, 80,* whole no. 609.

Roy, D.F. (1991). Improving recall by eyewitnesses through the cognitive interview: Practical applications and implications for the police service. *The Psychologist: Bulletin of the British Psychological Society, 4,* 398–400.

Rutter, M. (1972). *Maternal deprivation reassessed.* Harmondsworth, UK: Penguin.

Rutter, M. (1981). *Maternal deprivation reassessed (2nd Edn).* Harmondsworth, UK: Penguin.

Rutter, M., & The ERA Study Team (1998). Developmental catch-up and deficit following adoption after severe early privation. *Journal of Child Psychology and Psychiatry, 39,* 465–476.

Rymer, R. (1993). *Genie: Escape from a silent childhood.* London: Michael Joseph.

Sabini, J., Siepman, M., & Stein, J. (2001). The really fundamental attribution error. *Psychological Inquiry, 12,* 1–15.

Sagi, A., & Lewkowicz, K.S. (1987). A cross-cultural evaluation of attachment research. In J.W.C. Tavecchio & M.H. van IJzendoorn (Eds), *Attachment in social networks: Contributions to the Bowlby–Ainsworth attachment theory.* Amsterdam: Elsevier.

Sagi, A., van IJzendoorn, M.H., & Koren-Karie, N. (1991). Primary appraisal of the Strange Situation: A cross-cultural analysis of the pre-separation episodes. *Developmental Psychology, 27,* 587–596.

Salkovskis, P.M., Clark, D.M., & Gelder, M.G. (1996). Cognition–behaviour links in the persistence of panic. *Behaviour Research and Therapy, 34,* 453–458.

Salkovskis, P.M., Clark, D.M., Hackmann, A., Wells, A., & Gelder, M.G (1999). An experimental investigation of the role of safety-seeking behaviours in the maintenance of panic disorder and agoraphobia. *Behaviour Research and Therapy, 37,* 559–574.

Santee, R.T., & Maslach (1982). To agree or not to agree: Personal dissent amid social pressure to conform. *Journal of Personality and Social Psychology, 42,* 690–700.

Sbarra, D.A., Law, R.W., & Portley, R.M. (2011). Divorce and death: A meta-analysis and research agenda for clinical, social, and health psychology. *Perspectives on Psychological Science, 6,* 454–474.

Schaffer, H.R., & Emerson, P.E. (1964). The development of social attachments in infancy. *Monographs of the Society for Research on Child Development* (Whole no. 29).

Schliefer, S.J., Keller, S.E., Camerino, M., Thornton, J.C., & Stein, M. (1983). Suppression of lymphocyte stimulation following bereavement. *Journal of the American Medical Association, 250,* 374–377.

Segerstrom, S.C. (2010). Resources, stress, and immunity: An ecological perspective on human psychoneuroimmunology. *Annals of Behavioral Medicine, 40,* 114–125.

Segerstrom, S.C., & Miller, G.E. (2004). Psychological stress and the human immune system: A meta-analytic study of 30 years of inquiry. *Psychological Bulletin, 130,* 601–630.

Selye, H. (1936). A syndrome produced by diverse nocuous agents. *Nature, 138,* 32.

Selye, H. (1950). *Stress.* Montreal, Canada: Acta.

Selye, H. (Ed.) (1980) *Selye's guide to stress research.* New York: Van Nostrand Reinhold.

Shaffer, D.R. (1993). *Developmental psychology.* Pacific Grove, CA: Brooks/Cole.

Shallice, T., & Warrington, E.K. (1970). Independent functioning of verbal memory stores: A neuropsychological study. *Quarterly Journal of Experimental Psychology, 22,* 261–273.

Shaver, P.R., & Hazan, C. (1993). Adult romantic attachment: Theory and evidence. In D. Perlman & W. Jones (Eds), *Advances in personal relationships Vol. 4* (pp. 29–70). London: Kingsley.

Shea, J.D.C. (1981). Changes in interpersonal distances and categories of play behaviour in the early weeks of preschool. *Developmental Psychology, 17,* 417–425.

Sher, L. (2004). Daily hassles, cortisol, and the pathogenesis of depression. *Medical Hypotheses, 62,* 198–202.

Sherif, M. (1935). A study of some factors in perception. *Archives of Psychology, 27,* 187.

Shotland, R.L., & Straw, M.K. (1976). Bystander response to an assault: When a man attacks a woman. *Journal of Personality and Social Psychology, 34,* 990–999.

Shpancer, N. (2006). The effects of daycare: Persistent questions, elusive answers. *Early Childhood Research Quarterly, 21,* 227–237.

Shuell, T.J. (1969). Clustering and organization in free recall. *Psychological Bulletin, 72,* 353–374.

Shute, R.E. (1975). The impact of peer pressure on the verbally expressed drug attitudes of male college students. *American Journal of Drug and Alcohol Abuse, 2,* 231–243.

Sigal, J.J., Rossignol, M., Perry, J.C., & Ouimet, M.C. (2003). Unwanted infants: Psychological and physical consequences of inadequate orphanage care 50 years later. *American Journal of Orthopsychiatry, 73,* 3–12.

Simon, H.A. (1974). How big is a chunk? *Science, 183,* 483–488.

Skinner, B.F. (1938). *The behaviour of organisms.* New York: Appleton-Century-Crofts.

Smith, E.E., & Jonides, J. (1997). Working memory: A view from neuroimaging. *Cognitive Psychology, 33,* 5–42.

Smith, P., & Bond, M.H. (1993). *Social psychology across cultures: Analysis and perspectives.* New York: Harvester Wheatsheaf.

Smyke, A.T., Koga, S.F., Johnson, D.E., Fox, N.A., Marshall, P.J., Nelson, C.A., et al. (2007). The caregiving context in institution-reared infants and toddlers in Romania. *Journal of Child Psychology and Psychiatry, 48,* 210–218.

Soutter, A. (1995). Case report: Successful treatment of a case of extreme isolation. *European Child and Adolescent Psychiatry, 4,* 39–45.

Spangler, G. (1990). Mother, child, and situational correlates of toddlers' social competence. *Infant Behavior and Development, 13,* 405–419.

Spector, P.E., Dwyer, D.J., & Jex, S.M. (1988). Relation of job stressors to affective, health, and performance outcomes. A comparison of multiple data sources. *Journal of Applied Psychology, 73,* 11–19.

Spence, I., Yu, J.J., Feng, J., & Marshman, J. (2009). Women match men when learning a spatial skill. *Journal of Experimental Psychology: Learning, Memory, and Cognition, 35*(No. 4), 1097–1103.

Sperling, G. (1960). The information available in brief visual presentations. *Psychological Monographs, 74* (whole no. 498), 1–29.

Spiers, H.J., Maguire, E.A., & Burgess, N. (2001). Hippocampal amnesia. *Neurocase, 7,* 357–382.

Spitz, R.A. (1945). Hospitalism: An inquiry into the genesis of psychiatric conditions in early childhood. *Psychoanalytic Study of the Child, 1,* 113–117.

Spitz, R.A., & Wolf, K.M. (1946). Anaclitic depression. *Psychoanalytic Study of the Child, 2,* 313–342.

Standing, L.G., Conezio, J., & Haber, N. (1970). Perception and memory for pictures: Single-trial learning of 2500 visual stimuli. *Psychonomic Science, 19,* 73–74.

Statham, J. (2011). *Grandparents providing child care: Briefing paper.* Loughborough: Childhood Wellbeing Research Centre.

Sterbin, A., & Rakow, E. (1996). *Self-esteem, locus of control, and student achievement.* Paper presented at the Annual Meeting of the Mid-South Educational Research Association, Tuscaloosa, Alabama.

Steblay, N.M. (1997). Social influence in eyewitness recall: A meta-analytic comparison. *Law and Human Behavior, 25,* 459–474.

Stevens, S., Hynan, M.T., & Allen, M. (2000). A meta-analysis of common factor and specific treatment effects across the outcome domains of the phase model of psychotherapy. *Clinical Psychology: Science and Practice, 7,* 273–290.

Stewart, S.A. (2005). The effects of benzodiazepines on cognition. *Journal of Clinical Psychiatry, 66*(Suppl. 2), 9–13.

Stirling, J.D., & Hellewell, J.S.E. (1999). *Psychopathology.* London: Routledge.

Stone, A.A., Reed, B.R., & Neale, J.M. (1987). Changes in daily life event frequency precede episodes of physical symptoms. *Journal of Human Stress, 13,* 70–74.

Strassberg, D.S., & Lowe, K. (1995). Volunteer bias in sexuality research. *Archives of Sexual Behavior, 24,* 369–382.

Stright, A.D., Kelley, K., & Gallagher, K.C. (2008). Infant temperament moderates relations between maternal parenting in early childhood and children's adjustment in first grade. *Child Development, 79,* 186–200.

Stroud, L.R., Salovey, P., & Epel, E.S. (2002). Sex differences in stress responses: Social rejection versus achievement stress. *Biological Psychiatry, 52,* 318–327.

Stuss, D.T., & Alexander, M.P. (2007). Is there a dysexecutive syndrome? *Philosophical Transactions of the Royal Society B, 362,* 901–915.

Sue, D., Sue, D., & Sue, S. (1994). *Understanding abnormal behaviour.* Boston, MA: Houghton Mifflin.

Sulin, R.A., & Dooling, D.J. (1974). Intrusion of a thematic idea in retention of prose. *Journal of Experimental Psychology, 103,* 255–262.

Szasz, T.S. (1960). *The myth of mental illness.* London: Paladin.

Szewczyk-Sokolowski, M., Bost, K.K., & Wainwright, A.B. (2005). Attachment, temperament, and preschool children's peer acceptance. *Social Development, 14,* 379–397.

Tajfel, H., & Turner, J.C. (1979). An integrative theory of intergroup conflict. In W.G. Austin & S. Worchel (Eds), *The social psychology of intergroup relations* (pp. 33–47). Monterey, CA: Brooks/Cole.

Takahashi, K. (1990). Are the key assumptions of the 'strange situation' procedure universal? A view from Japanese research. *Human Development, 33,* 23–30.

Tavris, C. (1974). The frozen world of the familiar stranger. *Psychology Today, June,* 71–80.

Tharyan, P., & Adams, C.E. (2005). Electroconvulsive therapy for schizophrenia. *Cochrane Database of Systematic Reviews,* April 18, CD000076.

Therriault, D., Lemelin, J.P., Tarabulsy, G.M., & Provost, M.A. (2011). Direction of effects between temperament of child and maternal sensitivity. *Canadian Journal of Behavioural Science, 43,* 267–278.

Thomas, L.K. (1998). *Multicultural aspects of attachment.* http://www.bereavement.demon.co.uk/lbn/attachment/ lennox.html. [See also Thomas, L.K. (1995). Psychotherapy in the context of race and culture. In S. Fernando (Ed.), *Mental health in a multi-ethnic society.* London: Routledge.]

Thompson, R.A. (2000). The legacy of early attachments. *Child Development, 71,* 145–152.

Tilker, H.A. (1970). Socially responsible behaviour as a function of observer responsibility and video feedback. *Journal of Personality and Social Psychology, 14,* 95–100.

Tizard, B. (1979). Language at home and at school. In C.B. Cazden & D. Harvey (Eds), *Language in early childhood education.* Washington, DC: National Association for the Education of Young Children.

Tollestrup, P.A., Turtle, J.W., & Yuille, J.C. (1994). Actual victims and witnesses to robbery and fraud: An archival analysis. In D.F. Ross, J.D. Read, & M.P. Toglia (Eds), *Adult eyewitness testimony: Current trends and developments.* New York: Wiley.

Tronick, E.Z., Morelli, G.A., & Ivey, P.K. (1992). The Efe forager infant and toddler's pattern of social relationships: Multiple and simultaneous. *Developmental Psychology, 28,* 568–577.

Tuckey, M.R., & Brewer, N. (2003a). How schemas affect eyewitness memory over repeated retrieval attempts. *Applied Cognitive Psychology, 7,* 785–800.

Tuckey, M.R., & Brewer, N. (2003b). The influence of schemas, stimulus ambiguity, and interview schedule on eyewitness memory over time. *Journal of Experimental Psychology: Applied, 9,* 101–118.

Turner, L.H., & Solomon, R.L. (1962). Human traumatic avoidance learning: Theory and experiments on the operant–respondent distinction and failures to learn. *Psychological Monographs, 76*(40; Whole no. 559).

Twenge, J.M., & Im, C. (2007). Changes in the need for social approval, 1958-2001. *Journal of Research in Personality, 41,* 171–189.

Twisk, J.W.R., Snel, J., Kemper, H.C.G., & van Mechelen, W. (1999). Changes in daily hassles and life events and the relationship with coronary heart disease risk factors: A 2-year longitudinal study in 27–29-year-old males and females. *Journal of Psychosomatic Research, 46,* 229–240.

Tyrell, J.B., & Baxter, J.D. (1981). Glucocorticoid therapy. In P. Felig, J.D. Baxter, A.E. Broadus, & L.A. Frohman (Eds), *Endocrinology and metabolism.* New York: McGraw-Hill.

Valentine, T., Pickering, A., & Darling, S. (2003). Characteristics of eyewitness identification that predict the outcome of real line-ups. *Applied Cognitive Psychology, 17,* 969–993.

Vandell, D.L., & Corasaniti, M.A. (1990). *Variations in early child care: Do they predict subsequent social, emotional, and cognitive differences?* Unpublished manuscript, University of Wisconsin, Madison. [Noted in Andersson, B-E. (1992). Effects of daycare on cognitive and socioemotional competence of thirteen-year-old Swedish schoolchildren. *Child Development, 63,* 20–36.]

van IJzendoorn, M.H., Goldberg, S., Kroonenberg, P.M., & Frenkel, O.J. (1992). The relative effects of maternal and child problems on the quality of attachment: A meta-analysis of attachment in clinical samples. *Child Development, 63,* 840–858.

van IJzendoorn, M.H., & Kroonenberg, P.M. (1988). Cross-cultural patterns of attachment: A meta-analysis of the Strange Situation. *Child Development, 59,* 147–156.

van IJzendoorn, M.H., Schuengel, C., & Bakermans-Kranenburg, M.J. (1999). Disorganised attachment in early childhood: Meta-analysis of precursors, concomitants, and sequelae. *Development and Psychopathology, 11,* 225–249.

Van IJzendoorn, M.H., Verfeijken, C.M.J., Bakermans-Kranenburg, M.J., & Riksen-Walraven, J.M. (2004). Assessing attachment security with the attachment Q sort: Meta-analytic evidence for the validity of the observer AQS. *Child Development, 75,* 1188–1213.

Van Os, J., Park, S., & Jones, P. (2001). Neuroticism, life events and mental health: evidence for person-environment correlation. *British Journal of Psychiatry, 178* (Suppl. 40), s72–s77.

Vaughn, B.E., & Waters, E. (1990). Attachment behaviour at home and in the laboratory: Q-sort observations and Strange Situation classifications of one-year-olds. *Child Development, 61*, 1965–1973.

Vermeer, H.J., & van IJzendoorn, M.H. (2006). Children's elevated cortisol levels at daycare: A review and meta-analysis. *Early Childhood Research Quarterly, 21*, 390–401.

Victor, B. (2003). *Army of roses: Inside the world of Palestinian women suicide bombers.* Emmaus, Pa: Rodale [distributed by St. Martin's Press].

Virtanen, M., Ferrie, J.E., Singh-Manoux, A., Vahtera, M.J., Marmot, M.G., & Kivimäki, M. (2010). Overtime work and incident coronary heart disease: The Whitehall II prospective cohort study. *European Heart Journal, 31*, 1737–1744.

Vogt, D.S., Rizvi, Shipherd, J.C., & Resick, P.A. (2008). Longitudinal investigation of reciprocal relationship between stress reactions and hardiness. *Personality and Social Psychology Bulletin, 34*, 61–73.

Wang, A.Y., & Thomas, M.H. (2000). Looking for long-term mnemonic effects on serial recall: The legacy of Simonides. *American Journal of Psychology, 113*, 331–340.

Wang, K., Shu, Q., & Tu, Q. (2008). Technostress under different organizational environments: An empirical investigation. *Computers in Human Behavior, 24*, 3002–3013.

Wang, K.S., Liu, X.F., & Aragam, N. (2010). A genome-wide meta-analysis identifies novel loci associated with schizophrenia and bipolar disorder. *Schizophrenia Research, 124*, 192–199.

Warr, P. (1996). Employee well-being. In P. Warr (Ed), *Psychology at work* (pp. 224–253). London: Penguin Books Ltd.

Warren, R., & Zgourides, G.D. (1991). *Anxiety disorders: A rational–emotive perspective.* New York: Pergamon Press.

Wartner, U.G., Grossmann, K., Fremmer-Bombik, E., & Suess, G. (1994). Attachment patterns at age six in South Germany: Predictability from infancy and implications for preschool behaviour. *Child Development, 65*, 1014–1027.

Watson, J.B., & Rayner, R. (1920). Conditioned emotional reactions. *Journal of Experimental Psychology, 3*, 1–14.

Weeks, D., & James, J. (1995). *Eccentrics: A study of sanity and strangeness.* New York: Villiard.

Weinfield, N.S., Whaley, G.J.L., & Egeland, B. (2004). Continuity, discontinuity, and coherence in attachment from infancy to late adolescence: Sequelae of organisation and disorganisation. *Attachment and Human Development, 6*, 73–97.

Weist, R.M. (1972). The role of rehearsal: Recopy or reconstruct. *Journal of Verbal Learning and Verbal Behavior, 11*, 440–450.

Weng, N.P. (2006). Aging of the immune system: How much can the adaptive immune system adapt? *Immunity, 24*, 495–499.

Westen, D. (1996). *Psychology: Mind, brain, and culture.* New York: Wiley.

Whyte, W.F. (1943). *Street corner society: The social structure of an Italian slum.* Chicago: University of Chicago Press.

Williams, J.M., & Warchal, J. (1981). The relationship between assertiveness, internal-external locus of control, and overt conformity. *Journal of Psychology, 109*, 93–96.

Wilson, G.T., & Davison, G.C. (1971). Processes of fear reduction in systematic desensitisation: Animal studies. *Psychological Bulletin, 76*, 1–14.

Wilson, K., Roe, B., & Wright, L. (1998). Telephone or face-to-face interviews? A decision made on the basis of a pilot study. *International Journal of Nursing Studies, 35*, 314–321.

Wilson, S., Brown, N., Mejia, C., & Lavori, P. (2002). Effects of interviewer characteristics on reported sexual behavior of California Latino couples. *Hispanic Journal of Behavioral Sciences, 24*(1), 38–62.

Windgassen, K. (1992). Treatment with neuroleptics: The patient's perspective. *Acta Psychiatrica Scandinavica, 86*, 405–410.

Wolfson, A. (2005). "Trial to start for $200 million lawsuit over strip-search hoax", *Louisville Courier-Journal*, 2007-09-09. See http://www.usatoday.com/news/ nation/2007-09-09-mcdonaldslawsuit_N.htm

Wolpe, J. (1958). *Psychotherapy by reciprocal inhibition.* Stanford, CA: Stanford University Press.

Wolpe, J. (1969). *The practice of behaviour therapy.* Oxford, UK: Pergamon Press.

Wright, D.B., & Loftus, E.F. (2008). Eyewitness memory. In G. Cohen & M.A. Conway (Eds), *Memory in the real world (3rd Edn)*. Hove, UK: Psychology Press.

Wright, D.B., & Stroud, J.N. (2002). Age differences in lineup identification accuracy: People are better with their own age. *Law and Human Behavior, 26*, 6, 641–654.

Young, S.D., Adelstein, B.D., & Ellis, S.R. (2007). Demand characteristics in assessing motion sickness in a virtual environment: Or does taking a motion sickness questionnaire make you sick? *IEEE Transactions on Visualization and Computer Graphics, 13*, 422–428.

Yuille, J.C., & Cutshall, J.L. (1986). A case study of eyewitness memory of a crime. *Journal of Applied Psychology, 71*, 291–301.

Zegoib, L.E., Arnold, S., & Forehand, R. (1975). An examination of observer effects in parent–child interactions. *Child Development, 46*, 509–512.

Zimbardo, P.G. (1973). On the ethics of intervention in human psychological research: With special reference to the Stanford prison experiment. *Cognition, 2*, 243–256.

Zimbardo, P.G. (1989). *Quiet rage: The Stanford Prison Experiment video.* Stanford, CA: Stanford University.

Subject Index

Bold indicates where key terms are defined.

Illustration Credits

Chapter 2

Page 24: From Peterson & Peterson (1959). Copyright © American Psychological Association. Reproduced with permission. Page 31: From Robbins et al. (1996). Reproduced with permission of Springer Science + Business Media. Page 33: From Klauer & Zhao (2004). Copyright © American Psychological Association. Reproduced with permission. Page 39 (top): Copyright © image100/Corbis. Page 41: Copyright © Guy Cali/Corbis. Page 51: Image courtesy of the National Archives and Records Administration. Page 56: From *Psychology for GCSE Level* by Diana Dwyer and Craig Roberts (2007). Copyright © Psychology Press.

Chapter 3

Page 63 and page 64 (top): From Harlow (1959). Reproduced with kind permission of Harlow Primate Laboratory, University of Wisconsin. Page 68: Copyright © Science Photo Library. Page 75: From Fraley & Spieker (2003). Copyright © American Psychological Association. Reproduced with permission. Page 89: Copyright © Auschwitz Museum/Handout/Reuters/Corbis. Page 91: Copyright © Bernard Bisson/Sygma/Corbis. Page 104: Copyright © Peter Dazeley/Getty Images.

Chapter 4

Page 112: Copyright © Richard T. Nowitz/Corbis. Page 140: Copyright © Hulton-Deutsch Collection/Corbis.

Chapter 5

Page 188: Kushch Dmitry/Shutterstock.com. Page 194: From de Jonge et al. (2010). © Springer, Part of Springer Science + Business Media.

Chapter 6

Page 214: Andrey Yurlov/Shutterstock.com. Page 225 (top): JustASC/Shutterstock.com. Page 225 (bottom): Reproduced with permission of P.G. Zimbardo Inc. Page 227: Image courtesy of the German Federal Archive. Page 228: From the film *Obedience* © 1968 by Stanley Milgram. Copyright © renewed 1991 by Alexandra Milgram and distributed by Penn State Media Sales. Permission granted by Alexandra Milgram. Page 239: Image courtesy of the National Archives and Records Administration. Page 250: Copyright © Bettmann/Corbis

Chapter 7

Page 257: godrick/Shutterstock.com. Page 267: Copyright © Dr Robert Friedland/Science Photo Library. Page 275: Reproduced with the kind permission of Benjamin Harris, University of New Hampshire. Page 285: Copyright © Sunset Boulevard/Corbis. Page 290: Copyright © Will McIntyre/Science Photo Library. Page 296: Copyright © CC Studio/Science Photo Library.